EDITED BY
ROBERT KIMBALL

COLE

A BIOGRAPHICAL ESSAY BY
BRENDAN GILL

DESIGNED
BY
BEA FEITLER

THE OVERLOOK PRESS
WOODSTOCK & NEW YORK

Library of Congress Cataloging-in-Publication Data
Porter, Cole, 1891–1964.
[Songs. Texts. Selections]
Cole / [edited by] Robert Kimball ; biographical essay by
Brendan Gill.
p. cm.
Originally published: New York ; Holt, Rinehart & Winston, 1971.
"Chronology of Cole Porter songs and productions": p.
Discography: p.
Includes index.
1. Musicals—Excerpts—Librettos. 2. Popular music—Texts. I.
Kimball, Robert. II. Gill, Brendan, 1914– III. Title.
ML54.6P7 K55 2000   782.1'4'0268—dc21   00-058449

Manufactured in Spain   D.L.TO: 1377-2000
9 8 7 6 5 4 3 2 1
ISBN 1-58567-063-4

SONG COPYRIGHTS

PHOTO CREDITS

CULVER PICTURES, INC.: 3 left, 4, 46, 69, 114,
115, 125 bottom, 139, 158, 159, 178, 189, 209,
216, 230, 248, 249
HERBERT GEHR, Life Magazine © Time Inc.:
198-199
GRAPHIC HOUSE: 152 bottom, 163, 164, 191,
192, 197, 200, 203, 205, 207, 210, 214, 220,
224, 226, 228, 231, 235, 237
MIAMI COUNTY, INDIANA, HISTORICAL SOCIETY:
2 top
MUSEUM OF THE CITY OF NEW YORK (Theatre
and Music Collection): 89, 90, 91, 160, 161,
162
THEATRE COLLECTION, The New York Public
Library, Astor, Lenox and Tilden Founda-
tions: 35, 37, 105, 142, 151, 170, 179, 180, 181,
187
VAN DAMM PHOTOS, Theatre Collection, The
New York Public Library, Astor, Lenox and
Tilden Foundations: 122, 123, 126, 136, 137,
138, 144, 152, 153, 184, 185, 186
YALE UNIVERSITY: 5, 6, 7, 8, 10, 11, 12, 14, 15, 16,
17, 19 insert, 20, 21, 22, 23
ZODIAC (Friedman-Abeles), Courtesy,
Gretchen Wyler: 244.
All other photos and exhibits are from the
Cole Porter Collections, Yale University and
the Library of Congress; the Cole family,
Peru, Indiana; and The Cole Porter Musical
and Literary Property Trusts and appear
with the permission of John F. Wharton,
Trustee.

Acknowledgment is made to Simon and
Schuster for permission to use selections
from the Foreword by Moss Hart in *The Cole
Porter Song Book.* Copyright © 1959 by
Simon and Schuster.
Charles Scribner's Sons for permission to
reprint excerpts from *Tender Is the Night* by
F. Scott Fitzgerald. Copyright 1933, 1934
Charles Scribner's Sons; renewal copyright
© 1961, 1962 Frances Scott Fitzgerald
Lanahan.

The number of people to be thanked
for their assistance in the compilation of this book
makes for a very long list indeed, but it is one
that sunnily justifies itself on several
counts. First of all, Cole doted on lists. Secondly, he
doted in particular on lists of notabilities, and
the names mentioned below give off a
sufficient glitter, even by Cole's high standards.
Thirdly, Cole, the best of hosts, would have
been delighted to serve as the occasion
for so many of his old friends finding themselves,
thanks to him, in such admirable
company, to wit:

Billy Baldwin, Rigel Barber, the late
Lt. Col. Sir Rex Benson, Spencer Berger, Irving Berlin,
Dorothie Bigelow, Eubie Blake, William Bolcom,
Harold Bone, Gregory Bonenberger,
Alice Bray, Deborah Brown, Rose Mary Chuley, James
O. Cole, Jules Omar Cole, Mr. and Mrs. George
B. Cortelyou, Jr., the late Albert B.
Crawford, Bosley Crowther, Joan C. Daly, Agnes de
Mille, Honoria Murphy Donnelly, Alfred Drake,
Vivien Friedman, Joseph Fuchs, Lawrence
Fuchsberg, George Gaynes, Vladimir Golschmann,
Stanley Green, Baron Nicolas de Gunzburg, John
Hammond, Mr. and Mrs. Basil Duke

Henning, Ginny Carpenter Hill, Robert Jackson, Miles
Kreuger, Florence Leeds, Roy Lester, William
Lichtenwanger, Goddard Lieberson,
Patricia Loewenberg, Vincent Lopez, Sidney Lovett,
Jack Meltzer, Ethel Merman, Geoffroy Millais,
Vassilia Moore, Paul Myers, Melvin
Parks, Sam Pearce, Henry C. Potter, Gordon Ramsey,
Dr. and Mrs. Norman Rosenthal, Brian Rust,
Richard Sawicki, Ann Scaffidi, Scroll and
Key, Bobby Short, Alfred Simon, Noble Sissle, Leo Smit,
Steven Smolian, Benjamin Sonnenberg, Carlos
Stoddard, Dorothy Swerdlove, Thornton
Thayer, Calvin Tomkins, Robert Wachs, Carroll Wade,
Fred Waring, Richard Warren, Jr., Betty Wharton,
Mr. and Mrs. Arnold Whitridge, Edward Wittstein,
Gretchen Wyler, and many helping hands at Yale.

We are grateful to the publishers of
Cole Porter's songs for permission to reproduce the
lyrics, and to John F. Wharton, trustee of The Cole
Porter Musical and Literary Property
Trusts, for his guidance and support. Finally, we thank
our editor and friend, Steven M. L. Aronson, who,
having impetuously willed this book into
existence, with unfailing patience shaped and improved
it at every point.

Begin with the face, familiar from so many photographs. It was small, round, smooth-skinned, delicately modeled, invincibly boyish. Even in age, after decades of suffering, it held hints of the implike, lovable child that we see pictured in a starched blouse and broad-brimmed straw hat at four, already eager to seek out and embrace the world. It was a world that would become his oyster, his champagne, his caviar, and in the small city of Peru, Indiana, in the flagrantly misnamed gay nineties, it must have been plain to the ambitious mother of the child if not to the child himself that the sooner one held out both arms to such a world the better.

People who hug life to them, though they grow older, never grow old: Cole carried with him to the grave not the ravaged face of an old man but the ravaged face of a young one. The family knack for longevity—his grumpy millionaire grandfather J. O. Cole lived to be ninety-five, his mother to ninety—proved a curse to him; he was ready for death, indeed he pleaded for it, but the stout heart inside his mutilated body indignantly refused to consent. Cole had not marched with conventional inattentive acquiescence into his late sad years; he had been battered into them by an intemperate and preposterous fate, and when he died, in 1964, at the age of seventy-three, he had endured no telling how many centuries of continuous physical pain. In the light of this dreadful fact, it is curious to observe in the last photographs, along with the looked-for signs of anguish, signs of an undiminished trustingness, as if the promises of a long life, however little they had happened to be fulfilled for him, remained, all touchingly and beautifully, promises for others.

We are haunted by the face in part because it is so unchanging—because, in a sense, it haunts itself, being its own at first jaunty and playful ghost and then its pitiful one. In any casual snapshot of an outing held who knows when in Paris, Cairo, Venice, or Hollywood, it is Cole that one instantly singles out and gives a name to. The face of the little boy on ponyback in the apple country and the face of the elderly, crippled recluse dividing his time between an apartment high in the Waldorf Towers and a cottage in Williamstown is the face of the debonair undergraduate at Yale, already an accomplished charmer, who by an adroit manipulation of exceptional talents and an exceptional intelligence is offered whatever he covets and avoids whatever he dislikes. What a spoiled young man he must be! But then what excellent value he gives! All his life he will be accused of being a snob and all his life he will deny the charge, but his snobbery, real or imaginary, is beside the point, which is that at every turn, unfailingly, he furnished the world with far more joy than he got back. In the unspoken bargain struck between genius and the rest of us, it is the rest of us who come home with full hands and, in this instance, dancing feet.

There are several classbook photographs of Cole, posing with this or that distinguished undergraduate group before a length of nineteenth-century wooden fence from the Old Campus at Yale. (The official college photographers kept this sacred remnant of fence, no more likely to be genuine than slivers of the True Cross, in their Chapel Street studio for football captains and other heroes to be propped against. Behind the fence was a backdrop of tastefully painted Old Campus elms, looking not unlike a rain forest in Brazil.) Cole is well-dressed, not to say dudeish, in these official photographs, and the face, under dark hair parted in the middle, is always in dead earnest. It is obvious that he is proud to be who he is and where he is, and why not? By a number of years, he has anticipated the ordeal and triumph of a favorite protagonist of Scott Fitzgerald's daydreams and fictions: a rich young nobody from the uncharted here-be-dragons hinterland West of the Alleghenies makes his way East and succeeds in taking the gilded citadel by storm. In Cole's case, the East consisted of New Haven and New York, but how much more mere territory was it necessary to capture in order to count as a somebody? As for the gold, to a newcomer from Pee-ru, to say nothing of St. Paul, it looked like the real thing. Both Cole and Scott would assert with Henry James "I can stand a good deal of gold."

That short, trim, rather bookish-looking boy, with his crisp tenor voice and his dislike of contact sports and indeed of any exercise except riding and swimming—surely it was odd in the Yale of that day, shortly before the First World War, that such a figure could have been a big man on campus. Yet Cole was. Dink Stover and Frank Merriwell were long past, but their descendants have a way of incarnating themselves continuously out of the damp night air of all those narrow one-syllable eighteenth-century New Haven streets—Elm and York and Grove and High and Wall—and one cannot help wondering what the handsome, burly athletes of the Porter era, with their suspicion of cleverness, their pursuit of the manly, their strenuous Christianity, thought of the exquisite pagan hedonist in their midst. Well, it appears that they liked him very much. He made Deke (thanks, it is true, to the influence of an upperclassman and fellow hedonist named Gerald Murphy), and he made Keys, and he was the Leader of the Glee Club and a member of the Whiffenpoofs, and he was also, in his nearest approach to the sweat and towel snapping of the locker room, a cheerleader. His best friends were Monty Woolley and Len Hanna, notable specimens of what were thought of euphemistically in those days as perennial bachelors. The Woolley-Hanna set was inclined to spoof the pieties of Mother Yale and their favored habitat was New York, to which Cole often accompanied them; nevertheless, he was friendly enough with the Stovers to win their admiration with a couple of football songs —*Bingo Eli Yale* and *Bull Dog*—that to this day remain the best-loved musical furniture in the minds of many Old Blues.

We glimpse the bright, mascotlike face smiling above elegant white tie and tails when at Christmas the Glee Club would travel its thousands of miles by rail around the country and Cole at the piano would bring down the house with a series of encores consisting of his own perky (and shrewdly self-censored) ditties. We glimpse the face again when Cole, back in New Haven, attends a meeting of an arcane and prankish group known as the Pundits. Having spoken of ghosts, one is tempted to linger a moment over that quizzical Pundit face of his and to impose on its unmarked freshness all that we know will someday befall it. Among the courses that Cole took at Yale, and neglected less than he did others, was William Lyon Phelps's celebrated "T & B," the then universally recognized abbreviation of "Tennyson and Browning." Billy Phelps was a bravura performer, who manifested a shameless, endearing pleasure in his platform skills; his students never forgot that they had taken a course with him, though what he had taught them might soon slip from memory. Phelps had founded the Pundits, limiting the club to ten undergraduates, and he considered Cole an ideal member. The motto of the Pundits pretended to conceal itself from the barbarian world by being reduced to initials: "T.B.I.Y.T.B." These initials stood for "The best is yet to be" and came from Browning's famous and once frequently quoted exhortation from "Rabbi Ben Ezra": "Grow old along with me!/The best is yet to be,/ The last of life, for which the first was made."

Browning, incomparably skilled at rhyme and a master of syncope and of what Hopkins called sprung rhythm, made a profound impression on Cole. Long before he went off to New Haven, his father read Browning to him and urged Browning upon him. (Samuel Fenwick Porter, whom everyone in the family, including Cole, appears to have either pitied or disliked, was a remarkable man. He began life as a good-looking, penniless druggist and his marriage to the heiress Kate Cole ought to have proved a stroke of good fortune. He had a strong literary bent and a passion for agricultural experiments, which he was able to indulge with the help of his wife's wealth. He seems to have been slowly crushed to death between the fiercely go-getting Kate and his powerful, contemptuous father-in-law, neither of whom made any bones about preferring the cheerful son to the sorry father.) Browning's unquestionable influence upon Cole can be found in many of the more acrobatic of Cole's lyrics; indeed, the chances are that he learned at least as much from Browning as he did from another and more obvious source, W. S. Gilbert, and from his younger contemporary, Ogden Nash. By an agreeable coincidence, Cole was to spend several summers at the Palazzo Rezzonico, where Browning died. It is hard to resist speculating on what Cole made of Browning's incorrigible optimism when his dark days came. With what a wry mockery he must have repeated to himself in his last years the Pundit motto, "The best is yet to be." In spite of Browning and Billy Phelps and Mother Yale, life had not turned out that way.

(‖ ‖)

Ten or twelve years pass, and the face is still uncannily that of a stripling. The smooth skin is tanned now, for the season in the photographs is nearly always summer and the place nearly always somewhere in France or Italy, as like as not the Lido. Cole is said to have considered himself unprepossessing; a man's opinion of his looks, especially if it is unfavorable, is not to be trusted over his photographs, and in his Venetian period Cole is downright handsome. His eyes are his best feature—large and dark brown and slightly popped, with heavy lids and something lemur-like in their playful, darting alertness. Also rather simian, and appealingly so, is the big mouth open in laughter, with its formidable array of square white teeth. In these carefully preserved snapshots, Cole is a healthy, happy animal, his bare body, slender and nut-brown, shining with the oil that protects it from the Mediterranean sun; he stands or sits or lies on the endless blazing Lido beach, mugging into the camera, while behind him we make out serried rows of bathing cabanas, with perhaps a jacketed servant emerging from between the rows with drinks on a tray and, in the middle distance, Monty and Noël making silly faces.

If Cole has a reputation in the nineteen twenties, it is not that of a composer who happens to be having an awfully good time on the side but that of an international playboy who writes an occasional witty song to be played and sung by him in the corner of one or another of the innumerable fashionable parties he gives or goes to; subsequently, the song may be allowed to drift out and down into the ordinary workaday world and gain a certain vogue there among a deliberately limited cult. (Of all the songs that Porter wrote up to, say, 1925, only one became what is known in music-publishing circles as a standard, a tinkly little tune called *Old-Fashioned Garden*, which was a hit in the Raymond Hitchcock revue, "Hitchy-Koo of 1919.") Cole's reputation at that time could be summed up in the facile accusation that he was being "social" instead of "serious"; like most reputations, this contains a truth and deforms the truth, for Cole was, in fact, being both at once. Social in his tastes but Middle-Western-

Protestant-Puritan in the seriousness of his aspirations, he was every bit as eager to make good as his mother and grandfather had been before him. Although he took care to uphold the tiresome undergraduate tradition that to be seen to be working hard is bad form, in truth he worked very hard indeed. In Paris, he studied composition under the austere classicist Vincent d'Indy and familiarized himself with the entire range of nineteenth-century "art" songs, particularly the *lieder* of Schubert and Schumann. At the same time, he was making friends with a number of black musicians and performers in Paris. Well ahead of most of his white contemporaries, he began to experiment with jazz rhythms, and his clever pastiche, *The Blue Boy Blues*—a song inspired by the sale of Gainsborough's painting, "The Blue Boy," to an American millionaire— was, for a while, highly popular in England. In 1923, Porter composed the score of a ballet for the Swedish Ballet company; the book was by his old Deke sponsor Gerald Murphy, who also designed the sets and costumes. The ballet, a triumph in Paris, was regarded with almost equal admiration in America, where it was given over sixty times in the course of a two-month tour. It was Cole's first and last public appearance as a "serious" composer. The ballet, entitled "Within the Quota," anticipated certain musical ideas that were to cause a stir when, several months later, they found expression in *Rhapsody in Blue*, by Cole's friend George Gershwin. Cole undertook to write a second ballet, for which Bakst was to provide the costumes. Bakst died, and Cole abandoned work on the ballet. The score of "Within the Quota," which Cole himself believed had been lost forever with the dissolution of the Swedish Ballet, was brought to light in 1970 and the ballet given a revival in New York. Many musicologists find the score of interest, and not alone because of its historic significance.

To remain a sort of gentleman-composer, moving at a measured height above the squalid scramble of the market place, was important to Cole as a young man and proved a considerable stumbling block to his career. Irving Berlin warned him that if he wanted to get work from theatrical producers he had better acquaint himself with the corner of Broadway and 42nd Street, where, if his name was recognized at all in the twenties, he was written off as an expatriate highbrow. Seeking to avoid Broadway and yet hoping to be pursued by it, Cole would go so far as to rent a large and costly apartment on Fifth Avenue and invite theatrical people to parties there, but it appears not to have occurred to him that, except geographically, Fifth Avenue was even farther from Broadway than Paris and the Lido were. The desire to seem a charming amateur who just happened to enjoy all the perquisites of a hardened professional was based less on a sense of caste and class than on a deep-seated and, as it proved, ineradicable lack of confidence in himself. This was an emotion that, if it was unknown to Cole's mother and grandfather, must have been familiar enough to the father he despised. It directly contradicts the principle enunciated by Freud to the effect that no man who has been his mother's favorite knows what it is to fear failure. (The teasing of one's dead betters is often an irresistible temptation; let it be noted that Freud himself was his mother's favorite. In his seventies, white-bearded and world-famous, he was "*mein goldener Sigi*" to Frau Freud, who contrived to live even longer than Kate Porter did and to keep her beloved closer to her apron strings. Not all mama's boys have been great men, but a remarkable number of great men have been mama's boys.)

Cole wished ardently to succeed; still more ardently, he wished not to be known to have failed. Hints of this double goal are to be found scattered everywhere throughout his life. He was to give ample proof of his courage, but his refusal to defend his own work in the rough-and-tumble of preparing a show led more than one Broadway director to describe him flatly as a coward. At the peak of his popularity, if someone connected with a Porter show in rehearsal expressed skepticism about a song, Cole always preferred discarding it to rewriting it; a fresh start struck him as the safest way to avoid the odious close give-and-take of criticism. The discarded song might turn up years later, slightly altered, in a new show or movie; meanwhile, the moment of dangerous self-doubt had been got past. Cole's passion for travel may have been a covert method of problem-solving for him. Who can tell what the tireless sightseer has left unexamined at home? Cole was never to be offered as much work as he wanted, or claimed to want, but he rejected many of the projects that agents and producers brought to him because he doubted that he would be able to bring them off. Not that he would give this as a reason; it was an aspect of the discipline he practiced in respect to fear that it seemed to the casual observer an emotion totally alien to him. Gentlemen had no nerves, and on the opening night of a Porter show he made a point of sitting well down front with a party of friends, laughing and applauding the show as if he hadn't the slightest doubt of its success. His behavior was gallant, and it was also protective: by wearing a mask of unshatterable aplomb, he was putting himself beyond reach of critics and envious rivals, to say nothing of a public always eager to observe who in the pecking order is the latest to be made to bleed. The finest of the musicals he was to write—"Kiss Me, Kate"—was the one he hesitated longest over committing himself to; he pretended that the reasons for his hesitation were that the project was too intellectual, that revivals of Shakespeare never did well at the box office, and that he didn't understand the book that Bella and Samuel Spewack had prepared. The truth was that Cole had had a couple of failures and was aware that people were saying he was through; he was simply afraid that "Kiss Me, Kate" would prove to be beyond his powers.

Playboy. Expatriate. Highbrow. Snob. The names flung at him in his youth he slowly, manfully outgrew by the exercise of an extraordinary musical talent working in the closest possible union with high intelligence. (The Porter lyrics, composed at the same time as his music and indissolubly wedded to it bar by bar, syllable by syllable, were a product of intense intellectual concentration; the seemingly effortless rhymes came not from heaven but from a rhyming dictionary.) Cole literally sweated to make good, though it was part of what was later to become known as a "life style" for him never to be observed to be sweating at all: a mild Mediterranean glow was the permissible limit. In Venice, back of the drawn blinds of the Palazzo Rezzonico while the rest of the household napped, or in Paris, in the chaste, art-deco elegance of the silvery house at Number 13, Rue Monsieur, or in New York, on the forty-first floor of the Waldorf Towers, he gave himself to his difficult craft. It was donkey work, but he did it, and as far as one can tell at this distance in time the person who, after unfalteringly loyal "Ma" in far-off Peru, gave him the courage to persist in his years of largely unrecognized and unrewarded labor was Linda, his wife.

For Cole, astonishingly, had married. Unlike most of his close companions and without, it appears, disturbing his relations with these companions, he had fallen in love with and courted and won an American divorcée named Linda Lee Thomas. She was a good many years older than Cole and, perhaps because of her uncertain health, looked older than she really was; she was also far richer than he, for his millions were to sift down to him only after the deaths of his grandfather and mother. (Cole always doted on the rich, and, everything else being equal, he preferred what he called the "rich-rich" to the single, unhyphenated, and, in effect, poverty-stricken rich, like himself.) At one time, Linda had been described as the most beautiful woman in the world; when Cole met her, in 1918, the superlative, though reduced in scale, was still impressive: she was spoken of as the most beautiful woman in Europe. A compendium of the qualities that Cole then admired most in people, she was well-born, intelligent, and what was then known as sophisticated; she could manage a large household with her left hand; she gave amusing parties; and she gossiped amusingly about other people's parties. She was said to have perfect taste and perfect manners and, knowing everyone that mattered, she passed her days in the company not only of decorative idlers but of such ideal companions as Berenson, Lord Carnavon, Bakst, Churchill, and Shaw. Does all that sound, to our ears, sufficiently impressive? To young Cole, it must have seemed everything.

As an eighteen-year-old belle from Louisville, Kentucky, Linda had married a "fast" young Yale man of proper lineage named Edward Russell Thomas, destined to enter history as the first husband of Cole Porter's wife and, still more unluckily, as the first person in the United States known to have killed somebody with an automobile. Thomas soon proved an indefatigable philanderer; according to rumor, he was also something of a sadist in the discharge of his conjugal obligations, and it is possible that by the time Linda won a divorce from him, in 1912, she had had enough of the sexual side of marriage. Be that as it may, having accepted a handsome settlement from Thomas, she moved to Paris and became a leader of what, even during the years of the First World War, was a lively international social set. It was in Paris that Cole met her and in 1919, to the surprise of many friends on both sides, they were married. The marriage lasted for thirty-five years, until Linda's death from emphysema, in 1954. She had wished to be buried in Williamstown, where, in a house called Buxton Hill, they had passed happy summer days. Cole chose, instead, to bury her in the family plot in Peru, arranging matters so he could lie in death between Kate and Linda. He was always compulsively neat.

The marriage was not without intermittent warfare and cobbled-up truces. A recurring crisis concerned Hollywood, which Linda (perfect manners . . . perfect taste) disliked and which Cole adored, in part because of its climate and in part because he was genuinely interested in the sharklike ignoramuses and ex-fur salesmen who had swarmed up out of the gutter to assume control of the movie industry. Like any Keys man, he had a certain curiosity about the gutter. When a song he wrote for the movie "Rosalie"—*In the Still of the Night*—made Louis B. Mayer weep, Cole was beside himself with pleasure; he had a high opinion of Mayer's aggressive animality, and to see such a bully in tears! Linda was not impressed by bullies. It was one thing for her to play den mother to Cole's entourage in Venice or Paris or Williamstown or New York, but it was another to play that not always pleasant role in Hollywood. She was a model of the accommodating aristocrat, yet there were limits. An awareness of limits, she might have said, is precisely what distinguishes aristocrats from the lower orders, and it was a bad mark against Cole for him not to have kept this necessary social truth in mind. No doubt Cole had merry days beside the sun-struck swimming pool in Brentwood, but over him and his young friends fell, for her, the shadow of innumerable Mayers and Warners and Harry Cohns. To Linda, they and their imitative myrmidons were so many foul-mouthed, cigar-chomping Genghis Khans, and if it had not been for Cole's accident, in the autumn of 1937, she would almost certainly have left him.

(▐▐▐)

Cole's accident. It is the central episode of his life—not the most important one but the one that everything else stands in relation to. We ask of a Porter song or movie or party or broken friendship or newly decorated apartment whether it was before or after the dreadful October morning at the Piping Rock Club, in Locust Valley (the setting met the usual Porter requirements in respect to social cachet). Cole's old friend, the Duke di Verdura, designer of the celebrated bejeweled cigarette cases that Linda gave Cole to mark the openings of new Porter shows, was a member of the houseparty that had gathered at the Countess di Zoppola's that weekend on Long Island, and he recalls that Cole, with a characteristic impetuous need to *do* something, had worked absurdly hard at organizing a group to go horseback riding. "He hadn't been riding in a long time," the Duke has said. "It was a sudden caprice, but Cole's caprices seemed sometimes to be made of steel." Against the advice of a groom at the stable at Piping Rock, Cole chose for his mount a mettlesome, nervy horse. A few minutes out along the bridle path, the horse shied at some bushes, reared, and fell back upon Cole, who, being out of practice, found himself unable to disengage his feet from the stirrups. As the horse struggled to get up, it fell back upon Cole and crushed one of his legs. Again, the horse sought to rise and again it fell back, this time rolling over and crushing Cole's other leg.

The accident took but a few seconds, and Cole maintained afterwards that he scarcely realized that he had been hurt. A member of the riding party, Benjamin Moore, was the first to reach Cole. Although Cole made light of the accident, Moore saw at once that he was terribly injured, and he galloped off to get help. As Cole later told the story—and he liked a good story —lying there, he took out a pencil and notebook and set to work on the lyrics of a song that became *At Long Last Love*.

In the ambulance that Moore summoned and that carried Cole to a nearby hospital, he went into shock and remained unconscious for two days. The attending doctors were convinced that both legs would have to be amputated. Linda was in Paris (by an ironic chance, she and Cole were not speaking to each other at this desperate moment in their lives) and on being notified of the accident and of the threat of amputation, Linda insisted that no decision be reached until she arrived in New York. She consulted with Kate Porter in Indiana by long-distance telephone and between them they decided that, no matter what the doctors said, Cole's legs must not be amputated. (By a further ironic chance, Linda had been living apart from her first husband when he, too, suffered a grievous accident and was threatened with the loss of a leg. Linda returned to Thomas, forbade the doctors to cut off his leg, and nursed him back to health before leaving him for good, several years later. She must have thought she could do as much for Cole.) In respect to the recommended amputations, Linda and Kate reasoned that Cole would die of despair if with his pride in his body he were to be so conspicuously maimed and humiliated, and perhaps they were right. In any event, they had no way of knowing then that Cole's legs were never to mend; that after some thirty-five operations on both legs, one of them would have to be amputated at last; and that in the twenty-seven years left to Cole from the time of his accident until his death, there would scarcely be a day that he was free of pain.

Cole was forty-six when the accident happened. Given his preternaturally youthful appearance, he seemed a man who was only just beginning to approach his prime. It amounts to a miracle that even following the accident the boyish face did not vanish altogether; there comes to mind a photograph of him being carried into a theater in white tie and tails a couple of years after Piping Rock—a rueful, dapper banty of a man, held high by chauffeur and valet, one foot heavily bandaged, the other in a brace—and to this day there are people who speak with awe of seeing him hobble, with the help of two canes, into a Hollywood nightclub on Sunset strip, his eyes black and enormous with suffering and his mouth grinning with glee—with glee!—in anticipation of an evening's pleasure. He was brave, oh, he was very brave, but as Kate's son and Linda's husband he had little choice: to those unbending nineteenth-century aristocrats, courage was an assumed commonplace. Moreover, they were sure that the important thing was for Cole to go on working hard and playing hard, and he did. By no telling what power of concentration of mind and dismissal of body, he provided the scores for more Broadway musicals and Hollywood movies after the accident than he had done before it; among the musicals were such substantial hits as "Leave It to Me," "Panama Hattie," "Kiss Me Kate," "Can-Can," and "Silk Stockings." The number of Porter songs to achieve the status of standard continued to mount. Berlin, Rodgers, and he were said to be the three most popular composers in America. Cole's earnings from ASCAP threatened to move him out of the familiar category of rich into what he considered the much more appealing category of rich-rich. In his late years, Cole learned with delight that, according to an ASCAP survey, five of his songs had made a list of the thirty most popular songs of all time. He shook his head over that: not bad for a highbrow.

Which was Cole's way of saying that of course he never *had* been a highbrow. Applied to him, the tag was as unjust as the tag of lowbrow applied to those of Cole's contemporaries who, lacking his musical scholarship, seemed to stumble upon their beguiling tunes by serendipity. Cole was delighted to be popular and he was all the more delighted because his popularity was so unexpected: who would have guessed that the style he had spent so long forging and refining— a style idiosyncratic, making no concessions to the then common taste, and often difficult to play and sing correctly—would become, along with Gershwin's, the most readily recognizable voice of the American musical theater in the thirties? Of all decades, the thirties, with its sour aftertaste of the extravagant twenties and its gritty grayness of prolonged, unliftable depression, would seem the least apt to choose the wealthy, playful, and totally apolitical Cole for a spokesman, but so it happened. Porter musical comedies encompass the period with a Porter neatness. Cole wrote the score for the last Broadway musical of the twenties, "Wake Up and Dream," which opened on December 30, 1929, and boasted the hit song, *What Is This Thing Called Love?* He also wrote the score for the last Broadway musical of the thirties, "Du Barry Was a Lady," which opened on December 6, 1939, and offered, among its twenty-odd songs, *Well, Did You Evah!*, *Friendship*, *But in the Morning, No*, and *Do I Love You?*

Between those pleasing parentheses, in the sullen year 1932, there arrived "Gay Divorce," with Fred Astaire singing *Night and Day*, and two years later was born the quintessential Porter musical, "Anything Goes"—to the extent that such things can be defined, the quintessential American musical of the period. In the cast were Ethel Merman, William Gaxton, and Victor Moore, and among its hit songs were *I Get a Kick Out of You*, *All Through the Night*, *You're the Top*, and *Anything Goes*. A year later came "Jubilee," with *Begin the Beguine, Why Shouldn't I?* and *Just One of Those Things*, and in 1936 there was "Red, Hot and Blue" with *Ours, Down in the Depths (on the Ninetieth Floor)*, and *It's De-Lovely*. The list of hits is so long that it threatens to become simply a list and therefore to strike us as less fantastic than it really is. There were to be plenty of other hits in the forties and a few in the fifties as well, but Cole had changed and the country had changed, and with age and sickness it was harder and harder for him to take in what was happening beyond his high fortress at the Waldorf and the little fortress in Williamstown. For the movie, "High Society," besides the title song, he wrote *I Love You, Samantha, You're Sensational, True Love*, and *Who Wants to Be a Millionaire?* Under the circumstances, it was a remarkable score. Because Louis Armstrong was in the cast,

Cole wrote a song for him called *Now You Has Jazz*. He worked on it like a schoolboy on a term paper, diligently but without confidence; he was no longer sure what such a song should be, and, as always, he dreaded being seen to have failed. The year was 1956, but to Cole it felt like the year 2000.

True, Cole had stayed younger longer than most, but now he was growing old earlier than most. He was often petulant and forgetful and lonesome, and there were times when he was irrational, as when he claimed in unbecoming panic to be going broke. Nevertheless, there were good days, or, rather, good hours, or hours that managed to be simultaneously good and bad. An old Yale classmate, the historian Arnold Whitridge, would come to dinner at the Waldorf with his wife Janetta (it was Cole who had introduced the Whitridges to each other in those long-past Paris days), and in an attempt to cheer Cole up Whitridge would sing from memory, stanza after stanza, some Porter song from an undergraduate smoker of forty-odd years before. And Cole would smile and say, in the saddest voice, "Did I write that? Is that really mine?"

#

End with the last song Cole ever wrote. It was for a television musical entitled "Aladdin," broadcast in 1958 and roundly deplored by the critics. The song was supposed to be sung by the Emperor of China, and Cole called it *Wouldn't It Be Fun!* It is an amusing song to us, as it must have been to Cole, because it stands everything he believed in right on its head. Never can Cole have uttered so succinctly and merrily a credo the direct opposite of his own. The song outrageously asks

> Wouldn't it be fun not to be famous,
> Wouldn't it be fun not to be rich!
> Wouldn't it be pleasant
> To be a simple peasant
> And spend a happy day digging a ditch!
> Wouldn't it be fun not to be known as an important VIP,
> Wouldn't it be fun to be nearly anyone
> Except me, mighty me!

The song is like a casual, mocking wave of the hand, where a proper farewell would have proved unbearable, both to him and to us. "Mighty me!" The voice is that of the elfin boy in the straw hat and starched blouse, Kate's son, Linda's husband, lover and friend of many; the face and the voice and the songs are one and they will never grow old, never die.

BRENDAN GILL

Broadway, the main street of Peru, shortly before the turn of the century. Cole was born in a small house on a side street to the left of this view: a few years later, the Porter family moved out to Grandfather Cole's big place in the country. Peru is evidently an ambitious town. Broadway is yet to be paved, but its latest buildings—the so-called business "blocks"—reflect the new fashion for carved Romanesque stonework and bold Renaissance gables. These are embodiments of a splendor that looks East to New York and even to Europe and, in expense and intention, are very remote from the humble brick buildings of the post-Civil War period, some of which are still to be glimpsed in this photograph. One such brick building housed the drugstore owned and run by Cole's father, the clever and eccentric Sam Porter.

Peru, Indiana, 1900

Grandfather Cole

Kate

First composition, 1900

First published work, 1902

"I remember him as he first arrived in Worcester . . . a precocious youngster with enthusiasm sparkling from his bright eyes and even then he was full of music. He was the first student I can remember who either desired or was allowed to have a piano in his room. You can imagine that that room soon became overflowing with song and jollification."—a Worcester Academy schoolmate

Cole Porter.

COLE ALBERT PORTER was born June 9, 1893, in Peru, Indiana. His father, Samuel Fenwick Porter, was born in Indiana. He graduated from Indiana University, and is now retired. Mrs. Porter was Kate Cole.

Porter prepared for Yale at Worcester Academy. He was on the Freshman Glee Club, on the University Glee Club three years, and Leader in Senior Year. He was a member of the Dramatic Association, having taken part in "Robin of Sherwood," and written the music for the Smoker Play in 1912 and in 1913. Football Cheer Leader, 1912. Corinthian Yacht Club, University Club, Wigwam and Wrangler Debating Club, Hogans, Whiffenpoofs, Pundits, Grill Room Grizzlies, Mince Pie Club. Delta Kappa Epsilon. Scroll and Key. Freshman Year he roomed alone in 242 York Street; Sophomore Year in 112 Welch; Junior Year in 499 Haughton; Senior Year with H. Parsons in 31 Vanderbilt.

Porter expects to enter the Harvard Law School, after which he will go into either mining, lumbering or farming. His permanent address is Westleigh Farms, Peru, Indiana.

Like many celebrated people, Cole early took care to make himself seem even more precocious than he was. His actual birthdate was June 9, 1891.

College Street

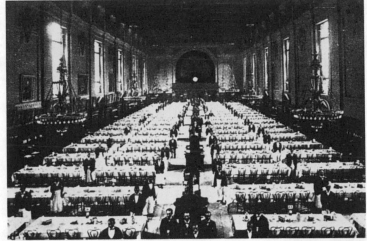

The Yale Dining Hall

York Street

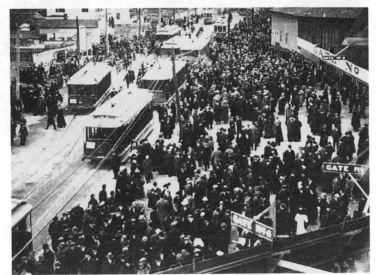

Crowds entering Yale Field for a football game, 1912

During freshman year, Cole lived at Garland's Rooming House, 242 York Street

The oldest surviving songs for which Cole wrote both music and lyrics were composed at 242 York Street in the spring of his freshman year (1910) and sent to his mother in Peru. The manuscripts were found after Cole's death tucked away in a scrapbook that Kate Porter kept of her son's college years.

WHEN THE SUMMER MOON COMES 'LONG

VERSE 1

If you want to wed a little girl
Simply wild about her
Couldn't live without her
If your heart's completely in a whirl
Just want to love and spoon
Don't propose while winter-time is here
Wait till stars are gleaming
Winking, blinking, beaming
Now's the time to ask your little dear
Under the summer moon.

REFRAIN

First select a small canoe
Where there's only room for two
You'll love her and she'll love you
You could never get in wrong
While the stars are shining bright
In the silv'ry dreamy night
You can hold her fold her tight
When the summer moon comes 'long.

VERSE 2

When you've popped the question to her too
After you have kissed her
She'll only be your "sister"
Then declare that you're completely through
Paddle her back home soon
Drift along until you've met a queen
Some one who will marry
Won't put off or tarry
Take her to the spot where you've just been
Under the summer moon.

Garland's Group: Cole is standing in the back row, directly behind his classmate, W. Averell Harriman.

Football Song Writing:

Cole Porter, Latest Yale Composer of Big Game Choruses, Looks to New Hits "Bull Dog" and "Eli" to Cheer Team to Victory Next Week.

It organized cheering, swinging football songs, good leaders or marches is the best can have any part in winning a championship, Yale will win out the year over Harvard and Princeton.

Not since "Down the Field" was written for the late James J. Hogan, eleven have their been so many good football songs as there this year. It is probable that "Down the Field" still ranks as a football song. There is none in any other college that can compare with it for the purpose and none has been written at Yale. But there have been several songs since "Down the Field" was written that have voiced a season and then been forgotten. The songs this year seem to have some qualities which will make them last for more than a year, as some of them are written in such a way that they can be used at any time.

"Down the Field" was distinctly a song for Hogan's team. It was written by W. W. O'Connor, who by the way has just written a new one "Yale Forever," and who is coming here to teach it to the men. Everybody knows "Down the Field," and its use has just been peculiar to Yale in the past few years. It is one of the greatest college marches ever written. The line: "Give a long cheer for Hogan's men" is still heard at the games, though the name substituted there is the successive years were Sheffin, Morse, Biglow, Burch, Coy, Daly and this year Howe. The song was written for that team. It took Yale men, undergraduates and graduates by storm and was learned everywhere. The name Hogan stuck to it, and probably will for years.

"BINGO!"

Bingo! Bingo!
Bingo! Bingo! Bingo! that's the lingo.

CHORUS OF THE BULL DOG SONG.

Chorus.

Bull dog! Bull dog! Bow, wow, wow, E-li Yale,
Bull dog! Bull dog! Bow, wow, wow, Our team can nev-er
fail, When the sons of E-li break thr

When Princeton Has the Ball on the Yale Five Yard Line.

"BRIGHT COLLEGE YEARS."

Bright college years, with pleasure rife,
The shortest, gladdest years of life,
How swiftly are ye gliding by,
Oh, why does time so quickly fly?
The seasons come, the seasons go,
The earth is green or white with snow,
But time and change shall nought avail
To break the friendships formed at Yale.

In after years should troubles rise
To cloud the blue of sunny skies,
How bright will seem through mem'ry's haze
Those happy, golden, by-gone days.
Then let us strive that ever we
May let these words our watch cry be,
Wherever upon life's sea we sail,
"For God, for country, and for Yale!"

Eli's bound to win.
There's to be a victory,
So watch the team begin.
Bingo! Bingo!
Princeton's team can naught avail.
Fight! Fight! Fight with all your might!
For Bingo! Bingo! Eli Yale!

Mr. Porter had no musical education, but had natural ability along this line. Some of the peculiar and distinctive features of his work have been explained by the fact that he has spent several years in the mountains of Roumania and heard many strange birds while up there. But it was probably the sight of Bill Howe's dog "Beans," which used to be in a continual brawl at Yale field last spring, but which had quieted down on the gridiron this fall, which inspired the following song which has been chosen as one of the official songs for the fall:

"BULLDOG."

Bull-dog! Bull-dog!
Bow wow wow!
Eli Yale!
Bull-dog! Bull-dog!
Bow wow wow!
Our team can never fail.
When the sons of Eli break through the line,
That is the sign we hail.
Bingbang! Bull-dog!
Bow wow wow!
E—li Yale!

Mr. Porter's third song is very short, but can be used at critical moments when some opposing team strikes near the Yale goal line. The song goes back to the beginning of things at Yale and is named "Eli." It follows:

"ELI."

E—li! E—li!
We are warriors ever glorious,
Enter the fray with hearts victorious,
Cheering for E—li. E—li!
Forever old Eli Yale.

Mr. Porter's work, it should be stated is not confined to writing football songs. He has just been engaged to write an opera for the summer colony at Easthampton, L. I., for which "Spud" Murphy of the class of 1908 will write the words. Another light opera by him is shortly to be produced. He proved the feature of the Glee club trip last winter and of various college banquets because of his versatile style of entertainment.

Another song which has been chosen as an official one for the fall and which will be sung at the big game is "Here Comes the Tiger," by Henry T. Rogers, Jr. of Cleveland. This song is longer and also has a good swing to it. Rogers is a member of the sophomore class in the academic department. He submitted his song with the others to the cheer leaders, and it was one of those selected, quite an honor for a sophomore. It follows:

HERE COMES THE TIGER.

Here comes the Tiger from Nassau,
Shouting his battle cry, "Waw! Waw! Waw! Waw!"
Eli will tame his roar
By rolling up a score.
Watch the blue go smashing through the orange line.
Princeton will soon be in mourning,
World is at the tiger's tail,
O'er the field victorious,
Make a touchdown glorious,
Win again for Eli Yale.

Other songs have been written this fall, but were not chosen by the powers for the official ones. Some of them have been printed and have been put on sale in music stores.

Beside these songs there will be "Whoop It Up for Yale," "Boola," by Hirsch, and others which have proved popular in years past. The two so called great Yale songs will also be sung at the games. "Bright College Years" and "Mother of Men," the latter the Herald prize song. The music was written by Seth Bingham of this city, and the words by Brian Hooker, formerly an English instructor at Yale, who wrote the words for Prof. Horatio Parker's opera, "Mona," last summer.

The songs have been practiced at the mass meeting in the university dining hall during the past week. There will be two or three mass meetings this week and the same number the following week preceding the Harvard game for the hundreds of students who will accompany the team to Cambridge.

The mass meeting for the practicing of cheers and learning the songs used to be held in Alumni hall at the northeast corner of the campus. But alumni hall has now been torn down and the Wright Memorial is being built in its place. The dining hall has proved the best available place for the singing and cheering. In order not to tire the boys' throats too much before the games, the men are given a rest for a while during the mass meeting and short addresses pleading for support, a plea entirely unnecessary are delivered by graduates. At the meeting Friday night there were brief speeches by Tom Shevlin, Jack Field and Capt. Howe, who are probably the biggest men to the undergraduate mind in the country at the present time.

The selection of the cheer leaders this year is particularly fortunate, both the academic and the Sheff men being very good. The leaders have had practice together and showed yesterday that they could lead cheering together with quality which has been rarely seen in Yale cheer leaders in the past.

The chief cheer leaders is Robert A. Gardner, leader of the Glee club, and crack pole vaulter, and former national golf champion. The other leaders are Stew Pittman, Vin Murphy, Len Burdette, George Thompson, Johnny Caldwell and Bill Osborn. Pittman wasn't at the field yesterday. The leaders will accompany the Yale cheering section to Cambridge after providing here next Saturday.

Differing from other colleges the Yale cheering is very simple and as in former years practically the only cheer used will be the so-called frog chorus from the opera written by the late Mr. Aristophanes.

COLE PORTER.

Who Drew Inspiration From Roumania's Birds and Bill Howe's Bull Dog.

Porter Stewart Wagoner Harper Derrick Chauncey Platt Meacham

1912 FOOTBALL CHEER LEADERS

BRIDGET MC GUIRE

VERSE 1

Bridget McGuire was a scullery maid.
And she worked in a home way up town
Patrick O'Brien was just simply dyin'
To marry and then settle down.
Most ev'ry night Pat on Bridget would call,
Thus he passed the long ev'nings away.
Soon Miss McGuire didn't mind it at all
Or the "Blarney" when Patrick would say

REFRAIN

Bridget—Bridget
Sweet Colleen Bawn!
'Faith and I'm feelin' so sad and forlorn
Won't you just smile at me
Once in a while at me?
Sure! And my heart is on fire;
I never met a girl that I liked better
Come on—Bridget,
Out for a lark,
We'll go meandering all through the park,
Ah! You're far too delicious
To wash and wipe dishes,
Miss Bridget, Bridget McGuire.

VERSE 2
(First Version)

Pat struck it rich and the two were soon wed
In the Church 'round the corner one day
All was complete, when they moved to their suite
In a huge hotel down on Broadway.
'Most every night you can see them about
For they go to the shows right along.
Perhaps that is Pat, who's asleep over there,
If it is, he'll wake up to this song.

VERSE 2
(Second Version)

Mister Pat had good luck, but to Bridget he stuck,
And he wedded her one day in May
When they were married, Miss Bridget was carried
To a house of his own, people say.
Now she has steam yachts and motors galore,
And though happy she often will long
To hear Pat's "blarney," as in days of yore
And to have him again sing that song—

★★★★★★★★★★

In the fall of 1910 Porter submitted *Bingo Eli Yale* in
the annual football song competition. *Bingo* was formally
introduced by Eddie Wittstein and his orchestra at
the Yale Dining Hall dinner concert on
October 29, 1910. The words of the song were
printed in the *Yale Daily News* and the song itself was
successfully tried out at several football rallies.

BINGO ELI YALE

Bingo! Bingo!
Bingo! Bingo! Bingo! That's the lingo.
Eli's bound to win,
There's to be a victory,
So watch the team begin.
Bingo! Bingo!
Princeton's team cannot prevail,
Fight! Fight!
Fight with all your might
For Bingo,
Bingo, Eli Yale!

★★★★★★★★★★

Eddie Wittstein, who conducted other Porter
premieres—including his first musical comedy, "Cora"—
remembers that Cole was "a good pianist, and
though not an especially talented singer he
was excellent at putting over his own lyrics. I
always liked him and played a lot of his football songs at
the dining hall and the Yale Proms."
In his junior year Cole wrote *Bull Dog, Eli, Beware
of Yale, Fla-de-dah,* and *Hail to Yale* (lyrics only). By
senior year he was a cheerleader and, as chairman
of the football committee, arbiter of all new
Yale football songs.

RECOLLECTIONS OF GERALD MURPHY, YALE '12

*There was this barbaric custom of going around
to the rooms of the sophomores and talking with them,
to see which ones would be the right
material for the fraternities. I remember going
around and seeing several nights running, a sign on one
boy's door saying, "Back at ten PM. Gone to football song practice." Gordon Hamilton, the
handsomest and most sophisticated boy in the
class, was enormously irritated that anyone would have
the gall to be out of his room on visiting night, and
decided not to call on him at all. But one
night I was passing his room and went in, just to
say hello. There was a single electric light bulb in the
center of the ceiling, wicker furniture, which was
considered a bad sign at Yale in 1911, a
piano with a box of caramels on it, and a little dark
man with his hair parted in the middle and slicked back,
wearing a salmon-pink tie and a checked suit,
looking like a westerner dressed up for the
east. He told me that he had lived on an enormous
apple farm in Indiana and that he had a cousin called Des-
demona and they both used to ride to market on the
apple trucks. He said yes, he had submitted
a song for the football team and that it had just
been accepted. We had a long talk about music and composers—we were both crazy about Gilbert and
Sullivan. I got the Glee Club to take him in
as a sophomore—something that was almost never*

*done—so that he could sing a new song he had written
which he performed on the tour that year. It was
the hit of the show, a wonderful satire on
the joys of owning an automobile. He came out
front and sang it perfectly, without any sort of act, just
folded his hands behind him and sang it in the
simplest way, while the seniors and juniors
behind him on the stage went "zoom, zoom, zoom."*

THE
MOTOR CAR

Off we go to take a ride, take a ride, take a ride,
All the fam'ly jam inside,
Mercy, what a clatter!

Something breaks and out gets Pa,
        out gets Pa, out gets Pa,
Now he crawls beneath the car,
What can be the matter?

Oh! What was that awful crack, awful crack,
        awful crack?
Hit the trolley in the back,
Trolley's system's twisted.

What makes father look so queer,
        look so queer, look so queer
His nose is hiding behind his ear,
His whole expression's shifted.

Oh, the lovely motor car,
What a wreck it's made of Pa!
Over twenty doctor chaps
Worked on him in his collapse:
Mother wears a sickly grin
Where her face is dented in:
What do we care as long as we are
Having a ride in the motor car?

★★★★★★★★★★

Cole played, sang, and acted out *Yellow
Melodrama*, one of his Glee Club specialties, to the
accompaniment of crashing chords, in the
style of a silent movie pianist.

YELLOW
MELODRAMA

I'm so bored at going to the theater,
Modern drama isn't worth a penny.
Rostand has no charms for me,
Maeterlinck I cannot see—
Chanticleer and bluebirds are too many.
Oh, I know, it's hardly *comme il faut*
But a melodrama fills my soul with bliss.
My tastes may be plebeian
But efforts herculean
Can never change my taste for plays like this.

Yale Clubs Charm Audience
Concert Is Brilliant Success

FRANK L. WOODWARD greeting Cole Porter, president of the Yale Glee
club, upon the arrival of the club at Union depot in Denver yesterday
afternoon.

Oh, picture me a poor girl alone in London;
Darkness, nightfall and not a sailor in sight.
Would that I were back in the United States of America,
Back among the cowboys, the buffaloes, and the
        families.
Hark! Someone is coming on horseback.
A knock at the door.
What if it were Victor Lambert?
Why, Daddy!

Yes, my litle girl, it is your Dad.
For while hunting woodchucks in the south pasture,
I struck gold, and now I'm worth two thousand dollars.

Oh Daddy, isn't it great to be rich?
And now that you have come to take me
Back to the portals and arms
Of my house and my mother respectively,
Let me tell you what it was
That dragged me from our home.
It was love—love for a dirty villain
Who called for me each afternoon
At the factory in a plush-lined barouche.
But he could not win me by his wiles,
For I had a far greater love—
A love for my own native country.

Oh, oh, that yellow melodrama
Nowadays considered out of date
I really fear that no more we'll hear
The distant mail train calling to its mate.
No more we'll see the villain cutting capers
With Lady Vere de Vere
Because he knows she has the papers.
They were grand old days.
They were wonderful plays.
Oh, that yellow melodrama for me.

Yale Glee Club Wins Denver's Heart With Old College Songs and Music

SENTIMENT ATTACHING TO AFFAIR ADDS TO ENJOYMENT OF PROGRAM.

BY ELEANOR DAVIDSON.

The Yale concert last night was everything that one would want a college concert to be. The big Central Presbyterian church was brave with Yale banners, 1898 being the remotest date that I discovered emblazoned on the blue ground, while a mighty Y-A-L-E hung from the organ loft and made itself into a stage setting for the gree, banjo and mandolin clubs which form the concert organization.

The music was good, excellent of its kind, but that isn't really the chief reason for going to a college concert. If you are under 25 you go to see the fellows you know, or to see fellows like those you know. If you are—well past 25, you go to renew your youth. Yes, that is the secret of the fascination of the 'varsity chap. You like him, singly or jointly, because he is young and clean, enthusiastic and optimistic. He is so sure that he is going to please you—and the world is as surely to be his; your own enthusiasm and optimism rise to the occasion. Your toes begin to want to tap the time and you hum "Clementine" or "We Won't Go Home Till Morning" with the same old-young spirit that you did 10, 20 or 30 years ago. So a college concert is worth while, tremendously worth while, even were it not the fashionable affair that it always is with us, and with most cities.

FINE PROGRAM PROVES
DELIGHT TO AUDIENCE.

And these Yale chaps are a fine looking set. You feel that you would like your sister to know them; and they are exceptionally well trained. From the first chorus "Mother of Men, Old Yale!" to the last "Bright College Years" for which every Yale man in the house went to the stage and joined his voice to that of the club, both in the song and in the final yells of "Yale" and for "Denver," from first to last the big audience was delighed.

There were so many good things one is embarrassed in trying to name the best. "Wedding Glide," by the banjo club, and a "Laughing Song" (written by Goodale, '89), sung by the glee club, led up to, or down to, "Tutti Frutti," exploited by the glee and mandolin clubs. As you might guess, this number offered opportunity for a variety of stunts, the most ambitious, perhaps, being a baseball game played by M. B. Flynn, the 'varsity fullback. Mr. Flynn, I would guess, can get an engagement on the Orpheum circuit whenever he feels in need of funds. He caught all the kinds of balls I ever heard of and then some more, finally making a home run in as good style as do Ben-Hur's horses win their race in the play. There were a couple of boys who did a bit of good ragging too, and won applause, much of it.

To my mind the most effective music given was an encore played by the mando-

Members of the Yale Glee club, which drew one of the most fashionable audiences ever gathered in Denver. Left to right: Cole Porter, president; S. S. Colt, assistant manager, and H. H. Parsons, manager.

lins, "After Vespers," with its distant chimes and delicate shadings was as ethereal and exquisite as are our own new cathedral spires against the setting sun.

Of course there were bits of a dozen old songs, "In the Wildwood," "Three Blind Mice," "He Sighed," "When I've Nothing Else to Do," and so through a long list. The banjos in a Yale medley introduced a number of exclusively Yale airs.

Cole Porter of 1913, is president of the concert club and leader of the glee club. He also can secure a place on the Orpheum program when he is so inclined. "A Football King" is entirely his own idea, and when he and the club had finished it, he sat down to the piano and one after another responded to three or

four encores. His recitative work is clever.

But after all we come back to the youth and to the happiness of it all. Not the least attractive feature was the football rush with which the boys always left the stage, and then that last picture, with the old boys and the young boys joining hands and voices for the Alma Mater. It was a mighty good thing to see. I remember an evening when in company with one of the old boys of a German university I saw Mansfield in Old Heidelberg and looking up to comment on one of the songs I met eyes suffused with tears, and the old boy said, "This recalls almost too poignantly, the happiest days of my life." This, I think, is what the college concert means to most of us.

After *Bull Dog*, Cole's most celebrated Yale song
was *Antoinette Birby*, also known as *Sweet Alice Kirby*
and *Annabelle Birby*.

ANTOINETTE BIRBY

VERSE 1

Miss Antoinette Birby lived way out in Derby,
    a maid divinely fair.
She found it no heaven retiring at seven;
    her heart was filled with care.
'Twas truly a pity that a maiden so pretty
    should milk the cows all day,
So she took a notion to get into motion
    and packed her trunk right away.
As the train pulled out of the station,
    she gave forth this explanation:

REFRAIN 1

I'm off for New Haven, so long, goodbye,
I'm off for New Haven, I don't know why.
This leaving the family really makes me very sad,
For they are by far the best pa and ma I ever had.
    But I've got to sling hash at the Taft Hotel,
As a waitress I never shall fail.
For I have a cravin' for dear old New Haven
    and Yale, Yale, Yale.

VERSE 2

Arrived in the city, this maiden so pretty
    did walk down Chapel Street,
And then a young fellow to whom she said "Hello"
    our heroine did meet.
Now he was a villain, but Nettie was willin',
    she loved him right away.
Her scruples foresook her,
    the villain he took her into a swell cafe.
As she took down her first few swallows,
    she was heard to murmur rather
    incoherently as follows:

REFRAIN 2

I'm strong for New Haven, believe me, kid,
For this is the town where there ain't no lid.
The life in New Haven makes Derby seem so very tame,
I've learned sev'ral things
    that I never knew before I came.
I'm going to learn all that there is to know,
At least if I keep out of jail,
As a fountain of knowledge believe me some college
    is Yale, Yale, Yale.

VERSE 3

Next morn at eleven, instead of at seven,
    she woke up in dismay.
Her bean it was addled, her brain had skedaddled,
    for she had passed away.
The warden he brought her a pail of ice water,
    her thirst was so intense;
Her spirit was stricken, her conscience was pricken,
    her head it felt immense

As she left the police station,
    she gave out this information:

REFRAIN 3

I'm going back to Derby, so long, goodbye,
I'm going back to Derby, you all know why.
When I came to New Haven I was
    so very good and sweet and true,
But I've done sev'ral things
    that a girlie shouldn't oughta do.
So it's back to the milking for Antoinette,
A sadder but wiser female.
No maiden that's pretty should come to the city
    and Yale, Yale, Yale.

★★★★★★★★★★

Cole's own favorite Glee Club number was his parody of
Marie Dressler's treatment of the popular ballad, *Heaven
Will Protect the Working Girl.*

As enthusiastic audiences brought him back
again and again he often held the stage for over thirty
minutes, giving as many as twelve encores
before the Glee Club returned to conclude the
concert. Cole's act, with its assortment of original compositions, burlesque, humorous patter, and typical
allusions, had all the ingredients of first-class vaudeville.

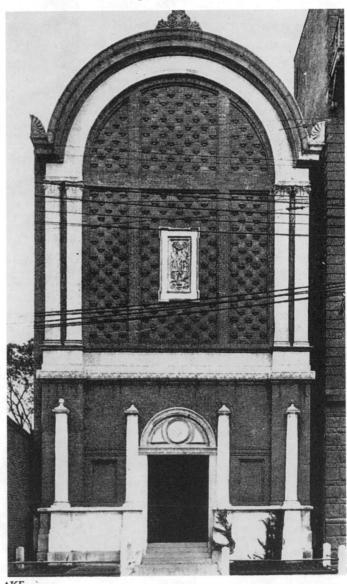

ΔKE

The Phi Theatre

York Street

R. A. Gardner and J. Coleman, Inc.

Proprietors and Managers.

—◄·•·►—

THE PHI OPERA CO.
DIRECTION OF
MESSRS. THOMAS AND PORTER
PRESENTS

 CORA.

A Musical Farce in Two Acts.

Book by T. Gaillard Thomas, 2nd.

Music and Lyrics by Cole Porter.

Staged by Peter C. Bryce.

Cole's first musical comedy, performed November 28, 1911

CORA (1911)

HELLO, MISS CHAPEL STREET

He: Hello, Miss Chapel Street
    You look very sweet tonight
She: Great damn,
    I'm sweet as sugar jam,
    And how is lovey-dovey,
    Little Willie wise boy?
He: I'm not so very well.
    I'm low as hell,
    For I can barely walk about a bit, dear
    Since we 'quit, dear,
    I'm not feeling very fit.
She: Well-a, well-a, who's to blame?
    I waited for an hour in the pouring rain.

He: But you didn't wait 'til eight.
She: I had a date with a freshman.
He: What's that you say
    That you had a date with a freshman?
She: Yesh, Man.
He: On my word,
    But that's absurd.
She: That's enough funny stuff;
    Cut the rough!
He: When can we have a party for two, dear?
She: That's up to you; any time will do.
He: Will you meet me to-night alone?
    For I've an awful lot of love
    That's simply hunting for a home.
She: Well, I'll be there,
    A-waiting on the square.
He: We'll have a drunken revel
She: Good night, you little devil.
He: We mustn't raise a riot.
She: Then kiss me on the quiet.
    Bring a low-necked hack and a bottle of Rye.
He: Oh, won't I!
    Goodbye.

POKER

Poker, poker forever
That's a grand old game
Of course it's rather hard on father
For sending checks is such a bother
And we'll confess, yes
Poker's expensive
But we're not to blame.
Though it may be dissipation
We need our recreation
So poker's the game

CONCENTRATION

Oh, it's awfully hard to concentrate at college.
Oh, it's awfully hard to concentrate at Yale.
Though we came with the one idea to get some knowledge,
We seem to fail, fail, fail.
Now, our families never guess we have a snap-a.
They think we'll trap-a
Phi Beta Kappa.
But really that's too dumb
For the extra curriculum
Makes the gay life at Yale.

SATURDAY NIGHT

Saturday night Saturday night
This is the one time we all get plenty of
Liquor, liquor just a wee flicker
So order a gallon and don't stop to bicker
We'll all sing something
Any old tune's all right
I love, I love the rest of the week
But oh! You Saturday night.

AND THE VILLAIN STILL PURSUED HER (1912)

Cole's second show, "And the Villain Still Pursued Her," a Yale Dramatic Association "smoker," was performed in the spring of 1912, with Monty Woolley starring as "The Villain."

I'M THE VILLAIN

VERSE

Now, I'm the kind of villain that you hear about,
Why, Satan is a saint compared to me;
Now, I'm the kind of villain that you'd fear about,
As much as any other you could see.
I never seek the open when the stars are shining bright,
But only when the streets are dark and solemn;

So if you ever wander in the dead and stilly night
Beware, or I shall twist your spinal column!

REFRAIN

Oh, I'm the villain,
The dirty little villain;
I leave a pool of blood where e'er I tread,
I take delight
In looking for a fight
And pressing little babies on the head
    till they're dead.
I have gotten
A rep for being rotten
I put poison in my mother's cream of wheat.
Tradition I base much on;
The family escutcheon
Is meat . . . raw meat.

THE POT OF GOLD (1912)

During the summer, Cole began work on the lyrics and music of a show that would be produced as the ΔKE fall initiation play. From Peru he wrote to his collaborator, Almet F. Jenks, Jr.:

In Cole's day, Scroll and Key was perhaps the most "social" of the secret societies at Yale, as Bones was the most august and reputedly the most powerful.

Cole is said to have written several anthems for Scroll and Key; if so, they have vanished forever behind all that ivy.

The Berkeley Oval where Cole lived in junior year

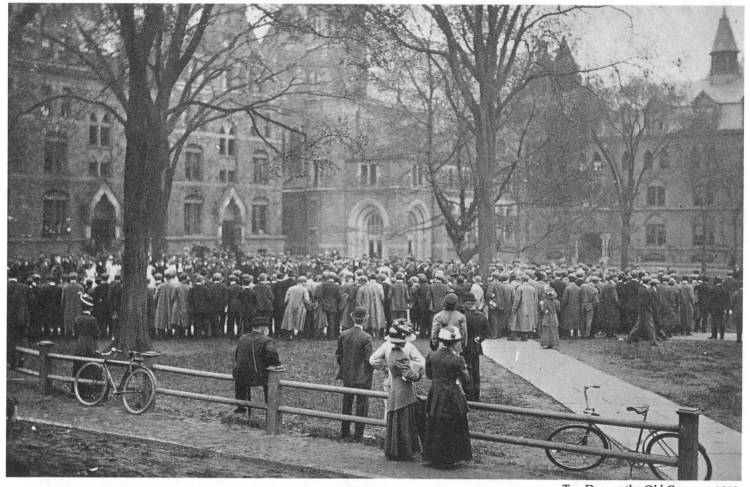

Tap Day on the Old Campus, 1913

Senior Society
C. S. P.

C. C. J.

John Adams Appleton
Reginald LaGrange Auchincloss
Walter Camp, Jr.
John Coleman
Albert Beecher Crawford
Robert Ovens Derrick
Lytton Warnick Doolittle

Anson Blake Gardner
Charles Henry Marshall
Henry Humphrey Parsons
Cole Porter
Jesse Spalding
Theodore Gaillard Thomas, II.
Vanderbilt Webb
Arnold Whitridge

The "tomb" of the secret Senior Society, Scroll and Key, designed in 1870, by Richard Morris Hunt, who subsequently conjured up a number of Renaissance castles for the Vanderbilts. The oldest of the secret societies at Yale, Skull and Bones, possessed a tomb in the Egyptian style; here Hunt's conscientious exoticism outdoes Egypt by echoing Byzantium. Tombs of other secret societies were later to resemble Greek temples (Book and Snake) and Cotswold manor houses (Wolf's Head).

★★★★★★★★★★

Westleigh on the Mis-sis-sin-e-wa,

Peru, Indiana

My Dear Almet,

I do hope you will be obvious and uninteresting. Otherwise we will suffer defeat, for my music was never the result of inspired imagination.

All I can ask is that you dash off a scenario and send it to me so I can work on opening choruses. Also tell me whom you select for different parts, and I can write fitting songs the more easily.

Don't forget color. We must have lots of that. Be naif and I can join you.

Goodbye.

Devotedly,
Cole

★★★★★★★★★★

Almet, My Dear

I am delighted I received a letter from you in which you showed a descent from the ethereal.

As for the title The Pot of Gold being trite, I think it is truly wonderful. A title is good only when it means nothing until the fall of the final curtain, and you must admit that in this case, the final curtain must fall. As for the cast, it seems rather large, but I suppose you consider it necessary. Of course with so many, rehearsals will be exceedingly difficult. Then, too, a chorus girl is worth more than a small useless part.

I love your two Russian Nihilists. As a matter of fact I have written your motif already. It combines the splendor of Wagner and the decadence of Strauss.

You speak of three acts. I beg you—Don't! Three would be either interminable or choppy. Remember what a change of costume and scene means! It is a terrible thought always, and if possible try to condense your action to two acts. I wish we could make this play a little masterpiece in its own foolish way. Take it horribly seriously, and I will join you. It really is important, for after all it can never happen again.

The minute you finish it send it to me, I have a great deal to do when I return to college, and I must have most of this play in black & white by Oct. 1st. As soon as college opens I shall begin rehearsing songs, & by the second week you can begin.

If you have written the opening of the first act, send it at once. Also write me the cast again, with the names of each member more plainly, so I can use them in verses of songs.

You have no idea how delighted I am that you have gone at this play so hard. We ought to open a few eyes.

Goodbye, Almet, & thank you.

Devotedly,
Cole

Aug. 23rd

★★★★★★★★★★

My Dear Almet:

Needless to say, I am delighted with the first act. The plot is excellent, the characters delightfully drawn, and most of the lines pertinent and witty.

I have written down the Overture. It begins with the motif—Chlodoswinde's yearning for Larry; then follows the waltz representing her pangs on finding him false, ending in the motif of supreme happiness, which appears again at the end of the play. Following this comes Larry's love song. Then a thing in 5/4 time introducing the foreign influence on the hotel, modulating into a death march representing the monotony and decadence of the place. This is connected with the opening chorus by a movement which grows more excited as it progresses. The opening chorus is the Rainbow song, which could be sung by guests who depart at the end of it.

If you get done soon enough (& by that I don't expect you to tear it off) I can have incidental music, an overture, an entre' acte, combined motifs, melodrama, etc.

Perhaps I sound altogether too serious about it, but I feel that it is up to you to show New Haven a little of that brain. You have no idea how much is expected. You have a reputation.

I can never thank you enough for accomplishing so much good work. Would it be possible to have the second act take place in the lobby also?

Goodbye, Almet. Write me if anything dramatic happens.

> *Devotedly,*
> *Cole*

Monday

****

My Dear Almet:

Of course I was delighted to hear from you that the second act doesn't require a switch, and I think your idea of contrast is wonderful. I feel duty bound to tell you how much work I have done because you must believe me enjoying the wilds of Maine. The truth is that I have manuscripted practically all of the first act. Immediately upon reaching New Haven Humphrey [Parsons] is going to try to persuade Dave Smith of the Music School to orchestrate it for about ten instruments.

As for getting together, I wish we could dine someplace Friday night and go through the members of each class and pick out ability. Don't you think we could confine the chorus to bell-boys and feminine guests? I shall leave the cast almost entirely to you, but of course those who can't sing can't have songs.

You have no idea how grateful I am for your play. I think we ought to get an awful lot of satisfaction in seeing it well done.

I can begin rehearsing songs Monday night, and you ought to begin getting separate parts typewritten as soon as you return.

I have had to insert arrows indicating the approach of certain songs, at which points the conversation must "lead up," but otherwise there are practically no changes.

I am so anxious to see you and talk over the whole thing, having thought of so little else during the past fortnight.

Finish that second act. I can do nothing until you do. You see my only means of making the songs relevant is by writing verses which give the idea of belonging to the person that sings them.

We shall meet very soon, but until then farewell.

> *Devotedly,*
> *Cole*

Sunday

We leave for New Haven tomorrow morning. Let me know the minute you arrive.

Late September, 1912

****

WHEN I USED TO LEAD THE BALLET

VERSE

Now you'd never infer
That as Premier Danseur
I was madly adored by the Russians
But when leading the ballet
My dance Bacchanale
Excited tremendous discussions,
With a negligee uniform
Over my puny form,
Thousands I made with delight rock!
In the get up I had on
I looked like the "ad" on
A bottle of sparkling White Rock!

Chorus: He was paid to say that,
           He was paid to say that,
           He was paid to say that about White Rock

REFRAIN

When I used to lead the ballet.
When I used to lead the ballet.
In costume so scanty
The world dilettante
Pronounced me a perfect joy.
Those wonderful days are over
When I danced with the fair Pavlova.
For I was her lordkin,
Her lambkin, her Mordkin.
Her beautiful ballet boy.

LONGING FOR DEAR OLD BROADWAY

VERSE

Gee what a place to waste a day in
Gee what a place to fade away in
Were I but free
Would I could be
Back where the world's alive
Some people pine for mountain green'ry
Never for mine this lonesome scen'ry
I'd like to walk
Start for New York
Back where the lobsters thrive

REFRAIN

For I'm longing for dear old Broadway
Longing for dear old town
Yes I'm longing to stroll on Broadway
Watching the world go 'round
To be back where the boys all know me
Back where the girls all bow
For I'm lonesome lonesome
Longing for Broadway now.

In his senior year Cole lived in 31 Vanderbilt Hall,
the room directly over the archway

Manuscript of the opening of "The Pot of Gold"

Whiffenpoofs ready for Brown game. Cole as "Pavalowa" in the front row

THE WHIFFENPOOFS

Bonnell   Kelleher

Sawyer   Marshall   Harper   Stevens   Krech   Porter   Tilney

THE NEW HOTEL
OF AMERICA

AN ESSAY
WRITTEN AND DELIVERED
BY COLE AT
SCROLL AND KEY,
JANUARY 16, 1913

It seems only fitting when the Taft Hotel is about to celebrate its first birthday to immortalize the celebration by writing an essay on The New Hotel of America.

Of course every town in the country with a sense of decency has a new hotel in these days. You may travel to the little city and look for the shabby hotel whose plush parlors you used to dread, only to find instead a wonderful skyscraper on the main street making all the early Victorian shops about it fairly black with rage.

The minute you arrive, the native who meets you begins booming the hotel to the skies. You are told with hushed awe of the interior decoration, and of the vulgar display of bathrooms. Then after leading up gradually, he ends by giving you the prize package—he mentions the grill—for there is always a grill. This is perhaps the most typical feature of the New Hotel—the grill—a low-ceilinged, rotingly ventilated cellar where the piece de resistance is rarebit, where the vintage is Budweiser all of which is accompanied by an orchestra from Long Branch taking the name of Robert E. Lee in vain.

With the coming of the new type of hotel, we have lost the dear old American plan—the famous gorge— the delight of the really hungry—which required no imagination to satisfy the appetite. Do you remember the days when a heavily betray-ed waiter used to place your plate on the table and then encircle it with little bathtubs—the whole giving the impression of a sun surrounded by a myriad of satellites? And will you ever forget the old menu that reveled in its number of vegetables, and gloated over its variety of pie? But those have passed now, and in its stead, we are presented with an aesthetic European plan menu wearing a cover on which is painted a lady in an impossible de-colleté gown rising out of a glass of champagne.

But these abuses which beset us are as nothing compared with the architectural evil in the typical New Hotel. And of course, New York is blamed again, when really the whole trouble lies with the owners of the hotels in our little towns. Every little village hotel owner decided to imitate the innocent metropolis to a T. As a result of this we see such a spectacle as the Hotel Taft which completely demoralizes the effect of a New England college campus.

But we rejoice to say that our American taste shows signs of improvement. This is a new era of hotels in America. Perhaps in a few years we shall return as graduates and refer to the dear old days when the Taft stood there.

The old New Haven House, for many years New Haven's principal hotel

The Hotel Taft built on the site of the old New Haven House

"The New Hotel of America" is even more interesting in the light of the fact that Cole was to spend much of his life in hotels. The little essay reveals Cole's irrepressible preoccupation with alliteration, syncopation, plays on words, puns, and rhymes.

THE
KALEIDOSCOPE
(1913)

"The Kaleidoscope" celebrates the dream of a boy intending to enter college. The first act depicts the prom of the past; the second invokes the prom of the future. "Cole Porter's production," said the *Yale Daily News*, "is a complete success, the music being superior to that of most Broadway musical shows. It makes your feet tingle and shake."

WE'RE A GROUP OF NONENTITIES

(Boom, boom) We're a group of nonentities,
(Boom, boom) Can't you guess our identities?
    We're but a fraction of a number graduated
    Who found their abilities
        were underestimated,
    And soon lost their jobs
        and (then) became intoxicated,
    And so (Diddle-dee-dum)
        sought the shelter of the street
    (Be-boom boom boom)
(Boom, boom) Known at Yale as the upper set
(Boom, boom) We were kings of the supper set,
    Gorging at restaurants expensive and luxurious,
    Racing to Wallingford in motors fast and furious,
    And now, down and out, we must admit
        we're rather curious
    To know (Diddle-dee-dum)
    Where to get a bite to eat.
    (Be-boom-boom-boom)
(Boom, boom) It's a hard life, (Boom) it's a weary one
    (Boom) When the dogs begin to bark.
(Boom, boom) It's a sad life, (Boom) it's a dreary one,
    (Boom) When you're sleeping in the park.
    Death hangs o'er us like the
        threatening sword of Damocles,
    We're so poor we can't afford
        a box of Rameses.
    (Boom) It's a hard life. (Boom)
        It's a weary one.
    Damn! Damn! Damn!

OH, WHAT A PRETTY PAIR OF LOVERS

VERSE

He: Let's live once more the day of
    warriors' surging fable.
She: When no one ran away,
    and King Arthur ran a table.
He: I love you so, my dear,
    I swear I ne'er shall doubt you.
She: Alas, I greatly fear
    I'm incomplete without you.
He: My heart is out of key
    It yearns for you to tune it.
She: How happy we shall be
    When once a perfect unit.
Both: Like lovers of the moyen age are we
    Singing silly persiflage are we:

REFRAIN

Both: Oh! What a pretty pair of lovers
    We two shall be.
    Side by side
    And always tied
    In a true blue lover's knot we.
    We don't care what the thoughts of
        the rabble are,
She: I'll be Eloise.
He: I'll be Abelard.
Both: Words of love with hints
        interlinear,
He: I'll be Paul,
She: And I Virginia.
Both: Climb the balcony by the
        trellis and
He: I'll be Pelleas.
She: I'll be Melisande.
Both: We don't care if the
        Round Table talks a lot.
She: I'll be Guinevere,
He: I'll be Launcelot.
Both: So cemented, quite unprecedented,
    Oh! What a pretty pair of lovers
        we two shall be!

The Elizabethan Club was founded at Yale in 1911 "to promote among its members and in the community a larger appreciation of literature and the arts and of social intercourse founded upon such appreciation." The Club's original purpose has been strengthened by its great library, which consists of over 250 volumes of first and notable editions of literary works of the Tudor and Stuart periods, including all the Shakespeare Folios and many of the Quartos. The Club was established by Alexander Smith Cochran, Yale '96, in tribute to "Billy" Phelps, who became its first president. Among the traditions of the Elizabethan Club are daily afternoon teas and, in the spring, lawn bowling and croquet in the garden.

A MEMBER OF THE YALE ELIZABETHAN CLUB

VERSE

I'm a member very noted
Of a club that's often quoted
As the most exclusive club in college.
My medulla oblongata
Has an awful lot of data
On the sources of our springs of knowledge.
I delight in being chatty
With New Haven's literati
On the subject of a brand new binding.
All the critics sing my praises
In illuminated phrases;
As a literary light I'm blinding.
As a literary light, as a literary light
    he's blinding!
Did you get that metaphor?
I confess I could do better for—

REFRAIN

I'm a member of the Yale Elizabethan Club
In a very hypocritical way.
By belonging to the Yale Elizabethan Club
I've a terrible political sway.
I convert New Haven
To the bard of Avon,
And a highbrow must I be;
For I give support
To the latest college sporto,
Tea by the quart
And editions by the quarto.
Good Gadzooks! But I love those books.
With a fol, with a fol,
With a hey, with a hey,
With a toureloure tourelourelay,
With a tralalalala,
With a tralalalala,
And a noney, noney, noney noney, ney,
For a member of the Yale Elizabethan Club am I!

PARANOIA (1914)

In the fall of 1913 Cole enrolled at the Harvard Law School. For a month or so he applied himself to his legal studies and even submitted a brief to the Williston Law Club, which he dutifully sent home to Indiana. Nevertheless music remained his chief interest and was the occasion for many late night parties in his room at 404 Craigie Hall. The following year, at the suggestion of the Harvard Law Dean, who heard him perform at a smoker, Cole switched from Law to the School of Music.

During his first year in Cambridge, Cole made friends with a fellow Keys man, T. Lawrason Riggs, Yale '10, who was then in the Harvard Graduate School. Riggs, who shared Cole's enthusiasm for Gilbert and Sullivan, had a good knowledge of literature, especially of the work of the romantic poets.

In 1914 Riggs' close friend Monty Woolley, who had just been appointed director of the Yale Dramat, invited him and Cole to write the Dramat play for the spring. The result was "Paranoia, or Chester of the Yale Dramatic Association," originally titled "The Belle of the Balkans." The work, performed at the Hotel Taft on April 24, anticipated by exactly two months the assassination of Archduke Ferdinand and his wife as they drove through the streets of Sarajevo, the capital of just the sort of Balkan kingdom depicted in "Paranoia."

Though the book, music, and lyrics were listed under joint authorship, the music was all Cole's and the book almost all Riggs'.

PROFESSOR WILLIAM LYON PHELPS

Johnfritz Achelis
William Christian Bullitt, Jr.
Carroll Chevalier Carstairs
George Herbert Day, Jr.
Jesse Holliday Philbin

Cole Porter
Allan Shelden
Aaron Augustus Vanderpoel
Ewing Thruston Webb
Arnold Whitridge

WILLISTON LAW CLUB.

C. D. Exum)
)
   vs.   )   BRIEF FOR THE PLAINTIFF.
)
X. Y. Jones)
                 Coram W. McAfee, C. J.

     Defendant and his friend Brown were standing on a street corner waiting for a car when Brown said to Defendant, "Tell me what you know about the murder in South Boston." Thereupon Defendant spoke the following words intending that only Brown should hear them. "I see from the morning paper that Exum is strongly suspected of the crime. Much evidence tends to show that he is the guilty man, but from the facts stated in the newspaper there is not sufficient evidence to warrant saying he is guilty. Still I would suspect the rascal anyway. My friend Smith says he is guilty and I believe him!"

     The truth was that there were two morning papers and one of them charged A. B. Exum with the crime and the other the plaintiff. Jones and Brown did not know the plaintiff and both had A. B. Exum in mind. A. B. Exum was in fact guilty. One person in the crowd, waiting for the car, overheard the conversation between the defendant and Brown and, having read the paper which charged the plaintiff with the crime, reasonably believed that the plaintiff was the man the defendant was speaking of, but he had been with the plaintiff on the night of the murder and knew in fact that he (the plaintiff) was not guilty.

     The plaintiff now sued the defendant for slander. The defendant demurred but was overruled and brings the case upon appeal.

BRIEF.

(I) The words are actionable *per se*, in that they impute a crime.
       Pollard v. Lyon. 91 U. S. 225.

   (a) They need not state a charge with all the precision of an indictment.
       Oldham v. Peake. 2 W. Bl, 959.

   (b) General Damages need not be specifically proved.
       Palm v. N. Y. News Pub. Co. 31 N. Y. App.Div.210.

(II) The words were published -- made known to persons other than plaintiff.
       See - Salmond, Torts, 3rd ed. §137, Par. 1.

     It is no defence that words were spoken confidentially and overheard. Negligence is no excuse.
       Shepheard v. Whitaker. L. R. 10 C. P. 502.
       See Odger, Libel & Slander, 5th ed. p. 163, &
          1st case under "Illustrations," on p. 163.
       Cockburn J. R. v. Tanfield. 42 J.P. p. 424.
       Hedley v. Barton, 4 F. & F. 224.

(III) The words referred to plaintiff. It is sufficient if those who heard the slander made out that the plaintiff was the person meant.
       H. & Co. v. Jones. 1910 A. C. 20.
       Le Fahu v. M. 1 H. L. C. 668.

(IV) It is immaterial that the only person to whom the words were published, knew that they were not true.

     THEREFORE, as the words spoken by the Defendant are actionable *per se*, as these words were published, and were reasonably interpreted to refer to the Plaintiff, it is the Plaintiff should have judgment against the Defendant for slander.

          · Respectfully submitted,

               Cole Porter

               Counsel for Plaintiff.

I WANT TO ROW ON THE CREW

VERSE

Now when Willie was still an obtuse Montesorri-an,
Having heard of Yale victories early Victorian,
He was mad to show oarsmanship ichthyosaurian,
On the Yale University Crew.
What a "Bright College Years" thing to do!
Though his mother regarded his scheme as chimerical,
And referred to his prospects in accents satirical,
Little Willie would chant in apostrophes lyrical
To the Yale University Crew.
Swing, swing, together!
In a voice that might rival Apollo's,
He expressed his intentions as follows:

REFRAIN

I want to row on the crew, mama.
That's the thing I want to do, mama.
To be known throughout Yale when I walk about it,
Get a boil on my neck (tail) and then talk about it.
I want to be a big bloke, mama,
And learn that new Argentine stroke, mama.
You'll see your slim son putting crimps in the crimson,
When I row on the (Brek-ek-coax-coax
    Brek-ek-coax-coax Parabalou)
When I row on the Varsity Crew.

August 1913, touring the English countryside: Cole, Peter Cooper Bryce, Charles Marshall, and Gurney Smith

WE'RE ALL DRESSED UP AND WE DON'T KNOW HUERTO GO (1914)

The Eleventh Annual Meeting of the Associated Western Yale Clubs was held in Cincinnati on May 22 and 23, 1914. Cole and several other members were invited to prepare a show—a spoof on the Mexican revolution.

The late Johnfritz Achelis, '13, the President of the Yale Dramat during Porter's senior year, recalled that the organizers of the evening . . .

were looking around for some entertainment and our show was suggested. Upon being approached we said we would be glad to come, but there were certain conditions, viz: we had to have first class accommodations, cards for all clubs, unlimited signing privileges, invitations to all parties, etc. etc. Well, the grads certainly came through in fine style. We had a car of our own which also served as hotel. Each one of us was presented with cards to five clubs, we attended the final polo matches, and many parties. Cliff

Wright was the local manager and it was for this occasion that Cole wrote C-I-N-C-I-N-N-A-T-I.

CINCINNATI

There's a place that I want to G-O
On the banks of the O-H-I-O.
What's the name of the C-I-T-Y?
C-I-N, C-I-N, N-A-T-I.
Let's go off for a T-R-I-P
Neath the flag that is B-L-U-E,
To the town that is not D-R-Y,
C-I-N, C-I-N, N-A-T-I.
There you'll probably S double E
Every drunken old G-R-A-D,
Get it way up his N-O-S-E.
S-O-S, P-D-Q, R-S-V-P.
In Cincinnati, in Cincinnati,
From hill and dale
Gathers Yale
To develop tissue fatty
On the beer here, beer there, beer everywhere
Flowing from the fountain in the public square
In Cincinnati, in Cincinnati,
The way they sing
Everything
Would make Adelina Patti
Give the kitchen stove and the derby of brown
To that Ohio town.

"Inspiration—Guy, Lytton, myself, and Lawrason"

"Perspiration—myself and Lawrason"

Apparently we were a success because a few years later the reunion was in Cleveland, and we were again asked to assemble the show. Len Hanna was the manager. We arrived in Mentor at 6 AM in cold, cold weather. Len was there and led us to the waiting room where we were liberally served hot rums. Some of us were put up at the Tavern Club and the rest at the other end of "Liquid" (Euclid) Avenue at Len's house. For this occasion Cole wrote Cleveland. *He wired the words to us in New York and we learned them on the train. As I remember, there were six or eight pages to the telegram.*

We had one more performance. The wives were curious to see the show so Buddy Marshall arranged a production at the Marshall Field House on Park Avenue and 69th Street. They put on a great party for us.

CLEVELAND

VERSE 1

Listen my dearie
Out on Lake Erie
I know the grandest town
Cleveland, Ohio
Oh me oh my-oh
A place of great renown
Cleveland—that's the title of my ditty
Cleveland—it's the famous Forest City
Cleveland—where they have the ammunition
Cleveland—to prohibit prohibition
Cleveland—praise the Lord and sing Hosannah
Cleveland, it's the home of Hoyt and Hanna
Cleveland, Cleveland, Cleveland, Cleveland, C L E V E L A N D.

REFRAIN

Oh Cleveland—let's make it Cleveland
It's such a gay old town
Chock full of real he-men
Y-A-L-E men
The kind who drink it down, way down

They're slicker at drinking liquor
Than any men I know
So we won't go beggin'
When we go bootleggin'
Out in Cleveland O-hio.

VERSE 2

Some say Toledo
Is full of speed-o
And rate Alliance
By quarts and pi-ants
In Marietta
Folks who know better
Are growing wetter and wetter and wetter
The wine in Akron
Is full of saccharin
The beer is cooler
In Ashtabula
The drinks in Dayton
More stimulatin'
But just you wait an' see
Oh, Cleveland, etc.

YALE MAN, SONG WRITER, HAS A FINE FUTURE

"I consider Cole Porter, your Yale graduate, who is now writing his first professional music, the most promising composer of light opera that I have ever encountered," declared Miss Elizabeth Marbury, the well-known dramatic agent and producer, who was here to witness the first night of Lew Field's new play for which Mr. Porter has supplied several numbers. Miss Marbury, who is known from coast to coast, and is a recognized authority on matters theatrical, was the one who first induced Mr. Porter, who was graduated from Yale only last year, and is now taking a special musical course at Harvard, to "write for the profession."

"It may seem that I am making a large order for the young man," she went on, "but I am convinced that Mr. Porter is the one man of the many who can measure up to the standard set by the late Sir Arthur Sullivan. This looks like a boast, but watch him.

"Hands Up," New Haven Evening Register,
June 8, 1915

Cole and cast of Cleveland show

CAMBRIDGE MASS APL 9TH 15.

S. F. PORTER, WESLEIGH FARMS, PERU IND.

CHECK ARRIVED LAST WEEK THANK YOU GOT OFFER TO WRITE JUNIOR

LEAGUE SHOW FOR NEXT YEAR COULD NOT ARRANGE MEETING

WITH COMMITTEE UNTIL MONDAY NIGHT   WILL COME HOME AS SOON

AFTER AS POSSIBLE MEETING MISS MARBURY TOMORROW AFTER-NOON LOVE..

NEWYORK ADDRESS SIX EAST SEVENTY SEVENTH CARE C. H. MARSHALL...

COLE...

APL 10TH-----8;12AM.......

10 5 W. 40 C

Miss Marbury

10 30 Monday

123 Fifty-fifth Street, East

MISS ELISABETH MARBURY
105 WEST 40TH STREET
NEW YORK

April 12,1915

Dear Mr. Porter,

Will you please meet me,
to play over your songs, to-morrow,
Tuesday, at 12 o'clock, at "Chez Maurice",
Wintergarden Building, Broadway, between
50th and 51st Street.

Sincerely Yours,

Elisabeth Marbury

KR-- NEWYORK N Y 11;28AM APL 12TH 15.

MRS. S. F. PORTER, WESTLEIGH FARMS, PERU,INDIANA.

MARBURY DELIGHTED PRODUCTION ASSURED FOR NEXT YEAR MEETING WEBER AND

FIELDS MANAGER TOMORROW IN REGARD TO INTERPOLATING SEVERAL OF MY

OLD SONGS IN THEIR NEW SHOW MEETING JUNIOR LEAGUE COMMITTEE

TONIGHT LEAVE FOR HOME TOMORROW AFTER-NOON....

COLE ...

SEE AMERICA FIRST (1916)

WESTERN UNION

WESTERN UNION AND CABLE

DAY LETTER

THEO. N. VAIL, PRESIDENT

Form 2589

RECEIVED AT

31 CH 43 BLUE

CH BOSTON MASS 710PM MAY 25, 1915

MRS J O COLE
    PERU IND

JUST RETURNED AFTER SIX DAYS WITH MARBURY, SHOW TO BE PRODUCED IN

OCTOBER, TELL GRANDAD LEW FIELDS GAVE ME 50 DOLLARS FOR EACH SONG

I SOLD HIM AND FOUR CENTS ON EACH COPY, FOUND YOUR WIRE WAITING.

THANK YOU SO MUCH WRITING

        COLE
        642PM

RECEIVED AT   3 CH B 37 ...

CAMBRIDGE MASS   3;10PM DEC 15TH 15

MRS. F. W. PORTER, PERU INDIANA.

JUST RETURNED FROM NEWYORK UNLESS SOMETHING EXTRAORDINARY HAPPENS

SHOW WILL GO INTO REHEARSAL IN A FEW WEEKS PRODUCED BY MARBURY

AND MOROSCO BUT DONT BE OVER CONFIDENT TELL GRANDAD AND BESSIE

TERRIBLY SORRY YOU ARE NOT WELL ..

        COLE PORTER...

RECEIVED AT JACKSON BOULEVARD AND LA SALLE ST., CHICAGO.

A60 NY 20 NL

    UD NEWYORK 24

  MRS F PORTER

      1309 ASTOR ST CHICAGO ILLS

SHOW GOING BEAUTIFULLY FRIGHTFULLY BUSY WILL WRITE SOON GIVE MY

LOVE TO DIXIE AND DOCTOR MISS YOU A LOT GOODBYE

        COLE.

Form 1204

CLASS OF SERVICE	SYMBOL
Day Message	
Day Letter	Blue
Night Message	Nite
Night Letter	N L

If none of these three symbols appears after the check (number of words) this is a day message. Otherwise its character is indicated by the symbol appearing after the check.

WESTERN UNION TELEGRAM

NEWCOMB CARLTON, PRESIDENT

GEORGE W. E. ATKINS, VICE-PRESIDENT   BELVIDERE BROOKS, VICE-PRESIDENT

CLASS OF SERVICE	SYMBOL
Day Message	
Day Letter	Blue
Night Message	Nite
Night Letter	N L

If none of these three symbols appears after the check (number of words) this is a day message. Otherwise its character is indicated by the symbol appearing after the check.

RECEIVED AT 18 CHM 23 BLUE.

UD NEW YORK NY 650PM FEB 14,1916

MR S F PORTER
    WESTLEIGH FARM
        PERU IND

EVERYTHING GOING BEAUTFULLY REHEARSING FROM

TEN IN MORNING UNTIL TWELVE AT NIGHT TIRED BUT CONTENTED WILL

WRITE AT EARLYEST OPPOPTUNITY.LOVE TO ALL

COLE-852PM

SA-- SCHENECTADY N Y FEBY 20TH 16

MRS. S. F. PORTER,

WEST-LEIGH FARMS,

PERU,INDIANA.

OPEN SCHENECTADY TUESDAY MATINEE PLAY ALBANY THURSDAY FRIDAY SATURDAY

NEXT WEEK ROCHESTER FOLLOWING WEEK RETURN TO NEWYORK AND REHEARSE

NEWYORK OPENING SHOULD BE MARCH FOURTEENTH IF EVERYTHING GOES WE LL

CAN MAKE NO PREDICTIONS LOVE TO ALL.

COLE .

RECEIVED AT

1 CH B   28 ...

SCHENECTADY N Y 9;22PM FEBY 22ND 16

MRS. S. F. PORTER,

WESTLEIGH FARMS, PDRU INDIANA.

SHOW MOST ENTHUSIASTICALLY RECEIVED HAVE HIGH HOPES FOR BRILLIANT

OPENING IN NEWYORK USUAL WORK PREPARATORY TO PREMIERE NOW BEGINNING

BIGELOW SCORES TREMENDOUS HIT DONT WORRY LOVE TO ALL...

COLE.

Dorothie Bigelow, Cole's first leading lady

RECOLLECTIONS
OF DOROTHIE BIGELOW

*My two sisters were married and living
in New York and I was studying singing with the famous
Miss Nellie Rowe in London, when the war of 1914
broke out.*

*I'd had a number of good prospects for the Autumn—a
revival of "Veronique" and several private concerts
—but these plans naturally went by the
board. We now bent our talents to concert parties
for soldiers and sailors in our part of England. It seemed a
minute part to play but evidently gave pleasure.*

*After about a year and a half of war-
time London my family began to agitate. So just
before 1916 I arrived in New York and was treated more
or less as a refugee.*

*Mrs. O. H. P. Belmont asked me to sing
the lead in a musical that she was producing in aid
of the Woman's Suffrage movement. The music was being
composed by the talented Miss Elsa Maxwell,
whom I accordingly went to see.*

*Just then Bessie Marbury and Cole Porter
erupted into my life. Inevitable that he and I should meet
at a party for, after leaving Yale, Cole had become
the pet of New York society. He had an
utterly charming Leprechaun personality which,
coupled with his gift of song, endeared him to everyone.*

*Soon after this Bessie Marbury was at my sister's,
where I was singing to them after tea and
she stayed behind to ask me if I'd like to go into
Cole Porter's musical which she was producing. I said
"Yes" and with apologies to Mrs. Belmont and
Elsa, embarked upon "See America First."*

*Under Bessie's aegis, Mr. Cole Porter and I met
again, unsocially, along with Lawrason Riggs, his collaborator, and the real star of the set-up, Benrimo. A
well known actor, he had created the role
of the Sheriff in "The Girl of the Golden West."
Next he'd taken the country by storm with his play "The
Yellow Jacket." He was an arresting personality.*

*Lawrason Riggs was charming. On the dif-
fident side—a complete contrast to the ebullient
Cole—shy and reserved but never failing in courtesy.*

*After this get-together we went into rehearsal.
My family seemed surprised but not unduly shaken.*

SEE AMERICA FIRST

Of European lands effete,
A most inveterate foe
My feelings when my camp I greet
Are such as patriots know
Condemning trips across the blue
As dollars badly dispersed
I hold that loyal men and true
Including in the category all of you

Should see America first
Should see America first.

All hail salubrious sky
All hail salubrious sky
Observe when I invoke the sky
It echoes reassuringly
That one should try to see America first
To see America first.

Of course, it's really not the sky
But just a repetition of his battle cry
To see America first
To see America first

So ev'ry true American
Whether white or red or black or tan
Should push this patriotic plan
To see America first.

This version was discarded and an entirely new
title song was substituted. It had a distinctly
Cohanesque quality.

VERSE

Of the sturdy Middle West I am the patriotic cream,
I'm the enemy of European Kings,
On the slightest provocation I can make the
        eagle scream,
When the Senate to my oratory rings.
He can talk for a week—
When he once starts to speak!
And I've thundered many times

That a trip to foreign climes
Is a thing no true American will seek.

REFRAIN

Don't leave America,
Just stick around the U.S.A.
Cheer for America
And get that grand old strain of Yankee Doodle
In your noodle;
Yell for America,
Altho' your vocal cords may burst;
And if you ever take an outing,
Leave the station shouting:
"See America First!"

I'VE A SHOOTING-BOX IN SCOTLAND

VERSE 1

Nowadays it's rather nobby
To regard one's private hobby
As the object of one's tenderest affections;
Some excel at Alpine climbing,
Others have a turn for rhyming,
While a lot of people go in for collections.

Such as Prints by Hiroshigi,
Edelweiss from off the Rigi,
Jacobean soup tureens,
Early types of limousines,
Pipes constructed from a dry cob,
Baseball hits by Mister Ty Cobb,
Locks of Missus Browning's hair,
Photographs of Ina Claire,
First editions still uncut,
Daily pranks of Jeff and Mutt,
Della Robbia singing boys,
Signatures of Alfred Noyes,
Fancy bantams,
Grecian vases,
Tropic beetles,
Irish laces,
But my favorite pastime
Is collecting country places.

REFRAIN 1

I've a shooting-box in Scotland,
I've a chateau in Touraine,
I've a silly little chalet
In the Interlaken Valley,
I've a hacienda in Spain,
I've a private fjord in Norway,
I've a villa close to Rome,
And in traveling
It's really quite a comfort to know
That you're never far from home!

"See America First" was Clifton Webb's first Broadway show.

VERSE 2

Now it's really very funny
What an awful lot of money
On exorbitant hotels a chap can squander;
But I never have to do so,
Like resourceful Mister Crusoe,
I can find a home however far I wander.

REFRAIN 2

I've a bungalow at Simla,
I've an island east of Maine,
If you care for hotter places,
I've an African oasis
On an uninhabited plain;
I've a houseboat on the Yangtse,
I've an igloo up at Nome,
Yes in traveling
It's really quite a comfort to know
That you're never far from home!

VERSE 3

Having lots of idle leisure
I pursue a life of pleasure,
Like a rolling stone in constant agitation
For tho' stay-at-homes may cavil,
I admit I'd rather travel,
Than collect a crop of mossy vegetation!

REFRAIN 3

I've a shanty in the Rockies,
I've a castle on the Rhine,
I've a Siamese pagoda,
I've a cottage in Fashoda,
Near the equatorial line!
On my sable-farm in Russia
O'er the barren steppes we'll roam,
And in traveling,
It's really quite a comfort to know
That you're never far from home.

During the tryout of the show, Cole wrote
a parody of *Shooting-Box*, which
was recalled by one of his good friends,
the late Lt. Col. Sir Rex Benson:

I've had shooting pains in Scotland
I've had measles in Touraine
I've had horrible malaria
When going through Bavaria
That suddenly turned to ptomaine
I've had Bright's Disease in Denmark
I've had whooping cough in Rome
But when traveling the continent
It's pleasant to know
That there's leprosy at home.

"Cole always referred to it as Shooting Pains
in Scotland, *but was quite upset when the chorus pronounced 'fjord' as 'Ford.'"* —D.B.

LADY FAIR, LADY FAIR

Lady fair, Lady fair
I have an intellect absurdly rare
Unsurpassed I am
At an epigram
And my verses have a note that's new
People weigh what I say
Posing as the critic of a book or play
On the whole it's plain
I've a brilliant brain
So I ought to be the man for you

Gentle Sir, gentle Sir
Culture is a quality I much prefer
I have always frowned on the sentimental sort
For I'm Queen uncrowned of a literary court
In that learned Massachusetts city
Where the stockings all are blue
So I'm sure I'd get along with you

Lady fair, Lady fair
I am a victim of the open air
I have cups galore
For my golfing score
For I always do a hole in two
Cheers I catch when I snatch
Goals by the dozens at a polo match
All the world agrees I'm a Hercules
So I ought to be the Man for you

Gentle Sir, with your notions I concur
For I love to be a stir
In some dashing sort of a sport
For pleasures athletic, peripatetic,
I excel in
Ev'ry game I figure well in
And you'll find very few
So competent to get along with you

Lady fair, Lady fair
I tell the tailors "what the men will wear"
In the swagger set
I'm a pampered pet
For my dancing is a joy to view
Fashion's knee bends to me
Begging for the pleasure of my company
Unapproached am I
As a butterfly
So I ought to be the Man for you

Gentle Sir
I've a tender passion for expensive Paris frocks
Gentle Sir
No one sees the Opera when I am in my box
Though its demands are not light
I love the social spot light
You must admit it's very true
I'd get along with you

Please give a quick consent
Thanks for the compliment
But though it could never be disputed

Dorothie Bigelow: "My hero was John Goldsworthy; a well-trained English actor with a good baritone and tall enough for me."

"The sextette was an important feature of the show. Billy Raymond, a concert singer and good looking. Wilfred Seagram, ditto. Clifton Webb, then utterly unknown, had a really nice voice and danced well. Mrs. John Charles Thomas (divorced) was enchanting-looking with long hair hanging below her waist—in fact she was a Vertès girl, long before the type had been invented. June, long golden hair. Gipsy Spain, piquante and new to the stage. In a day when the chorus was not noted for its PhD's, as they seem to be now, the girls were all charming and very young."—D.B.

Each to each is beautifully suited
Life would be very very dull
Very very dull
Very very dull
Why not try this obvious solution
Let's attempt a little substitution
I'll take you
You'll take me

Oh how much more interesting life will be!
Oh how much more interesting life will be!

*We rehearsed and rehearsed—shifting
scenes—new numbers for the sextette—everything in
short except the need for a first rate book, tailored to
Lawrason's very original, very amusing idea. During
the show I was conscious of Cole, Bessie, and Elsie de Wolfe
hanging out of their box, watching me. After the
curtain, they all clustered around—
touching but unnecessary. It was only later that it
dawned on me—I had no understudy.*

*After a matinee, the sextette and I were asked to stay
and were handed a new number, to go into the show
that evening. Plus a soft-shoe dance for
me. Never having studied "soft shoe," the efforts
of two chorus boys were unable to teach me
in one uneasy lesson.*

*By the time the number went into the
show, everyone was glassy-eyed. The chorus boy
who had to cue me into "Buy her a box at the opera," with
the line: "I'm sorry for you, Miss Huggins," approached
me in a daze, saying: "I'm sorry for you, Miss
Bigelow."*

The number was withdrawn the following day.

*We were in New Haven for one night only, which was
of course a bean-o with a terrific shebang after the show.*

*Then New York. A lay off. Benrimo
and tutti were sure that the lessons of the road had
registered and that now Lawrason would agree to
rewrite—anonymous or otherwise. But no. It was
announced that I would have a new wardrobe
from Madame Frances. Except for the Lion
Tamer, I didn't need a new wardrobe and I'm sure
that the sum spent would have paid for the play doctor.*

*What we were all waiting for was to be called
to rehearsal with a new book. When the
call came, it was just the same, only worse. And
so we progressed to the first night.*

*Unknown to us poor play actors, Bessie had evolved
the idea of a first night that would be all SOCIETY
—sans critics. We couldn't understand the
lack of reviews the following day but soon found
out when the critics were admitted. They weren't too kind
and you can't blame them. And so we moved
towards our slow death in that lovely
little theatre. Benrimo produced his "Willow
Tree" with tremendous success. Clifton Webb became
a brilliant revue artist and later an equally brilliant movie
actor. Lawrason Riggs eventually became a priest—
I'm sure a very good one.*

*Not embittered by his trying experience, Cole Porter
progressed to world-wide fame and acclaim.—D.B.*

"SEE AMERICA FIRST."

Maxine Elliott's (George J. Appleton, mgr.)
—*See America First*, a comic opera by T. Lawrason
Riggs and Cole Porter. Produced by Elisabeth
Marbury, on Tuesday night, March 28, 1916.

Lo, the Poor Indian............Henry Red Eagle
Notonah.........................Jeanne Cartier
Percy...........................Clifton Webb
Guy.............................Leo Gordon
Marmaduke.......................Lloyd Carpenter
Cecil, Duke of Pendragon...John H. Goldsworthy
Sarah Perkins...................Clara Palmer
Algernon........................Algernon Greig
Chief Blood-in-his-Eye..........Felix Adler
Ethel...........................Roma Juno
Gwendolyn.......................Betty Brewster
Muriel..........................Gypsy O'Brien
Polly Huggins...................Dorothie Bigelow
Senator Huggins.................Sam Edwards
Dancing with Clifton Webb...Mlle. Jeanne Cartier
SCENES.—Act I—At the Mesa. Act II—In the
Forest.

Staged by Benrimo.

We fear that "See America First" is not long
for Broadway, for the piece, which is billed as a
comic opera, is weak in both book and score.
The music is head and shoulders above the book.
The song, "See America First," is really one of
the most tuneful heard in the theatre this season,
and there are several other songs that are praise-
worthy.

A year after the closing of "See America First,"
Cole was studying music under the distinguished Pietro
Yon. He lived for a time at the Yale Club
of New York and then took an apartment on East
19th Street. After serving as an usher at the wedding of
Alice Huntington and his friend Charles Marshall
on June 2, 1917, he sailed for Europe to parti-
cipate in the work of the Duryea Relief Organization.

THE PERU REPUBLICAN.
FRIDAY, OCTOBER 5, 1917.

LETTER FROM COLE PORTER AT THE FRONT.

A very interesting letter from Cole
Porter, who is personal aid to the
president of the Duryea Relief party
now at the battle front in France,
written to his mother, Mrs. S. F. Porter, of this city, gives interesting and
valuable first-hand glimpses of the
war and his own work. He gives a
description of the latest German infernal machine, the caterpillar, a
string of burning torches shot from
the ground to hit the French air-
planes. We are permitted to copy
parts of the letter:

Dear Mother: An awfully cheery
letter arrived from you today (September 4) dated August 13.

Life here continues to offer great
surprises. For instance, yesterday I
went to inspect the village of Fresnoy.
As I was walking along the road of
the town I passed the entrance of an
abri (shelter in case of air raids).
But it looked so much better than
most of them that I opened the door
to it. I peered down the steps (they
are usually about twenty feet below
the surface) and there, at the bottom
stood a woman of about sixty years
smiling up at me. She asked me to
come down, which I did, and found an
immaculately clean room, a dirt floor
swept to a polish, and this was her
home. She told me her story—how
she was all alone in the world, her
husband and her son having been
killed, but, until the Boches had come,
she had lived in her brick house, on
her farm, with thirty cows (she had
prizes for cattle on her walls in the
cave). Then, the invasion She fled,
but was taken prisoner, sent to Prussia to work, grew ill and was returned

to France by way of Switzerland, went back to her home at Fresnoy, found it had completely disappeared, and she happened on this German abri as the only shelter she could find. Of course it was an astounding adventure 'she'd had, but the amazing part was her gaiety and her charm. I love this French race. They're so attractive, so amusing, so wonderfully brave, and so simple—just like children, all of them. So, we being without a cook, and I being tired of opening canned beans, asked her if she could cook. And she said, "Oh, Monsiur of course I can cook." So I said, "Pack up your things and jump in the motor." So here she is, this extraordinary old sport, living in the house with us, working like a Trojan, and cooking delicious omelettes, rabbit chops and compotes. And she has forgotten her trouble and we've forgotten ours!

Last night being very clear and calm, I went out to the aviation camp with the commandant of this canton, to see a glimpse, at least, of the only attractively exciting side of the whole war. I stood there and saw sixty aeroplanes rise, one by one, and make for St. Quentin. Before each aviator mounted his plane he would come up to his captain, shake his hand, and cry, "Au revoir, mon Capitaine!" and run off to his job. It was very, touching, mother, to see all this and to know that nearly every night one of these aeroplanes either never returns or else fails and kills its occupants.

A little later we saw three German caterpillars. The caterpillar is the newest German atrocity. It consists of a string of burning torches which is shot from the ground. It rises quickly and if it hits the French aeroplane it wraps itself about it and burns the plane and the occupants in the air. The French are completely "up in the air" about it. They fear it as nothing else and they can't understand how it is made.

I spent today in Erchen, and tomorrow I go to Amiens. I'm gradually getting awfully well acquainted with this country in the zone-des-armees, and I've worked so hard over my Ford camion that it runs perfectly. I know "Sammie" will be glad to hear that I really am developing into quite a mechanic.

A letter from headquarters today says that the reports from the French officers here in charge were pleased with the thoroughness and the speed of my inspections. I've interviewed over a thousand people and on finishing up here they want me to take charge of an inspection tour in the Vosges Mountains.

Arnold Whitridge is a captain on Gen. Pershing's staff. I have seen him.

I am so glad that your garden has been such a success. I can see you eating those delicious things now. Oh, I'd love to run out to Westleigh for about two weeks and then bring you back to France with me. I like my job and my health was never better.

Lots of love to all of you.

Affectionately,

COLE.

Roye-sur-Somme.
September 4, 1917.

Cole's war record was a modest one. He carried a zither around France with him:

About the famous zither, this was given to me by Charles A. Munn of Philadelphia, who gave it to me as I embarked for France. He was an old friend of mine and a major stockholder in Lyon & Healy, the music firm in Chicago. The zither had a piano keyboard about 2½ feet wide. In form it looked like a Baby Grand piano with collapsible legs. It had a big strap on it so that I could swing it over my back. He had had it made especially for me. I took this with me everywhere I went and in case I became too tired to keep it on my back any more, another soldier was always delighted to take it on. It was easy to keep it in tune as it had a key attached and whenever we had moments of leisure, I'd open it up and play popular French and American songs of the period, and everybody would sing.

It was later said that he had joined the French Foreign Legion as a romantic gesture of renunciation following the failure of "See America First." Cole's description makes his joining the Legion seem more commonplace:

In regard to joining the Foreign Legion, I went to a little office in Paris for my physical examination after having asked to enlist. There was an officer of the Legion there and several soldiers. The officer looked up my name and then asked me to get on the scales. After I had been weighed he said to me, "Now you're in the Foreign Legion." That was all there was to it and afterwards I was sent immediately to Limoge to go through preliminary training before being sent to the front.

Cole wrote a parody of Jerome Kern's standard, *They Didn't Believe Me*, which he called *War Song*. It became well known in England and can be heard with only one or two word changes as the finale of "Oh, What a Lovely War." The music is credited to Jerome Kern and the author of the parody lyric is listed as "unknown."

WAR SONG

And when they ask us how dangerous it was
We never will tell them, we never will tell them.
How we fought in some cafe
With wild women night and day.
'Twas the wonderfullest war you ever knew.
And when they ask us, and they're certainly going to ask us,
Why on our chests we do not wear the Croix de Guerre,
We never will tell them,
We never will tell them,
There was a front, but damned if we knew where.

Lt. Col. Sir Rex Benson recollecting Cole during the war years:

I met Cole for the first time when I was a subaltern in the 9th Lancers and very occasionally was given a day or two's leave from the north to go to Paris. I saw a good deal of Cole particularly in late 1917 and throughout 1918 when I was Liaison Officer between Sir Douglas Haig and Marshal Pétain. This enabled me to get into Paris fairly often and we had a little coterie of friends consisting of Cole, Alan Graham (an English officer), the Kingsland brothers, Count Antoine Sala, Monty Woolley, and Howard Sturges who used to meet frequently at 22 Place Vendome or latterly at Linda's house, and listen to Cole playing the piano and writing his songs.

KATIE OF THE Y.M.C.A.

Katie
That dainty little creature from the Y.M.C.A.
Katie, such a captivating creature, giving suppers away.
I'll ne'er forget that time we met
She asked me if I wanted doughnuts
And although I hate 'em
All the same I ate them
Simply because I was so nuts
On Katie
That willing little worker with the wile in her smile.
Katie

— — — — — — — — — —

And when this doggone war is through,
I'll build an all-night canteen for two.
So that's of course why I am for the Y.M.C.A.

IT PUZZLES ME SO

Who on earth was Mr. Pankhurst?
Who is Mr. Humphrey Ward?
Oh, I'd like to know, 'cause it puzzles me so.

Who is Duff Cooper?
Not Lady—but Lord.
Who was Mr. Langtry?
Yes, I'd like to know for it puzzles me so.
Who will I be if I marry you?

Linda and Cole met at a breakfast reception at the Ritz following the marriage in Paris of Ethel Harriman and Henry Russell, January 30, 1918.

VANITY FAIR

A Monthly Magazine of The Stage, Society, Sports, Fashions, The Fine Arts
PUBLISHED BY THE VANITY FAIR PUBLISHING COMPANY, INC.
449 FOURTH AVENUE, NEW YORK

August 6, 1915.

Dear Linda:—

Scrap books! How pathetic!

Just think of it; Linda and Nina pasting little pictures into albums; folding up ribbons in top bureau drawers, reading The Old Testament, feeding skimmed milk to the cat, reading the social jottings in the local papers; a cup of weak tea at five; a hymn and a little organ music at nine; knitting Afghans up to ten o'clock; and then a prophylactic, a Now I Lay Me, a quick look under the bed, a leap on the Ostermoor, a blow at the candle, and then the little pink toes under the little white sheets.

What a picture!!!

Are these the same little girls that used to take the big strong men on Fifth Avenue, at the Ritz, at Mrs. Mills's, at the Broadway cabarets, and punch the everlasting life out of them?

Those were the days when no man in New York was safe — with Linda and Nina loose on the town. And now they are pasting pictures in little scrap books. And here are the titles of some of the pictures:

Fast Asleep and Wide Awake; A Health to the Bride I'M Gran'ma Now; The Lover's Letter Box; The Toy-Makers of Nuremburg; Santa Claus on the Bowery; Patty Cake, Patty Cake; Man the Life Boats; Her Mother's Voice; A Sweet, Sad Song of

VANITY FAIR

A Monthly Magazine of The Stage, Society, Sports, Fashions, The Fine Arts
PUBLISHED BY THE VANITY FAIR PUBLISHING COMPANY, INC.
449 FOURTH AVENUE, NEW YORK

—2—

Long Ago; Grandpa's Darling; Who'll Drive Dobbin to the Fair; Pansies and Rue; The Young Master Comes of Age.

In a day or two I am going to Plattsburgh, to the military camp, to be a brave soldier boy. When I come back I am going to look like a Howard Chandler Christy book wrapper. If I don't shoot myself to death, I shall be back in three weeks.

My secretary, who is looking at me patiently while I dictate this letter, will send you the Vogues and Vanity Fairs by express. I have begged her to put in some extra magazines.

I am very old now and I have passed the age of passionate loving, but what little stock of love I have on hand (I should say, conservatively, about ten cents worth) I am sending to you and Nina in this letter.

Please remember that I once cared deeply for you both. There was something quite winning about you when you were young and pretty, but now that the scrap books have got you, I really cannot promise much of anything, although — being a gentleman — I shall of course always do my best.

Yours ever,

Mrs. Lee Thomas,
Colorado Springs, Colo.

Born abroad of Boston Brahmin parents and early translated to New York, Frank Crowninshield was the urbane editor of a witty, handsome, and expensively got-up magazine called "Vanity Fair," which, after twenty-two years, fell a victim to its natural enemy, the Great Depression. At the time of this letter, Linda Thomas was in her early thirties and Crowninshield was forty-three. His teasing was not *all* teasing; much as he pretended to admire women, he took care never to marry, and in his late years golf became his none-too-fastidious mistress.

Linda Lee Thomas c. 1910

Linda in Colorado Springs with Elsie de Wolfe, seated, and Nina Crosby Eustis. Elsie de Wolfe abandoned a moderately successful career as an actress to become one of America's first interior decorators. She joined her friends Anne Morgan and Elisabeth Marbury in founding the Colony Club, whose first headquarters she designed. The three went to France and bought the Villa Trianon outside Paris, which Elsie's taste and industry made into a show place of the world. With Elisabeth Marbury, Anne Morgan, and Mrs. W. K. Vanderbilt, she transformed two tenement-ridden districts along the East River into Beekman Place and Sutton Place. A confirmed bachelor until she was over sixty-five, Elsie astonished everyone by marrying Sir Charles Mendl, the press attaché to the British Embassy in Paris. Both Noël Coward and Cole Porter paid tribute in their lyrics to her skill in acrobatics. She was believed to be in her nineties at the time of her death in 1950.

Linda by Baron de Meyer

Linda and the Duke of Alba

Linda

HITCHY-KOO OF 1919

Raymond Hitchcock, star of "Hitchy-Koo of 1919"

WHEN I HAD A UNIFORM ON

VERSE

Now since the Allied banners gave
    a lesson in good manners
To the Kaisers and crown princes,
And von Hindenburgs, von Ludendorffs,
Von Falkenhayns, von Mackensens,
Von Tirpitzes, von Klucks,
The youth of all the nations
Finds its greatest recreations
Drinking Pol Roger and Pommery,
Veuve Cliquot, Louis Roederer,
Ruinart, Piper Heidsick,
Montebello, Mumm's and Cooks,
But while I watch the other fellows
    throwing up their hats,
And crying that at last the
    world's made safe for democrats,
For me the road seems rocky
For they've stripped me of my khaki,
And since I've been demobilized

REFRAIN

I find that life's not what it used to be
When I had a uniform on,
For all the lovely ladies fell for me
When I had a uniform on.
And in those days of glory I was the beau
Of ev'ry doggone musical show.
Each night you'd see me supping somewhere
With a dainty little star upon my Croix de Guerre;

Into their inmost hearts they'd let me strike
When I had a uniform on.
But now the war is o'er
They don't quite like me any more,
And it's a bore;
For they used to bound around me in millions,
But now, somehow that I'm in civilians,
They pass me by.
Gee, I wish I
Could start another war.

SINCE MA GOT THE CRAZE ESPAGNOLE

VERSE

Now I've always known that dear mother was prone
To be rather too ultra-progressive.
Her one idea was to go in for everything new.
However of late it's approaching a state
When her fads are becoming excessive.
Really my dear I don't quite see what we're going to do
To show to what limits our nerves have been taxed
Why she just had the bathroom done over by Bakst.
And for instance tho' only two servants we have
Yet the cook's Czecho-Slovak, the maid's Yugoslav.
Why in order to cure father's stroke of paralysis,
She chucked Christian Science for psychoanalysis.
But the fad she's got now makes all hope for her vanish
For she's taken a fancy for anything Spanish.

REFRAIN 1

And since Ma got the craze Espagnole
It's impossible quite to control her
For she races the heath
With a rose in her teeth
Crying, "Please find me some beau
Like Christy Columbo!"
O'er the Fandango she's gone so silly
That the parlor floor's getting all hilly
And in order to practice that bull-fighting game
Why she fights with our cow which is almost the same
And the way that poor cow looks today is a shame
Since Ma got the craze Espagnole.

REFRAIN 2

Since Ma got the craze Espagnole
It's impossible quite to control her
For she rants 'round the home
Simply clad in a comb
Shouting, "I'm Isabella
Where's that Ferdinand fella?"
She's learning the Carmen libretto,
So we all have to dodge her stiletto.
And old granny sits over her porridge and frets,
For she's tied all the spoons up to make castanets
Even small Baby Jane rolls her own cigarettes
Since Ma got the craze Espagnole.

THAT BLACK
AND WHITE BABY
OF MINE

VERSE

Now since my sweetheart Sal met Miss Elsie de Wolfe,
The leading decorator of the nation,
It's left that gal with her mind simply full'f
Ideas on interior decoration.
For instance she assumes
That the colors of our rooms
Are a most important factor in our lives
And that if a lot of bedrooms
Were pink instead of red rooms
There might be many more contented wives
And so she's put all color from her sight
And ev'rything she owns is black and white.

REFRAIN

She's got a black and white dress,
        a black and white hat
A black and white doggie and
        a black and white cat
Why, she's gone so far that
        she's started to look
Thro' the daily advertisements
        for a black and white cook
She's got a black and white shack
And a new Cadillac
In a black and white design
All she thinks black and white
She even drinks Black and White
That black and white baby of mine.

OLD-FASHIONED
GARDEN

VERSE

One summer day I chanced to stray
To a garden of flow'rs blooming wild,
It took me once more to the dear days of yore
And a spot that I loved as a child;
There were the Phlox,
Tall Hollyhocks,
Violets perfuming the air,
Frail Eglantines,
Shy Columbines,
And Marigolds everywhere.

REFRAIN

It was an old-fashioned garden,
Just an old-fashioned garden,
But it carried me back
To that dear little shack
In the land of long ago.
I saw an old-fashioned missus
Getting old-fashioned kisses,
In that old-fashioned garden
From an old-fashioned beau.

This song became Cole's first "standard." In England, where horticultural accuracy is of considerable importance, Cole was criticized for conflating the blooming seasons of the flowers.

With the success of "Hitchy-Koo" and the royalties from *Old-Fashioned Garden,* Cole returned to Paris. On December 19, 1919, the Paris *Herald* announced:

The marriage of Mr. Cole Porter of Peru, Indiana, who served with the French Army during the war, and Mrs. Lee Thomas of Louisville, Ky., was celebrated yesterday at the Mairie of the Eighteenth Arrondissement. After a brief visit to cities in the south of France, Mr. and Mrs. Porter will make their home in Paris.

A charcoal drawing of Cole, dated March 3, 1919, by the Engish artist Wilfrid De Glehn, who enjoyed a brief wartime vogue on the strength of his skill in drawing uniforms; he was especially admired for his way with Sam Browne belts.

Cole began the twenties by returning to his musical studies. He enrolled at the Schola Cantorum at 269 Rue St. Jacques. Founded in 1894 by Vincent d'Indy, the Schola stressed the fundamentals—harmony, counterpoint, and orchestration. It was the most rigorous form of education that Cole had ever consented to. Here he was introduced to the repertory of nineteenth-century romantic music, especially the songs of Schubert, Schumann, Faure, and Tchaikovsky. In May, 1920, he was assigned to orchestrate a Schumann piano sonata. Meanwhile, his work in the field of musical comedy dwindled almost to nothing. The music to three numbers for a London musical called "A Night Out" was his only contribution to the commercial theater of 1920.

In February, 1921, Cole, Linda, Howard Sturges, and Marthe Hyde chartered the *Chonsu* for a journey up the Nile. Linda, an ardent and knowl-edgeable Egyptologist, had made a similar voyage with her first husband, Ned Thomas, in 1909. Now, from Abydos to the Assuan Dam, with a formidable retinue of servants, they steamed upriver, stopping at Luxor and Karnak, at Tel el Amarna and Dier-el-Bahri; under the guidance of such authori-ties as Linda's friend, Lord Carnarvon, and of Howard Carter and T. Eric Peet, they went on side trips to inspect important new diggings.

"Sturge," Yale '08, an amiable bachelor from Providence, had come to Paris to study music and devoted himself, instead, to having a good time. He said of his periodic drinking bouts: "They cost me two fortunes. Luckily I had a third."

Howard Sturges on deck

Linda and Cole on the *Chonsu*

RUINS

Ruins, ruins, ruins.
Ev'rywhere we go they show us ruins.
We saw a pile in Carthage—
In Rome, another lot,
While here, apart from bugs and fleas,
The only thing they've got
Is ruins, ruins, ruins.
They constitute our daily doin's,
We're off again, thank heaven,
This afternoon at four,
To sail across the water
For Egypt's balmy shore,
And when we get to Luxor
We'll be dragged to see some more
Ruins, ruins, ev'rywhere we go, they show us
Ruins, ruins, ruins.

Linda, Sturge, and Cole set out from Karnak for an orange grove

Linda in the Temple of Amon at Karnak

Linda, Marthe Hyde, Cole, and Sturge at the Assuan Dam

Linda: "Cole being dreadful," in sarcophagus at Dier-el-Bahri

Gerald and Sara Murphy

The hotel and its bright tan prayer rug of a
beach were one. In the early morning the distant image of
Cannes, the pink and cream of old fortifications,
the purple Alp that bounded Italy, were
cast across the water and lay quavering in the
ripples and rings sent up by sea-plants through the clear
shallows. . . . Of all the region only the beach stirred
with activity. Three British nannies sat knitting
the slow pattern of Victorian England, the pattern of
the forties, the sixties, and the eighties, into sweaters
and socks, to the tune of gossip as formalized as
incantation; closer to the sea a dozen persons
kept house under striped umbrellas, while their
dozen children pursued unintimidated fish through the
shallows or lay naked and glistening with
cocoanut oil out in the sun. . . .

Obviously each family possessed the strip of sand immediately in front of its umbrella; besides there
was much visiting and talking back and
forth—the atmosphere of a community upon
which it would be presumptuous to intrude. . . . A young
woman lay under a roof of umbrellas making out
a list of things from a book on the sand. Her
bathing suit was pulled off her shoulders and her
back, a ruddy, orange brown, set off by a string of creamy
pearls, shone in the sun. Her face was hard and
lovely and pitiful. . . . Beyond her was a
fine man in a jockey cap and red-striped tights. . . .
After a while she [Rosemary] realized that the man in the
jockey cap was giving a quiet little performance
for this group; he moved gravely about with
a rake, ostensibly removing gravel and meanwhile
developing some esoteric burlesque held in suspension by
his grave face. Its faintest ramification had become
hilarious, until whatever he said released
a burst of laughter. Even those who, like herself,
were too far away to hear, sent out antennae of attention
until the only person on the beach not caught up
in it was the young woman with the string
of pearls. Perhaps from modesty of possession she
responded to each salvo of amusement by bending closer
over her list. . . .

"I fell in love on the beach," said Rosemary.
"Who with?"
"First with a whole lot of people who looked
nice. Then with one man."
"Did you talk to him?"
"Just a little. Very handsome. With reddish hair." She
was eating, ravenously. "He's married though—
it's usually the way."

F. Scott Fitzgerald, Tender Is the Night

Once again in Paris, the *Colporteurs*, as they were
sometimes punningly called, resumed their roles as
conspicuous members of the international set.
One of their acquaintances, the opera
singer Mary Garden, suggested that they summer
on the French Riviera, where, in July, 1921, they rented a
large, vine-covered white villa at La Garoupe near
the still undefiled beach area of Antibes.
There they entertained, among many others, Sara
and Gerald Murphy.

"Cole always had great originality about
finding new places," Gerald Murphy told his biographer,
Calvin Tomkins, "and at that time no one ever
went near the Riviera in summer. The
English and Germans—there were no longer any
Russians—who came down for the short spring season
closed their villas as soon at it began to get warm.
None of them ever went in the water, you
see. When we went to visit Cole, it was hot, hot
summer, but the air was dry, and it was cool in the evening, and the water was that wonderful jade-and-
amethyst color. Right out on the end of
the Cap there was a tiny beach—the Garoupe—
only about forty yards long and covered with a bed of
seaweed that must have been four feet thick.
We dug out a corner of the beach and
bathed there and sat in the sun, and we decided
that this was where we wanted to be. Oddly, Cole never
came back, but from the beginning we knew we
were going to."

Their small group was joined by Sir Charles Mendl,
the British press attaché in Paris, and William Crocker,
Yale '15, of the San Francisco banking and
railroad family. Crocker lent Cole money during
the years that his grandfather, hoping to
force Cole to abandon music in favor of a more "useful"
career, kept him on what amounted, in Cole's set, to
a meagre allowance. Cole later repaid Crocker's
loans and, by way of thanks, named the energetic
leading character in "Anything Goes" Billy Crocker.

54

The villa at La Garoupe

The gardens

Linda

PILOT ME

VERSE

I've got an aeroplane,
Entirely new,
A cosy, narrow plane,
Just built for two.
I'll let you drive it, dear,
And when you do,
Up where it's private, dear,
We'll bill and coo.

REFRAIN

Pilot me,
Pilot me,
Be the pilot I need.
Please give my ship
A maiden trip,
And we'll get the prize for speed.
So cast away your fears,
Strip my gears,
Let me carry you through.
And when afraid you are
Of going too far,
Then I'll
Just pil—
—Ot you.

Linda in flight

Linda, second from left, and Sir Charles
Mendl, far right, seated; Gerald, Monty Woolley, and Sara
standing. "Monty," Edgar Montillion Woolley, was
the son of the owner-manager of the Grand
Union Hotel in Saratoga Springs, New York.
A member of the class of 1911 at Yale, where
he was President of the Dramatic Association, Monty
was to direct several Broadway shows, including
Cole's "Fifty Million Frenchmen" and "The New Yorkers."
Famous for his portrayal of Sheridan Whiteside
in both the play and film, "The Man Who
Came to Dinner," Monty is remembered also
for his affability and his beard.

Paris was home but the Porters were never at
home for long. In London, in 1922, Cole was able to place
several songs in Charles B. Cochran's ambitious but
ill-fated "Mayfair and Montmartre," one of which,
The Blue Boy Blues, was inspired by a major event in
the art world.

In 1922, Sir Joseph Duveen, acting on behalf of
the Duke of Westminster, negotiated the sale of Gainsborough's "The Blue Boy" to Henry E. Huntington,
the American railroad magnate, for $620,000.
Ninety thousand people came to the National Gal-
lery to pay an affectionate farewell to what they considered a national treasure. The lamentation in
England over the departure of "The Blue
Boy" moved Cole to elegy.

Sara and Linda

THE BLUE BOY BLUES

VERSE

As a painting you must have heard a lot about me,
For I lived here for many happy years;
Never dreaming that you could ever do without me
In spite of all my tears.
It's a long way from gilded galleries in Park Lane
To the wild west across the winter sea.
If you don't know quite what I mean,
Simply ask Sir Joseph Duveen
And he'll tell you what he gave 'em for me.

Nellie Taylor singing *The Blue Boy Blues*

REFRAIN

For I'm the Blue Boy;
The beautiful Blue Boy;
And I am forced to admit
I'm feeling a bit depressed.
A silver dollar took me and my collar
To show the slow cowboys
Just how boys
In England used to be dressed.
I don't know what I shall do
So far from Mayfair;
If Mister Gainsborough knew,
I know he'd frown.
As days grow fewer,
I'm bluer and bluer;
For I am saying "good-bye" to London town.

Chorus:　We've got those Blue Boy blues,
　　　　　We've got the dog-gone Blue Boy blues.
　　　　　We fairly feel it oozing from our heads
　　　　　　　Down to our shoes.
　　　　　So won't you tell us what to do, boy?
　　　　　We've got the Blue Boy blues.
　　　　　We've got those Blue Boy blues.
　　　　　We've got those dog-gone Blue Boy blues.
　　　　　We fairly feel it oozing from our heads
　　　　　　　Down to our shoes.
　　　　　So won't you tell us what to do, boy?
　　　　　We've got the Blue Boy blues.

ENCORE

Chorus:　Don't be so blue
　　　　　Always so blue

We never saw such a cry baby
　　　cry baby
Why don't you smile
Once in a while
Say Willie what silly book ever sold
　　　you that collar
Boo-hoo! Boo-hoo!
That's all you know to do
Boo-hoo! Boo-hoo!
Why don't you try something new
Powder your nose
Buy some new clothes
And stop longing for London town.

The Porters "opened in Venice," in 1923—the Palazzo Barbaro

　　　*. . . the warmth of the southern summer was
still in the high, florid rooms, palatial chambers where
hard, cool pavements took reflections in their
lifelong polish, and where the sun on the
stirred sea-water, flickering up through open
windows, played over the painted "subjects" in the
splendid ceilings—medallions of purple and
brown, of brave old melancholy color,
medals as of old reddened gold, embossed and
beribboned, all toned with time and all flourished and
scolloped and gilded about, set in their great
moulded and figured concavity (a nest
of white cherubs, friendly creatures of the air),
and appreciated by the aid of that second tier of smaller
lights, straight openings to the front, which did
everything . . . to make of the place an
apartment of state.*

　　　Henry James, The Wings of the Dove

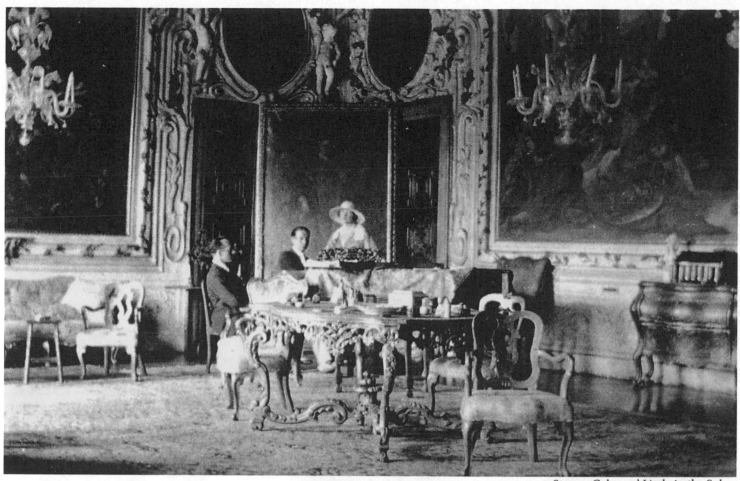

Sturge, Cole, and Linda in the Salon

Cole, Linda, Bernard Berenson, and Sturge. "B.B." greatly admired the elegance of dress and manners displayed by Linda

Tallulah

Bernard Berenson

Mary Garden

On the Lido

POOR YOUNG MILLIONAIRE

After hunting all over for pleasure
With some measure of success,
I've decided the pace known as rapid
Leads to vapid nothingness.
And I'm tired of betting,
Tired of sporting,
Tired of flirting,
Tired of courting,
Tired of racing,
Tired of yachting,
Tired of loafing,
Tired of rotting,
Tired of dining,
Tired of wining,
Tired of teaing.
Tired of being
Tired, tired, tired.
Oh won't somebody care
For a poor young millionaire.
If you knew what blues meant
You'd find me amusement.
I've had every thrill
From a Rolls-Royce to a Ford.
And there's no concealing
The fact I'm feeling
Bored, bored, bored.

Monty

Bored with the beach . . .

They drive to the country . . .

Which proves moderately amusing.

Cole was a great friend and very devoted to my mother Rue Carpenter. I remember him with pleasure and warmth, and the gratitude one feels toward a friend of the family who treats the young with respect and interest . . . I always felt that Cole had a quality of living alone and apart from the long procession of endless people who lunched or dined with him. He loved surprises. Some were more successful than others. He arranged that I should sit for Marie Laurencin to "surprise" my mother with a gift of a portrait. A great success! He gave me once in Venice a very large, very untrained puppy to keep in my hotel room. Not a success!

The last time I saw him was many years ago when I sat next to him at a large dinner party in Newport. My mother was then very ill, and Cole suggested that he come here to see her as a "surprise."

He also made a remark to me during that same evening, that with all his success he would give anything if he had one tenth of my father's knowledge and genius for orchestration (my father was John Alden Carpenter). He said, "My latest musical is very light. I have little knowledge. John is a serious composer, and I would give my soul if I could believe that I was."

Ginny Carpenter Hill (Mrs. Patrick Hill)

Elsie de Wolfe, Linda, and Marthe Hyde

Ginny Carpenter

Rue Carpenter

Elsie   The Murphys

"La Princesse de Polignac, dans sa gondole, quitte le jardin de son palais. Elle est habillée de blanc; ses gondoliers sont également entièrement vêtus de blanc, ce qui forme une jolie harmonie et très lumineuse."

Princesse Edmond de Polignac, the former Winnaretta Singer of Yonkers, occupied an important place in the cultural life of Paris for more than half a century. The oldest daughter of the sewing machine magnate Isaac Singer, she was educated in Europe, became an accomplished painter, pianist, and organist, and devoted her fortune and energy to an astonishing variety of artistic, scientific, and social concerns. A canvas painted by her was often mistaken for a Manet; she was a friend of Proust, Verlaine, and Marie Curie; and she commissioned works by Faure, Ravel, Satie, Poulenc, Stravinsky, de Falla, Milhaud, and Weill. She helped support the Salvation Army, archaeological excavations in Greece, the Nadia Boulanger Orchestra, and the Ballet Russe. *Chez* "Winnie," Cole met Darius Milhaud, who arranged for the Ballet Suedois to commission "Within the Quota," for which Gerald Murphy provided the book and Cole the music.

Linda, Gerald, and Lady Cynthia Mosley

Gerald, Cole, and Sir Charles

Gerald, Ginny, Cole, and Sara

WITHIN THE QUOTA (1923)

Within The Quota, a "ballet-sketch" in 1 Act, presented by Les Ballets Suedois. Music: Cole Porter. Libretto, scenery, and costumes: Gerald Murphy. Choreography: Jean Borlin. World premiere: Theatre des Champs-Elysees, Paris, October 25, 1923. American premiere: Century Theatre, New York, November 28, 1923.

An immigrant lands in America and meets successively a variety of American types—part real, part mythical—with which he is already familiar through visits to the cinema. His pleasure in these types (a millionairess, a strutting colored vaudevillian, a jazz baby, a cowboy), is interrupted by repeated appearances of the American puritan who masquerades in turn as social reformer, revenue agent, uplifter, and sheriff. Finally, he makes the acquaintance of The Sweetheart of the World, a Mary Pickford-type, who embraces him and to the accompaniment of clicking cameras oversees his transformation from a raw immigrant to a movie star, an inevitable result which brings the ballet to its conclusion.

"Within the Quota" was a satire on American life and the mythology of instant success. Cole's music, displaying the influences of Stravinsky, Milhaud, and American jazz, is full of parody and exaggeration. One of the first symphonic jazz compositions, it predated Gershwin's *Rhapsody in Blue* by several months. Murphy's setting was a single back-drop shaped as a page from an American newspaper. "Within the Quota's" reception in Paris was described as "triumphal" by *Figaro* and its American premiere was also successful. Deems Taylor called it "amusing and colorful, blessedly brief, and spiced with the satire that consists in presenting slightly exaggerated facts. Mr. Porter's music comprised some very good jazz and some polytonal dissonances that were evidently meant to be as funny as they sounded." After its New York appearance Les Ballets Suedois toured America until March, 1924. A year later the company disbanded. Cole believed that his score was lost.

Gerald Murphy's backdrop for "Within the Quota"

Finale: Cowboy, Jazz Baby, Sweetheart of the World, Immigrant, Colored
Gentleman, Millionairess, and Sheriff-Reformer

Manuscript of the opening page of "Within the Quota"

GREENWICH VILLAGE FOLLIES (1924)

TWO LITTLE BABES IN THE WOOD

VERSE 1

There's a tale of two little orphans who
    were left in their uncle's care,
To be reared and ruled and properly schooled
Till they grew to be ladies fair.
But, oh, the luckless pair!
For the uncle, he was a cruel trustee,
And he longed to possess their gold;
So he led them thence to a forest dense,
Where he left them to die of cold.
That, at least, is what we're told.

REFRAIN 1

They were two little babes in the wood,
Two little babes, oh, so good!
Two little hearts, two little heads,
Longed to be home in their two little beds,
So—two little birds built a nest
Where the two little babes went to rest,
While the breeze, hov'ring nigh,
Sang a last lullaby
To the two little babes in the wood.

VERSE 2

They were lying there in the freezing air,
When fortunately there appeared
A rich old man in a big sedan,
And a very, very fancy beard.
He saw those girls and cheered,
Then he drove them down to New York town,
Where he covered them with useful things,
Such as bonds, and stocks, and Paris frocks,
And Oriental pearls in strings,
And a show case full of rings.

REFRAIN 2

Now those two little babes in the wood,
Are the talk of the whole neighborhood
For they've too many cars, too many clothes,
Too many parties, and too many beaux,
They've learned that the fountain of youth
Is a mixture of gin and vermouth,
And the whole town's agreed
That the last thing in speed
Is the two little babes in the wood.

Two Little Babes in the Wood (The Dolly Sisters)

I'M IN LOVE AGAIN

VERSE 1

Why am I
Just as happy as a child?
Why am I
Like a race horse running wild?
Why am I
In a state of ecstasy?
The reason is 'cause
Something's happened to me.

REFRAIN 1

I'm in love again
And the Spring is comin',
I'm in love again,
Hear my heart strings strummin',
I'm in love again,
And the hymn I'm hummin',
Is the "Huddle Up, Cuddle Up Blues!"
I'm in love again,
And I can't rise above it,
I'm in love again,
And I love, love, love it:
I'm in love again,
And I'm darn glad of it,
Good news!

VERSE 2

Someone sad,
Had the awful luck to meet,
Someone bad,
But the kind of bad that's sweet.
No one knows
What a glimpse of paradise,
Someone who's naughty
Showed to someone who's nice.

REFRAIN 2

I'm in love again,
And with glee I bubble.
I'm in love again,
And the fun's just double.
I'm in love again.
If I got in trouble,
I'll be cursin' one person I know.
I'm in love again
I'm a lovebird singin'
I'm in love again.
I'm a spring lamb springin'
I'm in love again
Weddin' bells are ringin'
Let's go.

Mammammamma,
I want to tell you a curious story.
Three years ago, when I was writing the
Greenwich Village Follies, I gave them a tune called I'm In
Love Again. *This tune I had written before and*
had sung it around Paris, and always with
howling success, as the melody was very simple and the
sentiment appealed to everyone.
The great powers of The Greenwich Village Follies
thought less then nothing of this song, and
never would allow it in the show. So it lay in a drawer at
Harms, and I thought it was dead for ever. But one
thing very funny about that little song, no
matter where I traveled to, I'd always hear someone
singing it. Last year, in New York, I heard it at Maurice's
cabaret. They played it over and over again,
simply the one refrain, as no one knew the verse. I went to
the band leader and asked him who wrote it, and he
said "Oh a Harlem nigger wrote it."
Everybody in Paris knows it, and it's almost as well known
in London and in Rome. But practically no one
knows that I wrote it.
Now, suddenly out of a clear sky, comes a wire from
Harms, offering me an excellent royalty to publish
this song and do everything they can to
make a big hit out of it. And I have sent them a verse and
a second refrain, and its coming out immediately
as a popular song. As Harms usually only
publish songs in productions, and never launch a song
unless they make a big hit of it, I shall be surprised
if I dont make a lot of money out of it.
Dont you think its a funny story, that poor little
deserted song suddenly landing on her feet.
I've no news except that I'm as happy as a lark, and so
is Linda. We are staying here until the last week in
March, when we leap in the motor and go
all over Spain, ending up at Seville, at the Albas, for
an Easter house-party. The Prince of Wales is going too,
and it will be very gay.
I have written a lot of new songs, and I
believe excellent ones, which I am going to send to
Harms, and I hope they will publish them. Also, I have
just finished two more paintings on glass of
Spanish bullfights, and now I'm doing a big one of a
beautiful nude lady, sailing away from New York
in a balloon.
Paris is empty and charming. We have had beautiful
spring weather, and the Bois is crowded.
I can't thank you enough for your Christmas check. You
were very sweet to send it to me, and I had a grand
time spending it on totally useless things.
Goodbye and lots of love from us both. Linda said you
were the gayest person she saw in New York, and
that after being with you, everyone else
seemed dead. And Weston said "Oh sir, you have no idea
how chic Mrs. Porter looked in New York."
Give my love to Sammie, my papa, and to Bessie and
Dixie. I'd love to see you so much. Do you
want me to come over in the spring and bring you to
Venice? Think that over.

Cole, February 2, 1927

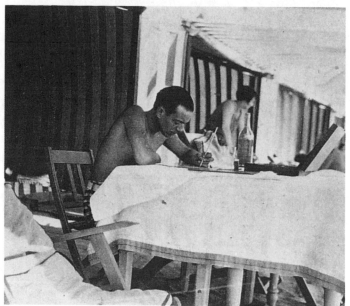

Painting on glass

"The Acrobats," a painting by Cole

OUT O' LUCK

ANNUAL SHOW OF
THE YALE DRAMAT, 1925

RECOLLECTIONS
OF H. C. POTTER,
YALE '26

*Looked at in the cold light of today, the show
(by Tom Cushing—'02, I believe), the songs—and, very
probably, the individual performances too, for
that matter—would seem terribly naive,
démodé and . . . "campy," the youth of today would
call it. However, we all thought it was wonderful, the New
Haven audiences ate it up and the 1925 Christmas
Tour was a huge success wherever we
played—so much so that the Dramat took the
show out the following Christmas for another series of
highly successful "one-nighters" throughout the
East and Middle West.*

*All concerned, including Tom Cushing and Cole,
felt that a great measure of the play's success was due to
the vigorous and incredibly skillful staging by
Monty Woolley. But Cole's songs clinched it.*

*"Out o' Luck" was a comedy-melodrama con-
cerning a group of American "dough-boys" (and one
French "girl," played by William Hinkle '27,
and very well played too) in France during
the last days of WW I.*

*Cole's songs were sandwiched into Act II, during an
impromptu "show" being put on by some of
the soldiers, dressed in spangled, chorus-
girl "tutus" (but still wearing their GI boots).
There were three of them:*

   Butterflies—an "opening Chorus"
   Mademazelle—comedy love-song
   Opera Star—a "special material" comedy song
*I played the lead and sang the first two. The third,
Opera, was especially written for John Hoysradt,
'26, President of the Dramat, who did his
very funny and adroit falsetto burlesques of
current divas for Cole one day at rehearsal; within a week
Cole delivered Opera, incorporating John's burlesques; Opera proved to be what used
to be called "a wow."*

*The two songs that I sang, while great for the show and
the period, and while perfectly good examples of
1925 "pop" songwriting, have no lasting
value—as I am sure Cole would have been the first
to admit, and as one can see from the lyrics themselves—
except that they do possess, here and there, that
Cole Porter flip of phrasing and rhyming
that was so uniquely his. Opera lived a little longer:
John Hoysradt (today John Hoyt—at the request of Paramount Pictures which insisted that "Hoysradt"
would get him nowhere) used it for
several years in his nightclub act.*

*But the really interesting thing about Cole and "Out o'
Luck" is this: Cole's involvement with the Dramat's*

72

show, and the success of the songs,
undoubtedly played a part in getting him out of
the doldrums which plagued him in the long and unpro-
ductive period between, say, Two Little Babes in
the Wood and Night and Day. Monty
Woolley had often told me of Cole's despondency,
how he felt that his style was hopelessly outmoded and
old-fashioned, his conviction that he would never
be able to "get with" the music that was
then being written. I know that Monty had to use
every bit of the exuberant enthusiasm and persuasion that
was so wonderfully his to nudge Cole out of what
he himself considered virtual retirement.
Incidentally, Cole and Monty's great friend Herman
Oelrichs was also instrumental in getting Cole to write
these songs. I remember well, one evening "after
hours" when those of us in the Dramat sat
around with Cole, singing and doing little skits,
imitations of Jolson and so on. I did an imitation of some
currently popular vaudeville "sob-ballad" singer.
When I finished, Cole laughed; then his
face grew somber and he said: "But do you know?
I wish I could write songs like that."

Thank God he didn't. But not too many years
after that evening along came Night and
Day and all the glorious rest. And we Dramat
'25—'26-ers have always thought that perhaps we had
helped a little.

OPERA STAR

VERSE

If the critics have dominion
Over popular opinion
I'm the opera's most sensational soprano.
It's because I have a fashion
Of my own for putting passion
In the roles that I portray for Otto Kahn-o.
All the smart set go as far as
Wearing top hats and tiaras
Every time they come to see me do a rave.
And commuters enter rushing
From their furnished flats in Flushing,
To encourage me to mis . . . be . . . have.
As an opera vamp I've reached the very top,
But in private life my technique is a flop:

REFRAIN

I'm a great success making love on the stage,
But a terrible failure at home.
I can find a nice fellow once in an age
But in no time he starts in to roam.
'Round the fireside I'll admit I'm much too tame
But they call the fire department
    when I sing "Boheme":

[burlesqued bit from the opera]

I'm a great success making love on the stage
But a terrible failure at home.

Palazzo Rezzonico, where the Porters spent four summers

"Robert Browning . . . died in the
splendid Rezzonico, the residence of his son and a wonderful
cosmopolite 'document,' which, as it presents itself,
in an admirable position, but a short way
farther down the Canal, we can almost see, in spite of the
curve, from the window at which we stand. This
great seventeenth-century pile, throwing
itself upon the water with a peculiar florid assurance, a
certain upward toss of its cornice which gives it
the air of a rearing sea-horse, decorates
immensely—and within, as well as without—the wide
angle that it commands."—Henry James, "Italian Hours"

The Launch

The Grand Staircase

"A wave of entertaining has swept over
Venice within recent weeks. One of the most elaborate balls
was given this week by Mr. and Mrs. Cole Porter in
the Rezzonico Palace, the residence occupied
by the Robert Brownings on the Grand Canal. The guests
entered from the canal, ascending the steps between
gondoliers attired in red and white costumes
instead of the usual liveried footmen. Mediaeval torches
replaced the usual electric lights."

The Ballroom

"The ball was representative of four
periods of the 19th Century. Paper costumes representing
the four epochs of the century were distributed.
    Preceding the ball a dinner was given
in honor of Mr. and Mrs. Porter by Miss Elsa Maxwell at the
Grand Hotel. Among the guests were: Conte and
Contessa Volpi, Lady Diana and Mr. Duff
Cooper, Princess San Faustino, Countess Zoppola, Miss
Dorothy Fellowes-Gordon, Signorina Volpi, Principe
Aldobrandini, M. and Mme. Henri Bernstein,
Count and Countess Andrea Robilant, Count and Countess
Dentice Frasso, Duca di Sangro, Lady Wimborne,
the Hon. Evelyn Fitzgerald and Mrs.
Fitzgerald, Princess Boncompagni, Marchese and Marchesa
Sommi-Piccenardi, Don Guido Branco, Princesse
Polignac, M. and Mme. Agnelli, Prince
Pignatelli, Baron de Gunsburg, Prince and Princesse Faucigny-
Lucinge, Mme. Toulmin, Lord and Lady Northesk,
and Mr. Billy Reardon."

THEY'RE ALWAYS ENTERTAINING

VERSE

Run, run, run, rush,
Mop, dust, sweep, brush,
Work ,work, work until you drop.
All day, all night,
No sleep in sight,
Dio mio, when will it ever stop?
Since the fam'ly of Americans have taken this Palazzo,
We work so hard that ev'ryone is practically pazzo,
Yet when we suggest
We need a little rest,
They look at us and laugh at us and say to us,
"Is that so?"

REFRAIN

They're always entertaining, these Americans
Who come to town.
Forever entertaining, it's no wonder we're a bit
Run down.
Ev'ry day they ask a bunch
Of celebrities for lunch
If you think that that is all,
Ev'ry night they give a ball,
So excuse us for complaining,
But these Americans are always entertaining.

Italian and British Nobility and U.S. Heiress Perform for Charity

August 29, 1926

VENICE.—Principessa di San Faustino can be counted on to produce something good every year in the way of charity entertainment and this year's amateur vaudeville, given on Monday night in the ballroom of the Excelsior Hotel, even surpassed those of other years in its almost professional quality.

Scions of proud old Italian houses, members of the British nobility and daughters of American magnates combined in a jazz revue which for swing and pep would yield place to no amateur show.

Mr. Billy Reardon appeared first on the program with one of his clever dancing numbers, followed by Miss Storrs and Marchese de Portago in a beautiful waltz; Duca della Verdura heading a trio giving a most amusing eccentric dance; Miss Caroline and Miss Anne Storrs dancing together pleasingly, Miss Elizabeth Millhiser and Prince Jit of Kapurthala in a lively ukelele number, assisted by several other youths, Miss Mary Corday, whose dancing was received with the enthusiasm that always characterizes her appearance; Lady Northesk and Mr. Billy Rearden dancing together brought down the house and were obliged to give an encore.

Hit of the Evening.

The hit of the evening was furnished by Miss Elsa Maxwell who, clad in a bathing-suit with a curly blonde wig covering her cropped head sang, "Just a Lonely Little Lady on the Lido" with such stupendous effect that she was forced out from behind the scenes again and again and finally repeated it.

The final number was a Charleston chorus composed of Lady Wimborne, Lady Northesk, the Hon. Mrs. Fitzgerald, Mrs. Emmett, Mrs. Sturges, Miss Aileen Flannery, Miss Lila Emery, Miss Blanche Vogel, Miss Mary Corday, Contessa Zoppola, Contessa Robilant, Contessa Buccino, the Misses Storrs, Marchese di Portago, Duca Dello Verdura, Conte Robilant, Mr. Billy Rearden, Baron de Gunsburg, Conte Celani, Marchese Salina, Conte Buccino, M. Ronvier.

With Lady Diana Cooper in the role of a champagne vendor, also Contessa Frasso, Mrs. Cole Porter, Lady Abdy and Marchesa Sonuni-Picciardi, the bar did a rushing business.

After the performance there was dancing on the terrace in the moonlight.

Among those present were Prince Frederick Leopold of Prussia, Baroness d'Erlanger, Mrs. Payne Thompson, Major and Mrs. James Sullivan, Miss Sullivan and her guests Miss Bartlett and Miss Coolidge, of Boston; Sir Charles and Lady Mendl, Mrs. Clarence Millhiser, Mr. Richard Tobin, American Minister at the Hague; Mrs. Townsend, Major and Mrs. Feildin, Mr. and Mrs. Arthur Osborne, Mrs. Henry Cooper, Mr. Samuel Dennett, and Mr. and Mrs. Richard Brown.

MR. WILLIAM REARDON AND LADY NORTHESK
Who were amongst those who gave such
valuable aid at the amateur cabaret show recently given
at the Excelsior Hotel at the Lido in aid of charity.
Mr. Reardon's and Lady Northesk's
exhibition dancing was one of the hits of the production.

A SOCIETY BEAUTY CHORUS ON THE LIDO, VENICE
Some of those who assisted at the
amateur cabaret show included Lady Northesk
and Lady Wimborne. Lady Northesk
was Jessica Brown of the Ziegfeld Follies.

THE
SCAMPI

Once there lived a nice young Scampi
In a canal that was dark and damp, he
Found his home life much too wet,
And longed to travel with the supper set.
Poor little Scampi.

Fate was kind for very soon a—
Long came the chef from the Hotel Luna,
Saw that Scampi lying there,
And said, "I'll put you on my bill of fare."
Lucky little Scampi.

See him on his silver platter,
Hearing the Queens of the Lido chatter.
Getting the latest in regard
To Elsa Maxwell and Lady Cunard.
Thrilled little Scampi.

See that ambitious Scampi we know
Feeding the Princess San Faustino.
Think of his joy as he gaily glides
Down to the middle of her Roman insides.
Proud little Scampi.

After dinner the Princess Jane
Said to her hostess, "I've such a pain.
"Don't be cross, but I think I shall
"Go for a giro in a side canal."
Scared little Scampi.

Off they went through the troubled tide,
The gondola rocking from side to side.
They tossed about till that poor young Scampi
Found that his quarters were much too crampy.
Up comes the Scampi.

Back once more where he started from
He said, "I haven't a single qualm,
"For I've had a taste of the world, you see,
"And a great Princess has had a taste of me."
Wise little Scampi.

Princess San Faustino,
the former Jane Campbell of New Jersey

Venice Innovation

July, 1926

VENICE.—One of the charms of Venice is that it is never dull. Just when one begins to feel the need of an innovation, out of the hat, like a rabbit, it springs. This time it is out of the heads of four members of the younger set in Venice, Count Andrea Robilant, Marquis di Salina, Baron Franchetti, and Mr. Cole Porter, who are successfully launching the Dance Boat.

A large barge, which has been specially constructed, containing facilities for serving supper, will float out into the lagoon and, on still nights, even into the open sea. A negro jazz orchestra is being brought from Paris to play and there will be dancing.

Invitations have been sent to a number of members of the summer colony, and the subscription list is to be limited to 150 members, with the proceeds going to several Venetian charities.

Saturday, August 7, 1926
Hotel des Bains
Lido, Venice

. . . We have stopped at the
Hotel des Bains because the fracases at
the Excelsior make life intolerable.
The whole of Venice is up in
arms against Cole Porter because of
his jazz and his Negroes. He has started
an idiotic night club on a boat moored
outside the Salute, and now the
Grand Canal is swarming with the
very same Negroes who have made us
all run away from London and Paris.
They are teaching the "Charleston" on the Lido Beach! It's dreadful!
The gondoliers are threatening to massacre
all the elderly American women here.
The very fact of their (Linda and
Cole Porter's) renting the Palazzo Rezzonico is considered characteristic
of nouveaux riches.

> *Boris Kochno-*
> *Diaghilev and the*
> *Ballets Russes,*
> *New York, 1970*

Hutch (the piano-vocalist Leslie Hutchinson) and his band

THE TRAGICAL HISTORY OF YOUNG KING COLE

BY DIDYMUS BELCAMPUS

BALLAD

Young King Cole
Was a jolly youthful soul,
And a jazz-band king was he.
He launched a dainty barge
On the fashionable marge
Of the Adriatic Sea.

Young King Cole
Whom the ladies all extol
For his hospitality,
Gave parties of a sort
That the fishes of the port
Jumped high in the air to see.

Young King Cole
— I confess I find it droll —
Composed when his hours were free;
And graciously he'd strum
On the soft melodious drum,
His dusky-toned harmony.

Young King Cole
Bought a gondolier's pole
And sent for his minstrelsy.
Their hands of jet-black hue
Sawed the slender timber through,
And made of it parts thrice three.

Young King Cole
Kept in splendour on the dole
An expert in sorcery.
The nine sticks mute as stones
Were transformed to saxophones
By his arts of devilry.

Young King Cole
— Sacred fury in his soul —
Now blared all day at the sea.
Each morn he'd syncopate
Every night he'd ululate
To a grateful Italy.

Young King Cole
Winds might howl or waters roll,
Played on without stop till he
Had roused the Doges dead
From their ever-lasting bed,
To join in the jamboree.

Young King Cole
Slightly losing that control
We expect of royalty,
Now cabled to the moon
To perform on the lagoon,
Offering a fine fat fee.

Young King Cole
Quite misunderstood the role
Of that lone divinity;
Her sober virgin state
Had for long been out of date
In our smart society.

Young King Cole
Who was rather in a hole
For a tip-top novelty
Sent two aërial cars,
One for Venus, one for Mars,
In the charge of Mercury.

Young King Cole
Felt a quiver through the whole
Of his proud anatomy:
When closely neck to neck
Waltzed the Gods around his deck
And bunny-hugged rapturously.

Young King Cole
Do you know that on his scroll,
Deathless Immortality
Is writing hard your name,
And your killing little game
To delight posterity?

Young King Cole
Though you must one day pay toll
To the fateful sisters three;
Your jazz and cocktail barge
Will be rescued from the marge
By the Venice Signiory.

At the conclusion of the *Ballad*,
the author, "Didymus Belcampus"
(better known in English
translation as Sir Thomas
Beecham) announces
that Young King Cole has been
hurled violently from his barge into
the Venetian waters by a blast
from the nine saxophones
and has then been swept out to
sea and drowned. And then:

They scrapped the old Bucentaur —
— And who could now lament her?
T' was high time that they sent her
To the bottom of the sea.
They manned the brave Coleporter
To sail the Lido water;
While down below her author
Jazzed and jazzed in ecstasy.

Noël Coward

Lady Diana Cooper

Noël and Linda

Linda

Cole

Cole

Lady Abdy

Baroness de Meyer

Linda and Millicent Sutherland

Countess Buccino

Billy Reardon

Elsa and Cole

Noël and Jack Wilson

"Just Married" Elsie de Wolfe
and Sir Charles Mendl

Elsa and "Tookie" (Countess di Zoppola,
the former Edith Mortimer)

Jack, "Noëly and Coëly," as Elsa
dubbed them

Front row: Countess Buccino, Fanny Brice, Lela Emery, Dorothy Fellowes-Gordon ("The Dicky"). Second row: Linda, Princess Jane, Elsa, Dolly

O'Brien, Count Buccino, Linda Lee (Linda's cousin). Standing: Cole, Jay O'Brien, and others

Lady Diana Cooper. Enid Bagnold,
in her *Autobiography*, describes Lady Diana Manners (the
then unmarried daughter of the Duke of Rutland)
making an entrance at "One-Three-Nine-Pic,"
Baroness Catherine d'Erlanger's London house: "One night,
on those stairs, there was a flutter, a commotion, a loud
gay voice and a group of men. Diana
Manners came down the stairs like a muslin swan. Her blind
blue stare swept over me. I was shocked—in the sense
of electricity. Born to the city I wanted
to storm, the Queen of Jericho swept past me."

Fanny, Chalto Elizaga, Princess Jane, Grace Moore, and Roger Davis

Fanny Brice visited Venice in 1926,
when my wife and I were living in the Palazzo Rezzonico.
At this time in my life I had given up all hope of
ever being successful on Broadway and had
taken up painting but Fanny, whom we grew to know
very well, asked me to write a song for her.
This was the reason for Hot-House Rose. *When I finished*
it, I invited her to the Rezzonico to hear it and
afterwards she always told friends how wonderfully
incongruous it was, that I should have demonstrated to
her this song about a poor little factory girl
as she sat beside me while I sang and played it to her on a
grand piano that looked lost in our ballroom, whose
walls were entirely decorated by Tiepolo
paintings and was so big that if we gave a Ball for less
than a thousand people they seemed to be
entirely lost. She never sang the song.

Cole Porter, 1953

Milly, Linda, and Cole

HOT-HOUSE ROSE

VERSE

No wonder that the rose to me's
The fairest flow'r that grows
My fam'ly name is Rosenbaum,
My other name is Rose,
So yesterday
When I got my pay
I went to a park I know,
And walked around
'Till I fin'lly found
The place where the roses grow.
When I saw those flowers all in bloom,
I almost forgot my basement room.

REFRAIN 1

I'm hot-house rose from God knows where,
The kind that grows without fresh air.
The whistle blows and work is done
But it's too late for me to get the sun.
They say that when you dream a lot,
You always dream of what you haven't got,
That's why I dream of a garden, I s'pose,
'Cause I'm only a hot-house rose.

Seated: Fanny, Elsa, Cole, Grace, Lela Emery. Standing:
Linda Lee, "The Dicky," Charlto, Jay O'Brien

Elsa pursues a beach ball in front of the Excelsior, Venice, 1927

Cole and Chalto

REFRAIN 2

I'm hot-house rose from God knows where,
The kind that grows without fresh air.
A summer breeze I never get,
The morning dew has never kissed me yet.
I bought an ounce of nice perfume
And now I smell just like a rose in bloom.
But why take trouble when ev'ryone knows
That I'm only a hot-house rose.

★★★★★★★★★★

Dear Cole:

*I'm writing—or trying to record—some
of the outstanding experiences of my life and one of them
is that fabulous (am deathly sick of that word but I
can't think of any other that so clearly
describes it) trip back on the Paris (or was it the
S. S. France?) in 1927, I believe. I was dead tired after a
really gala few weeks abroad, and expected to go to bed to
rest up on the way home so that I wouldn't
look as though I had had too good a time to Frederic
[her husband], when the boat docked in
New York. I was leaving the purser's office where I had
gone to try and change a hot stuffy little room up
forward, which I had obtained with quite
some difficulty at the last minute—when down the grande
escalier came Cole Porter, Howard Sturges, Sydney
Smith and two other dream boats I have
forgotten the names of—yelling with flattering
enthusiasm "Irene"!!! Throwing all my good intentions
about resting right out a porthole—there began the
gayest, most entertaining, warm and friendly
days I have ever spent anywhere. We sat up every night
until the lounge was almost entirely free of
passengers so that you could play—and play you did until
the wee small hours—new and old things you had
written until we were steeped in that
original, brilliant, melodious "aurora" that is only, and
can be—a Cole Porter evening!! Remember our
efforts at ducking Barotra? And my Paris
dress that brought about the big chase in my cabin which
reminded me of the old silent picture days of Lillian
Gish and "the villain still pursued her." We
all sat out on deck next day while I described the scene in
detail—the panting—the French and Spanish
imploring etc., remember? It was such a wonderful,
memorable crossing. Who were the other two? Give my
love to Howard when you see him—and much
love to you dear Cole. Blessings,*

Irene Castle, April, 1956

Linda by Steichen

84

William Baldwin, universally
known as "Billy," was to become the most celebrated
of American decorators after the Second World
War. In the nineteen fifties, he
decorated Cole's apartment in the Waldorf
Towers and his cottage in Williamstown. Baldwin
has said of the house in the Rue Monsieur,

"Though I never saw it when the Porters
owned it, of course I used many fine things out of
it in my later designs. As we can tell by the
pictures, the rooms were timeless;
not a false touch anywhere. They were beautiful
in the nineteen twenties and, if they had been preserved,
we would find them equally beautiful now."

If the beauty of these interiors strikes us as a trifle austere, it is because the evidence of the photographs is incomplete; we must fill the rooms, as the Porters did, with a crowd of talented and amusing people. It was here that Linda arranged for the first lessons in the Charleston to be given in Paris, when that dance craze crossed the Atlantic. One imagines reflected in the polished floor rolled stockings kicking frantically back and forth, a criss-cross of hands over silken knees, and, at the piano, some gifted boy out of who knows what desolate American tank town playing *Black Bottom* and *Yes, Sir, That's My Baby!*

Birthday Girl

THE LAZIEST GAL IN TOWN

VERSE

I've a beau, his name is Jim,
He loves me and I love him,
But he tells me I'm too prim,
That means I'm too slow.
I let him rant, I let him rave,
I let him muss my permanent wave,
But when he says "let's misbehave,"
My reply is "no!"

REFRAIN

It's not 'cause I wouldn't,
It's not 'cause I shouldn't,
And, Lord knows, it's not 'cause I couldn't,
It's simply because I'm the laziest gal in town.
My poor heart is achin'
To bring home the bacon,
And if I'm alone and forsaken,
It's simply because I'm the laziest gal in town.
Though I'm more than willing to learn
How these gals get money to burn,
Ev'ry proposition I turn down,
'Way down,
It's not 'cause I wouldn't
It's not 'cause I shouldn't,
And, Lord knows, it's not 'cause I couldn't,
It's simply because I'm the laziest gal in town.

LET'S MISBEHAVE

VERSE

You could have a great career,
And you should.
Only one thing stops you, dear,
You're too good.
If you want a future, darling,
Why don't you get a past?
'Cause that fatal moment's coming,
At last.

REFRAIN

We're all alone
No chaperone
Can get our number,
The world's in slumber,
Let's misbehave.
There's something wild
About you, child,
That's so contagious,
Let's be outrageous,
Let's misbehave.
When Adam won Eve's hand,
He wouldn't stand for teasin',
He didn't care about
Those apples out of season.
They say that spring

Means just one thing
To little love birds,
We're not above birds,
Let's misbehave.

It's getting late
And while I wait,
My poor heart aches on,
Why keep the brakes on?
Let's misbehave.
I feel quite sure,
Un peu d'amour
Would be attractive,
While we're still active,
Let's misbehave.
You know my heart is true,
And you say, you for me care;
Somebody's sure to tell,
But what the heck do we care?
They say that bears
Have love affairs,
And even camels;
We're merely mammals
Let's misbehave.

LA REVUE DES AMBASSADEURS (1928)

OMNIBUS

Guide: Do you wanna see Paris?
Do you wanna see Paris?
If you wanna see Paris,
You'd better come with me.
Flappers: We wanna see Paris.
We wanna see Paris.
Millionaire: And see how Paris
Compares with Kankakee.
Guide: Then get aboard my omnibus.
Flappers: First, how much is it, sonny?
Guide: Its only fifty francs apiece.
Millionaire: What's that in American money?
Guide: Well, fifty francs, divided by three,
And multiplied by seven
Makes let me see, let me see.
Millionaire: Why you damn fool, eleven.
Flappers: Is that all? Is that all?
You're talking through your hat.
Millionaire: You couldn't get a ride in a baby-carriage,
in the U.S.A. for that.
Guide: We now are going up the Champs Elysees,
if you please.
You see those poles sticking out the ground,
those are trees.
Flappers: Poor little trees, they've got some awful disease.
Guide: That building there, upon the right,

Is the famous Hotel Claridge.
It's where the ladies go at night,
When they get fed up with marriage.

Flappers: Hurrah for the Claridge, and down with marriage.

Guide: And now, before you, straight ahead, the
     Arc de Triomphe stands,
To commemorate the victories of France
     in many lands.
It was built in eighteen hundred and five by Napoleon
     the Great.

Flappers: 'Swonderful. 'Smarvelous. It'd make such a nice
     front gate.

Guide: It's a hundred and sixty four feet high, and a hundred
     and fifty wide,
And exactly seventy-two feet deep.

Flappers: Well, we'll say you're some guide.

Guide: This great arcade
Sits all alone,
But unafraid
A flower full-blown,
Entirely made of
Of solid stone.

Millionaire: I'll buy it.

Guide: Before you stands the Eiffel Tow'r, a
     monument adored.

Millionaire: Then what does that sign mean, Citroen?

Guide: Citroen is French for Ford.

Flappers: Aux armes, Citroen.
Citroen is French for Ford.

Guide: Do you realize this famous tow'r
Will be all lit up, in another hour,
By a light of a million candle-pow'r?

Millionaire: I'll buy it.

Guide: Kneel in pray'r
And doff your hat.
And cease your remarks profane.
The building there
You're looking at
Is the famous church of the Madeleine.

Flappers: Hallaluyah, Hallaluyah.
It's the famous Madeleine.

Millionaire: We've got a church in Kankakee,
But this one is a riot.
So if you'll send it C.O.D.
I'll buy it.

Guide: If you're really connoisseurs,
I've got a treat for you.
We're now at the Ambassadeurs,
To see the new Revue.

Flappers: Oh this is swell.
Is this the Ambassadeurs?

Guide: Yes, this is the reason why Chanel
Invented summer furs.

Flappers: And who's that little lonely
Fellow sitting down?

Guide: Why, that man is the only
Frenchman left in town.

Millionaire: You see that lovely lady with a young man
     sitting by 'er?
Well, she's a famous beauty here, that all
     the men admire.
They tell me she has ev'rything a lover could require.

Millionaire: I'll buy her.

All: Now that we've seen Paris, it's time that we begin
To pack our trunks and buy our bunks on a fast train
     to Berlin.
The next day to Vienna, and then a day in Rome.
And after that we'll hurry back to home sweet home.

PARIS (1928)

LET'S DO IT, LET'S FALL IN LOVE

VERSE

When the little blue-bird,
Who has never said a word,
Starts to sing "Spring, spring,"
When the little blue-bell,
In the bottom of the dell
Starts to ring "Ding, ding,"
When the little blue clerk,

In the middle of his work,
Starts a tune to the moon up above,
It is nature, that's all,
Simply telling us to fall
In love.

REFRAIN 1

And that's why Chinks do it, Japs do it,
Up in Lapland, little Laps do it,
Let's do it, let's fall in love.
In Spain, the best upper sets do it,
Lithuanians and Letts do it,
Let's do it, let's fall in love.
The Dutch in old Amsterdam do it,
Not to mention the Finns,
Folks in Siam do it,
Think of Siamese twins.
Some Argentines, without means, do it,
People say, in Boston, even beans do it,
Let's do it, let's fall in love.

REFRAIN 2

The nightingales, in the dark, do it,
Larks, k-razy for a lark, do it,
Let's do it, let's fall in love.
Canaries, caged in the house, do it,
When they're out of season, grouse do it,
Let's do it, let's fall in love.
The most sedate barnyard fowls do it,
When a chantacleer cries,
High-browed old owls do it,
They're supposed to be wise,
Penguins in flocks, on the rocks, do it,
Even little cuckoos in their clocks, do it,
Let's do it, let's fall in love.

REFRAIN 3

Romantic sponges, they say, do it,
Oysters, down in Oyster Bay, do it,
Let's do it, let's fall in love.
Cold Cape Cod clams, 'gainst their wish, do it,
Even lazy jelly-fish do it,
Let's do it, let's fall in love.
Electric eels, I might add, do it,
Though it shocks 'em, I know,
Why ask if shad do it?
Waiter, bring me shad roe.
In shallow shoals, English soles do it,
Gold-fish, in the privacy of bowls, do it,
Let's do it, let's fall in love.

REFRAIN 4

The dragon flies, in the reeds, do it,
Sentimental centipedes do it,
Let's do it, let's fall in love.
Mosquitos, heaven forbid, do it,
So does ev'ry katydid, do it,
Let's do it, let's fall in love.
The most refined lady-bugs do it,
When a gentleman calls,
Moths in your rugs, do it,
What's the use of moth-balls?

Locusts in trees do it, bees do it,
Even highly educated fleas do it,
Let's do it, let's fall in love.

REFRAIN 5

The chimpanzees in the zoos do it,
Some courageous kangaroos do it,
Let's do it, let's fall in love.
I'm sure giraffes, on the sly, do it,
Heavy hippopotami do it,
Let's do it, let's fall in love.
Old sloths who hang down from twigs do it,
Though the effort is great,
Sweet guinea-pigs do it,
Buy a couple and wait.
The world admits bears in pits do it,
Even pekineses in the Ritz, do it,
Let's do it, let's fall in love.

WHICH

Which is the right life,
The simple or the night life?
When, pray, should one rise,
At sunset or at sunrise?
Which should be upper,
My breakfast or my supper?
Which is the right life,
Which?
If the wood nymph left the park,
Would Park Avenue excite her?
Would the glow-worm trade her spark
For the latest Dunhill lighter?
Here's a question I would pose,
Tell me which the sweeter smell makes,
The aroma of the rose
Or the perfume that Chanel makes?

Irene Bordoni and Eric Kalkhurst

Which land is dreamier,
Arcadia or Bohemia?
Who'll tell the answer,
The daisy or the dancer?
Which life is for me,
The peaceful or the stormy?
Which is the right man,
Walt Whitman or Paul Whiteman,
Which?
Should I read Euripides or continue with the Graphic?
Hear the murmur of the breeze or the roaring of the traffic?
Should I make one man my choice
And regard divorce as treason,
Or should I like Peggy Joyce,
Get a new one ev'ry season?
Which is the right life,
The simple or the night life?
When, pray, should one rise,
At sunset or at sunrise?
Which should be the upper,
My breakfast or my supper?
Which is the right life,
Which!

Irene Bordoni and Arthur Margetson

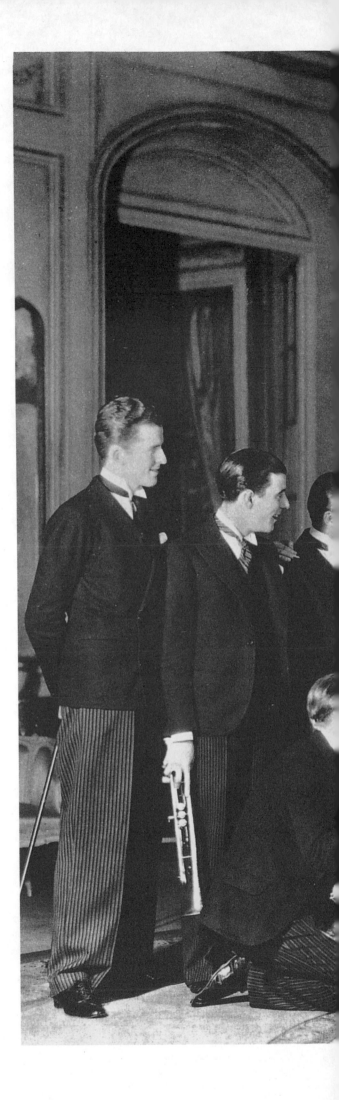

Irene Bordoni with Irving Aaronson's Commanders

WAKE UP AND DREAM (1929)

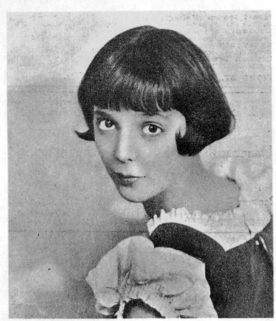

Miss Jessie Matthews

I LOVED HIM BUT HE DIDN'T LOVE ME

VERSE 1

The gods who nurse
This universe
Think little of mortals' cares.
They sit in crowds
On exclusive clouds
And laugh at our love affairs.
I might have had a real romance,
If they'd given me a chance.

REFRAIN 1

I loved him,
But he didn't love me.
I wanted him,
But he didn't want me.
Then the gods had a spree,
And indulged in another whim.
Now he loves me
But I don't love him.

VERSE 2

I told this tale
With its weary wail
To sev'ral devoted wives.
They said, "You're young,
You have simply sung
The story of all our lives."
So maybe there are couples here
Who have had the same career.

REFRAIN 2

You loved him,
But he didn't love you.
You wanted him,
But he didn't want you.
Then the gods saw you two,
And indulged in another whim,
Now he loves you,
But you don't love him.

REFRAIN 3

You loved her
But she didn't love you.
You wanted her,
But she didn't want you.
Then the gods saw you two,
And you both felt a change occur.
Now she loves you,
But you don't love her.

I wrote Looking at You *for Clifton Webb,*
when I was doing a revue at Les Ambassadeurs in Paris.
Clifton did it so well that I put it in the score of
"Wake Up and Dream" in London, where it was sung by
Sonnie Hale to Jessie Mathews. Later when
Jack Buchanan starred in "Wake Up and Dream" on
Broadway he sang this song.

Cole Porter

LOOKING AT YOU

VERSE

I've gone afar,
Collecting objets d'art,
I know the whole game by heart.
Why, Joe Duveen
Will tell you what I mean
'Twas I who gave him his start.
But since I looked, dear, in your direction,
I've quite forgotten my art collection.
To be exact,
You simply prove the fact
That nature's greater than art.

"What Is This Thing Called Love?"

REFRAIN

Looking at you,
While troubles are fleeing.
I'm admiring the view,
'Cause it's you I'm seeing.
And the sweet honey-dew
Of well being settles upon me.
What is this light
That shines when you enter?
Like a star in the night,
And what's to prevent 'er
From destroying my sight,
If you centre all of it on me?
Looking at you
I'm filled with the essence of
The quintessence of
Joy.
Looking at you,
I hear poets tellin' of
Lovely Helen of
Troy, darling.
Life seemed so grey
I wanted to end it,
Till that wonderful day
You started to mend it.
And if you'll only stay?
Then I'll spend it looking at you.

WHAT IS THIS THING CALLED LOVE?

VERSE 1

I was a humdrum person,
Leading a life apart.
When love flew in through my window wide
And quickened my humdrum heart.
Love flew in through my window,
I was so happy then.
But after love had stayed a little while,
Love flew out again.

REFRAIN

What is this thing called love?
This funny thing called love?
Just who can solve its mystery?
Why should it make a fool of me?
I saw you there one wonderful day.
You took my heart and threw it away.
That's why I ask the Lord in heaven above,
What is this thing called love?

VERSE 2

You gave me days of sunshine,
You gave me nights of cheer,
You made my life an enchanted dream
Till somebody else came near.
Somebody else came near you,
I felt the winter's chill
And now I sit and wonder night and day
Why I love you still.

"What Is This Thing Called Love?" The girl (Tilly Losch), the man (Toni Birkmayer), and the idol (William Cavanagh)

I'M A GIGOLO

VERSE

I should like you all to know,
I'm a famous gigolo.
And of lavender, my nature's got just a dash in it.
As I'm slightly undersexed,
You will always find me next
To some dowager who's wealthy rather than passionate.
Go to one of those night club places
And you'll find me stretching my braces.
Pushing ladies with lifted faces 'round the floor.
But I must confess to you
There are moments when I'm blue.
And I ask myself whatever I do it for.

Tilly Losch as a Manchu Marchioness (costume by Oliver Messel)

REFRAIN

I'm a flower that blooms in the winter,
Sinking deeper and deeper in "snow."
I'm a baby who *has*
No mother but *jazz*,
I'm a gigolo
Ev'ry morning, when labour is over,
To my sweet-scented lodgings I go,
Take a glass from the shelf
And look at myself,
I'm a gigolo.
I get stocks and bonds
From faded blondes
Ev'ry twenty-fifth of December.
Still I'm just a pet
That men forget
And only tailors remember.

Yet when I see the way all the ladies
Treat their husbands who put up the dough,
You cannot think me odd
If then I thank God
I'm a gigolo.

FIFTY MILLION FRENCHMEN (1929)

YOU DO SOMETHING TO ME

VERSE 1

I was mighty blue,
Thought my life was through,
Till the heavens opened,
And I gazed at you.
Won't you tell me, dear,
Why, when you appear,
Something happens to me
And the strangest feeling goes through me?

REFRAIN

You do something to me,
Something that simply mystifies me.
Tell me, why should it be
You have the pow'r to hypnotize me?
Let me live 'neath your spell,
Do do that voodoo that you do so well,
For you do something to me
That nobody else could do.

VERSE 2

If I seem to stray
When you talk this way
It's because I'm wondering
What I ought to say
I could cry, please don't
But I believe I won't
For when you talk to me
Such a soothing feeling goes through me.

YOU'VE GOT THAT THING

VERSE

Since first you blew in like a boisterous breeze
I often have wondered, dear,
Why gentlemen all seem to fall on their knees
The moment that you appear?
Your fetching physique is hardly unique,
You're mentally not so hot;
You'll never win laurels because of your morals,
But I'll tell you what you've got

Betty Compton and Jack Thompson

REFRAIN 1

You've got that thing, you've got that thing,
That thing that makes birds forget to sing;
Yes, you've got that thing, that certain thing.
You've got that charm, that subtle charm
That makes young farmers desert the farm,
'Cause you've got that thing, that certain thing.
You've got what Adam craved when he
With love for Eve was tortured,
She only had an apple tree,
But you, you've got an orchard.
You've got those ways, those taking ways
That make me rush off to Cartier's
For a wedding ring;
You've got that thing.

REFRAIN 2

You've got that thing, you've got that thing,
That thing that makes vines prefer to cling.
Yes, you've got that thing, that certain thing.
You've got those looks, those fatal looks,
That make book-censors enjoy their books
'Cause you've got that thing, that certain thing.
Just what made Samson be, for years,
Delilah's lord and keeper?
She only had a pair of sheers.
But you, you've got a reaper.
You've got that pow'r, that pow'r to grip
That makes me map out a wedding trip
For the early spring,
You've got that thing.

REFRAIN 3

You've got that thing, you've got that thing,
That thing that makes bees refuse to sting,
Yes, you've got that thing, that certain thing,
You've got that kiss, that kiss that warms,
That makes reformers reform reforms,
'Cause you got that thing, that certain thing.
They tell us Trojan Helen's lips
Made ev'ry man her slavey
If her face launched a thousand ships
Well, yours could launch a navy
You've got that love, and such a lot
It makes me think you're prepared for what
Any stork might bring.
You've got that thing.

I WORSHIP YOU

VERSE

Back in the days when Greece was mighty,
Men used to worship Aphrodite.
When the Phoenicians threw a party
The driest host drank a toast to Astarte.
The big Egyptian sacrifices
Were made to please the goddess Isis,
And one of my most ancient vices
Is my worship of you.

REFRAIN

I don't love you, dear,
I swear it's true,
I don't love you, dear,
I worship you.
Must I modify
My point of view?
Why should I be odd if I
Worship you?
On that sacred day
When you become mine,
Somewhere, far away
I'll build you a shrine.
There I'll put you, dear,
And when I do,
I'll get on my knees
And worship you.

Evelyn Hoey

FIND ME A PRIMITIVE MAN

VERSE

Now before this modern idea had burst
About the women and children first,
The men had much more charm than they have today.
And if only one of that type survived,
The very moment that he arrived
I know I'd fall in love in a great big way.
I can't imagine being bad
With any arrow collar ad,
Nor could I take the slightest joy
In waking up a college boy.
I've no desire to be alone
With Rudy Vallee's megaphone
So when I'm saying my pray'rs I say:

REFRAIN

Find me a primitive man
Built on a primitive plan;
Some one with vigor and vim,
I don't mean the kind that belongs to a club,
But the kind that has a club that belongs to him.
I could be the personal slave
Of some one just out of a cave.
The only man who'll ever win me
Has gotta wake up the gypsy in me.
Find me a primitive man,
Find me a primitive man.
Trouve moi un homme primitif.
Trouve moi un garcon naif.
Quelqu'un tout plein de vigeur,
Ces p'tits maquereaux qu'on appelle gigolos ne
Pourraient jamais me donner le vrai bonheur.
J'ai besoin d'un bel animal
Pour chauffer mon chauffage centrale.
Et l'homme qui me veut pour capitane
Devrait reveiller mon sang tzigane,
Trouve moi un homme primitif, vif,
Trouve moi un homme primitif.

WHERE WOULD YOU GET YOUR COAT?

VERSE

As a buyer for a firm that deals in ladies' fur coats
I get sort of pessimistic now and then
'Cause so many women who invest in our coats
Spend so many evenings out with other men
I wish they'd simply take a few notes
From the animals who make their coats.

REFRAIN 1

For if dear little ermines in Siberia
On their dear little husbands didn't dote
If the dear little 'possum
Didn't let their husbands boss 'em
Tell me where would you get your coat?
If the dear little caraculs in Syria

All their time to their mates did not devote
If the dear little sables ever told their husbands fables
Tell me where would you get your coat?
If you modern wives led more domestic lives
And started singing home sweet home
There'd be no more divorce in Paris and
Of course there'd be no more annulments in Rome
For if the dear little foxes had hysteria
When their mates fondly grabbed them by the throat
If the dear little rabbits weren't so bourgeois in their habits
Tell me where would you get your coat?

William Gaxton and girls

REFRAIN 2

If the dear little lamb in Lithuania
Ever had a flirtation with a goat
If home life didn't thrill a South American chinchilla
Tell me where would you get your coat?
If the dear little skunk in Pennsylvania
Over her dear little husband didn't gloat
If the dear little beaver
Were in birth control a believer,
Tell me where would you get your coat?
Now if each wife I see
Would only try to be
Content to make her husband's bed,
Cholly Knickerbocker might have nothing more to write
And Town Topics would cease to be read
For if the dear little mink should get a mania
For some hell raising gigolo of note
If the dear little squirrel
Quit her mate
'Cause he was virile
Tell me where would you get your coat?

THE TALE OF AN OYSTER

Down by the sea lived a lonesome oyster,
Ev'ry day getting sadder and moister,
He found his home life awf'lly wet,
And longed to travel with the upper set.
Poor little oyster.
Fate was kind to that oyster we know,
When one day the chef from the Park Casino
Saw that oyster lying there,
And said, "I'll put you on my bill of fare."
Lucky little oyster.
See him on his silver platter,
Watching the queens of fashion chatter.
Hearing the wives of millionaires
Discuss their marriages and their love affairs.
Thrilled little oyster.
See that bi-valve social climber
Feeding the rich Mrs. Hoggenheimer,
Think of his joy as he gaily glides
Down to the middle of her gilded insides.
Proud little oyster.
After lunch Mrs. H. complains,
And says to her hostess, "I've got such pains.
I came to town on my yacht today,
But I think I'd better hurry back to Oyster Bay."
Scared little oyster.
Off they go thru the troubled tide,
The yacht rolling madly from side to side,
They're tossed about till that poor young oyster
Finds that it's time he should quit his cloister.
Up comes the oyster.
Back once more where he started from.
He murmured, "I haven't a single qualm,
For I've had a taste of society
And society has had a taste of me."
Wise little oyster.

Helen Broderick and William Gaxton

YOU DON'T KNOW PAREE

VERSE

You come to Paris, you come to play;
You have a wonderful time, you go away.
And, from then on, you talk of Paris knowingly;
You may know Paris, you don't know Paree.

REFRAIN

Though you've been around a lot,
And danced a lot, and laughed a lot;
You don't know Paree.
You may say you've seen a lot,
And heard a lot, and learned a lot;
You don't know Paree.
Paree will still be laughing after
Ev'ry one of us disappears;
But never once forget her laughter
Is the laughter that hides the tears.
And, until you've lived a lot
And loved a lot, and lost a lot,
You don't know Paree,
You don't know Paree.

I'M UNLUCKY AT GAMBLING

VERSE

I went to Monte Carlo the other day,
I went to Monte Carlo to have some play;
I went to Monte Carlo and, straight-a-way
I went and fell in love with a croupier.
The croupier advised me to back the red,
The croupier was handsome, I lost my head;
And when the game was over and love was dead,
I realized I'd played on the black instead.

REFRAIN

For, I'm unlucky at gambling,
And I'm unlucky in love.
Why should I go on scrambling
To get in heaven above?
It's bad enough to lose your purse
But, when you lose your heart, it's even worse.
Oh, I'm unlucky at gambling
And I'm unlucky in love.

VERSE 2

I took the croupier to a picture show,
I took the croupier to a picture show,
And though I snuggled close when the lights
        were low,
The croupier impressed me as rather slow
I said I like John Gilbert a lot, don't you?
I said I like John Gilbert a lot, don't you?
He didn't answer but when the show was through
I realized that he liked John Gilbert too.

Larry Ceballos' Hollywood Dancers

The Longchamps scene

E. RAY GOETZ

COLE PORTER
Writer of the Words and Music

The producer, composer-lyricist, and featured performers of "The New Yorkers"

THE NEW YORKERS (1930)

WHERE HAVE YOU BEEN?

VERSE

If ever you love again,
If such luck could be,
You must fall in love again
With nobody but me;
For now that I see you, I know
That we should have met long ago.

REFRAIN

Where have you been?
I want to know where have you been?
My life was a losing fight
Till the lucky night,
Baby, you happened in.
From what I had heard about love,
I thought it was all sorrow and sin,
But now that we meet at last,
I forget the past,
Baby, where have you been?
I was alone, unbefriended,
In the depths of despair,
When out of the blue you descended
And somehow ended ev'ry care.
So if you will give me a break,
And order the love-scene to begin,
So close to your side I'll stay
You can never say
"Baby, where have you been?"

THE GREAT INDOORS

VERSE

When the weekend comes,
All my dearest chums
To the country go tearing off,
To improve their frames
Playing dam-fool games
Such as Polo and Tom Thumb golf.
While they're breaking ground,
Biffing balls around,
And perspiring to beat the band,
I am sitting pretty
In the great big city,
With a cool drink in my hand.

REFRAIN

From Saturday until Monday
I'm what the sportsman abhors,
A weekend hater
Thanking my creator

For the great indoors.
While all the others are rushing
From bathing suits to plus-fours,
You'll find this mamma's still in her pajamas
For the great indoors.
The breeze may die,
But what care I,
I've got a big electric fan.
If passing by,
Come in and try
Biting your initial on my artificial tan.
Instead of wrecking my system
By playing games with old bores,
I take no chances,
Sitting on my Frances,
In the great indoors.

LOVE FOR SALE

VERSE

When the only sound in the empty street
Is the heavy tread of the heavy feet
That belong to a lonesome cop,
I open shop.

Hope Williams and the team of Clayton, Jackson, and Durante in "The New Yorkers," 1930

When the moon so long has been gazing down
On the wayward ways of this wayward town
That her smile becomes a smirk,
I go to work.

REFRAIN

Love for sale,
Appetizing young love for sale.
Love that's fresh and still unspoiled,
Love that's only slightly soiled,
Love for sale.
Who will buy?
Who would like to sample my supply?
Who's prepared to pay the price
For a trip to paradise?
Love for sale.
Let the poets pipe of love
In their childish way,
I know ev'ry type of love
Better far than they.
If you want the thrill of love,
I've been thru the mill of love,
Old love, new love,
Ev'ry love but true love.
Love for sale,
Appetizing young love for sale.
If you want to buy my wares
Follow me and climb the stairs,
Love for sale.

★★★★★★★★★★★

A frightened vocalist, Miss Kathryn
Crawford sings a threnody entitled Love for Sale *in*
which she impersonated a lily of the gutters,
vending her charms in trembling accents,
accompanied by a trio of melancholy female crooners.
When and if we ever get a censorship, I will give
odds that it will frown upon such an honest thing.

> *Percy Hammond*
> *New York* Herald Tribune
> *December 9, 1930*

. . . Love for Sale, as sung by Kathryn
Crawford, June Shafer, Ida Pearson, and Stella Friend,
was in the worst possible taste.

> *Charles Darnton*
> *New York* Evening World
> *December 9, 1930*

★★★★★★★★★★★

Percy Hammond's fears were confirmed
when the song was banned on the radio. Recordings by
Libby Holman and Fred Waring and
the Three Girl Friends as well as
many night club renditions assured a widespread audience for the song, but the attitude of critics such
as Charles Darnton had its effect on the
authors, who changed the setting to the Cotton Club
and the singer to a "colored girl."

Scene in one Exterior of Cotton Club.
Pedestrians walking into Cotton Club.
Newsboys selling papers.

Newsboys: Morning papers, morning papers.
        Gang chief killed when explosion occurs
        Six months bride says that child isn't hers
        Admiral Byrd's bought a new set of furs.
           Morning papers
           Morning papers
           Morning papers
           Morning papers
        Well-known clubman is put in the pen
        Clara Bow seen with several men
        Aimee McPherson socks her mother again.
        Morning papers, morning papers.

Two colored boys doing dancing specialty.

Colored Girl sings *Love for Sale*

LET'S FLY AWAY

VERSE

He: I've such a hate on Manhattan lately,
     That I'd gladly die;
She: Your conversation excites me greatly,
     For so have I.
He: I'm tired of the telephone always ringing.
She: I'm tired of hearing Rudy Vallee singing.
He: I'm tired of the Paramount's gaudy gilding.
She: I'm tired of looking up to the Chrysler Building.
He: I'm tired of having Texas Guinan greet me.
She: I'm tired of having Grover Whalen meet me.
He: There's only one solution, dear.
She: Let's calmly disappear.

REFRAIN

Let's fly away,
And find a land that's warm and tropic;
Where prohibition's not the topic
All the live long day.
Let's fly away,
And find a land that's so provincial,
We'll never hear what Walter Winchell
Might be forced to say.
I'll make your life sublime,
Far across the blue;
I'll take up all your time
Compromising you.
Let's not delay,
Make mother nature our Messiah;
New York is not for us,
Let's fly away.

Ann Pennington, dancing star of "The New Yorkers" and of "The Ziegfeld Follies," "George White's Scandals," and Warner Brothers film musicals

Happy in the success of E. Ray Goetz's new musical show,"The New Yorkers," which recently opened at the new Broadway Theatre, Cole Porter, who wrote the music and lyrics, has sailed away to Monte Carlo for a vacation. The whole town is whistling and singing the big song hits in"The New Yorkers"written by Porter and a song which caused Porter to wireless Goetz from mid-ocean when he was two days out at sea, the title being I Happen to Like New York.

New York Evening Journal
December 23, 1930

I HAPPEN TO LIKE NEW YORK

I happen to like New York.
I happen to like this town.
I like the city air, I like to drink of it,
The more I know New York the more I
    think of it.
I like the sight and the sound and even the
    stink of it.
I happen to like New York.
I like to go to Battery Park
And watch those liners booming in
I often ask myself: why should it be
That they should come so far
From across the sea.
I suppose it's because they all agree with me
They happen to like New York.
On Sunday afternoon
I took a trip to Hackensack
But when I gave Hackensack the onceover
I took the next train back
I happen to like New York.
I happen to like this burg
And when I have to give the world
A last farewell
And the undertaker
Starts to ring my funeral bell
I don't want to go to heaven
Don't want to go to hell.
I happen to like New York.
I happen to love New York.

STAR DUST (1931)

In 1931 Cole completed the score for a musical with a book by Herbert Fields. The show, which Goetz was to produce and which was to star Peggy Wood, never went into production. The exceptionally fine score included several of Cole's best previously discarded numbers. Three of the songs turned up a year later in "Gay Divorce." Another, *I Get a Kick Out of You*, was one of the hits of "Anything Goes" in 1934. One outstanding song never got into any show: *Pick Me Up and Lay Me Down*.

"WILL YOU COME AS YOUR OPPOSITE TO MY PARTY IN HONOUR OF THE MOST UNATTRACTIVE MAN IN NEW YORK, MR. COLE PORTER, IN CRYSTAL ROOM, RITZ HOTEL, DECEMBER TENTH, ELEVEN-THIRTY P.M. PLEASE ANSWER—ELSA MAXWELL." Thus, by telegram, came the invitations to the most amusing party in New York this winter. Half of New York's three-ring social circus went. Miss Maxwell herself as President Hoover, Mrs. William Averell Harriman as Peggy Hopkins Joyce, Prince Vassili of Russia as a Communist, Mrs. Henry Gray as Elinor Glyn, Jack Pratt as his mother, the Hon. Ruth Pratt, Fannie Brice as an ingénue, Mr. Schuyler Parsons as Brigham Young, Princesse Chlodwig Hohenlohe-Schillingsfürst and Mrs. Baldwin Preston as nuns, Miss Eleanor Barry as Ann Pennington—on and on, ad infinitum. The only decorations were huge posters satirizing books and plays by the guests.

Ina Claire as Leonore Ulric, Cole as an 1890's halfback, and Mrs. George F. Baker, Jr., as a *demi-mondaine*

PICK ME UP AND LAY ME DOWN

VERSE

A certain yearning
That's burning me up
I never felt before.
Ideas within me
Are churning, concerning
Returning to nature once more.
I want to study the pea, the bean, the beet,
From omega to alpha,
And get acquainted with corn and oats and wheat,
Not to mention alfalfa.
So—

REFRAIN

Pick me up and lay me down
On a sleepy farm.
Where the cares that weigh me down
Can do no more harm.
Let the sun behind the hill

Be my cue to yawn,
Let me rival the rooster
As a booster
Of the dawn.
I want to gaze at
Gardens of green,
I want to hoe potatoes,
I want to learn the diff-rence between
Tomahtoes and tomatoes.
If you know of such a spot
Not too far from town,
Pick me up and lay me down.

★★★★★★★★★★★

One of Cole's most celebrated jokes
was his invention of a bogus social-climbing couple,
Mr. and Mrs. S. Beach Fitch. He began to send
notices to various society editors in Paris
of the comings and goings of the Fitches.
Cole and his friends were responsible for many letters
agreeing and disagreeing with the Fitches. The hoax,
which was eventually exposed by Walter Winchell and
Cholly Knickerbocker, inspired the song.

In the spring of 1931 Elsa borrowed Baron Nicolas de Gunzburg's farm for "Un Bal Champêtre
—Des Fêtes D'Esprit et De Gaieté"

Here is the market gardener's entrée at the fête champêtre. Seated on the cart is Mr. Cole Porter, with the Princesse Ilyinsky and Mrs. Porter. Mr. Billy Reardon, the Duc de la Verdura, the Marquis Salina Amorini, and Mr. Howard Sturges are dressed as peasants

Why Flag Is Lowered.

Paris, July 27.

To the Editor of The New York Herald:

Writers such as Edward Empire annoy me as they seem to glory in their ignorance. All governments have about the same regulations regarding the official colors. For example, government vessels, such as those of the navy, lower the colors at sunset. In the U.S.A. this rule holds good for all Government buildings and offices where and when flags are flown.

In the U.S. army the garrison flag is flown from a staff when a parade is held and colors are lowered at sunset. In France, where a garrison flag is not used, the regimental colors are carried at parade and after "La Marseillaise" is played, the colors are put away with fitting ceremony.

W. A. R.

Introducing Mr. King.

Nice, August 1

To the Editor of The New York Herald:

As a hundred-percenter and a nephew of Mr. S. Beach Fitch (my mother having been a Fitch) I wish to congratulate publicly my relation on his patriotic point of view.

The idea of Americans becoming Europeanized is to me nothing short of disgusting. It is the duty of every travelling citizen of the U.S.A. to make foreigners realize the gorgeous advantages of American civilization and to work towards the Americanizing of Europe. This rather than letting ourselves become demoralized by the effete influence of this Continent.

It was wonderful to read in the issue of July 29 the fine list of artists; it is well for all to know that the U.S.A. is able to take the lead in artwork, music and writing as well as in business, politics and warfare.

I know what I am writing about for I have lived in Europe for nearly eight years but that is on account of taxes, prohibition, expenses and my one desire here that they should know all about the glory of Uncle Sam.

C. S. KING.

Mr. Fitch Retorts.

Carlsbad, July 14.

To the Editor of The New York Herald:

As a 100 per cent. American, I read Mr. Edward Empire's letter in your Tuesday issue, concerning Old Glory, with indignation.

Why we citizens of the "land of the free and the home of the brave" should copy the habits of foreign countries I fail to understand, and it seems to me that what Mr. Empire needs is a trip back home before he forgets that the U.S.A., to all good Americans, always has been and always will be the greatest country on earth.

S. BEACH FITCH.

A Question of Greatness.

Siegsdorf, August 1.

To the Editor of The New York Herald:

Mr. S. Beach Fitch, writing to you in defence of 100 per cent. Americans, includes in his letter a list of persons, born 'neath the Stars and Stripes, who are also, in his opinion, "Grade A artists."

Alas for Mr. Fitch! He produces a queer kettle o' fish. For if Ella Wheeler Wilcox must forever hold her own, thanks to her burning-heart quality, her soaring idealism and the tender lullaby of her verse, as one of the glories of American literature and American womanhood, what are we to think of following up her name with that of Michael Strange, a clever but (in the 1890 sense of the word) "decadent" writer. And, if Mr. Fitch considers Zane Grey "the greatest of them all," where, may one ask, does he place Louis Bromfield?

If Mr. Fitch would condescend to imbibe a little more of what he calls "the exhausted culture of Europe," his values might be less muddy.

CLARA B. ALLEN.

Cocktails and Demoralization.

Paris, August 4.

To the Editor of The New York Herald:

I wish to congratulate C. S. King upon his sense of humor, as I can hardly believe that he meant his letter seriously. But it would be more amusing, I think, if he would exercise this sense of humor in another direction instead of poking fun at the gorgeous advantages of American civilization.

Does he mean the cocktail? I happened to read in the Mailbag that this is America's one and only contribution to civilization. I don't agree with this at all, but perhaps C. S. King does. If so, then why admit that he has lived over here for eight years because of prohibition and other reasons?

That is hardly the way to contribute to the glory of Uncle Sam. He also wants to Americanize Europe. That would be his undoing, according to his own words. There would be prohibition, higher taxes and everybody would know all about the glory of Uncle Sam. Then where would he go?

I have also lived over here for eight years, but have not noticed the demoralizing influence of this continent yet. Perhaps C. S. King knows better through experience.

NOT DEMORALIZED.

Mr. and Mrs. S. Beach Fitch, who are visiting Mr. and Mrs. Cole Porter at the Koenigsvilla at Carlsbad, were the guests of honor at a dinner given Wednesday by Mrs. Martha Hyde at the Restaurant Konigin Louise. Mr. and Mrs. Fitch will be joined shortly by their daughter, Miss Sonia B. Fitch, when they will go to visit the Count and Countess Laszlo Szechenyi in Hungary, following which they will be the guests of the Countess Potocka in Poland. In the early autumn Mr. and Mrs. Fitch and Miss Fitch will go to Rome to stay with the Marquis de Talleyrand, who has arranged for them an audience of the Pope.

Woe to 100 Per Centers.

Paris, July 22.

To the Editor of The New York Herald:

More than a week ago I wrote hoping that some reader could help me out with information concerning the vague origin of the custom of lowering Old Glory, our nation's flag, at sunset, which tradition has puzzled me for years.

The only response was that gouty outburst from Mr. S. Beach Fitch at Carlsbad, which enlightened contribution to your columns had no bearing whatever on my Old Glory trouble and, besides, threw me into such a rage that I decided to just leave Mr. Fitch, without even bothering to question why he isn't patronizing one of the various homeland spas out in the desolate stretches of Indiana, where everybody is 100 per cent. American.

Today I read Mr. Herbert Fitch's letter and felt that I, who had, although innocently enough, more or less started this all, ought to step in to help him (Mr. Herbert Fitch), not that he necessarily needs any support, because every clear-visioned, far-thinking person, whether he be 100 per cent. American or not, knows that it is just such 100 per cent. Americans as Mr. S. Beach Fitch who are the fundamental cause of all the misunderstandings between nations, unspeakable wars, financial depressions, unemployment, bootlegging, misery and bad art that we have in the world today.

Can Mr. Herbert Fitch tell me why the Stars and Stripes has to be brought in at night? EDWARD EMPIRE.

Forgetting American Artists.

Munich, July 25.

To the Editor of The New York Herald:

When Edward Empire writes that 100 per-cent. Americans are responsible for all the bad art in the world today, he touches upon a subject that no loyal son of Uncle Sam can ignore.

For, in one sentence, he tries to sweep aside such artists as Ella Wheeler Wilcox, Michael Strange, Frances Hodgson Burnet, George Barr McCutcheon, Ethelbert Nevin, Carrie Jacobs Bond, Jo Davidson, Mrs. Harry Payne Whitney, Maxfield Parish and Howard Chandler Christy, all of whom are Grade A artists and everyone of them is a 100-per-cent. American. Also the greatest of them all, Zane Grey.

I think Edward Empire and Herbert Fitch should shake hands, and not waste further time imbibing the exhausted culture of Europe.

S. BEACH FITCH.

What They Think of Each Other.

Paris, August 7.

To the Editor of The New York Herald:

The great intellectual battle now waging at reduced wages (pardon the lisp) within S. B. Beach's Grade A milk-fed brain should not be fought from the ringside concerning the values, if any, of Lady Zane Gray and Blanche (Michael) Strange Oelrichs Thomas Barrymore and what else (not to be confused with Marjorie Oelrichs).

What or what not Dame Clara Butt-Allen thinks about the above and Louis Bromfield? No, indeed. It is what Louis Bromfield has to say concerning the qualities of Ring Lardner, Thomas Beer, and "H. D.," the only American writers who, to my mind, can compete in quality, if not substance, with Virginia Woolf and Edith Sitwell. The best Anglo-Saxons are gone: Elinor Wylie, Katherine Mansfield and Thomas Hardy. George Moore, of course, remains, much to the distress, I am sure, of our dear little left (and how) bank.

For the good of international relations I would like to see a few words on the subject by Mr. Bromfield (himself) and Paul Valéry, Salvador de Madariaga and Jean Giraudoux. And let us hear what Jean Hugo thinks about Peter Arno, what George Luks thinks of Kisling and what George (doesn't kiss and tells) Moore thinks of George B. (don't kiss but write) Shaw, who might have something to say about George Gissing. As Clarence Mackay said to Irving Berlin: "Don't write songs, telegraph." SYLVIA LYON.

What We Act Like.

Nice, July 18.

To the Editor of The New York Herald:

May another "Fitch," not 100 per cent. American, retort to Mr. Beach Fitch, of Carlsbad?

Although my tribe settled in Lynn, Reading, Bedford, Boston and Fitchburg, almost 300 years ago, I cannot enthuse over this idea of "the land of the free and the home of the brave" because I cannot see that there has been much "freedom" in the U.S.A. since people from central, eastern and southern Europe, along with the Irish, got practical control through the votes.

I don't even know that I am brave, although I have been in some tight places. I don't even know that the "U.S.A. to all good Americans," as Mr. Fitch says, is the "greatest country on earth." I have lived in Europe, Asia, Africa, South America, Australasia, and in almost every one of the larger islands of this earth, and I have yet to see that any race is "superior" to another.

Darwin, I think, saw us in our stark nakedness, better than most people of this day. We do not actually climb trees, now, but we act like those who did, it seems to me.

HERBERT FITCH.

THE MYSTERY about Mr. and Mrs. Fitch deepens. Were they really killed in that motor accident outside Rome, or was it all just a ghastly jest? Or is Mrs. Fitch haunting places?

Most of the history of Mr. and Mrs. Fitch is well known. They were the creation of Cole Porter, who amused himself and his friends on the Riviera by sending out society items about the Fitches of Tulsa, Okla. Soon the imaginary couple became international society figures.

Things got so complicated that Porter arranged for their deaths. He and Lady Mendl paid for an obituary notice. The Fitches, it was announced, were killed in an auto crash. Then Porter wrote an amusing song, "Mr. and Mrs. Fitch," for "Gay Divorce."

BUT—! Among the canvases shown until Thursday at the Wildenstein Galleries, in an exhibit of would-be artists organized by Mrs. Charles Morgan Jr., there was a certain painting. A very crude water color. It's still there because, though the exhibit was generally a great success, nobody bought it.

The artist's name is on the back —Mrs. S. B. Fitch of Tulsa, Okla.

Evidently Porter and Lady Mendl botched their motor killing. It was a sloppy job anyway, because they forgot, at the time, that the Fitches had a daughter, Sonia B. Fitch. She wasn't in the accident.

Sonia must be wandering about Europe somewhere, while her mother has been dabbling in water colors.

Those who are already back from Paris are full of talk about the Fitches. You don't know about the Fitches? They are the latest personalities in Paris society. One reads about them in the papers almost every day. The Cole Porters have given them a dinner, and they are in all the charity lists. But I will tell you a secret about them—they don't exist. Cole Porter invented them. He first wrote a song that went something like this: "They came to the big city and started to play. Every one wanted to meet the green, socially ambitious, but rich Mr. and Mrs. Fitch. When they called for the drinks, the drinks arrived. When they called for a plane, the plane arrived. A private train, the train arrived. But when they called for cash, the crash arrived . . . etc., etc." Now, everybody asks, "which Fitches?" And the answer is, "THE Fitches. You know, the Fitches from Tulsa." Now, when we are asked to dinner and are already engaged, we say, "Dear, I am so sorry, but I am dining with the Fitches." Only the other day, some one sent me a clipping from Paris, which read: "Mr. and Mrs. Cole Porter and Mr. Howard Sturges left yesterday for Carlsbad to take the cure. They will be joined Saturday by the Baron Nicolas de Gunzburg and Mr. and Mrs. S. B. Fitch, his house-guests here in Paris."

Regarding your piece about Cole Porter fooling reporters with the spurious name of S. B. Fitch while in Yurrop, Porter wrote a ditty about them, now a hit over there . . . Louella Gear will sing it in "The Gay Divorce," the new play due soon. .

Cholly Knickerbocker Says:

Cole Porter, who, in Paris, has a music room with lacquer walls, chairs covered with white kid and zebra rugs thrown over the highly polished floors, is in New York looking after the details of his newest musical comedy.

Last Summer, in Paris, Cole played a rather shabby trick on one of my confreres, the editor of a society column in an American daily published in Paree.

Mr. Winchell has told, in his column, a part of the story: how Cole invented a family and named them "Mr. and Mrs. S. B. Fitch" and then proceeded to send reams of publicity to the society editor in question concerning the polite activities of Mr. and Mrs. Fitch.

The story spread all over the Continent. "Mr. Fitch" even penned letters to the "Voice of the People," or whatever it is called, column, and those not in the know began to wonder about the Fitch family.

It just so happens that the society editor in question once served as my secretary. So, upon arriving in Paris and hearing the story of the Fitches from Lady Mendl (Elsie de Wolfe) I determined to save my former secretary some trouble—and her job.

For she had unsuspectingly printed all the dribble sent in about the mythical Fitches.

What Mr. Winchell did not tell was that one morning several weeks ago, Cole and the rest of the razzle-dazzle American set in Paree were astounded to read, in their favorite Paris journal, a notice in the obituary column announcing the sudden death in Rome of Mr. and Mrs. S. B. Fitch!

That notice was inserted and paid for by "Cholly Knickerbocker" and ended the career of Mr. and Mrs. Fitch.

And were those who perpetuated the joke surprised, ask me!

MISTER AND MISSUS FITCH

VERSE

On a farm far from pleasant,
No pair was more peasant
Than Mister and Missus Fitch.
Their days, each one duller,
Were so lacking in color,
They didn't know which was which.
When suddenly tilling the soil
Mister Fitch struck oil.

REFRAIN

Mister and Missus Fitch one day
Hit town, determined to play.
Mister and Missus Fitch were green,
Ambitious, but rich.
And soon the crowd they call "elite"
Were fighting madly to meet
The young, attractive, and rich,
Mister and Missus Fitch.
When they called for champagne
Champagne arrived.
An aeroplane,
The plane arrived.
A private train,
The train arrived.
But when they called for cash
The *crash* arrived.
Now men who once knew Missus Fitch
Refer to her as a bitch.
While the girls who once loved Mister Fitch
Say he always was a son of a bitch,
So love and kisses,
Mister and Missus Fitch.

GAY DIVORCE (1932)

Cole claimed, no telling how seriously, that
the music was inspired by a Mohammedan
call to worship that he had heard in Morocco.
The song was completed on the beach
at Newport.

NIGHT AND DAY

VERSE

Like the beat beat beat of the tom tom when the jungle
        shadows fall
Like the tick tick tock of the stately clock as it
        stands against the wall
Like the drip drip drip of the raindrops when the
        sum'r show'r is through
So a voice within me keeps repeating You—You—You.

REFRAIN

Night and day you are the one,
Only you beneath the moon and under the sun,
Whether near to me or far
It's no matter darling where you are
I think of you night and day.
Day and night, why is it so
That this longing for you follows wherever I go?
In the roaring traffic's boom
In the silence of my lonely room
I think of you night and day.
Night and day under the hide of me
There's an, oh, such a hungry, yearning burning
        inside of me
And its torment won't be through
Till you let me spend my life making love to you
Day and night, night and day.

IRVING BERLIN

Jan. 3rd, 1933

Dear Cole:

I am mad about NIGHT AND DAY, and I think it is
your high spot. You probably know it is being
played all over, and all the orchestra leaders
think it is the best tune of the year -- and I
agree with them.

Really, Cole, it is great and I could not resist
the temptation of writing you about it.

Love from us to you and Linda.

As ever,

Cole Porter, Esq.,
13 Rue Monsieur,
Paris, France

JANUARY MUSIC SURVEY

THIS TABLE SHOWS THE LEADING SIX SELLERS IN SHEET MUSIC AND PHONOGRAPH RECORDS GATHERED FROM THE REPORTS
OF SALES MADE DURING JANUARY BY THE LEADING MUSIC JOBBERS AND DISC DISTRIBUTORS IN THE TERRITORIES

6 Best Sellers in Sheet Music
Reported by Leading Jobbers

	NEW YORK	CHICAGO	LOS ANGELES
SONG—No. 1	'Little Street Where Old Friends Meet'	'Little Street Where Old Friends Meet'	'Love in the Moonlight'
SONG—No. 2	'My Darling'	'My Darling'	'Moon Song'
SONG—No. 3	'Night and Day'	'Rockabye Moon'	'Play, Fiddle, Play'
SONG—No. 4	'Play, Fiddle, Play'	'Fit as a Fiddle'	'My Darling'
SONG—No. 5	'Willow Weep for Me'	'I'm Sure of Everything But You'	'Willow Weep for Me'
SONG—No. 6	'Rockabye Moon'	'Play, Fiddle, Play'	'Night and Day'

3 Leading Phonograph Companies Report 6 Best Sellers

Side responsible for the major sales only are reported.   Where it is impossible to determine the side responsible for the
sales, both sides are mentioned:

	NEW YORK	CHICAGO	LOS ANGELES
BRUNSWICK—No. 1	'Night and Day,' 'Did You Mean What You Said Last Night' (Eddie Duchin Orch.)	'Street of Dreams' (Guy Lombardo)	'Night and Day' (Eddie Duchin Orch.)
BRUNSWICK—No. 2	'Waltzing in a Dream,' 'Please' (Bing Crosby with Anson Week Orch.)	'Just an Echo' (Bing Crosby)	'Just a Little Home for the Old Folks' (Guy Lombardo)
BRUNSWICK—No. 3	'Street of Dreams,' 'I Called to Say Goodnight' (Guy Lombardo Orch.)	'Night and Day' (Eddie Duchin Orch.)	'Eadie Was a Lady' (Ethel Merman)
BRUNSWICK—No. 4	'Eadie Was a Lady' (Ethel Merman)	'Please' (Bing Crosby)	'Fit as a Fiddle' (Three Keys)
BRUNSWICK—No. 5	'Street of Dreams,' 'It's Within Your Power' (Bing Crosby)	'Till Tomorrow' (Eddie Duchin Orch.)	'Just an Echo in the Valley' (Bing Crosby)
BRUNSWICK—No. 6	'I Gotta Right to Sing the Blues,' 'That's What I Hate About Love' (Cab Calloway)	'It's Winter Again' (Hal Kemp Orch.)	'Harlem Holiday' (Cab Calloway)
COLUMBIA—No. 1	'Just an Echo in the Valley,' 'The Language of Love' (Rudy Vallee)	'Linger a Little Longer in the Twilight' (Rudy Vallee)	'Play, Fiddle, Play' (Ted Lewis Orch.)
COLUMBIA—No. 2	'Street of Dreams,' 'A White House of Our Own' (Ben Selvin Orch.)	'May I Have This Dance, Madame' (Enrique Madriguera Orch.)	'Here It Is Monday' (Rudy Vallee)
COLUMBIA—No. 3	'At the Baby Parade,' 'Waltzing in a Dream' (Enrique Madriguera Orch.)	'Hell's Bells' Art Kassel)	'Hell's Bells' Art Kassel)
COLUMBIA—No. 4	'Jazz Pie,' 'One Note Trumpet Player' (Joe Haymes Orch.)	'Street of Dreams' (Ben Selvin Orch.)	'What a Perfect Combination' (Eddie Cantor)
COLUMBIA—No. 5	'Look Who's Here,' 'California Here I Come' (Claude Hopkins Orch.)	'Baby Parade' (Enrique Madriguera)	'New Farewell Blues' (Ted Lewis Orch.)
COLUMBIA—No. 6	'May I Have This Waltz With You,' 'Sing, Brothers' (Enrique Madriquera)	'Just an Echo' (Rudy Vallee Orch.)	'You're Getting to Be a Habit With Me' (Ben Selvin Orch.)
VICTOR—No. 1	'Night and Day,' 'I've Got You on My Mind' (Leo Reisman Orch.)	'Night and Day' 'Leo Reisman Orch.)	'We've Got a Moon and Sixpence' (Ray Noble's London Mayfair Orch.)
VICTOR—No. 2	'The Girl in the Little Green Hat,' 'My Fraternity Pin' (George Olsen)	'Hobo, You Can't Ride on This Train' (Louis Armstrong Orch.)	'Night and Day' (Leo Reisman Orch.)
VICTOR—No. 3	'Willow Weep for Me,' 'At Last It's Come to This' (Paul Whiteman)	'Willow Weep for Me' (Paul Whiteman Orch.)	'Moon Song' (Jack Denny Orch.)
VICTOR—No. 4	'Along Came Love,' 'My Darling' (Don Bestor Orch.)	'Look Who's Here' (Ted Weems Orch.)	'With All My Love and Kisses' (Ray Noble's London Mayfair Orch.)
VICTOR—No. 5	'Eadie Was a Lady,' 'You're an Old Smoothy' (Paul Whiteman)	'Eadie Was a Lady' (Ramona and Whiteman Orch.)	'Underneath the Harlem Moon' (Joe Rines Orch.)
VICTOR—No. 6	'I've Told Every Little Star,' 'The Song	'You'll Wish You Were Never Born'	'Speak to Me of Love' (Don Bestor

I shall always be grateful to After You
because I had been engaged by Dwight Wiman for "Gay
Divorce." Our great hope was to persuade Fred
Astaire to play the lead. We were living
in Paris at the time and I asked Fred over to the house
to hear what I had written so far. Once I had
played After You, *he decided to do the show.*
> *Cole Porter*

AFTER YOU, WHO?

VERSE

Though with joy I should be reeling
That at last you came my way,
There's no further use concealing

That I'm feeling far from gay
For the rare allure about you
Makes me all the plainer see
How inane, how vain, how empty—life without you would be.

REFRAIN

After you, who
Could supply my sky of blue?
After you, who
Could I love?
After you, why
Should I take the time to try
For who else could qualify
After you, who?
Hold my hand and swear you'll never cease to care
For without you there what could I do?
I could search years but who else could change my tears
Into laughter after you?

To Cole + Linda — from — Fred 1933

I'VE GOT YOU ON MY MIND

VERSE

She: You can't be much surprised to hear
He: I think you're sweller than swell,
     But granting all your virtues, dear,
     You've certain failings as well.
She: You don't sing enough, you don't dance enough,
He: You don't drink the great wines of France enough!
She: You're not wild enough,
He: You're not gay enough,
She: You don't let me lead you astray enough.
He: You don't live enough, you don't dare enough,
     You don't give enough,
She: You don't care enough,
He: You don't make my sad life sunny enough.
She: Yet, sweetheart, funny enough.

REFRAIN

She: I've got you on my mind
     Although I'm disinclined,
     You're not so hot, you,
     But I've got you on my mind.
He: I'd thank the Gods above
     If I could only love
     Somebody not you
     But I've got you on my mind.
She: Let my poor upset leisure be
     Otherwise my pet treasure be
He: And arrange to let pleasure be
     A bit less refined.
Both: For, darling, not until
     I get that famous thrill
     Will I be resigned.
     I've got you on my mind.

HOW'S YOUR ROMANCE

VERSE

Tonetti: In Italia the signori are so very amatory,
         That their passion, apriori is, l'amor.
Girls: Is it always l'amor?
Tonetti: Si sempre l'amore.
         And from Napoli to Pisa, ev'ry man has
         On his knees a
         Little private Mona Lisa
         To adore
Girls: As he once said before,
       It's always a l'amore,
Tonetti: The result is when Italians meet a friend
           who's been away
         Instead of saying, "How's your health?"
         They say—

REFRAIN

How's your romance?
How is it going?
Waning or growing,
How's your romance?

Does she or not love you an awful lot?
Cold, tepid, warm, or hot,
How's your romance?
Do you from the moment you met her
Never, never, never, forget her?
Do you when she sends you a letter,
Begin to go into a dance,
Break me the news,
I'm with you win or lose,
So tell me how's and who's your romance?
Girls: Do you from the moment you met him
       Never, never, never forget him?
       Do you when he wants you to let him
       Begin to go into a dance.
All: Break me the news,
     I'm with you win or lose,
     So tell me how's and who's your romance?

Cole wrote *Thank You So Much,
Mrs. Lowsborough-Goodby* and
Miss Otis Regrets to amuse his friends.

THANK YOU SO MUCH, MRS. LOWSBOROUGH-GOODBY

VERSE

Mrs. Lowsborough-Goodby gives week-ends
And her week-ends are not a success,
But she asks you so often
You finally soften and end by answering "yes."
When I left, Mrs. Lowsborough-Goodby's
The letter I wrote was polite
But it would have been bliss
Had I dared write her this
The letter I wanted to write

REFRAIN

Thank you so much, Mrs. Lowsborough-Goodby,
    thank you so much.
Thank you so much for that infinite week-end with you.
Thank you a lot, Mrs. Lowsborough-Goodby,
    thank you a lot
And don't be surprised if you suddenly should be
    quietly shot
For the clinging perfume
And that damp little room
For those cocktails so hot
And the bath that was not
For those guests so amusing and mentally bracing
Who talked about racing and racing and racing
For the ptomaine I got from your famous tin salmon
For the fortune I lost when you taught me backgammon
For those mornings I spent with your dear but
    deaf mother
For those evenings I passed with that bounder,
    your brother
And for making me swear to myself there and then
Never to go for a week-end again,
Thank you so much, Mrs. Lowsborough-Goodby,
    thank you, thank you so much.

Claire Luce, Fred Astaire, and Erik Rhodes (Tonetti)

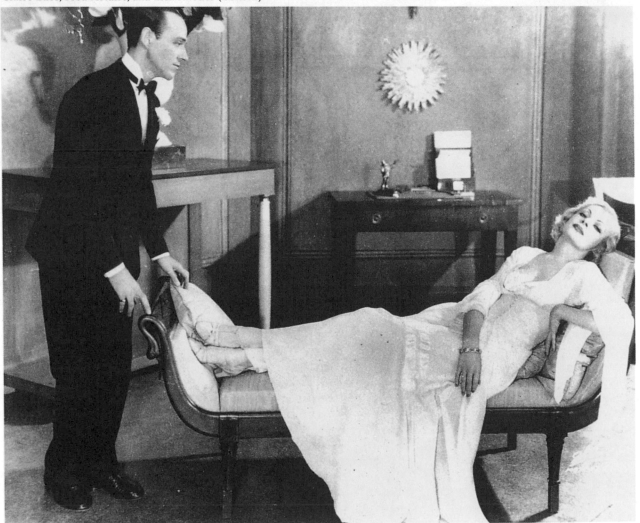

"In 'Gay Divorce' you will see Mr. Fred Astaire fluttering his winged dogs nimbly accompanied by Miss Claire Luce, whose elegant feet and legs are also, figuratively speaking, feathered. To gay or pensive music by Mr. Cole Porter they take several heavenly flights in the course of the play, swirling, swooping, and soaring as if their home was the air."
—Percy Hammond, New York *Herald Tribune*

From the chorus

MISS OTIS REGRETS

(Dedicated to Elsa)

Miss Otis regrets she's unable to lunch today,
Madam, Miss Otis regrets she's unable to lunch today.
She is sorry to be delayed,
But last evening down in lover's lane she strayed,
Madam, Miss Otis regrets she's unable to lunch today.

When she woke up and found
That her dream of love was gone,
Madam, she ran to the man
Who had led her so far astray,
And from under her velvet gown
She drew a gun and shot her lover down,
Madam, Miss Otis regrets she's unable to lunch today.

When the mob came and got her
And dragged her from the jail,
Madam, they strung her upon
The old willow across the way,
And the moment before she died
She lifted up her lovely head and cried
Madam, "Miss Otis regrets she's unable to lunch today."

Faltboating on the Rhine, 1934

```
15   Bier                        7.65
 1   Emmentaler 1 Butter         1.40
 3   Suppen                      1.20
 2   Mocca                       1.00
 2   Slibovitz                   -.80
13   St. 30 g Marken             3.90
20   Sport                       1.00
 1   Suppe                        30
 2   Kalbsgullasch m. Nudln      3.60
 2   Marken                       64
 3   Mocca                       1.50
 2   Slibovitz                   -.80
 2   Bier                       v1.10
Brode                           -.40
                              -----------
                               25.29
     10%    Service              2.50
                              -----------
                               27.79

Spielkarten                     6.50
Pfeifenstierer                   30
                              ---------
               S       34.59
```

Dinner Bill
18 VII 33.
melk

HUGO SCHÖFFER
HOTEL ZUM GOLDENEN OCHSEN
MELK a. d. DONAU

"Blossom Time." Cole and Michael Strange,
Danube trip, 1933. Born Blanche Oelrichs of Newport,
Michael Strange, poet and actress, was one
of the great figures of her day. She was married
first to Philadelphian Leonard Thomas; next to John
Barrymore, by whom she had a daughter, Diana;
and then to the distinguished lawyer, Harrison Tweed.

Gertrude Lawrence in "Nymph Errant"

NYMPH ERRANT (1933)

EXPERIMENT

VERSE

Before you leave these portals
To meet less fortunate mortals,
There is just one final message
I would give to you.

You all have learned reliance
On the sacred teachings of science,
So I hope, through life, you never will decline
In spite of Philistine
Defiance
To do what all good scientists do.

REFRAIN

Experiment.
Make it your motto day and night.
Experiment
And it will lead you to the light.
The apple on the top of the tree
Is never too high to achieve,
So take an example from Eve,
Experiment.

Be curious,
Though interfering friends may frown.
Get furious
At each attempt to hold you down.
If this advice you always employ
The future can offer you infinite joy
And merriment.
Experiment
And you'll see.

IT'S BAD FOR ME

VERSE

Your words go through and through me
And leave me totally dazed,
For they do such strange things to me
They nearly make me gloomy,
For you, dear, are so clever
So obviously "the top,"
I wish you'd go on forever,
I wish even more you'd stop.

REFRAIN

For it's bad for me, it's bad for me,
This knowledge that you're going mad for me,
I feel certain my friends would be glad for me,
Still it's bad for me.
It's so good for me, so new for me
To see someone in such a stew for me,
And when you say you'd do all you could for me
It's so good for me, it's bad for me.

I thought I'd been, till you met me,
Completely put on the shelf,
But since you started to pet me
I'm just crazy about myself.
Oh, it's sweet for me, it's swell for me
To know that you're going through hell for me,
Yet no matter however appealing
I still have a feeling
It's bad for me.

THE PHYSICIAN

VERSE

Once I loved such a shattering physician,
Quite the best looking doctor in the state.
He looked after my physical condition,
And his bed-side manner was great,
When I'd gaze up and see him there above me,

Looking less like a doctor than a Turk,
I was tempted to whisper, "Do you love me,
Or do you merely love your work?"

REFRAIN 1

He said my bronchial tubes were
        entrancing,
My epiglottis filled him with glee,
He simply loved my larynx
And went wild about my pharynx,
But he never said he loved me.
He said my epidermis was darling,
And found my blood as blue as could be,
He went through wild ecstatics,
When I showed him my lymphatics,
But he never said he loved me.
And though, no doubt,
It was not very smart of·me,
I kept on a-wracking my soul
To figure out
Why he loved ev'ry part of me,
And yet not me as a whole.
With my aesophagus he was ravished,
Enthusiastic to a degree,
He said 'twas just enormous,
My appendix vermiformis,
But he never said he loved me.

REFRAIN 2

He said my cerebellum was brilliant,
And my cerebrum far from N.G.
I know he thought a lot a'
My medulla oblongata,
But he never said he loved me.
He said my maxillaries were marvels,
And found my sternum stunning to see.
He did a double hurdle
When I shook my pelvic girdle,
But he never said he loved me.
He seemed amused
When he first made a test of me
To further his medical art,
Yet he refused
When he'd fix up the rest of me,
To cure that ache in my heart.
I know he thought my pancreas perfect,
And for my spleen was keen as could be,
He said of all his sweeties,
I'd the sweetest diabetes,
But he never said he loved me.

REFRAIN 3

He said my vertebrae were "sehr schöne,"
And called my coccyx "plus que gentil,"
He murmured "molto bella,"
When I sat on his patella,
But he never said he loved me.
He took a fleeting look at my thorax,
And started singing slightly off key,
He cried, "May Heaven strike us,"
When I played my umbilicus,
But he never said he loved me.
As it was dark,

I suggested we walk about
Before he returned to his post,
Once in the park,
I induced him to talk about
The thing I wanted the most.
He lingered on with me until morning,
Yet when I tried to pay him his fee,
He said, "Why, don't be funny,
It is I who owe you money,"
But he never said he loved me.

THE COCOTTE

VERSE

While the lucky ones sit together
With nothing to curse but weather,
Permit me to tell you of my sad fate.
For due to my great discretion
In practising my profession,
I suddenly wake up to find I date.
When ladies still had propriety,
Women like me were covered with glory,
But now, since these damned society
Women invaded my territory.

REFRAIN 1

A busted, disgusted cocotte am I,
Undesired on my tired little bottom, I,
While those fat femmes du monde
With the men whom once I owned
Splash around like hell-bound hippopotami.
Since only dames with their names on
        their cheques appeal
To modern men, instead of sex, I now
        have ex-appeal.
What will ma say to me
When she sees I've turned out to be
An annoyed, unemployed cocotte?

REFRAIN 2

A cheated, defeated cocotte am I,
On the page of this age, just a blot am I.
Since the girls known as chic
Have invented new technique,
I'm afraid, in my trade, not so hot am I.
As ladies smart make love's art
        so delectable,
The boys about won't take me out—
        I'm too respectable
And on my tombstone, I trust,
Will be written "Excuse the dust
Of a fast but out-classed cocotte."

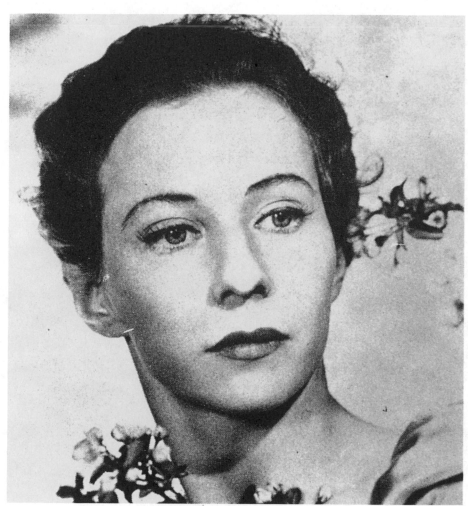

"Nymph Errant" was Agnes de Mille's first major choreographic assignment

NYMPH ERRANT

VERSE

Men,
I used to take you
So seriously.
Then,
I dreamed about you
Deliriously.
But now I've gone so far
I know how harmless you are;
So I'm off to follow the voice
That whispers mysteriously.

REFRAIN

Nymph errant, go wandering on,
You've lived and loved
Your illusions are gone;
Nymph errant, forget your blues,
You've all to gain,
And nothing to lose;
So, climb the hill

And cross the dale,
Like the pale moon above
And go sailing gaily on and on,
Forever on and on—
Laughing at love.

SI VOUS AIMEZ LES POITRINES

VERSE

Trav'llers I've seen
Say the prettiest poitrines
Are the ones you find in Poona.
Others are these
Say the buxom Balinese
Have the greatest goona-goona.
Spaniards maintain
That the kind you find in Spain
Are so fair that ev'ry man tumbles.
While not long ago
A boy in Eastbourne I know

Simply raves about those on the crumbles.
Ces belles poitrines sau-vage
May be very fair perchance
But why should one voy-age
When the best of them are made in France?

REFRAIN

Si vous aimez les poi-trines
Come to gay Paree.
Si leur beaute vous a-nime
Come and call on me.
I will show you how di-veene
Parisiennes poi-trines really are,
If you promise me, you naughty boy,
Not to go too far.
Si vous voulez d'la ten-dresse
Et d'la volupte,
Let me give you my ad-dresse
For a rainy day.
And when zat feeling comes a-stealing
You know what I mean?
Mais oui, monsieur,
Come and play wiz me in gay Paree,
Si vous aimez les poitrines.

Les Poitrines

"I shouldn't care for those nights in the air/ That the fair Mrs. Lindbergh goes through" was an early version. Cole's revision was necessitated by the kidnapping of the Lindbergh baby.

William Gaxton and Bettina Hall

ANYTHING GOES (1934)

I GET A KICK OUT OF YOU

VERSE

My story is much too sad to be told,
But practically ev'rything leaves me totally cold.
The only exception I know is the case
Where I'm out on a quiet spree
Fighting vainly the old ennui
And I suddenly turn and see your fabulous face.

REFRAIN

I get no kick from champagne.
Mere alcohol doesn't thrill me at all,
So tell me why should it be true
That I get a kick out of you.
Some get a kick from cocaine.
I'm sure that if I took even one sniff
That would bore me terrific'ly too
Yet I get a kick out of you.
I get a kick ev'ry time I see
You're standing there before me.
I get a kick though it's clear to me
You obviously don't adore me.
I get no kick in a plane.
Flying too high with some guy in the sky
Is my idea of nothing to do,
Yet I get a kick out of you.

ALL THROUGH THE NIGHT

VERSE

The day is my enemy,
The night my friend,
For I'm always so alone
Till the day draws to an end.
But when the sun goes down
And the moon comes through,
To the monotone of the evening's drone
I'm all alone with you.

REFRAIN

All through the night I delight in your love.
All through the night you're so close to me.
All through the night from a height far above,
You and your love bring me ecstasy.
When dawn comes to waken me,
You're never there at all.
I know you've forsaken me

William Gaxton, Ethel Merman, and Victor Moore

Ethel Merman and William Gaxton sing *You're the Top*

Till the shadows fall;
But then once again I can dream I've the right
To be close to you all through the night.

If I stopped to think twice
I know I'd hurry away,
But it all is so nice
So I'll only think once and stay.
All through the night I delight in your love.
All through the night, oh so close to me.
All through the night, under bright stars above
You and your love will bring ecstasy.
When dawn's overtaken us, we'll sadly say goodbye,
Till dreams re-awaken us and the moon is high.
And then, once again, will I know I was right
Staying close to you, all through the night.

KATE THE GREAT

Katherine of Russia, that potentate,
Knew that her job was to fascinate.
Some people called her a reprobate,
But still she's known as Kate the Great.
To sessions of Congress she wouldn't go;
Never heckled the crowd on the radio.
She never would mix in affairs of state,
But in affairs of the heart, how Kate was great.
As few
Lovely ladies today,
She knew where woman should stay.
She never laid a five year plan,
But was there ever such a girl at laying—a plan—
     for a man?
So drink
To that jovial jade
And think of the history she made.
Why she made the Congress,
She made the Premier,
She made the clergy,
And she made 'em cheer.
She made the butler,
She made the groom,
She made the maid who made the room.
She made the Army,
She made the Marines,
Made some of them princes,
And some of them queens.
And when she was still discontent,
Kate'd create a new regiment.
So beautiful ladies, before too late,
Follow the lead of this potentate,
Give up arranging affairs of state
And stay in the hay like Kate the Great
Hay-de-hay hay-de-hay hay-de-hay
Stay in the hay like Kate the Great.

YOU'RE THE TOP

VERSE 1

At words poetic, I'm so pathetic
That I always have found it best,
Instead of getting 'em off my chest,
To let 'em rest unexpressed.
I hate parading
My serenading
As I'll probably miss a bar,
But if this ditty
Is not so pretty,
At least it'll tell you
How great you are.

REFRAIN 1

You're the top!
You're the Colosseum.
You're the top!

You're the Louvre Museum.
You're a melody from a symphony by Strauss,
You're a Bendel bonnet,
A Shakespeare sonnet,
You're Mickey Mouse.
You're the Nile,
You're the Tow'r of Pisa,
You're the smile
On the Mona Lisa.
I'm a worthless check, a total wreck, a flop,
But if, Baby, I'm the bottom
You're the top!

VERSE 2

Your words poetic are not pathetic
On the other hand, boy, you shine
And I can feel after every line
A thrill divine
Down my spine.
Now gifted humans like Vincent Youmans
Might think that your song is bad,
But for a person who's just rehearsin'
Well I gotta say this my lad:

REFRAIN 2

You're the top!
You're Mahatma Gandhi.
You're the top!
You're Napoleon brandy.
You're the purple light of a summer night in Spain,
You're the National Gall'ry,
You're Garbo's sal'ry,
You're cellophane.
You're sublime,
You're a turkey dinner,
You're the time
Of the Derby winner.
I'm a toy balloon that is fated soon to pop,
But if, Baby, I'm the bottom
You're the top!

REFRAIN 3

You're the top!
You're a Ritz hot toddy.
You're the top!
You're a Brewster body.
You're the boats that glide on the sleepy Zuider Zee,
You're a Nathan panning,
You're Bishop Manning,
You're broccoli.
You're a prize,
You're a night at Coney,
You're the eyes
Of Irene Bordoni.
I'm a broken doll, a fol-de-rol, a blop,
But if, Baby, I'm the bottom
You're the top!

REFRAIN 4

You're the top!
You're an Arrow collar.
You're the top!
You're a Coolidge dollar.
You're the nimble tread of the feet of Fred Astaire,

You're an O'Neill drama,
You're Whistler's mama,
You're Camembert.
You're a rose,
You're Inferno's Dante,
You're the nose
On the great Durante.
I'm just in the way, as the French would say
"De trop,"
But if, Baby, I'm the bottom
You're the top.

REFRAIN 5

You're the top!
You're a Waldorf salad.
You're the top!
You're a Berlin ballad.
You're a baby grand of a lady and a gent,
You're an old Dutch master,
You're Mrs. Astor,
You're Pepsodent.
You're romance,
You're the steppes of Russia,
You're the pants on a Roxy usher.
I'm a lazy lout that's just about to stop,
But if, Baby, I'm the bottom
You're the top.

REFRAIN 6

You're the top!
You're a dance in Bali.
You're the top!
You're a hot tamale.
You're an angel, you, simply too, too, too diveen,
You're a Botticelli,
You're Keats,
You're Shelley,
You're Ovaltine.
You're a boon,
You're the dam at Boulder,
You're the moon over Mae West's shoulder.
I'm a nominee of the G. O. P.
or GOP,
But if, Baby, I'm the bottom,
You're the top.

REFRAIN 7

You're the top!
You're the Tower of Babel.
You're the top!
You're the Whitney Stable.
By the River Rhine,
You're a sturdy stein of beer,
You're a dress from Saks's,
You're next year's taxes,
You're stratosphere.
You're my thoist,
You're a Drumstick Lipstick,
You're da foist
In da Irish svipstick.
I'm a frightened frog
That can find no log
To hop,
But if, Baby, I'm the bottom
You're the top!

Billy Reardon, Jay O'Brien, Celia Von Rath, and Cole

Birthday Boy

Ethel Merman and ensemble in "*Blow, Gabriel, Blow*"

BLOW, GABRIEL, BLOW

VERSE

(Trumpet call)

      Reno: Do you hear that playin'?
    Chorus: Yes I hear that playin'.
      Reno: Do you know who's playin'?
    Chorus: No, who is that playin'?
Reno & Cho. Why it's Gabriel, Gabriel playin'
             Gabriel, Gabriel sayin',
      Reno: "Will you be ready to go when I blow my horn?"

REFRAIN

Reno: Oh, blow, Gabriel, blow,
     Go on and blow, Gabriel, blow!
     I've been a sinner, I've been a scamp,
     But now I'm willin' to trim my lamp,
     So blow, Gabriel, blow!
     I was low, Gabriel, low,
     Mighty low, Gabriel, low.
     But now since I have seen the light,
     I'm good by day and I'm good by night,
     So blow, Gabriel, blow.
     Once I was headed for hell,
     Yes once I was headed for hell;
     But when I got to Satan's door
     I heard you blowin' on your horn once more,
     So I said, "Satan, farewell!"
     And now I'm all ready to fly,
     Yes, to fly higher and higher!
     'Cause I've gone through brimstone and I've
          been through the fire,
     And I've purged my soul and my heart too,
     So climb up the mountain top and start to
     Blow, Gabriel, blow.
     Go on and blow, Gabriel, blow!
     I want to join your happy band
     And play all day in the Promised Land,
     So blow, Gabriel, blow!

ANYTHING GOES

VERSE

Times have changed
And we've often rewound the clock
Since the puritans got a shock
When they landed on Plymouth Rock,
If today
Any shock they should try to stem,
'Stead of landing on Plymouth Rock,
Plymouth Rock would land on them.

REFRAIN 1

In olden days, a glimpse of stocking
Was looked on as something shocking,
But now, God knows,
Anything goes.
Good authors too who once knew better words
Now only use four-letter words,
Writing prose,
Anything goes.
If driving fast cars you like,
If low bars you like,
If old hymns you like,
If bare limbs you like,
If Mae West you like,
Or me undressed you like,
Why, nobody will oppose.
When ev'ry night, the set that's smart is intruding
     in nudist parties in
Studios,
Anything goes.

REFRAIN 2

When missus Ned McLean (God bless her)
Can get Russian reds to "yes" her,
Then I suppose
Anything goes.
When Rockefeller still can hoard enough money
     to let Max Gordon
Produce his shows,
Anything goes.
The world has gone mad today
And good's bad today,
And black's white today,
And day's night today,
And that gent today,
You gave a cent, today
Once had several chateaux.
When folks who still can ride in jitneys
Find out Vanderbilts and Whitneys
Lack baby-clo'es,
Anything goes.

REFRAIN 3

If Sam Goldwyn can with great conviction
Instruct Anna Sten in diction,
Then Anna shows
Anything goes.
When you hear that Lady Mendl standing up
Now turns a handspring landing upon her toes,
Anything goes.
Just think of those shocks you've got
And those knocks you've got
And those blues you've got
From that news you've got
And those pains you've got
(If any brains you've got)
From those little radios.
So Missus R., with all her trimmins
Can broadcast a bed from Simmons
'Cause Franklin knows
Anything goes.

WORLD CRUISE

ON BOARD
CUNARD WHITE STAR
"FRANCONIA".

MISS LINDA'S YOUNG GENTLEMEN!.

An   Address
By

Mr. Moss Hart

An   Old   Alumnus

Made One The Occassion
Of
The Opening Of The 102nd. Term
Of
Miss Linda's School For Young Gentlemen.

My dear young friends. As I gaze at the array of happy and expectant
young faces before me this evening, my mind goes back to just such an
evening as this many, many, years ago. Then, as now the odour of the
jasmine wafted gently in thru the open windows, then as now the bright
and shining faces were turned toward the platform, and then as now Miss
Linda sat in her large gilt chair, smiling and radiant. That was a
great many years ago, dear children,.....more years perhaps than Miss
Linda and myself would like to admit. It was, in fact, the evening of
the beginning of my first term at Miss Linda's school, and my young
heart beat, mayhap as all of yours do now, just a little faster. For I
was brought up on Miss Linda. Far, far, back -- ever since I can remember, I recall my old nurse or my dear Mother saying: "Now if
you don't stop that immediately, Miss Linda'll come and get you!" And
it was enough. All through my young childhood the mere mention of Miss
Linda's name was enough to freeze my blood. -- enough to make me behave, so it was small wonder than that when I was finally packed up and
sent here in my tenth year I was so filled with horror that if the
devil himself had appeared and said: "I am Miss Linda" I would not have
been surprized. And I am sure, dear children, that is how many of
you feel to-night. Imagine my astonishment, then, when a smiling old
lady slid out onto the platform, (yes, Miss Linda used to slide in
those dear old days) and shouted: "Has anybody here seen Kelly -- Kelly
with the green neck-tie!" Well, you could have knocked us all
over with a Huntley & Palmer Biscuit. But that was only the beginning!

Linda and travel writer William Powell, Sturge, Monty, Cole, and Moss Hart as the *Franconia* passes through the Panama Canal

*I dined twice with the Porters during
my ten-day stay in Paris and fell in love, as everyone
did, with Linda Porter. To fall in love with Linda
Porter was as much a part of a young
man's first trip to Paris as eating snails at Fouquet's or
climbing the Eiffel Tower. They were a wonderful
pair, the Cole Porters. They were rich,
they were gifted, and they moved about with infinite
ease and lightheartedness in two worlds—the
worlds of fashion and glitter and the
pantaloon world of the theater. Their house in Paris was
exquisite, one of the most beautiful houses I have
ever seen, and Linda Porter, a legendary
beauty herself, lent something of her own radiance and
splendor to their life together so that everything
and everyone in their house seemed to
shine and sparkle with a little of her own special grace.
She was a woman of immense delicacy, with an
enchanting turn of mind, as easily beguiled
by a chorus girl as by a duchess and equally at home
with both. Together, the Porters bloomed in a
scintillating world that seemed uncom-
monly festive, and I thought to myself on my last
evening with them, What fun it would be to do
a musical with Cole Porter. . . . Less than
two years later, that is exactly what happened. We did
do a musical together. Moreover, we sailed around
the world to write that musical, and I
learned to my chagrin that the jaunty and debonair
world of Cole Porter disappeared completely when
he was at work, and that Linda Porter,
who accompanied us, was as stern and jealous a
guardian of that work as Cole Porter himself.*

Moss Hart in The Cole Porter Song Book
Simon and Schuster, New York, 1959

Moss on deck

Bill Powell, Monty, Cole, Linda, and Sturge at
Volcano House, Hilo, Hawaii

Monty, Sturge, and Cole at Kalabahai, March 15, 1935

Monty, Tudor House, Mombasa, April, 1935

The *Franconia* at anchor near the village of
Kalabahai, in the island of Alor (Sunda Islands) on the
"Sea of Flowers," March, 1935. Cole wrote *Begin the
Beguine* sailing from Kalabahai to the Fiji Islands.

Clifford Sabrey, Sturge, Monty, and Cole,
New Zealand, February, 1935

With Papuan chieftain, New Guinea, March, 1935

Garden Party given by Robert Buell, U.S. Consul in
Ceylon, for Cole Porter and Moss Hart, 1935. Standing: Robert
Buell, Mrs. John Ott of Chicago, Vice Consul George W.

Renchard, Linda, Monty, Mrs. George Carter
of Honolulu, and Sturge. Seated: Moss, Cole,
John N. Ott, and Bill Powell

The lights of Rio. "At night, when the sun goes down . . . when the sky pales and the pale light fades, and the thick-clustering tropical stars come out, and are met below by the semi-circle of warm yellow sparks . . . you will find yourself holding on to the picture almost fiercely with your eyes, for fear that they shall ever lose it."—*Franconia Cruise Book*

Bad news in Singapore, March, 1935

Durban, April, 1935

Good news in Madagascar, April, 1935

JUBILEE (1935)

I suddenly recalled the time I had first heard it sung by Cole Porter himself, sitting at the upright piano in his cabin as the boat sailed toward the Fiji Islands.

Moss Hart

BEGIN THE BEGUINE

When they begin the beguine
It brings back the sound of music so tender,
It brings back a night of tropical splendor,
It brings back a memory ever green.
I'm with you once more under the stars
And down by the shore an orchestra's playing,
And even the palms seem to be swaying
When they begin the beguine.
To live it again is past all endeavor
Except when that tune clutches my heart.
And there we are, swearing to love forever,
And promising never,
Never to part.
What moments divine, what rapture serene,
Till clouds came along to disperse the joys we
        had tasted,
And now when I hear people curse the chance that
        was wasted,
I know but too well what they mean;
So don't let them begin the beguine!
Let the love that was once a fire remain an ember.
Let it sleep like the dead desire I only remember
When they begin the beguine.
Oh yes, let them begin the beguine, make them play
Till the stars that were there before return above you,
Till you whisper to me once more "darling, I love you!"
And we suddenly know, what heaven we're in,
When they begin the beguine.

A PICTURE OF ME WITHOUT YOU

VERSE

From being merely
A necessary luxury
And someone sympathetic to have about,
Why, now you're nearly
A luxurious necessity
I couldn't imagine ever living without,
I suppose I could somehow struggle through,
But I'd hate to picture myself without you.

REFRAIN 1

Picture Henry Ford without a car,
Picture heaven's firmament without a star,
Picture Fritzy Kreisler without a fiddle,
Picture poor Philadelphia without a Biddle,
Picture Central Park without a sailor,
Picture Mister Lord minus Mister Taylor,
Mix 'em all together, and what have you got?
Just a picture of me without you.

REFRAIN 2

Picture H. G. Wells without a brain,
Picture Av'rill Harriman without a train,
Picture Tintern Abbey without a cloister
Picture Billy the Oysterman without an oyster,
Picture good cigars without Havana,
Picture Huey Long less Louisiana,
Mix 'em all together, and what have you got?
Just a picture of me without you.

REFRAIN 3

Picture Ogden Nash without a rhyme,
Picture Mr. Bulova without the time,
Picture Staten Island without a ferry,
Picture little George Washington without a cherry,
Picture Brother Cain without his Abel,
Picture Clifton Webb minus Mother Mabel,
Mix them all together and what have you got?
Just a picture of me without you.

REFRAIN 4

Picture Paul Revere without a horse,
Picture love in Hollywood without divorce,
Picture Barbara Hutton without a nickel,
Picture poor Mister Heinz, my dear, without a pickle,
Picture City Hall without boondogglin',
Picture Sunday tea minus Father Coughlin,
Mix 'em all together and what have you got?
Just a picture of me without you.

REFRAIN 5

Picture Lilly Pons without a throat,
Picture Harold Vanderbilt without a boat,
Picture Billy Sunday without a sinner,
Picture dear Missus Corrigan without a dinner,
Picture Hamlet's ghost without a darkness,
Picture Mother Yale minus Father Harkness,
Mix 'em all together and what have you got?
Just a picture of me without you!

June Knight and Charles Walters dance the beguine

WHY SHOULDN'T I?

VERSE

All my life I've been so secluded
Love has eluded me,
But from knowing second-hand what I do of it,
I feel certain I could stand a closer view of it.
Till today I studied love discreetly,
But now that I'm completely free,
I must find some kind persona grata
To give me data personally.

REFRAIN

Why shouldn't I
Take a chance when romance passes by?
Why shouldn't I know of love?
Why wait around
When each age has a sage who has found
That upon this earth
Love is all that is really worth
Thinking of.
It must be fun, lots of fun
To be sure when day is done
That the hour is coming when
You'll be kissed and then you'll be kissed again,
Each debutante says it's good,
And ev'ry star out in far Hollywood
Seems to give it a try—
So why shouldn't I?

June Knight sings *Begin the Beguine*

Charles Walters, June Knight, Mark Plant,
May Boley, Derek Williams, Margaret Adams, Melville
Cooper, and Mary Boland

"Why, Henry! They're playing your favorite song!
Me and Marie! Came out the year we were married. They
must be reviving it for the Jubilee! You used to
drive me crazy with it."—Mary Boland and Melville Cooper

Finale: "Jubilee"

ME AND MARIE

VERSE

On Saturday night when my work is through,
I always call for Marie.
Then we hop on a bicycle built for two
And go scorching down to the sea.
After one or two whirls to the German Band
We go strolling under the moon
Till we find a good spot on the silv'ry sand
Then, gee whiz, how we spoon.

REFRAIN

You ought to see little me and Marie
By the old sea-side.
By the ocean we set
And we pet and we pet
Till we get swept out by the tide.
You may have been to Paris
And had both of your eyes opened wide,
But you ought to see
Me and Marie
By the old sea-side.
If you want to see a thing of beauty
You should see me spoonin' with my little cutie
By the old sea-side.
For when once we get the proper settin'
We begin a-pettin' and go on a-pettin'
Till we end by gettin' such an awful wettin'
From the tide.
First we talk about that and this a bit
Then we walk about
And hug and kiss a bit
Till we finally
Find a spot where we
Can hide,
Then until the crowin' of the chickens
Me and my Marie proceed to raise the dickens
By the old sea-side.

★★★★★★★★★★

The weekend before rehearsals were
scheduled to begin, I accompanied him to Leonard
Hanna's farm in Ohio for a last respite before
the frenzy that lay just ahead. On
Saturday afternoon as we walked through the quiet
September countryside, inevitably discussing
the only topic that held any interest for
either of us, I brought out into the open a nagging
thought I had long held—that the score still
lacked a major song in the second act.
He was surprised, but quickly agreed with me. There-
after silence fell and the withdrawal began. I
might just as well have been strolling
through the woods by myself. Early on, I might have
mistaken this for annoyance, but I knew by now
that he was already at work. Mentally I
made a note that, with luck, we might have the song for
the third week of rehearsal. It is unwise to count
on predictability in people, more particularly

*in anyone as unpredictable as Cole Porter. The next
morning he called me into the living room and
closed the doors. He placed a scribbled
sheet of paper on the music rack of the piano and then
played and sang the verse and chorus of* Just One
of Those Things. *No word of either verse
or chorus was ever altered. It has been played and sung
through the years exactly as I heard it on
that Sunday morning in Ohio, a song written overnight.*
　　　　Moss Hart *in* The Cole Porter Song Book

JUST ONE OF
THOSE THINGS

VERSE

As Dorothy Parker once said to her boyfriend,
"Fare Thee Well,"
As Columbus announced when he knew he was bounced,
"It was swell, Isabelle, swell,"
As Abelard said to Héloise,
"Don't forget to drop a line to me, please,"
As Juliet cried in her Romeo's ear,
"Romeo, why not face the fact, my dear?"

REFRAIN

It was just one of those things,
Just one of those crazy flings,
One of those bells that now and then rings,
Just one of those things.
It was just one of those nights,
Just one of those fabulous flights,
A trip to the moon on gossamer wings,
Just one of those things.
If we'd thought a bit
Of the end of it,
When we started painting the town,
We'd have been aware
That our love affair
Was too hot not to cool down.
So goodbye, dear, and amen.
Here's hoping we meet now and then,
It was great fun,
But it was just one of those things.

BORN TO
DANCE
(1936)

In late 1935, after a vacation in Bermuda,
the Porters rented the Richard Barthelmess house in
Hollywood while Cole waited for his first
assignment from MGM. Linda disliked
the film colony but Cole, in the words of columnist
Dorothy Kilgallen, "went Hollywood quickly
and completely." "I like it here," he told
her. "It's like living on the moon, isn't it? When I first
came here they told me 'You'll be so bored you'll

die; nobody talks about anything but
pictures.' After I was here a week, I discovered I didn't
want to talk about anything else myself."

During the first half of 1936 Cole kept
a diary that records in detail the planning of the film
"Born To Dance." One of the first songs he finished
was *Good-bye, Little Dream, Good-bye.*

*Thursday, March 12, 1936: Conference in
the office of Sam Katz. Present: Sam Katz, Jack
McGowan, Sid Silvers, Jack Cummings. I
played them all the numbers which I had
finished, including a new one that I wrote last night for
Frances Langford. It's called,* Good-bye, Little
Dream, Good-bye. *This number seemed to
have much greater success than I could have ever
expected. They sang it over and over again,
and at the finish Sam Katz said to me,
"You know, Cole, that song is beautiful, it's—why, it's
Jewish."*

Friday, March 13, 1936: As the result of
Good-bye, Little Dream, Good-bye, *Major Zanft asked
me to come to see him at his office. He told me
that people in the Katz unit had dined last
night with the powers at Paramount and they raved so
over this new song that Paramount had asked him
to offer me $50,000 for two months'
work on the next Crosby picture. . . .
　　Arthur Lyons called me up to tell me
about the excitement* Good-bye, Little Dream, Good-bye
*had caused on the MGM lot, and added that the
Katz outfit had hinted to him that they
would like to have me back next year for the same
length of time, but for $100,000 instead of the
paltry $75,000 that I am struggling along with now.*

Hollywood, 1936

GOOD-BYE, LITTLE DREAM, GOOD-BYE

VERSE

I first knew Love's delight,
When presto out of the blue,
A dream appeared one night
And whispered, "How do you do?"
I knew I was tempting fate,
But I took it straight to my heart,
My fears were right, and now we must part.

REFRAIN

Good-bye, little dream, good-bye,
You made my romance sublime, now it's time to fly,
For the stars have fled from the heavens,
    the moon's deserted the hill,
And the sultry breeze that sang in the trees,
    is suddenly strangely still.
It's done, little dream, it's done,
So bid me a fond farewell, we both had our fun.
Was it Romeo or Juliet, who said when about to die,
"Love is not all peaches and cream,"
Little Dream, good-bye.

Good-bye, Little Dream, Good-bye was
dropped from the film. Cole had confidence in the song
and resurrected it for Ethel Merman in "Red,
Hot and Blue!" but it was eventually dropped from
the show. Yvonne Printemps sang it in a London play,
"O Mistress Mine," and recorded it. The
recording is a collector's item.

By the end of May the score was finished. One
task remained.

★★★★★★★★★★

*Tuesday, June 2nd, 1936: Sam Katz
telephoned and said "Cole, will you do me a favor?",
and I said "Probably, what is it?", and he said
"Will you come out and play and sing your
score to Louis B. Mayer and Thalberg tomorrow
afternoon?" I said "Why?" and he answered
"Well, Cole, my boy, after all, they are
slightly interested." So I agreed to do it—however,
with dread.*

*Wednesday, June 3, 1936: After a stiff
whisky and soda, and my arms full of books which Miss
Moore had prepared, containing the lyrics in the
order in which they come in the picture,
I left for the studio. A few minutes later I was in Louis
B. Mayer's office. He was there, also Sam Katz,
Jack Cummings, Roger Edens, Sid Silvers,
Mrs. Koverman (L. B.'s secretary and an angel),
Eleanor Powell and Virginia Bruce. Suddenly the
door opened and in crept Thalberg,
looking more dead than alive, and obviously angry at
being disturbed to hear this score. I passed out
the lyric books and began. By the time
Rolling Home was over, I realized that the atmosphere
was friendly. When I finished Hey, Babe, Hey,*

*there was wild applause and L. B. began
jumping around the room, whispering to people. I
attacked Entrance of Lucy James next, and it
was during this that Thalberg suddenly
became a different person and began smiling. Then the
door opened and in walked Eddie Mannix
(General Manager of MGM), and L. B.
said "Cole, you've got to repeat Hey, Babe, Hey for
Eddie," which I did, and they all sang it. From
then on it was clear sailing and the moment
I finished the Finale, Thalberg leaped out of his seat,
rushed over to me, grabbed my hand and said
"I want to congratulate you for a magnificent
job, I think it's one of the finest scores I have ever
heard." He was followed by L. B., who came up
and put his arms around me and said
"Cole, how about coming into the next room and signing
your contract for next year," to which I replied,
"No, L. B., I don't understand money matters."
Then Mrs. Koverman said "Gentlemen, I think this is
worth a celebration, what do you all want to drink?"
So we ordered big whiskies and sodas,
and everybody stood around the piano and sang the
entire score over again. It was completely jubilant.
Then L. B. addressed the house and said
"Now, Sam, this material is so fine that I don't want you
to take any chances with it. I want every lyric
heard, and in order to assure that, I want
you to make 'rushes' of these numbers and then show
them in theatres as shorts to find out whether
audiences can understand every word.
And, another thing, this Finale is so brilliant, that I want
you to go to town and spend $250,000 on that
Number alone." When everybody had
hugged and kissed everybody else, I went over to Sam
Katz's office with Jack Cummings, to see the model
for the Lonely Hearts Club and the drawings
for the Finale. The model for the Lonely
Hearts Club was so beautiful that I wanted to join the
club at once. As for the Finale, it's staggering.
While this was going on, more whiskies
and sodas were brought in for everybody and I motored
home, exhausted and just a little bit tight.
On arriving home I found that the
minute I left L. B.'s office, he telephoned to Arthur
Lyons to come to the studio tomorrow and
arrange my contract for next year.*

★★★★★★★★★★

Easy to Love was written for William
Gaxton in "Anything Goes." Gaxton was uncomfortable
with the wide vocal range of the number and it
was dropped in favor of *All Through the Night.*

*Tuesday, April 14, 1936: Conference in
the office of Mr. Sam Katz. Present: Sam Katz, Max
Gordon, Jack McGowan, Sid Silvers, Jack
Cummings and Seymour Felix (dance director).
I played them a song which I had resurrected and
rewritten last night, called Easy to Love. The
response was instantaneous. They all*

grabbed the lyric and began singing it, and even called in the stenographers to hear it, their enthusiasm was so great. When this singing was finally over, Seymour Felix got on his knees in front of Sam Katz and said, "Oh, please Mr. Katz, let me stage that song when the picture is shot."

So left the office again very happy.

Friday, April 24, 1936: Conference in the office of Sam Katz. Present: Sam Katz, Sid Silvers, Jack McGowan and Jack Cummings.

I took in the verse to Easy to Love *and they seemed to feel that it would fit perfectly.*

Then the discussion began as to who would play the lead . . . After I returned home, I began thinking about James Stewart as a possibility for the male lead. I talked to Sam Katz about this on the telephone and he thought the idea was most interesting, if Stewart could sing. The next day Stewart came over to the house and I heard him sing. He sings far from well, although he has nice notes in his voice, but he could play the part perfectly.

EASY TO LOVE

VERSE

I know too well that I'm
Just wasting precious time
In thinking such a thing could be
That you could ever care for me.
I'm sure you hate to hear
That I adore you, dear,
But grant me, just the same,
I'm not entirely to blame, For

REFRAIN 1

You'd be so easy to love,
So easy to idolize, all others above,
    [or: To take on a honeymoon, all others above]
So sweet to waken with,
    [or: So sweet to watch the day awaken with]
So nice to sit down to eggs and bacon with,
We'd be so grand at the game,
So carefree together, that it does seem a shame
That you can't see
Your future with me,
'Cause you'd be, oh, so easy to love.

REFRAIN 2

You'd be so easy to love,
So easy to idolize, all others above,
So worth the yearning for,
So swell to keep any home fire burning for.
Oh, how we'd bloom, how we'd thrive
In a cottage for two, or even three, four, or five,
So try to see
Your future with me,
'Cause they'd be, oh, so easy to love.

REFRAIN 3

You'd be so easy to love,
So easy to worship as an angel above,
Just made to pray before,
Just right to stay home and walk the baby for,
I know I once left you cold,
But call me your "lamb" and take me back to the fold.
If you'll agree,
Why, I guarantee
That I'll be, oh, so easy to love.

I'VE GOT YOU UNDER MY SKIN

REFRAIN

I've got you under my skin,
I've got you deep in the heart of me,
So deep in my heart, you're really a part of me,
I've got you under my skin.

I tried so not to give in,
I said to myself "This affair never will go so well."
But why should I try to resist when, darling,
    I know so well
I've got you under my skin.

I'd sacrifice anything, come what might,
For the sake of having you near,
In spite of a warning voice that comes in the night,
And repeats and repeats in my ear
"Don't you know, little fool, you never can win,
"Use your mentality,
"Wake up to reality."
But each time I do, just the thought of you
    makes me stop, before I begin,
'Cause I've got you under my skin.

At a recording session

Ethel Merman and Jimmy Durante demanded equal billing. The flier demonstrates Cole's ingenious solution to the problem. The names changed position every two weeks to assure absolute fairness.

RED, HOT AND BLUE (1936)

Cole's gift to Linda for the opening of "Red, Hot and Blue": "Square platinum case. Lid paved with diamond sunburst set with numerous round and baguette diamonds on a divided field of faceted rubies and faceted sapphires and small diamond star motifs. End panels and bottom of case inlaid with gold stars. Bottom of case centering gold sunburst motif with crescent. From Verdura." (From description in Parke-Bernet Catalogue for Public Auction of Cigarette Cases, May 17, 1967)

There are two accounts by Cole of the genesis of *It's De-lovely*:

I took a world tour a couple of years ago, and I was in Java with Monty Woolley and Moss Hart. We'd just been served that famous eastern fruit—the mongosteen—and were all enjoying it mightily ... Moss Hart said, "It's delightful!" I chimed in with "It's delicious." And Monty Woolley said, "It's de-lovely!" and there's the title of the song.

★★★★★★★★★★

In 1935 when my wife and I and Monty Woolley were approaching the harbor of Rio de Janeiro by boat, it was dawn. My wife and I had risen especially for the event, but Mr. Woolley had stayed up all night to see it and during the night had enjoyed a few whiskys and soda.

As we stood on the bow of the boat my exclamation was "It's delightful!" My wife followed with "It's delicious!" And Monty, in his happy state, cried, "It's dee-lovely!" This last exclamation gave me the title for the song.

IT'S DE-LOVELY

VERSE 1

He: I feel a sudden urge to sing
The kind of ditty that invokes the spring,
So control your desire to curse
While I crucify the verse.

She: This verse you've started seems to me
The Tin-Pantithesis of melody,
So spare me, please, the pain,
Just skip the damn thing and sing the refrain.

He: Mi, mi, mi, mi,
Re, re, re, re,
Do, sol, mi, do, la, si,

She: Take it away.

REFRAIN 1

The night is young, the skies are clear,
So if you want to go walking, dear,
It's delightful, it's delicious, it's de-lovely.
I understand the reason why
You're sentimental, 'cause so am I,
It's delightful, it's delicious, it's de-lovely.
You can tell at a glance
What a swell night this is for romance,
You can hear dear Mother Nature murmuring low
"Let yourself go."
So please be sweet, my chickadee,
And when I kiss you, just say to me,
"It's delightful, it's delicious,
"It's delectable, it's delirious,
"It's dilemma, it's delimit, it's deluxe,
    it's de-lovely."

VERSE 2

She: Oh, charming sir, the way you sing
Would break the heart of Missus Crosby's Bing,
For the tone of your tra la la
Has that certain je ne sais quoi.

He: Oh, thank thee kindly, winsome wench,
But 'stead of falling into Berlitz French
Just warble to me, please,
This beautiful strain in plain Brooklynese.

She: Mi, mi, mi, mi,
Re, re, re, re,
Do, sol, mi, do, la, si

He: Take it away.

REFRAIN 2

Time marches on and soon it's plain
You've won my heart and I've lost my brain,
It's delightful, it's delicious, it's de-lovely.
Life seems so sweet that we decide
It's in the bag to get unified,
It's delightful, it's delicious, it's de-lovely.
See the crowd in that church,
See the proud parson plopped on his perch,
Get the sweet beat of that organ, sealing
    our doom,

"Here goes the groom, boom!"
How they cheer and how they smile
As we go galloping down that aisle.
"It's divine, dear, it's diveen, dear,
"It's de-wunderbar, it's de victory,
"It's de vallop, it's de vinner, it's de voiks,
    it's de-lovely."

REFRAIN 3

The knot is tied and so we take
A few hours off to eat wedding cake,
It's delightful, it's delicious, it's de-lovely.
It feels so fine to be a bride,
And how's the groom? Why, he's slightly fried,
It's delightful, it's delicious, it's de-lovely.
To the pop of champagne,
Off we hop in our plush little plane
Till a bright light through the darkness
    cozily calls
"Niag'ra Falls."
All's well, my love, our day's complete,
And what a beautiful bridal suite,
"It's de-reamy, it's de-rowsy,
"It's de-reverie, it's de-rhapsody,
"It's de-regal, it's de-royal, it's de-Ritz,
    it's de-lovely."

REFRAIN 4

We settle down as man and wife
To solve the riddle called "married life,"
It's delightful, it's delicious, it's de-lovely.
We're on the crest, we have no cares,
We're just a couple of honey bears,
It's delightful, it's delicious, it's de-lovely.
All's as right as can be
Till, one night, at my window I see
An absurd bird with a bundle hung on his nose—
"Get baby clo'es."
Those eyes of yours are filled with joy
When Nurse appears and cries, "It's a boy,"
"He's appalling, he's appealing,
"He's a polywog, he's a paragon,
"He's a Pop-eye, he's a panic, he's a pip,
    he's de-lovely."

REFRAIN 5

Our boy grows up, he's six feet, three,
He's so good looking, he looks like me,
It's delightful, it's delicious, it's de-lovely.
He's such a hit, this son of ours,
That all the dowagers send him flowers,
It's delightful, it's delicious, it's de-lovely.
So sublime is his press
That in time, L. B. Mayer, no less,
Makes a night flight to New York and tells him he should
Go Hollywood.
Good God!, today, he gets such pay
That Elaine Barrie's his fiancé,
"It's delightful, it's delicious,
"It's delectable, it's delirious,
"It's dilemma, it's delimit, it's deluxe, it's de-lovely."

Members of the cast including Vivian Vance,
Jimmy Durante, Ethel Merman, Bob Hope, and Grace Hartman

OURS

VERSE

He: The high gods above
     Look down and laugh at our love,
     And say to themselves "How tawdry it's grown."
     They've seen our cars
     In front of so many bars,
     When we should be under the stars,
     Together, but alone.
     Ours is the chance to make romance our own.

REFRAIN 1

He: Ours, the white Riviera under the moon,
     Ours, a gondola gliding on a lagoon,
     Ours, a temple serene by the green Arabian Sea,
     Or, maybe you'd rather be going ga-ga in gay Paree,
     Ours, the silent Sierras greeting the dawn,
     Or a sun-spotted Devonshire lawn dotted with flowers.
     Mine, the inclination,
     Yours, the inspiration,
     Why don't we take a vacation
     And make it all ours.

PATTER

She: Don't say "Venice" to me,
     Or suggest that old Riviera,
     Those faded hot spots fill me with gloom, somehow,
     As for a Hindu temple, my pet,

I wouldn't enter one on a bet.
Why I'd be afraid of being chased by a sacred cow.
Don't expect me to dream
Of the silent Sierras, dear,
Or to love that fattening cream
That they give you in Devonshire,
Don't mention the wilds of Paris,
Or, as you call it "gay Paree,"
I may not be right,
But New York is quite
Wild enough for me.

REFRAIN 2

She: Ours, the glitter of Broadway, Saturday night,
Ours, a box at the Garden, watching a fight,
Ours, the mad brouhaha of the Plaza's Persian Room,
Or, if this fills you with gloom,
We can go and admire Grant's tomb.
Ours, a home on the river facing the East,
Or on one of Park Avenue's least frightening tow'rs.
All the chat you're chattin'
Sounds to me like Latin,
Why don't we stay in Manhattan
And play it's all ours.

★★★★★★★★★★★

*Just last week while the new show
was playing in Boston, we all decided another song
should be added. It had to be done in a hurry,
of course, but I didn't have any difficulty,
as I knew the situation in the show perfectly. I got my
song in mind Tuesday, worked on it that night
and Wednesday, and it was in the show,
orchestrated, and sung by Ethel Merman on Thursday
night (October 15, 1936).*

Cole Porter, October 24, 1936

DOWN IN THE DEPTHS

VERSE

Manhattan—I'm up a tree,
The one I've most adored
Is bored
With me.
Manhattan, I'm awf'lly nice,
Nice people dine with me,
And even twice.
Yet the only one in the world I'm mad about
Talks of somebody else
And walks out.

REFRAIN

With a million neon rainbows burning below me
And a million blazing taxis raising a roar
Here I sit, above the town
In my pet pailletted gown.
      [or:
         Here I sit while deep despair
         Haunts my castle in the air.]
Down in the depths on the ninetieth floor,
While the crowds at El Morocco punish the parquet
And at Twenty-One, the couples clamor for more,

      [or:
         While the rounders at Leon and Eddie's
            "roll down the mountain"
         And the mobs that storm the Stork Club
            clutter the door]
      [or:
         While the crowds in all the night clubs
            punish the parquet
         And the bars are packed with couples
            calling for more]
I'm deserted and depressed
In my regal eagle nest
Down in the depths on the ninetieth floor.
When the only one you wanted wants another
What's the use of swank and cash in the bank galore?
Why, even the janitor's wife
Has a perfectly good love life
      [or:
         Why even the janitor's wife
         Has some sentiment in her life]
And here am I
Facing tomorrow
Alone with my sorrow
Down in the depths on the ninetieth floor.

RIDIN' HIGH

VERSE

Love had socked me
Simply knocked me
For a loop.
Luck had dished me
Till you fished me
From the soup.
Now, together,
We can weather
Anything.
So please don't sputter
If I should mutter:

REFRAIN

Life's great, life's grand,
Future all planned,
No more clouds in the sky,
How'm I ridin'? I'm ridin' high.

Some one I love,
Mad for my love,
So long, Jonah, goodbye,
How'm I ridin'? I'm ridin' high.

Floating on a starlit ceiling,
Doting on the cards I'm dealing,
Gloating, because I'm feeling
So hap-hap-happy,
I'm slap-happy.

So ring bells, sing songs,
Blow horns, beat gongs,
Our love never will die,
How'm I ridin'? I'm ridin' high.

PATTER

What do I care
If Missus Harrison Williams is the best
  dressed woman in town?
What do I care
If Countess Barbara Hutton has a
  Rolls-Royce built for each gown?
Why should I have the vapors
When I read in the papers
That Missus Simpson dined behind
  the throne?
I've got a cute king of my own.
What do I care
If Katie Hepburn is famous for the world's
  most beautiful nose,
Or, if I, for my sins
Don't possess underpins

Like the pegs "Legs" Dietrich shows?
I'm feeling swell,
In fact so well
It's time some noise began,
For although I'm not
A big shot,
Still, I've got my man.

SECOND PATTER

What do I care
If Missus Dorothy Parker has the country's
  wittiest brain?
What do I care
If little Eleanor Jarrett only swims in
  vintage champagne?
Why should I be a-flutter

When Republicans mutter
That Missus R gets pay to write her day,
If I could write my nights, hey, hey!
What do I care
If fair Tallulah possesses tons and tons of
  jewels from gents?
Or, if some one observes
That I haven't the curves
That Simone Simon presents?
I'm doin' fine,
My life's divine,
I'm living in the sun
'Cause I've a big date
With my fate,
So I rate
A-1.

NOTES ON THE MORNING AFTER AN OPENING NIGHT

By COLE PORTER

AM I made wrong? While Russel Crouse was pacing back and forth in the lounge of the Alvin Theatre during the opening performance of "Red, Hot and Blue!" giving a perfect take-off on all of the ten million ghosts, and Howard Lindsay was somewhere on his New Jersey estate getting quarter-hourly reports from his wife, I was in as good a seat as the management would give me, and, flanked by Mary Pickford and Merle Oberon, was having a swell time watching the actors. Russel claims this is being as indecent as the bridegroom who has a good time at his own wedding.

The morning after an opening of one of my own shows is more or less the same as any other morning—except that I sleep much later. In the case of "Red, Hot and Blue!" I broke my record by exactly ten minutes.

The reason for my behavior isn't that I'm confident of the play's success or that I'm totally without nerves. I'll put up my nerves against the best of them. But, for some reason, the moment the curtain rises on opening night, I say to myself: "There she goes," and I've bid good-bye to my baby.

* * *

During the months of preparation the piece itself has a way of becoming something of a person to me—not always a nice person, perhaps, but at least some one that I've grown fond of. The minute it is exposed to its première audience, however, I feel that it's no longer mine. It belongs to the performers. And I become just another $8.80 customer. That is why I take my friends along and make a night of it afterward.

The morning after is still a hangover of the holiday mood. One of the luxuries is to wake up to an inspired breakfast and then hunt for the notices. It is a pleasant feeling, this sensation of laziness which dictates that the entire day be dedicated to comfortable indolence, and nothing else but.

* * *

At any rate, there was I, my breakfast done and the notices half finished, when the telephone rang. It was Vinton Freedley, the girl at the desk announced: would I talk to him? I hesitated a moment. Whenever a producer calls up a song writer it always means trouble. And this was my day of rest. However, I weakened. I steeled myself for the inevitable barrage and decided to take the call.

"Hello, Cole, this is Vinton talking. How are you feeling?"

"I'm feeling fine. How are you feeling?"

"I'm feeling fine too."

And he hung up.

Considerate fellow, Vinton, when you get down to it.

Pleasantly relieved, I settled back to the notices again.

The telephone rang once more. "Ethel Merman," the girl at the desk announced.

I wasn't sure what to do. I love Ethel. I hope it will not be considered ungracious of me, in the face of the other very talented artists who have sung my songs and helped them along to popularity, to confess that I'd rather write for Ethel than any one else in the world. Every composer has his favorite, and she is mine. Her voice, to me, is thrilling. She has the finest enunciation of any American singer I know. She has a sense of rhythm which few can equal. And her feeling for comedy is so intuitive that she can get every value out of a line without ever overstressing a single inference. And she is so damned apt.

* * *

We decided in Boston one day that her first number in the show, whatever its melodic qualities might be, was too somber to start things off, and it became advisable to replace it. So that same afternoon I locked myself in my room and emerged the following morning with "Down in the Depths, on the Ninetieth Floor." The song was scored in the afternoon and that evening Ethel sang it in the show. And sang it beautifully. One thinks of these things, on the morning after an opening, with affection and gratitude. For, after all is said and done, a song writer is very much at the mercy of his interpreters, and it adds greatly to his sense of comfort to know that numbers are in capable hands.

These thoughts ran through my mind and still I hesitated, for usually when Ethel phones me it is to suggest changes in her songs, and this was one morning when I did not feel like doing anything of the kind.

However, I took the call.

"Hello. Cole. This is Ethel talking. How are you feeling?"

"I'm feeling fine. How are you feeling?"

"I'm feeling fine too."

And she hung up.

* * *

Cheerfully I returned to the notices. But again the phone interrupted, and this time it was Henry Spitzer of Chappell's. Henry is my music publisher. I like him very much in spite of the fact that he often talks business. Right now I did not feel like being bothered with details pertaining to restricting numbers on the radio, additional arrangements, foreign rights, special licenses and the like.

However, I had taken the other calls. I might just as well take his too.

"Hello, Cole. This is Henry talking. How are you feeling?"

"I'm feeling fine. How are you feeling?"

"I'm feeling fine too."

And he hung up. A pal to the end.

A couple of minutes later Jimmy Durante was on the phone. Jimmy had been after me to write him a song which he could sing with the girls in the show. Writing for Jimmy is not easy. It isn't the range of his voice, which is usually the major problem when turning out numbers for other performers, but rather catching that certain something which goes into the making of the Durante personality. The man who cleans up my apartment had several extra basketfuls of paper to cart out during the days I was fashioning "Little Skipper From Heaven Above" for Jimmy. But I took the call.

"Hello, Cole. This is Jimmy talking. How are you feeling?"

"I'm feeling fine. How are you feeling?"

"I'm feeling fine too."

And that was that.

By this time I was more or less finished with the notices. They ran according to form. I was considering the prospect of going back to bed when the telephone rang once more.

It was the press agent of the show.

"Hello," I said, beating him to the punch, "I'm feeling fine."

"That's fine, because then you'll be able to do a piece about it."

P. S. He was feeling fine too.

ROSALIE (1937)

Nelson Eddy introduced the song that is reputed to have made L. B. Mayer cry when he first heard Cole play it. Cole pretended that Mayer's tears were the highest compliment his music had ever received. "Imagine making L. B. Mayer cry," he told a friend. "What could possibly top that?"

IN THE STILL OF THE NIGHT

In the still of the night,
As I gaze from my window
At the moon in its flight,
My thoughts all stray to you.
In the still of the night,
While the world is in slumber,
Oh, the times without number,
Darling, when I say to you,
"Do you love me as I love you?
Are you my life-to-be, my dream come true?"
Or will this dream of mine
Fade out of sight
Like the moon
Growing dim
On the rim
Of the hill
In the chill,
Still
Of the night?

ROSALIE

NO. 6

VERSE

Since first you murmured your name to me,
Your name, in heaven designed,
The night no longer is the same to me
For I've only "Rosalie" on my mind.
Why does the sound of it thrill me
        through and through?
Is it my Song of Songs
Because it belongs
To

REFRAIN

Rosalie, Rosalie,
I keep repeating "Rosalie,"
Just a name, just a word,

Yet still the sweetest I ever heard.
On I go, never I tire,
For ev'ry syllable sets my heart a-fire.
What can be
The strange flame
That hallows thy name?
Rosalie, could it be love?

SERENADE VERSION

REFRAIN

Rosalie, dear,
You are my guiding star.
Rosalie, near,
Rosalie, near or far,
Why does a radiant halo gleam
        about you?
Why am I happier when I dream
        about you?
Oh, Rosalie, rare,
Rosalie, divine,
When can I say "Rosalie, mine?"
When will you be
My Rosalie?

NO. 7

VERSE

When knighthood was in flow'r
And a man wooed a maid,
Beneath her sacred bow'r
He sang a serenade.
I date,
I suppose,
It's late
Heaven knows,
It blows
And it snows,
But anyway, here goes:

REFRAIN

Rosalie, my darling,
Rosalie, my dream,
Since, one night, when stars danced
        above,
I'm oh, oh, so much in love.
So, Rosalie, have mercy,
Rosalie, don't decline,
Won't you make my life thrilling,
And tell me you're willing
To be mine, Rosalie, mine.

New York, May 9, 1946

Mr. Paul Whiteman
American Broadcasting Co.
New York, N.Y.

Dear Paul:
   This is the only story I have about the song *Rosalie*:
   In 1937 I was writing a picture for M-G-M called *Rosalie* and it was very important that the title song be good. I wrote six before I handed one in, but I was very proud of No. 6. Louis B. Mayer asked me to play the score for him and when I finished he said to me, "I like everything in the score except that song *Rosalie*. It's too highbrow. Forget you are writing for Nelson Eddy and simply give us a good popular song." So I took *Rosalie* No. 6 home and in hate wrote *Rosalie* No. 7. Louis B. Mayer was delighted with it, but I still resented my No. 6 having been thrown out, which to me seemed so much better.
   Six months later when the song became a hit, I saw Irving Berlin and he congratulated me on it. I said to him, "Thanks a lot, but I wrote that song in hate and I still hate it." To which Irving replied, "Listen, kid, take my advice, never hate a song that has sold a half million copies."
   This is the only story I have about *Rosalie*. I am delighted you are playing it and shall listen in with great interest.

                    Your old friend,
                    Cole Porter

At Kalser-Tauernhaus

At Murnau, Summer, 1937

HAMLET

Last photo before the accident

YOU NEVER KNOW (1938)

When this horse fell on me, I was too stunned to be conscious of great pain, but until help came I worked on the lyrics for a song called At Long Last Love.

Cole Porter

The song was introduced by Clifton Webb.

AT LONG LAST LOVE

VERSE

I'm so in love,
And though it gives me joy intense,
I can't decipher
If I'm a lifer,
Or if it's just a first offense.
I'm so in love,
I've no sense of values left at all.
Is this a play-time
Affair of Maytime,
Or is it a wind-fall?

REFRAIN 1

Is it an earthquake or simply a shock?
Is it the good turtle soup or merely the mock?
Is it a cocktail—this feeling of joy,
Or is what I feel the real McCoy?
Have I the right hunch or have I the wrong?
Will it be Bach I shall hear or just a Cole Porter song?
Is it a fancy not worth thinking of,
Or is it at long last love?

REFRAIN 2

Is it the rainbow or just a mirage?
Will it be tender and sweet or merely massage?
Is it a brainstorm in one of its quirks,
Or is it the best, the crest, the works?
Is it for all time or simply a lark?
Is it the Lido I see or only Asbury Park?
Should I say "Thumbs-down" and give it a shove,
Or is it at long last love?

REFRAIN 3

Is it a breakdown or is it a break?
Is it a real Porterhouse or only a steak?
What can account for these strange pitterpats?
Could this be the dream, the cream, the cat's?
Is it to rescue or is it to wreck?
Is it an ache in the heart or just a pain in the neck?
Is it the ivy you touch with a glove,
Or is it at long last love?

REFRAIN (Unfinished)

Is it in marble or is it in clay?
Is what I thought a new Rolls, a used Chevrolet?
Is it a sapphire or simply a charm?
Is it .... or just a shot in the arm?
Is it today's thrill or really romance?
Is it a kiss on the lips or just a kick in the pants?
Is it the gay gods cavorting above,
Or is it at long last love?

This Clifton Webb-Lupe Velez duet was the most widely acclaimed song in the show. After the enthusiastic reception of the song in New Haven and Boston, Cole added the encore refrains numbers four and five. J. J. Shubert referred to the song as *From Alfalfa to Omega*.

FROM ALPHA TO OMEGA

VERSE

You're such a ne plus ultra creature,
That if I had your photo,
I couldn't pick my fav'rite feature,
I like you so in toto.
In ev'ry way, from ev'ry angle,
You're the bangle I long to dangle,
For from basement to roof,
From Wagner op'ra to op'ra bouffe,

REFRAIN 1

From Alpha to Omega,
From A to Z,
From Alpha to Omega,
You're made for me.
From left hooks by Dempsey to Braddock's upper-cuts,
From Jericho to Kokomo, not to mention from soup to nuts,
From Journal until Mirror,
From coast to coast,
From Juliet to Norma Shearer,
You're what I like the most,
And from morning until evening
In mis'ry I shall pine,
Till from Alpha to Omega you're mine.

REFRAIN 2

From Alpha to Omega,
From A to Z,
From Alpha to Omega,
You're made for me.
From love songs by Schumann to hits by Jerry Kern,
From Sarawak to Hackensack, not to mention
  from stem to stern,
From dyah Missus Pat Campbell
To sweet Mae West,
You happen to be the mammal
This baby loves the best,
And from morning until evening,
Will you stun yourself with wine?
Certainly, till from Alpha to Omega you're mine.

Rex O'Malley, Clifton Webb, Lupe Velez, and Libby Holman in "You Never Know," 1938

Clifton Webb and Lupe Velez

REFRAIN 3

From Alpha to Omega,
From A to Z,
From Alpha to Omega,
You're made for me.
From Lou Gehrig's home-run to Lou Chiozza's bunt,
From Tripoli to Kankakee, not to mention from
    Lynn to Lunt,

From great eighty-pound codfish
To sardines canned,
You happen to be the odd fish
This lad would love to land,
And will you woo me and pursue me,
With sinker, hook, and line?
Yes, till from Alpha to Omega you're mine.
And will you chase me,
And embrace me,
And say that I'm divine?
Till from Alpha to Omega you're mine.

REFRAIN 4

From Alpha to Omega,
From A to Z,
From Alpha to Omega,
You're made for me.
From cotton ploughed under
To this year's bumper crop,
From Benzedrine
To Ovaltine,
Not to mention from go to stop.
From corn muffins to Triscuit
From fat to thin,
From Zev to the young Seabiscuit,
I'll bet on you to win.
And will you brunch me,
And then lunch me,
Then make me stay to dine?
Yes, till from Alpha to Omega you're mine.

REFRAIN 5

From Alpha to Omega,
From A to Z,
From Alpha to Omega,
You're made for me.
From old English Sherry
To very French Vermouth,
From Mozambique
To Battle Creek,
Not to mention from North to South.*
From great eagles to sparrows,
From large to small,
From Austins to big Pierce-Arrows,
Your rumble tops 'em all,
And will you beat me
And maltreat me,
And bend my Spanish spine?
Yes, till from Alpha to Omega you're mine.
*FROM COLE Note: Mr. Webb, go Southern,
and pronounce this Nauth and Sooth.

Finale
ACT II

From Martinis to brandy,
From East to West,
From Salomey to Sally Randy,
I like your fan the best,
And from morning until ev'ning,
The sun will never shine
Till from Alpha to Omega you're mine.

LEAVE IT TO ME (1938)

MY HEART BELONGS TO DADDY

VERSE

I used to fall
In love with all
Those boys who maul
Refined ladies.
But now I tell
Each young gazelle
To go to hell—
I mean, hades,
For since I've come to care
For such a sweet millionaire.

REFRAIN 1

While tearing off
A game of golf
I may make a play for the caddy.
But when I do
I don't follow through
'Cause my heart belongs to Daddy.
If I invite
A boy, some night,
To dine on my fine finnan haddie,
I just adore
His asking for more,
But my heart belongs to Daddy.
Yes, my heart belongs to Daddy,
So I simply couldn't be bad.
Yes, my heart belongs to Daddy,
Da-da, da-da-da, da-da-da, dad!
So I want to warn you, laddie,
Tho' I know you're perfectly swell,
That my heart belongs to Daddy
'Cause my Daddy, he treats me so well.
He treats it and treats it,
And then he repeats it,
Yes, Daddy, he treats it so well.

REFRAIN 2

Saint Patrick's day,
Although I may
Be seen wearing green with a paddy,
I'm always sharp
When playing the harp,
'Cause my heart belongs to Daddy.
Though other dames
At football games
May long for a strong undergraddy,
I never dream
Of making the team
'Cause my heart belongs to Daddy.
Yes, my heart belongs to Daddy,
So I simply couldn't be bad.
Yes, my heart belongs to Daddy,
Da-da, da-da-da, da-da-da, dad!
So I want to warn you, laddie,
Tho' I simply hate to be frank,
That I can't be mean to Daddy
'Cause my Da-da-da-daddy might spank.
In matters artistic
He's not modernistic
So Da-da-da-daddy might spank.

MOST GENTLEMEN DON'T LIKE LOVE

VERSE

When Mummy in her sixteenth year
Was dreaming of romance a lot,
She thought that she was Guinevere
And ev'ry boy Sir Launcelot,
But now that Mummy's more mature
And knows her way about,
She doesn't b'lieve in "Vive l'amour"
For Mummy's found out—

REFRAIN 1

Most gentlemen don't like love, they just like
    to kick it around,
Most gentlemen can't take love, 'cause most gentlemen
    can't be profound.
As Madam Sappho in some sonnet said
"A slap and a tickle
Is all that the fickle
Male
Ever has in his head,"
For most gentlemen don't like love.
I've been in love,
So I know what I'm talking of
And, oh, to my woe I have found
They just like to kick it around.

REFRAIN 2

Most gentlemen don't like love, they just like
    to kick it around,
Most gentlemen don't like love, 'cause most gentlemen
    can't be profound.
So just remember when you get that glance,
A romp and a quickie
Is all little Dickie
Means
When he mentions romance,
For most gentlemen don't like love,
They just like to kick it around.

REFRAIN 3

Most gentlemen don't like love, they just like
    to kick it around,
Most gentlemen don't like love, 'cause most gentlemen
    can't be profound.
In ev'ry land, children, they're all the same,
A pounce in the clover
And then when it's over
"So long and what is your name?"
'Cause most gentlemen don't like love,
They just like to kick it around.

REFRAIN 4

Most gentlemen don't like love, they just like
    to kick it around,
Most gentlemen don't like love, 'cause most gentlemen
    can't be profound.

So if your boy friend, some fine night, should say
He'll love you forever
And part from you never,
Just push him out of the hay, (way)
'Cause most gentlemen don't like love,
They just like to kick it around.

Mary Martin makes her Broadway debut singing
My Heart Belongs to Daddy. Gene Kelly, standing next to her, also
made his first Broadway appearance in "Leave It to Me."

Sophie Tucker in "Leave It to Me"

FAR AWAY

Now that there is no question
Of my not becoming your wife,
I've a certain suggestion
As to our married life.
If you only accept it
I shall prove my gratitude.
Go on, spring it,
If possible, sing it
For I'm in a lyrical mood.

REFRAIN 1

I'm not suggesting to you
A drafty cottage for two
By the side of a wide waterfall,
But you must grant me, sweetheart,
That it would be rather smart
To get away, far away from it all.
I'll make a row if you lease
A tumbling temple in Greece,
Or a hole in the ole China wall,
But when it's all said and done
I'll admit it would be fun
To get away, far away from it all.
What a joy not to fear,
As we wander 'neath the moon,
That some radio near
Will repeat that Berlin tune.
And to be certain, my dear,
That the readers of Heywood Broun
Are far away,
Far, far away,
But me from you
Never too
Far away.

REFRAIN 2

I'm not proposing we get
A tent atop of Tibet,
Or that we cross the sea in a yawl,
But, dear, with me as your mate
You'll agree it would be great
To get away, far away, from it all.
Please don't suggest that we test
The open spaces out West,
In a shack with no back to the hall,
But if we took some nice nook
I could watch you while you cook
And get away, far away from it all.
With the blue skies above,
And a peaceful habitat,
There'll be no danger of
Hearing Franklin give a chat.
And we'll know also, my love,
Grover Whelan and his hat
Are far away,
Far, far away,
But me from you
Never too
far away.

GET OUT OF TOWN

VERSE

The farce was ended,
The curtain drawn,
And I at least pretended
That love was dead and gone.
But now from nowhere
You come to me as before,
To take my heart
And break my heart
Once more.

REFRAIN

Get out of town,
Before it's too late, my love.
Get out of town,
Be good to me, please.
Why wish me harm?
Why not retire to a farm
And be contented to charm
The birds off the trees?
Just disappear,
I care for you much too much,
And when you are near,
Close to me, dear,
We touch too much.
The thrill when we meet
Is so bitter-sweet
That, darling. it's getting me down,
So on your mark, get set,
Get out of town.

TOMORROW

VERSE

Ladies and gentlemen, when my heart is sick
I've got a remedy that does the trick,
So, ladies and gentlemen, whenever you're blue
I advise you to try
My remedy too,
Just say

REFRAIN 1

Tomorrow, your troubles'll be done,
Tomorrow, your vict'ry'll be won,
Tomorrow, we're all gonna have fun,
'Cause there aint gonna be no sorrow, tomorrow.
Tomorrow, when the dawn appears, we all will be so good,
And so intent on doing just exactly as we should,
That there'll be no double crossing, even out in Hollywood,
'Cause there aint gonna be no sorrow, tomorrow.
Tomorrow, you poor Jerseyites, who got such awful jars,
When Orson Welles went on the air and made you all see stars,
I know you'll be relieved to hear we're giving him back to Mars,
'Cause there aint gonna be no sorrow, tomorrow.
Tomorrow, plumpish ladies who are heavier than whales,
Will wake to find that suddenly they're all as thin as rails,
So little Elsa Maxwell will no longer break the scales,
'Cause there aint gonna be no sorrow, tomorrow.
We'll have so much spare time that each of Maurice Evans' plays

Instead of lasting seven hours will last for days and days,
And to make all Federal projects even bigger, we propose
To throw out Harry Hopkins and instead hire Billy Rose.
Tomorrow, this dear world will be so beautiful a place,
And such a happy hunting ground for all the human race,
That you'll even see John L. Lewis with a smile upon his face,
'Cause there aint gonna be no sorrow, tomorrow.

REFRAIN 2

Tomorrow, your troubles'll be done,
Tomorrow, your vict'ry'll be won,
Tomorrow, we're all gonna have fun
'Cause there aint gonna be no sorrow, tomorrow.
Yes, Yes, tomorrow, it's all gonna be grand,
Tomorrow, you'll start leadin' the band,
Tomorrow, we'll live in a new land
'Cause there aint gonna be no sorrow, tomorrow.
There aint gonna be
No tears in your eyes,
You aint gonna see
No clouds in the skies,
You aint gonna have
No worries at all,
So why do you fret yourself iller?
You'll feel like a killer-diller
Tomorrow, you'll wake up and feel swell,
Tomorrow, you'll start ringin' the bell,
Tomorrow, we're all gonna raise hell
'Cause there aint gonna be no sorrow, tomorrow.
And so why borrow
Even a small cup of sorrow?
Instead, get in your head, mio caro,
There aint gonna be no sorrow, tomorrow.
No, no there aint gonna be
No sorrow for you and me
Tomorrow.

REFRAIN 3

Tomorrow, there'll be nothin' but peace—
Tomorrow, we'll all get a new lease,
Tomorrow, your trousers'll all crease,
'Cause there aint gonna be no sorrow, tomorrow.
Yes, Yes, tomorrow, the soldiers and their kits,
Tomorrow, will put war on the fritz,
Tomorrow, and move into the Ritz,
'Cause there aint gonna be no sorrow, tomorrow.
You girls who adore
New clothes on your backs,
You'll each own a floor
At Gimbel's and Saks.
You boys who are blue,
'Cause always it's true
When you see the girls,
You want to ensnare 'em,
You'll each have a Turkish harem.
Tomorrow, your dear hubby, madame,
Tomorrow, who's colder than a clam,
Tomorrow, will start pushin' a pram,
'Cause there aint gonna be no sorrow,
Tomorrow.

REFRAIN 4

Tomorrow, if blue, laddie, you are,

Tomorrow, 'cause she's gone away far,
Tomorrow, you'll meet Hedy Lamarr,
'Cause there aint gonna be no sorrow, tomorrow.
Yes, yes, tomorrow, dear lady with gray hair,
Tomorrow, if you'd like an affair,
Tomorrow, Bob Taylor'll be there
'Cause there aint gonna be no sorrow, tomorrow.
You're sure gonna meet
The one you'll adore,
Your heart's gonna beat
As never before,
It's all gonna change
From darkness to dawn,
So why do you squeal and feel so darn bitter?
You'll score like a Yankee hitter.
Tomorrow, the season'll be Spring,
Tomorrow, the birdies'll all sing,
Tomorrow, Dan Cupid'll be king,
So there aint gonna be no sorrow, tomorrow.
And so why trouble
Each time a pin bursts your bubble?
Just say, when you feel 'way below par, oh
"There aint gonna be no sorrow, tomorrow."

CODA

No, no there aint gonna be
No sorrow for you and me
Tomorrow.

★★★★★★★★★★

A request from George S. Kaufman and
Moss Hart to provide a "Noël Coward-type song"
for their forthcoming play, "The Man Who
Came to Dinner," resulted in the following
parody, sung by John Hoysradt (Beverly Carlton).

WHAT AM I TO DO

BY NOËL PORTER

VERSE

Off in the nightfall
I think I might fall
Down from my perilous height;
Deep in the heart of me,
Always a part of me,
Quivering, shivering light.
Run, little lady,
Ere the shady
Shafts of time
Barb you with their winged desire,
Singe you with their sultry fire.
Softly a fluid druid meets me,
Olden and golden the dawn greets me:
Cherishing, perishing, up to the stairs I climb.

REFRAIN

What am I to do
Toward ending this madness,
This sadness,
That's rending me through?
The flowers of yesteryear
Are haunting me,
Taunting me,
Darling, for wanting you.
What am I to say
To warnings of sorrow
When morning's tomorrow
Greets the dew?
Will I see the cosmic Ritz
Shattered and scattered to bits?
What not am I to do?

BROADWAY MELODY OF 1940

In the spring of 1939 MGM asked
Cole to write the score for "Broadway Melody
of 1939." The film took so long to
complete that Metro was forced to retitle
it "Broadway Melody of 1940."

BETWEEN YOU AND ME

VERSE

As you sail your glorious way
Like a shining star,
You don't know what havoc you play,
And how upsetting you are,
For so near you seem,
At night when I dream,
But when I waken, how far!

REFRAIN

Between you and me,
You're something spectacular,
Between you and me,
You're a prize,
Between you and me,
To use the vernacular,
You've got what they call "Oomph" in your eyes.
Till I make you mine
Your heart I'll bombard to get
No matter how hard to get
It may be.
So why not combine
And chuck the formality
Between Love and
Between you and
Me.

A gift to Cole from Monty, John Hoysradt, Moss Hart, and George S. Kaufman

Eleanor Powell and Fred Astaire dance to *Begin the Beguine* on a mirror covering just over 4,000 square feet

I CONCENTRATE ON YOU

Whenever skies look grey to me
And trouble begins to brew,
Whenever the winter winds become too strong,
I concentrate on you.
When Fortune cries "Nay, Nay!" to me
And people declare "You're through,"
Whenever the Blues become my only song,
I concentrate on you,
On your smile so sweet, so tender,
When at first my kiss you decline,
On the light in your eyes, when you surrender,
And once again our arms intertwine.

And so when wise men say to me
That Love's young dream never comes true,
To prove that even wise men can be wrong,
I concentrate on you,
I concentrate
And concentrate
On you.

DU BARRY WAS A LADY (1939)

Cole ended his most productive decade
by writing the score for the Ethel Merman-Bert Lahr
burlesque-extravaganza, "Du Barry Was a Lady."
The opening on December 6, 1939, was
the last musical comedy premiere of the thirties.

IT AIN'T ETIQUETTE

VERSE

Missus Emily Post
Who they tell me is most
Reliable,
For a helluva sum
Wrote a book that's become
My Bi-able.
And if only you look
At that Etiquette book
Of dear Emily's,
You can co-habitate
With America's great
Families,
Now for instance, Snooks,

REFRAIN 1

If you meet J. P. Morgan while playing golf
With the Long Island banking set,
Don't greet him by tearing your girdle off,
It ain't etiquette.
When invited to hear from an op'ra box
Rigoletto's divine quartet,
Don't bother your neighbors by throwing rocks,
It ain't etiquette.
When you're asked up to dine by
        some mean old minx,
And a meat ball is all you get,
Never say to your hostess,
"This dinner stinks,"
It ain't smart,
It ain't chic,
It ain't etiquette.

Fred and Eleanor

Betty Grable making her Broadway debut

It ain't smart,
It ain't chic,
It ain't etiquette.

REFRAIN 3

If a very proud mother asks what you think
Of her babe in the bassinette,
Don't tell her it looks like
    the missing link,
It ain't etiquette.
If you're asked up to tea at
    Miss Flinch's school
By some shy little violet,
Don't pinch poor Miss Flinch in the vestibule,
It ain't etiquette.
If you're swimming at Newport with some old leech
And he wrestles you while you're wet,
Don't call him a son of a Bailey's Beach,
It ain't smart,
It ain't chic,
It ain't etiquette.

★★★★★★★★★★★

*This song was written at the last moment
in Boston during the tryout of "Du Barry Was a Lady,"
when we all suddenly realized that Ethel Merman
didn't have quite enough material, as she
was so great in this show. This show was also
interesting for the fact that it was the first
time Betty Grable played Broadway,
and she made an instantaneous hit.*

          Cole Porter

GIVE HIM THE OO-LA-LA

REFRAIN 1

If you're fond of fancy things,
Diamond clips and em'rald rings.
If you want your man to come through,
Give him the Oo-la-la.
If your car is asked to stop
By some handsome traffic cop,
Lest you want a ticket or two,
Give him the Oo-la-la.
If poor Napoleon at Waterloo-la-la
Had had an army of debutantes,
To give the British the well-known Oo-la-la,
He'd have changed the hist'ry of France.
When your fav'rite Romeo
Grabs his hat and starts to go,
Don't reveal the fact you are blue,
Don't break down and start to boohoo,
There's but one thing for you-la-la,
To-la-la
Do-la-la,
Dance a hula
And give him the Oo-la-la!

REFRAIN 2

On arriving at one of those White House balls,
While you're touching up your toilette,
Don't write smutty jokes on the bathroom walls,
It ain't etiquette.
When the Chinese Ambassador's wife unfurls
After three drinks of anisette,
Don't ask if it's true about Chinese girls,
It ain't etiquette.
If you thought you were gypped at the
    Fair last year
And that Grover is just all wet,
Don't suggest what he do with the Perisphere,

La-la, la-la, la-la,
The Oo-la-la,
The Oo-la-la,
The Oo-la-la, Oo-la-la,
Oo-la-la, Oo-la-la,
Oo-la-la! Ha! Ha!

REFRAIN 2

If the tax man calls one day
And insists you pay and pay,
Just to cut your taxes in two,
Give him the Oo-la-la!
If your rich old uncle Ben,
Starts to make his will again,
Just before his lawyer is due,
Give him the Oo-la-la!
If Mr. Roosevelt desires to rule-la-la,
Until the year nineteen forty-four,
He'd better teach Eleanor how to Oo-la-la!
And he'll be elected once more.
If your bridegroom at the church,
Starts to leave you in the lurch,
Don't proceed to fall in a faint,
Don't run wild and crack up a saint,
There's but one thing for you-la-la,
To-la-la
Do-la-la,
Go Tallulah
And give him the Oo-la-la!
La-la, la-la, la-la,
The Oo-la-la,
The Oo-la-la,
The Oo-la-la, Oo-la,
Oo-la-la, Oo-la-la,
Oo-la-la!

DO I LOVE YOU?

VERSE

After that sweet summer afternoon
When for the first time I saw you appear,
Dreaming of you, I composed a tune,
So will you listen to it, dear?

REFRAIN

Do I love you, do I?
Doesn't one and one make two?
Do I love you, do I?
Does July need a sky of blue?
Would I miss you, would I,
If you should ever go away?
If the sun should desert the day,
What would life be?
Will I leave you never?
Could the ocean leave the shore?
Will I worship you forever?
Isn't heaven forevermore?
Do I love you, do I?
Oh, my dear, it's so easy to see,
Don't you know I do?
Don't I show that I do?
Just as you love me?

KATIE WENT TO HAITI

REFRAIN 1

Katie went to Haiti
Stopped off for a rest.
Katie met a natie
Katie was impressed.
After a week in Haiti
She started to go away,
Then Katie met another natie
So Katie prolonged her stay.
After a month in Haiti
She decided to resume her trip,
But Katie met still another natie
And Katie missed the ship.
So Katie lived in Haiti
Her life there, it was great,
'Cause Katie knew her Haiti
And practically all Haiti knew Katie.

REFRAIN 2

Katie stayed in Haiti
Spending all her pay.
Katie met a natie
Ev'ry other day.
Katie would tell the natie
That Katie was out for thrills
Each natie got a few for Katie
And Katie, she got the bills.
After a year in Haiti
She decided she should really go
But Katie had lived at such a ratie

That Katie had no dough
So Katie stuck to Haiti
Delighted with her fate
'Cause Katie still had Haiti
And practically all Haiti had Katie.

REFRAIN 3

Katie looked at Haiti
Feeling rather tired.
Katie met a natie
Katie was inspired.
After another natie
She sat down and wrote a book,
A guide-book for visitors to Haiti
Called "Listen, Stop, and Look!"
After the book by Katie
Had been published in the USA
The ratie of tourist trade in Haiti
Got bigger ev'ry day.
When Katie died at eighty
They buried her in state
For Katie made her Haiti
And practically all Haiti made Katie.

FRIENDSHIP

REFRAIN 1

He: If you're ever in a jam, here I am.
She: If you ever need a pal, I'm your gal.
He: If you ever feel so happy you land in jail,
    I'm your bail.
Both: It's friendship, friendship,
    Just a perfect blendship,
    When other friendships have been forgot,
    Ours will still be hot.
    Lahdle—ahdle—ahdle—dig, dig, dig.

REFRAIN 2

She: If you ever lose your way, come to May.
He: If you ever make a flop, call for Pop.
She: If you ever take a boat and get lost at sea,
    Write to me.
Both: It's friendship, friendship,
    Just a perfect blendship.
    When other friendships have been forgit,
    Ours will still be it,
    Lahdle—ahdle—ahdle—chuck, chuck, chuck.

REFRAIN 3

He: If you're ever down a well, ring my bell.
She: If you ever catch on fire, send a wire.
He: If you ever lose your teeth and you're out to dine,
    Borrow mine.
Both: It's friendship, friendship,
    Just a perfect blendship,
    When other friendships have ceased to jell
    Ours will still be swell.
    Lahdle—ahdle—ahdle—hep, hep, hep.

REFRAIN 4

She: If they ever black your eyes, put me wise.
He: If they ever cook your goose, turn me loose.
She: If they ever put a bullet through your brr-ain,
    I'll complain.

Ethel Merman

Singing *Katie Went to Haiti*

Both: It's friendship, friendship,
Just a perfect blendship.
When other friendships go up in smoke
Ours will still be oke.
Lahdle—ahdle—ahdle—chuck, chuck, chuck.
Gong, gong, gong,   Quack, quack, quack,
Cluck, cluck, cluck,   Tweet, tweet, tweet,
Woof, woof, woof,   Push, push, push,
Peck, peck, peck,   Give, give, give.
Put, put, put,
Hip, hip, hip.

REFRAIN 5

He: If you ever lose your mind, I'll be kind.
She: If you ever lose your shirt, I'll be hurt.
He: If you're ever in a mill and get sawed in half,
I won't laugh.
Both: It's friendship, friendship,
Just a perfect blendship,
When other friendships have been forgate,
Ours will still be great.
Lahdle—ahdle—ahdle—goof, goof, goof.

REFRAIN 6

She: If they ever hang you, pard, send a card.
He: If they ever cut your throat, write a note.
She: If they ever make a cannibal stew of you,
Invite me too.
Both: It's friendship, friendship,
Just a perfect blendship,
When other friendships are up the crick,
Ours will still be slick,
Lahdle—ahdle—ahdle—zip, zip, zip.

WELL, DID YOU EVAH!

VERSE

He: When you're out in smart society
And you suddenly get bad news,
You mustn't show anxiety
She: And proceed to sing the blues.
He: For example, tell me something sad
Something awful, something grave,
And I'll show you how a Racquet Club lad
Would behave.

But in the Morning, No

REFRAIN 1

She: Have you heard the coast of Maine
      Just got hit by a hurricane?

He: Well, did you evah! What a swell party this is.

She: Have you heard that poor, dear Blanche
      Got run down by an avalanche?

He: Well, did you evah! What a swell party this is.
      It's great, it's grand.
      It's Wonderland!
      It's tops, it's first.
      It's DuPont, it's Hearst!
      What soup, what fish.
      That meat, what a dish!
      What salad, what cheese!

She: Pardon me one moment, please,
      Have you heard that Uncle Newt
      Forgot to open his parachute?

He: Well, did you evah! What a swell party this is.

She: Old Aunt Susie just came back
      With her child and the child is black.

He: Well, did you evah! What a swell party this is.

REFRAIN 2

He: Have you heard it's in the stars
      Next July we collide with Mars?

She: Well, did you evah! What a swell party this is.

He: Have you heard that Grandma Doyle
      Thought the Flit was her mineral oil?

She: Well, did you evah! What a swell party this is.
      What Daiquiris!
      What Sherry! Please!
      What Burgundy!
      What great Pommery!
      What brandy, wow!
      What whiskey, here's how!
      What gin and what beer!

He: Will you sober up, my dear?
      Have you heard Professor Munch
      Ate his wife and divorced his lunch?

She: Well, did you evah! What a swell party this is.

He: Have you heard that Mimmsie Starr
      Just got pinched in the Astor Bar?

She: Well, did you evah! What a swell party this is!

REFRAIN 3

She: Have you heard that poor old Ted
      Just turned up in an oyster bed?

He: Well, did you evah! What a swell party this is.

She: Lilly Lane has louzy luck,
      She was there when the light'ning struck.

He: Well, did you evah! What a swell party this is.
      It's fun, it's fine,
      It's too divine.
      It's smooth, it's smart.
      It's Rodgers, it's Hart!
      What debs, what stags.
      What gossip, what gags!
      What feathers, what fuss!

She: Just between the two of us,
      Reggie's rather scatterbrained,
      He dove in when the pool was drained.

He: Well, did you evah! What a swell party this is.

She: Mrs. Smith in her new Hup
      Crossed the bridge when the bridge was up.

He: Well, did you evah! What a swell party this is!

REFRAIN 4

He: Have you heard that Mrs. Cass
      Had three beers and then ate the glass?

She: Well, did you evah! What a swell party this is.

He: Have you heard that Captain Craig
      Breeds termites in his wooden leg?

She: Well, did you evah! What a swell party this is.
      It's fun, it's fresh.
      It's post depresh.
      It's Shangrilah.
      It's Harper's Bazaar!
      What clothes, quel chic,
      What pearls, they're the peak!
      What glamour, what cheer!

He: This will simply slay you dear,
      Kitty isn't paying calls,
      She slipped over Niagara Falls.

She: Well, did you evah! What a swell party this is.

He: Have you heard that Mayor Hague
      Just came down with bubonic plague?

She: Well, did you evah! What a swell party this is.

BUT IN THE MORNING, NO

VERSE

He: Love affairs among gentility
      Hit the rocks with great agility
      Either because of income or incompatibility.

She: We've adjusted our finances,
      You run mine and I run France's,
      So there's only one question that's hot,
      Will we have fun or not?

REFRAIN 1

She: Are you fond of riding, dear?
      Kindly tell me, if so.

He: Yes, I'm fond of riding, dear,
      But in the morning, no.

She: Are you good at shooting, dear?
      Kindly tell me, if so.

He: Yes, I'm good at shooting, dear,
      But in the morning, no.
      When the dawn's early light
      Comes to crucify my night,
      That's the time
      When I'm
      In low.

She: Are you fond of wrestling, dear?
      Kindly tell me, if so.

He: Yes, I'm fond of wrestling, dear,
      But in the morning, no, no—no, no,
      No, no, no, no, no!

NOTE: This refrain, with ''boxing''
substituted for ''wrestling'' was the only
published refrain from the song.

REFRAIN 2

He: Do you like the mountains, dear?
   Kindly tell me, if so.
She: Yes, I like the mountains, dear,
   But in the morning, no.
He: Are you good at climbing, dear?
   Kindly tell me, if so.
She: Yes, I'm good at climbing, dear,
   But in the morning, no.
   When the light of the day
   Comes and drags me from the hay,
   That's the time
   When I'm
   In low.
He: Have you tried Pike's Peak, my dear?
   Kindly tell me, if so.
She: Yes, I've tried Pike's Peak, my dear,
   But in the morning, no, no—no, no,
   No, no, no, no, no!

REFRAIN 3

She: Are you fond of swimming, dear?
   Kindly tell me, if so.
He: Yes, I'm fond of swimming, dear,
   But in the morning, no.
She: Can you do the crawl, my dear?
   Kindly tell me, if so.
He: I can do the crawl, my dear,
   But in the morning, no.
   When the sun through the blind
   Starts to burn my poor behind
   That's the time
   When I'm
   In low.
She: Do you use the breast stroke, dear?
   Kindly tell me, if so.
He: Yes, I use the breast stroke, dear,
   But in the morning, no, no—no, no,
   No, no, no, no, no!

REFRAIN 4

He: Are you fond of Hot Springs, dear?
   Kindly tell me, if so.
She: Yes, I'm fond of Hot Springs, dear,
   But in the morning, no.
He: D'you like old Point Comfort, dear?
   Kindly tell me, if so.
She: I like old Point Comfort, dear,
   But in the morning, no.
   When my maid toddles in
   With my orange juice and gin,
   That's the time
   When I'm
   In low.
He: Do you like Mi-ami, dear?
   Kindly tell me, if so.
She: Yes, I like your-ami, dear,
   But in the morning, no, no—no, no,
   No, no, no, no, no!

NOTE: To satisfy the objections of some of the critics as well as the complaints of the Boston censors, Cole wrote the next two refrains:

REFRAIN 5

She: Are you good at football, dear?
   Kindly tell me, if so.
He: Yes, I'm good at football, dear,
   But in the morning, no.
She: Do you ever fumble, dear?
   Kindly tell me, if so.
He: No, I never fumble, dear,
   But in the morning, yes.
   When I start with a frown
   Reading Winchell upside down,
   That's the time
   When I'm
   In low.
She: Do you like a scrimmage, dear?
   Kindly tell me, if so.
He: Yes, I like a scrimmage, dear,
   But in the morning, no, no—no, no,
   No, no, no no, no!

REFRAIN 6

He: D'you like Nelson Eddy, dear?
   Kindly tell me, if so.
She: I like Nelson Eddy, dear,
   But in the morning, no.
He: D'you like Tommy Manville, dear?
   Kindly tell me, if so.
She: I like Tommy Manville, dear,
   But in the morning, no.
   When my maid says, "Madame!
   "Wake 'em up and make 'em scram,"
   That's the time
   When I'm
   In low.
He: Are you fond of Harvard men?
   Kindly tell me, if so.
She: Yes, I'm fond of Harvard men,
   But in the morning. no, no—no, no,
   No, no, no, no, no!

REFRAIN 7

She: Are you good at figures, dear?
   Kindly tell me, if so.
He: Yes, I'm good at figures dear,
   But in the morning, no.
She: D'you do double entry, dear?
   Kindly tell me, if so.
He: I do double entry, dear,
   But in the morning, no.
   When the sun on the rise
   Shows the bags beneath my eyes,
   That's the time
   When I'm
   In low.
She: Are you fond of business, dear?
   Kindly tell me, if so.
He: Yes, I'm fond of business, dear,
   But in the morning, no, no—no, no,
   No, no, no, no, no!

REFRAIN 8

He: Are you in the market, dear?
   Kindly tell me, if so.
She: Yes, I'm in the market, dear,
   But in the morning, no.
He: Are you fond of bulls and bears?
   Kindly tell me, if so.
She: Yes, I'm fond of bears and bulls,
   But in the morning, no.
   When I'm waked by my fat
   Old canary, singing flat,
   That's the time
   When I'm
   In low.
He: Would you ever sell your seat?
   Kindly tell me, if so.
She: Yes, I'd gladly sell my seat,
   But in the morning, no, no—no, no,
   No, no, no, no, no!

REFRAIN 9

She: Are you fond of poker, dear?
   Kindly tell me, if so.
He: Yes, I'm fond of poker, dear,
   But in the morning, no.
She: Do you ante up, my dear?
   Kindly tell me, if so.
He: Yes, I ante up my dear,
   But in the morning, no.
   When my old Gunga Din
   Brings the Bromo Seltzer in,
   That's the time
   When I'm
   In low.
She: Can you fill an inside straight?
   Kindly tell me, if so.
He: I've filled plenty inside straight,
   But in the morning, no, no—no, no,
   No, no, no, no, no!

REFRAIN 10

He: Are you fond of Democrats?
   Kindly tell me, if so.
She: Yes, I'm fond of Democrats,
   But in the morning, no.
He: Do you like Republicans?
   Kindly tell me, if so.
She: Yes, I like Republi-cans,
   But in the morning, no.
   When my pet pekinese
   Starts to cross his Q's and P's,
   That's the time
   When I'm
   In low.
He: Do you like third parties, dear?
   Kindly tell me, if so.
She: Yes, I love third parties, dear,
   But in the morning, no, no—no, no,
   No, no, no, no, no!

On the M.S. *Kungsholm*

★★★★★★★★★★

After the opening of "Du Barry Was a Lady," Cole escaped to the South Seas on the M. S. *Kungsholm. So Long, Samoa* was written for the enjoyment of his fellow passengers.

SO LONG, SAMOA

VERSE 1

Mrs. Lundbeck is in despair,
Mrs. Bunting is tearing her hair,
Mrs. Stowell is out of step.
Why, even Mrs. Browning is losing
    her pep.
And as for me
I'm as gloomy as can be.
Oh

VERSE 2

Mrs. Travers is in a fog,
Mrs. Samuels is biting her dog,
All the men folks have gone insane.
Why, even Mr. Nolan is buying
    champagne.
Those girls in huts
Drove 'em all completely nuts!
Oh

REFRAIN

So long, Samoa,
Lovely land so sweet, so serene,
So long, Samoa,
I've got to go back to the old routine.
But when the next time they tell me
That my income tax is over-due
'Stead of cursing F.D.R. as befoa,
Sweet Samoa, I'll return to you.

In the spring of 1940, Cole and Linda, who
had sold 13 Rue Monsieur, purchased "Buxton
Hill," an estate in Williamstown, Massachusetts.

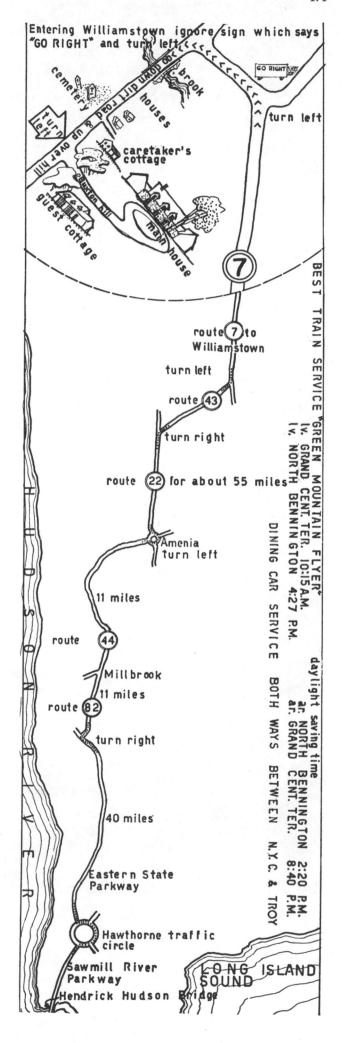

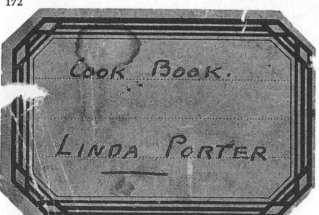

CHICI SAUCE

(Mrs. Wilson)

9 large ripe tomatoes

2 large onions

1/2 cup sugar

1/2 teaspoon cinnamon

1 teaspoon salt

2 green peppers

1 cup vinegar

1/2 teaspoon cloves (ground)

1/2 teaspoon allspice

Chop fine and boil until thick.

Dining room, "Buxton Hill"

SCHUYLER L. PARSONS, INC.
P. O. BOX 189
AIKEN, SOUTH CAROLINA

Shrimp South Side

1 lb. raw shrimp chopped
3 tbs. butter
2 tbs. flour
Cup cream
1 tsp. Worcestershire sauce
Tobasco to taste
1 tbs sherry
Salt and pepper to taste

Melt butter in double boiler, stir in flour, add cream,
stir until it thickens. Add raw shrimp. Add seasonings.
Just before serving add sherry. Serve on dry toast. Serves six.

LADY MENDL'S RECIPE
FOR
FISH SOUP

Fry thoroughly, golden brown, 4 or 5 onions (finely cut)
in oil in which has been diluted a coffee spoon of powder
of red sweet peppers. When the onions are well cooked,
add 6 tomatoes, fresh, peeled and seeded (or a box of
puree of concentrated tomatoes). Add a ladle-full of
bouillon, and stir well on the fire, adding salt and
pepper. Have on the side 10 or 15 potatoes, boiled
and peeled. Take a dish with high sides, glass that
will stand the fire, and butter well the inside. Cut
the potatoes in little rounds, put in the dish a layer
of potatoes, and pieces of butter, and squares of
Gruyere cheese (Swiss cheese) or (Port Salut) and some
spoonsful of cream, then a layer of the onions and
tomatoes already prepared, and pieces of carefully
boned and skinned fish of a firm flesh, one can add
also some mussels or crevettes or ecrevices, (or in
America, some clams or lobster and some mushrooms).

Do not fill the dish too full for one must add water
or milk, which will spill or boil over in the cooking.
The proportion of liquid is that of a soup - nice and
thick.

Put it to cook on a moderate fire, 1-1/2 hours.
Several minutes before you take it off, add hardboiled
quartered eggs and again some spoonsful of cream.

Serve in soup plates from the dish in which it is cooked.

Mrs. Lathrop's Cole Slaw

MRS. WILLIAM WALLACE
WALLACE HALL
NANTUCKET ISLAND, MASS.

½ teaspoon mustard
¼ cup sugar
Salt & pepper to taste
½ cup water — 1½ cup vinegar
Put these in double boiler let
come to a boil
Cream 2 tablespoons butter
with 1½ tablespoons flour
Stir these with the mustard
in double boiler and let cook
until it thickens — stirring then
then beat 2 eggs separately
until stiff
Take mixture off fire add the
2 egg yolks — mix thoroughly
and pour over cabbage
then add the beaten whites
let cool and just before serving
add 2 tablespoons of whipped
cream —
Use small head of cabbage
chop fine and use only tender
part

PANAMA HATTIE (1940)

I'VE STILL GOT MY HEALTH

VERSE 1

I wasn't born to stately halls
Of alabaster,
I haven't given many balls
For Missus Astor,
But all the same, I'm in the pink,
My constitution's made of zinc
And you never have to give this goil
Oil castor.

REFRAIN 1

I'm always a flop at a top-notch affair,
But I've still got my health, so what do I care!
My best ring, alas, is a glass solitaire,
But I've still got my health, so what do I care!
By fashion and fopp'ry
I'm never discussed,
Attending the op'ry,
My box would be a bust!
When I give a tea, Lucius Beebe ain't there,
Well, I've still got my health, so what do I care!

VERSE 2

In spite of my Lux Movie skin
And Brewster body,
I've never joined the harem in
Scheherazade,
But, if so far, I've been a bust,
I'm stronger than the Bankers Trust
And you never have to give this one
Hunyadi.

REFRAIN 2

No rich Vanderbilt gives me gilt underwear,
But I've still got my health, so what do I care!
I've never been dined by refined L. B. Mayer,
But I've still got my health, so what do I care!
When Barrymore, he played
With his wife of yore,
The lead Missus B played,
But I played Barrymore,
She chased me a block for a lock of my hair,
Well, I've still got my health, so what do I care!

REFRAIN 3

I haven't the face of Her Grace, Ina Claire,
But I've still got my health, so what do I care!
I can't count my ribs, like His Nibs, Fred Astaire,
But I've still got my health, so what do I care!
Once I helped Jock Whitney
And as my reward,
I asked for a Jitney—
In other words, a Ford,
What I got from Jock was a sock, you know where,
Well, I've still got my health, so what do I care!

REFRAIN 4

When I'm in New York, I'm the Stork Club's despair,
But I've still got my health, so what do I care!
No radio chain wants my brain on the air,
But I've still got my health, so what do I care!
At school I was noted
For my lack of speed,
In fact I was voted
"Least likely to succeed,"
My wisecracks, I'm told, are like old Camembert,
Well, I've still got my health, so what do I care!

VERSE 3

When Broadway first reviewed this wench,
The Press was catty,
They all agreed I'd even stench
In Cincinnati.
But, if I laid an awful egg,
I'm still as hot as Mayor Hague,
So in case you want to start a fire,
Wire Hattie.

REFRAIN 5

The hip that I shake doesn't make people stare,
But I've still got my health, so what do I care!
The sight of my props never stops thoroughfare,
But I've still got my health, so what do I care!
I knew I was slipping
At Minsky's one dawn,
When I started stripping,
They hollered "Put it on!"
Just once Billy Rose let me pose in the bare,
Well, I've still got my vitamins A, B, C, D,
E, F, G, H,
I
Still have my
Health.

I'M THROWING A BALL TONIGHT

VERSE

My life was simply hellish,
I didn't stand a chance,
I thought that I would relish
A tomb like General Grant's,
But now I feel so swellish,
So Elsa Maxwell-ish,
That I'm giving a dance.

REFRAIN

I feel like a million dollars,
I feel simply out o' sight,
So come on down, come on down,
I'm throwing a ball tonight.
I'm full of the old paprika,
I'm loaded with dynamite,
So come on down, come on down,
I'm throwing a ball tonight.
A certain person just brought some news,
And wow, was it great!
So, I'm rehearsin' my dancin' shoes
'Cause now, I can celebrate.
I feel like a million dollars,
I feel simply out o' sight,
So come on down, come on down,
I'm throwing a ball tonight.

PATTER 1

I invited Wendell Willkie,
I invited F.D.R.,
And for photographs,
I asked the staffs
Of Life, Look, Peek, Pic, Snap, Click, and
        Harper's Bazaar.
I invited Monty Woolley
And of course I asked Cliff Odets,
But to my surprise
Ev'ry one of those guys
Tendered his regrets.
And so I
Feel like a million dollars,
I feel simply out o' sight,
So come on down, come on down,
I'm throwing a ball tonight.

PATTER 2

I invited Gov'nor Lehman,
And Commishner Valentine,
And to do their stunts
I asked the Lunts
And Grace Moore, Bert Lahr, Mae West,
        and Father Divine.
I invited Gracie Allen
And, of course, I asked Fannie Brice.
But to all my bids
Ev'ry one of those kids
Wired back
"No dice!"

I've arranged a rhumba contest,
Just to make the party chic
And the winning ones
Will get two tons
Of Lux, Ponds, Teel, Squibbs, Mum, Zip,
        and Campho-phenique.
I invited Johnny Walker
And Haig and Haig I asked twice,
But to all my bids
Ev'ry one of those kids
Wired back

"No dice!"
And so I
Feel like a million dollars,
I feel simply out of sight,
So come on down, come on down,
Come on down,
Come on down,
Come on down,
I'm feeling magnific,
I'm throwing a turr-ific
Ball - - - - - - - - - - - - - - - to-night.

Panama Hattie

MAKE IT ANOTHER OLD-FASHIONED, PLEASE

VERSE

Since I went on the wagon, I'm
Certain drink is a major crime,
For when you lay off the liquor
You feel so much slicker,
Well, that is, most of the time.
But there are moments,
Sooner or later,
When it's tough, I've got to say,
Not to say
"Waiter,

REFRAIN 1

Make it another Old-Fashioned, please,
Make it another double Old-Fashioned, please,
Make it for one who's due
To join the disillusioned crew,
Make it for one of love's new
Refugees.
Once, high in my castle, I reigned supreme,
And oh! what a castle. built on a heavenly dream,
Then quick as a lightning flash,
That castle began to crash,
So make it another Old-Fashioned, please.

REFRAIN 2

Make it another Old-Fashioned, please,
Make it another double Old-Fashioned, please,
Make it for one who's due
To join the disillusioned crew,
Make it for one of love's new
Refugees.
Once I owned a treasure, so rare, so pure,
The greatest of treasures, happiness safe and secure,
But like ev'ry hope too rash,
My treasure, I find, is trash,
So make it another Old-Fashioned, please.
Leave out the cherry,
Leave out the orange,
Leave out the bitters,
Just make it a straight rye!"

LET'S BE BUDDIES

VERSE

Hattie: I get awful gloomy,
 Jerry: You mean, very gloomy,
Hattie: *Very* gloomy, now and then, in this town,
    'Cause it's always so hard
    To find a real pard
    Who'll play in your yard
    When you're down.
    But since the talk you and me,
    I mean, you and *I* have had,
    I've got a good friend, I see.

**Joan Carroll and Ethel Merman
(Jerry and Hattie) sing *Let's Be Buddies***

 Jerry: Well I'm not so very bad.

REFRAIN

What say, let's be buddies,
What say, let's be pals,
What say, let's be buddies,
And keep up each other's morales.
I may never shout it,
But many's the time I'm blue,
What say, how's about it,
Can't I be a buddy to you?

PATTER

 Jerry: Yes, with certain reservations.
Hattie: Will you try your best to go for this moll?
 Jerry: Hattie, what are you talking about?
Hattie: If you do, I'll buy a new dress for your doll.
 Jerry: But please let *me* pick it out.
Hattie: And I'll take you to hear the big cathedral bells.
 Jerry: Oh I hate those noisy old chimes.
Hattie: Well, instead then we'll go to see *Gone With The Wind*.
 Jerry: But I've already seen it four times.
Hattie: Would you like a big box of chocolate creams?
 Jerry: No, for candy I never did care.
Hattie: Then will you let me get you a cute little dog?
 Jerry: Would you mind making it a bear?
Hattie: Say, Jerry, old kid, you're a tough proposition.
    Are you sure your lid is in a healthy condition?
    Are you feelin' good, Jerry?
 Jerry: What me? Why very.
Hattie: Well, whether you are or not.

AMERICANS ALL DRINK COFFEE

VERSE

Oh, Americans and Englishmen,
How far they are from each other!
For England's child has gone so wild
That she's even wilder than her mother.
Yet they still have in common one quality,
    I find,
And 'twould take a master-mind to top it,
They're both too tolerant,
Both too kind,
But they both know when to say
"Stop it!"

REFRAIN 1

Americans all drink coffee,
Englishmen all drink tea,
When Englishmen say " 'Pon my Word!"
Americans say "Oh gee!"

Americans love their sunshine,
Englishmen love their fogs,
While Englishmen eat cold roast-beef,
Americans eat hot dogs.
Yet when some Dictator threatens
Johnny Bull or Uncle Sam,
An American
And an Englishman
Both say "Scram!"

REFRAIN 2

Americans all drink coffee,
Tea is for English chaps,
When Englishmen are shooting grouse,
Their cousins are shooting craps,
Americans don't like cricket,
Englishmen hate baseball,
The English love their ladies blonde,
Americans love them all.
Yet they're so alike in one way,
When a goat against 'em butts,
An American
And an Englishman
Both say "Nuts!"

REFRAIN 3

Americans all drink coffee,
England drinks tea a lot,
The English like their music sweet,
Americans like it hot.
Americans all drink cocktails,
Whiskey's what England drinks,
The English say a play is bad,
Americans say it stinks.
Yet they're so alike in one way,
When a mad dog comes to town,
An American
And an Englishman
Both say "Down!"

REFRAIN 4

Americans all drink coffee,
Tea is what England tries,
While England's making dreadful puns,
America's throwing pies.
America has its heat waves,
England by cold is cursed,
While England reads Lord Beaverbrook,
Americans still read Hearst,
Yet, they're so alike in one way,

In the chorus are Vera-Ellen and June Allyson

When encountered by a lout
An American
And an Englishman
Both say "Out!"

REFRAIN 5

Americans all drink coffee,
Tea is an English sin,
What England calls a one pound note,
America calls a finn.
America's sold on football,
England's a soccer fan.
While England's got its good King George,
America's got her man.
But when any fake magician
Tries to play them dirty tricks,
An American
And an Englishman
Both say "Nix!"

FINAL REFRAIN

Americans all drink coffee,
Englishmen tea prefer,
When Englishmen say "What a gel!"
Americans say "Get *her*!"
Americans all play poker,
Englishmen, solitaire,
When Englishmen their molars lose,
Americans lose their hair.
Yet they're so alike in one way,
When confronted by a rat,
An American
And an Englishman
Both say "Scat!"

FIRST ENCORE REFRAIN

Americans all drink coffee,
Tea is what England picks,
While England has her provinces,
America has her sticks.
America's palsy walsy,
England's a trifle smug,
While England does the stately waltz,
America cuts a rug,
But when any boasting bully
Tries to tell them what to do,
An American
And an Englishman
Both say "Screw!"

SECOND ENCORE REFRAIN

Americans all drink coffee,
Englishmen tea approve,
When England's feeling too divine,
America's in the groove.
Americans ride in street-cars,
Englishmen ride on trams.
What Englishmen call lovely legs
Americans call nice gams.
But when any goofy gangster
Starts to tread on either's toe,
An American
And an Englishman
Both say "Blow!"

YOU'LL NEVER GET RICH (1941)

SO NEAR AND YET SO FAR

VERSE

I so often dream
We might make a team,
But so wild a scheme
I must banish,
For each time I start
To open my heart
You vanish.
We might find some isle
Where lotuses smile
And our time beguile
Going native,
But how can we go
Unless you are co-
Operative?

REFRAIN

My dear, I've a feeling you are
So near and yet so far,
You appear like a radiant star,
First so near, then again so far.
I just start getting you keen on clinches
    galore with me,
When fate steps in on the scene and
    mops up the floor with me.
No wonder I'm a bit under par
For you're so near and yet so far.
My condition is only so-so,
'Cause whenever I feel you're close, oh
You turn out to be oh - - so - -
Far.

SINCE I KISSED MY BABY GOODBYE

VERSE

Oh, what nights, glory be,
When my baby and me
Used to ramble Lover's Lane
From sun-down to dawn,
Then a voodoo, I guess,
Put the jinx on our happiness,
And the mockin'-bird's refrain
Is done dead and gone.

REFRAIN

Evenin', creepin' down the mountain,
Wakes up Mister Fire-fly,
Bull-frog, settin' there,
Starts a-croakin', but I don't care,
Since I kissed my baby goodbye.
South-wind shakes the ole magnolia,
Moon-man lights the dingy sky,
Stars start sprinklin' gold
On the river, but still I'm cold
Since I kissed my baby goodbye.
Since my baby and me
Parted company,
I can't see what's the diff if I live
    or I die.
Oh, Lawd, I'm takin' such a beatin',
I'm no good, even cheatin',
Since I kissed my baby goodbye.

Cole with Rita and the director, Sidney Lanfield

Rita and Fred in "You'll Never Get Rich"

With Danny Kaye

LET'S FACE IT (1941)

At rehearsal

LET'S NOT TALK ABOUT LOVE

REFRAIN 1

Let's talk about love, that wonderful thing,
Let's blend the scent of Venice with Paris
    in Spring,
Let's gaze at that moon and try to believe
We're Venus and Adonis, or Adam and Eve,
Let's throw away anxiety, let's quite
    forget propriety,
Respectable society, the rector and his piety,
And contemplate l'amour in all its
    infinite variety,
My dear, let's talk about love.
Pretend you're Chopin and I'll be George Sand,
We're on the Grand Canal and, oh baby,
    it's grand!
Let's mention Walkures and helmeted knights,
I'm beautiful Brünnhilde, you're Siegfried
    in tights,
Let's curse the asininity of tribal
    consanguinity,
Let's praise the masculinity of Dietrich's
    new affinity,
Let's picture Cleopatra saying "Scram"
    to her virginity,
My dear, let's talk about love.
The weather's so warm and you are so cute,
Let's dream about Tahiti and tropical fruit,
I've always said men were simply deevine,
(Did you know that Peggy Joyce was once a
    pupil of mine?)
Let's gather miscellania on Oberon's Titania,
Or ladies even brainier who've moved to
    Pennsylvania,
(Bucks County, so I hear, is jest a
    nest of nymphomania)
My dear, let's talk about love.

My buddies all tell me selectees
Are expected by ladies to neck-tease,
I could talk about love and why not?
But believe me, it wouldn't be so hot,
So

REFRAIN 2

Let's talk about frogs, let's talk about toads,
Let's try to solve the riddle why chickens
    cross roads,
Let's talk about games, let's talk about sports,
Let's have a big debate about ladies in shorts,
Let's question the synonymy of freedom
    and autonomy,
Let's delve into astronomy, political economy,
Or if you're feeling biblical, the book
    of Deuteronomy,
But let's not talk about love.

Let's ride the New Deal, like Senator Glass,
Let's telephone to Ickes and order more gas,
Let's curse the Old Guard and Hamilton Fish,
Forgive me, dear, if Fish is your favorite dish,
Let's heap some hot profanities on Hitler's
    inhumanities,
Let's argue if insanity's the cause of
    his inanities,
Let's weigh the Shubert Follies with The Ear-rl
    Carroll Vanities,
But let's not talk about love.
Let's talk about drugs, let's talk about dope,
Let's try to picture Paramount minus Bob Hope,
Let's start a new dance, let's try a new step,
Or investigate the cause of Missus Roosevelt's pep,
Why not discuss, my dee-arie,
The life of Wallace Bee-ery
Or bring a jeroboam on
And write a drunken poem on
Astrology, mythology,
Geology, philology,
Pathology, psychology,
Electro-physiology,
Spermology, phrenology,
I owe you an apology
But let's not talk about love.

REFRAIN 3

Let's speak of Lamarr, that Hedy so fair,
Why does she let Joan Bennett wear all
    her old hair?
If you know Garbo, then tell me this news,
Is it a fact the Navy's launched all
    her old shoes?
Let's check on the veracity of Barrymore's
    bibacity
And why his drink capacity should get so
    much publacity,
Let's even have a huddle over Ha'vard
    Univassity,
But let's not talk about love.
Let's wish him good luck, let's wish him
    more pow'r,
That Fiorella fella, my favorite flow'r,
Let's get some champagne from over
    the seas,
And drink to Sammy Goldwyn,
Include me out please.
Let's write a tune that's playable,
    a ditty swing-and-swayable
Or say whatever's sayable, about the
    Tow'r of Ba-abel,
Let's cheer for the career of itty-bitty
    Betty Gra-abel,
But let's not talk about love.
In case you play cards, I've got some
    right here
So how about a game o' gin-rummy, my dear?
Or if you feel warm and bathin's your whim,
Let's get in the all-together and
    enjoy a short swim,
No honey, Ah suspect you all

Danny and Mary Jane Walsh

Of bein' intellectual
And so, instead of gushin' on,
Let's have a big discussion on
Timidity, stupidity, solidity, frigidity,
Avidity, turbidity, Manhattan, and viscidity,
Fatality, morality, legality, finality,
Neutrality, reality, or Southern hospitality,
Pomposity, verbosity,
You're losing your velocity
But let's not talk about love.

EV'RYTHING I LOVE

VERSE

If I were Lord Byron,
I'd write you, sweet siren,
A poem inspirin',
A killer-diller-oo,
Too bad, I'm no poet,
I happen to know it,
But anyway
Here's a roundelay
I wrote last night about you:

REFRAIN

You are to me ev'rything,
My life-to-be, ev'rything,
When in my sleep you appear,
Fair skies of deep blue appear,
Each time our lips touch again,
I yearn for you oh so much again,
You are my fav'rite star,
My haven in heaven above,
You are ev'rything I love.

A LADY NEEDS A REST

VERSE

I'm tired, I'm pooped,
I'm ready to drop,
I'd gladly cut my throat, I feel so bad.
For some unanswered reason,
This year, the social season
Has been the most
Overdosed
Season we ever had.

REFRAIN 1

Life is very far from easy
For a lady nowadays,
What with closing all the hot-spots
And opening all the plays,
What with ev'ry day a luncheon,
A dinner date ev'ry night,
What with keeping her children sober
And keeping her husband tight,
What with shopping tours
And manicures
And learning to bowl as well,
What with Philharmonics
And high-colonics
And giving the servants hell,
Add to this her wifely duty
Of letting him play the pest,
No wonder, now and then, a lady
    needs a rest.

REFRAIN 2

Life is very far from easy
For a lady nowadays,
What with posing for her photo
In all the best cafés,
What with burning up her mattress
With cigarettes she's endorsed,
What with getting her children married
And getting herself divorced,
What with fashion shows
And rodeos
And plugging for Billy Conn,
What with paying taxes
To beat the Axis,
And spraying her stockings on,
What with trying all the doodads
That Harpers and Vogue suggest,
No wonder, now and then, a lady
    needs a rest.

REFRAIN 3

Life is very far from easy
For a lady nowadays,
What with buying stocks in Woolworth's
And shopping at Cartier's.
What with eating only pot cheese
For fear of becoming stout,
What with keeping her children in nights
And keeping her husband out,
What with paying calls

And giving balls
And living beyond her means,
What with portrait sittings
And girdle fittings
And christening submarines.
Add to that a Latin boyfriend
She keeps in a private nest,
No wonder, now and then, a lady
    needs a rest.

REFRAIN 4

Rip Ra-Ti-Ra-Ti-Ra
Life is very far from easy
For a lady nowadays,
What with benefits unending
And charity matinees,
What with rooting for the Russians

Without being called a Red,
What with trying to read The Tribune
And doing her nails instead, a lady needs a
    two bar rest
Whata witha frocks to fit
And socks to knit
For the Britishers over-seas,
What with art collections,
Hormone injections
And walking her Pekinese, trees,
    trees, trees, trees
Add to this her constant worry
Of keeping her friends impressed,
No wonder, now and then a lady needs a—
Lady needs a—
Lady needs a rest cure
Now and then a lady needs a rest—sure
Now and then a lady needs a rest.

Edith Meiser, Eve Arden, and Vivian Vance sing
A Lady Needs a Rest

Farming: Jack Williams, Nanette Fabray, Danny Kaye, Sunnie O'Dea, and Benny Baker

Eve Arden, Danny Kaye, Edith Meiser, Benny Baker, Jack Williams, and Vivian Vance

FARMING

VERSE

Here's a bit of news that's quite a shocker
Proving Mother Nature still has charm,
Quoting Mister Cholly Knickerbocker,
"Get in the swim and buy a farm."
Acres of alfalfa, fields of clover
Suddenly enchant our top "Who's Who,"
So the moment all this row is over
What say if we go hay-seed too?
For

REFRAIN 1

Farming, that's the fashion,
Farming, that's the passion
Of our great celebrities of today.
Kit Cornell is shellin' peas,
Lady Mendl's climbin' trees,
Dear Mae West is at her best in the hay,
Stomping through the thickets,
Romping with the crickets,
Makes 'em feel more glamorous and more gay,
They tell me cows who are feeling milky
All give cream when they're milked by Willkie,
Farming is so charming, they all say.

REFRAIN 2

Farming, that's the fashion,
Farming, that's the passion
Of our great celebrities of today.
Monty Woolley, so I heard,
Has boll weevils in his beard,
Michael Strange has got the mange, will it stay?
Mussing up the clover,
Cussing when it's over,
Makes 'em feel more glamorous and more gay.
The natives think it's utterly utter
When Margie Hart starts churning her butter,
Farming is so charming, they all say.

REFRAIN 3

Farming, that's the fashion,
Farming, that's the passion
Of our great celebrities of today.
Fannie Hurst is haulin' logs,
Fannie Brice is feedin' hogs,
Garbo-Peep has led her sheep all astray,
Singing while they're rakin',
Bringing home the bacon,
Makes 'em feel more glamorous and more gay.
Miss Elsa Maxwell, so the folks tattle,
Got well-goosed while de-horning her cattle,
Farming is so charming, they all say.

REFRAIN 4

Farming, that's the fashion,
Farming, that's the passion
Of our great celebrities of today.
Don't inquire of Georgie Raft
Why his cow has never calfed,
Georgie's bull is beautiful, but he's gay!
Seeing spring a-coming,
Being minus plumbing,
Makes 'em feel informal and dégagé.
When Cliff Odets found a new tomater
He ploughed under the Group Theaytre,
Farming is so charming, they all say.

REFRAIN 5

Farming, that's the fashion,
Farming, that's the passion
Of our great celebrities of today.
Steinbeck's growing Grapes of Wrath,
Guy Lombardo, rumor hath,
Toots his horn and all the corn starts to sway,
Racing like the dickens,
Chasing after chickens,
Makes 'em feel more glamorous and more gay,
Liz Whitney has, on her bin of manure, a
Clip designed by the Duke of Verdura,
Farming is so charming, they all say.

(Among the discarded lines were the following:)
Farming, that's the fashion,
Farming, that's the passion
Of our great celebrities of today.
Digging in his fertile glen,
Goldwyn dug up Anna Sten,

Fred Astaire has raised a hare and its gray.
Clowning in their mittens,
Drowning extra kittens,
Makes 'em feel more glamorous and more gay.
Paul Whiteman, while he was puttin' up jelly,
Ate so much he recovered his belly,
Farming is so charming, they all say.

Farming, that's the fashion,
Farming, that's the passion,
Of our great celebrities of today.
Missus Henry Morganthau
Looks so chic behind a plow,
Mrs. Hearst is at her worst on a dray.
Tearing after possum,
Wearing just a blossom,
Makes 'em feel more glamorous and more gay,
Why Orson Welles, that wonderful actor,
Has Del Rio driving a tractor.
Farming is so charming, they all say.

Farming, that's the fashion,
Farming, that's the passion,
Of our great celebrities of today.
Just to keep her roosters keen,
Dietrich that great movie queen,
Lifts her leg and lays an egg, what a lay.
Going after rabbits,
Knowing all their habits,
Makes 'em feel more glamorous and more gay.
So Harpo Marx, in a moment of folly,
Had his barn repainted by Dali.
Farming is so charming, they all say.

Farming, that's the fashion,
Farming, that's the passion,
Of our great celebrities of today.
Lynn Fontanne is brandin' steer,
Sophie Tucker, so I hear,
Rides en masse upon an ass, hip-hooray.
Hoeing new potatoes,
Throwing all tomatoes,
Makes 'em feel more glamorous and more gay.
So Clifton Webb has parked his Ma, Mabel,
"Way Down East" in a broken-down stable,
Farming is so charming, they all say.

MAKE A DATE WITH A GREAT PSYCHOANALYST

VERSE

Listen girls, last Wednesday, I went to a matinee
And saw Gertrude Lawrence in "Lady in the Dark,"
       that wonderful play.
You know it was written by that wonder boy, called Moss Hart,
And *in it*, Gertie—that's what Ilka Chase calls her—
       plays the part
Of a magazine editor who knows so little of life,
That simply because the boys wouldn't romp with her
       when she was a child,
She got all mixed up in her love-life,

So she goes to see a brain doctor who lets her recline on a sofa
And talk about herself until she gets into such
       a perfect state of bliss,
That—well in any case—the point of that beautiful
Gertrude Lawrence play was this:

REFRAIN

If you've certain problems that must be solved,
If your love affairs have been involved,
If you're haunted by the way you look,
If your son has just eloped with your fav'rite cook,
Make a date with a great psychoanalyst and lie down.
If at winning at bridge you've lost your touch,
If you dream about Raymond Gram Swing too much,
If of late you're constantly in your cups,
If your peke's become the mother of poodle pups,
Ring the bell of a swell psychoanalyst and lie down.
If your nights are dreary and your days long
'Cause your boy friend has given you the gate,
Find a fancy doctor with a chaise-longue
And wait—simply wait.
If your lawyer's been sent to Alcatraz,
If you just found out that your husband has
Ev'ry day with a gay cutie-pie, a tryst,
I suggest it is best that you try a tryst
With some willing, eye-filling psychiatrist
And lie down.

At an opening

PETS

VERSE

Some folks collect paintings,
Some folks collect stamps,
Some are amassers
Of antimacassars
And other Victorian camps,
Some folks collect horses,
Others we know, Reno divorces,
But I, Little Me,
Well I just can't wait till you see my

REFRAIN 1

Pets,
I collect pets,
I collect ev'rything from mice to marmosets,
I've a whirling-mouse called Jumbo
And a cockatoo from Colombo
Who tells dirty jokes and smokes cigarettes,
I've a dinner-jacketed penguin who gives me
      lessons in poise,
And a very sexy old peacock who makes such an
      int'resting noise,
But the pride of my collection is my bevy of
      Harvard boys,
I'm like a child,
I'm simply wild
About my pets!

REFRAIN 2

Pets,
I collect pets,
I collect ev'rything from mice to marmosets,
I've a genuine chinchilla
And a rather chi-chi gorilla,
Who wears negligés and plays minuets,
I've a Persian kitten from Newport who only cares
      for whipped cream
And a pair of riotous rabbits, the way they behave
      is a scream!
And as soon as I've more cages
I'll take over the Dartmouth team,
I'm like a child,
I'm simply wild
About my pets!

REFRAIN 3

Pets,
I collect pets,
I collect ev'rything from mice to marmosets,
I've an acrobatic monkey
And a highly endowed young donkey
Who's played sev'ral shows
And knows Cliff Odets,
I've an op'ra-conscious canary
Who sings so loud that I'm deaf,
And an awf'lly fussy French poodle,
(Thank heaven I've got a French chef!)
And whenever Winston's willing
I'm adopting the R.A.F.,
I'm like a child,
I'm simply wild
About my pets!

SOMETHING TO SHOUT ABOUT (1943)

NEW YORK, FEBRUARY 4, 1942

    LINE FOR SONG   "SINCE THE DUPONTS CROSSED THE DELAWARE"
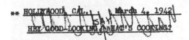

FEBRUARY 4, 1942

    MY FIRST LOVE

    NICE THINGS ALWAYS TAKE A LONG TIME.

FEBRUARY 6, 1942

    ~~YOU WOULD BE SO WONDERFUL TO COME HOME TO~~

February 9, 1942

    ~~SOME ONE TO COME HOME TO~~

~~WORDS FOR LYRIC   "Curdled   Marbled".~~

FEBRUARY 18, 1942

    THE MIRACLE OF YOU

    THEN CAME THE MIRACLE OF YOU

FEBRUARY 19, 1942

    SOMETHING TO KEEP ME WARM

** ~~HOLLYWOOD, CAL.,   March 4, 1942~~
~~HEY, GOOD-LOOKING, WHAT'S COOKING?~~

    MARCH 4, 1942

    IF YOU KNOW HOW TO ENTER AND WHEN TO LEAVE

    MARCH 9, 1942

TAKE ALONG MY HAPPINESS, BUT PLEASE BRING IT BACK ONE OF THESE DAYS

YOU'D BE SO NICE TO COME HOME TO

VERSE 1

He: It's not that you're fairer
      Than a lot of girls just as pleasin'
      That I doff my hat
      As a worshipper at
      Your shrine,
      It's not that you're rarer
      Than asparagus out of season,
      No, my darling this is the reason
      Why you've got to be mine:

REFRAIN

You'd be so nice to come home to,
You'd be so nice by the fire,
While the breeze, on high,
Sang a lullaby,
You'd be all that I
Could desire,
Under stars, chilled by the winter,
Under an August moon, burning above,
You'd be so nice,
You'd be Paradise
To come home to and love.

VERSE 2

She: I should be excited,
But, Lothario, why not own up
That you always chase
After ev'ry new face
In town?
I would be delighted
If we two could, some day, be sewn up
For if you behaved like a grown-up
And could only slow down.

SOMETHING FOR THE BOYS (1943)

THE LEADER OF A BIG-TIME BAND

VERSE

If a girl in any sector
Makes you feel like the puppy called Hector,
And you're longin' to subject 'er,
To elect 'er your wife and protect 'er,
If she's just as sweet as nectar,
But of your job she's no respecter,
Become a top band
Director and
You never, never will miss.

Veda Ann Borg, Jack Oakie, Cobina Wright, Jr., Don Ameche, and Janet Blair in "Something to Shout About"

REFRAIN 1

In the old days, when a maid desired to wed,
Any man who'd foot the bill could fill the bed,
But today the lad who's sure to win her hand
Is the leader of a big-time band.
Even gals who go for wrestlers quit 'em quick
When they meet some guy who sings and swings a stick,
For of late the only date they long to land
Is the leader of a big-time band.
When they hear Harry James
Make with the lips
The most Colonial Dames
Fracture their hips,
(So if Thee would like to be in great demand,
Be the leader of a big-time band.)

REFRAIN 2

In the gilded age, a Wall Street millionaire
Was the answer to a working maiden's prayer,
But today she'd chuck that yearly fifty grand
For the leader of a big-time band.
In the days when Casanova was the tops
All his rivals with the femmes were famous flops,
But today's who got that extra monkey gland?
Why, the leader of a big-time band.
When Goodman, champ of champs,
Goes blowin' blue,
Rum-ridden debutramps
Nearly come to,
'Cause there's nothing, when you're out,
    like being fanned
By the leader of a big-time band.

REFRAIN 3

In the days when old King Louie held the scene,
Any Jock who had the Jack could play the Queen,
But today who'd come and play that baby grand?
Why, the leader of a big-time band.
When, in Venice, Georgia Sand with Chopin romped,
Her libido had the Lido simply swamped,
But today who would be buried in the sand?
Why, the leader of a big-time band.
When Dorsey starts to tilt
That horn about,
Dear Missus Vanderbilt
Bumps herself out,
So, if, say, you still can play a one-night stand,
Be the leader of a big-time band.

REFRAIN 4

When in Reno ladies we know used to clown,
All the chaps who wore the shaps could wear 'em down,
But today the only rider they demand
Is the leader of a big-time band,
When Salome got John the B. and by the head,
It appears he wasn't kosher in da bed.
But today who'd be the goy she'd like to land?
Why, the leader of a big-time band.
When Cugat comes to tea

With Gypsy Rose,
She gets so het-up, she
Puts on her cloe's,
And she only turns one cheek while being scanned
By the leader of a big-time, jig-time,
    dig a-dig-time band.

COULD IT BE YOU?

VERSE

A white sea-shore in moonlight immersed,
A silent palm-tree swaying,
When out of nowhere you suddenly burst
And I found myself saying:

REFRAIN

Could it be you,
The one I'm fated for?
Could it be you,
The love I've waited for?
For lo, since you came along
And kindled the song in my heart,
Why bother pretending?
The song is unending,
Are you the dream
I always dream about?
Are we the team
I'm on the beam about?
Could be these rev'ries of mine
Are far too divine
To come true,
Or, could it be really you?

Ethel Merman in her fifth Porter show

Mike Todd, the producer of "Something for the Boys," 1943

He's a Right Guy

HE'S A RIGHT GUY

REFRAIN

I can see
He's happier without me,
It could be
My hopes were too high.
Obviously
He's not mad about me
But b'lieve you me
He's a right guy.
Yes, I can tell
He far from adores me,
I know but too well
That wandering eye,
I treat him swell
And still he ignores me,
But, what the hell,
He's a right guy.
They'll tell me I should say
"Goodbye and goodnight, guy,
Be on your way,
Just toddle along."
But I know one fine day

He'll prove he's a right guy,
And with a right guy
You can never go wrong.

TAG

Never, never,
Never, never,
Well, hardly ever
Go wrong.

BY THE MISSISSINEWAH

VERSE

Both: We're two little squaws from Indiana,
Who embarked on a trip for fun,
We're two little squaws who'll sing "Hosanna"
When the dog-gone trip is done.
No, no more we shall roam
Blossom: From our comfy, cozy, Hoosier home!

REFRAIN 1

Both: By the Miss-iss-iss-iss-iss-iss-iss-iss-inewah,
Blossom: There's a husband who waits for me,
Chiquita: And me!
Both: By the Miss-iss-iss-iss-iss-iss-iss-iss-inewah,
Blossom: There he waits in a wigwam built for three,
Chiquita: [spoken] Me, he and she!
Blossom: As it's one whole week since from our shiek
we've been awah
We're longing so for our co-papa,
Chiquita: Our co-dada!
Both: Thank the Lord this trip is brief
So we can leap on our heap-big chief
By the Miss iss-iss-iss-iss-iss-Inewah, Wah-wah!
By the Miss-iss-iss-iss-iss-iss-inewah.

PATTER

Chiquita: If we tried the Mississippi,
I am certain I'd go dippy
Blossom: If they moved us to the S'wanee,
I'd take "coke" or smoke "marrawanny."
Chiquita: Life would surely be a fluke on
That Alaskan stream, the Yukon,
Blossom: And as for the Rio Grande,
No its bed is much too sandy!
Chiquita: You'll agree that we two dames
Would not be F. F. V. on the James,
Blossom: I could never go to slumber-land
On the Kennebec or the Cumberland,
Chiquita: Would you like the old "Putomuck?"
Blossom: It would give me a pain in my "stowmuck."
Chiquita: Would the Missouri put you in a fury?
Blossom: Why, yuh houri, I'm from Missouri,
Chiquita: To the Delaware
I'm well aware
We could never, never move
Blossom: For beside our stream,
Life is such a sweet dream
That we're strictly in the groove.

[SEGUE INTO REFRAIN]

REFRAIN 2

Both: By the Miss-iss-iss-iss-iss-iss-iss-inewah,
Chiquita: There's a husband who waits for me,
Blossom: And me!
Both: By the Miss-iss-iss-iss-iss-iss-inewah,
Chiquita: There he waits in a wigwam built for three,
Blossom: [spoken] It's bigamy!
Chiquita: Since no love we've had since from that lad
we've been awah
Back by that stream, we will scream "Hoorah!"
Blossom: Hip, hip, hoorah!
Both: Yes, the moment we get in,
We'll blow the top with our pop red-skin,
By the Miss-iss-iss-iss-iss-iss-inewah, Wahoo!
By the Miss-iss-iss-iss-iss-iss-inewah,
Wah, wah, wah, wah
Wah, wahwah, wah, wah,
Wah!

REFRAIN 3

Both: By the Miss-iss-iss-iss-iss-iss-iss-iss-inewah,
There's a husband with whom we thrive and jive,
By the Miss-iss-iss-iss-iss-iss-iss-inewah,
There he waits for the day when we arrive,
Mister Ten-By-Five,
We're a total loss, since from the boss,
we've been awah,
'Cause for that Bo, we are so ga-ga,
completely blah,
Life will be a dream again
When we can laze in a daisy chain
By the Miss-iss-iss-iss-iss-iss-inewah, without a bra,
By the Miss-iss-iss-iss-iss-iss-inewah,
Wah, wah, wah,

REFRAIN 4

Both: By the Miss-iss-iss-iss-iss-iss-iss-iss-inewah,
Chiquita: Il m'attend mon charmant joujou,
Blossom: Are you kiddin'?
Both: By the Miss-iss-iss-iss-iss-iss-iss-inewah,
Chiquita: Il m'attend, dans une veegvam, mon p'tit chou,
Blossom: [spoken] Dig me, honey, dig me!
Chiquita: Je suis trés, trés glum since, from mon homme,
I've been awah
Et comme, je yearn to return la-bas,
Blossom: Mais, pourquoi, pas?
We'll be rootin' pour La France
When in we tucky with our lucky Alphonse,
Chiquita: Sur la Meess-eess-eess-eess-eess-eess-eenewah!
Blossom: Oo-la-la!
Both: Sur la meess-eess-eess-eess-eess-eess-eenewah.
Wah, wah, wah,
Wah, wahwah, wah, wah, wah!

REFRAIN 5

Both: By the Miss-iss-iss-iss-iss-iss-iss-inewah,
Chiquita: There's a husband who me adore,
Blossom: Me more,
Both: By the Miss-iss-iss-iss-iss-iss-iss-inewah,
Chiquita: There he waits in a wigwam built for four,
Blossom: [spoken] Are you expectin', too?
Chiquita: Though to sleep I try, since from that guy

I've been awah,
I have such awful insomnia,
Blossom: [spoken] Etcetera.
Chiquita: Oh that wigwam will be heaven
When we are one, two, three, four.
Blossom: [spoken] Five, six, seven,
Both: By the Miss-iss-iss-iss-iss-iss-inewah, howdy, Ma!
By the Miss-iss-iss-iss-iss-iss-inewah!
Wah, wah, wah,
Wah, wahwah, wah, wah, wah!

Two Indian squaws who share a husband "by the Mississinewah"

PUBLISHED VERSION

VERSE

I'm a poor little squaw from Indiana,
Who embarked on a trip for fun,
I'm a poor little squaw who'll sing "Hosanna,"
When the dog-gone trip is done.
No, no more shall I roam
From my comfy, cozy, Hoosier home!

REFRAIN 1

By the Miss-iss-iss-iss-iss-iss-iss-iss-inewah,
There's a husband to whom I'm true,
By the Miss-iss-iss-iss-iss-iss-iss-iss-inewah,
There he waits in a wigwam built for two,
Since no love I've had since from that lad I've been awah,
Back by that stream I will scream "hoorah!"
Thank the Lord this trip is brief
So I can leap on my heap-big chief
By the Miss-iss-iss-iss-iss-iss-inewah, Wah-wah!
By the Miss-iss-iss-iss-iss-iss-inewah!

REFRAIN 2

By the Miss-iss-iss-iss-iss-iss-iss-iss-inewah,
There's a husband to whom I'm true,
By the Miss-iss-iss-iss-iss-iss-iss-iss-inewah,
There he waits in a wigwam built for two,
I'm a total loss since from the boss I've been awah,
'Cause for that Bo, I am so ga-ga,
Yes, the moment I get in
I'll blow the top with my pop red-skin.
By the Miss-iss-iss-iss-iss-iss-inewah, Wah-wah!
By the Miss-iss-iss-iss-iss-iss-inewah!

MEXICAN HAYRIDE (1944)

I LOVE YOU

VERSE

If a love-song I could only write,
A song with words and music divine,
I would serenade you ev'ry night
Till you'd relent and consent to be mine,
But alas, just an amateur am I
And so I'll not be surprised, my dear,
If you smile and politely pass it by
When this, my first love-song you hear:

REFRAIN

"I love you"
  Hums the April breeze.
"I love you"
  Echo the hills.
"I love you"
  The golden dawn agrees
  As once more she sees
  Daffodils.
  It's Spring again
  And birds, on the wing again,
  Start to sing again
  The old melodie.
"I love you"
  That's the song of songs
  And it all belongs
  To you and me.

THERE MUST BE SOMEONE FOR ME

VERSE

If you're a maid men always quit
And with such velocity
That you're getting ready to commit
A ferocatrocity,
If you're blue because in each love-affair,
You have wound up on the shelf,
Simply learn this little old nurs'ry air
And repeat it to yourself:

REFRAIN 1

There's a boy cat for ev'ry girl cat,
There's a boy bat for ev'ry girl bat,
There's a boy rat for ev'ry girl rat,
So there must be someone for me.
There's a boy snail for ev'ry girl snail,
There's a boy quail for ev'ry girl quail,
There's a boy whale for ev'ry girl whale,
So there must be someone for me.
For each lassy hippo in the river-bed,

Say the rhymes of Mother Goose,
There's a laddie hippo she will shortly wed
So why in hell should I reduce?
There's a boy mouse for ev'ry girl mouse,
There's a boy grouse for ev'ry girl grouse,
There's a boy louse for ev'ry girl louse,
So there must be someone for me.

REFRAIN 2

There's a boy lamb for ev'ry girl lamb,
There's a boy clam for ev'ry girl clam,
There's a boy ham for ev'ry girl ham,
So there must be someone for me.
There's a boy trout for ev'ry girl trout,
There's a boy lout for ev'ry girl lout,
There's a boy scout for ev'ry girl scout,
So there must be someone for me.
Mister Charlie Chaplin, simply look at him,
He'll be sixty-three today,
Yet whenever Charlie's feeling full of vim
He gets another protégée.
There's a boy tot for ev'ry girl tot,
There's a boy hot for ev'ry girl hot,
There's no boycott on any girl cot,
So there must be someone for me.

REFRAIN 3

There's a boy chick for ev'ry girl chick,
There's a boy tick for ev'ry girl tick,
There's a boy hick for ev'ry girl hick,
So there must be someone for me.
There's a boy moose for ev'ry girl moose,
There's a boy goose for ev'ry girl goose,
There's a pa-poose for ev'ry ma-poose,
So there must be someone for me.
Mister John L. Lewis I could not begin
To imagine as my spouse,
Yet a lot of girls would love to slumber in
The bushes of his eye-brows.
There's a boy loon for ev'ry girl loon,
There's a boy prune for ev'ry girl prune,
There's a boy goon for ev'ry girl goon,
So there must be someone for me.

IT'S JUST YOURS

REFRAIN 1

Your charm is not like the still of ev'ning, dear,
Your glamour not like the sky when stars appear,
Your warmth is not like the moonlight on the moors,
It's just yours, it's just yours, it's just yours.
Your touch is not like the summer breeze, oh no!
Your sweetness, not like a song of long ago,
Your smile is not like the sun a-shine
But, darling, like this heart of mine,
It's just yours, it's just yours, it's just yours.

REFRAIN 2

Your walk is not like a graceful young gazelle's,
Your style is not what the chic Mainbocher sells,
Your voice is not Gracie Field's or Gracie Moore's,
It's just yours, it's just yours, it's just yours.

Your charm is not that of Circe's with her swine,
Your brain would never deflate the great Einstein,
Your laughter's not like a babbling brook,
But my love, believe me, Snook,
It's just yours, it's just yours, it's just yours.

REFRAIN 3

Your mouth is not like a rose-bud on the wall,
Your neck is not like a swan's, oh not at all,
Your nose is not early Greek like Dot Lamour's,
It's just yours, it's just yours, it's just yours,
Your skin is not like the virgin winter snow,
Your figure hardly excels Blondell's, oh no!
Your smile is not like the sun a-shine
But, lambkin, like this heart of mine,
It's just yours, it's just yours, it's just yours.

IT'S JUST LIKE THE GOOD OLD DAYS

VERSE

How's it, back in the homeland, Buzz?
I feel so far away.
Things are quite as they used to wuz
In fact I'm sure you would say

REFRAIN 1

It's just like the good old days,
Our country's just the same,
It's just like the good old days
We're still playing the game,
The landmarks we always loved
Haven't changed their charming ways,
The pet of the net-works is still Major Bowes,
Durante is still being paid through the nose,
Missus Harrison Williams is still wearing clo'es,
It's just like the good old days,
Miss Garbo remains as the Hollywood Sphinx
Monty Woolley's still bathing his beard
        in his drinks,
P.M. still assures us that ev'rying stinks,
It's just like the good old days.
Just like the good old days.

REFRAIN 2

It's just like the good old days,
Our country's just the same,
It's just like the good old days
We're still playing the game,
The landmarks we always loved
Haven't changed their charming ways,
Drew Pearson still worries the President most,
Walter Lippman still ruins your coffee and toast,
Martin Dies still refuses to give up the ghost,
It's just like the good old days,
At dear Wanamaker's the organ still plays,
At Morocco, it still is the woman who pays,
When Cornell doesn't jell there is still
        Helen Hayes,
It's just like the good old days,
Just like the good old days.

REFRAIN 3

It's just like the good old days,
Our country's just the same,
It's just like the good old days
We're still playing the game,
The landmarks we always loved
Haven't changed their charming ways,
The subway is still the most popular place,
George Nathan's still writing and so's Ilka Chase,
At the Met they do "Carmen" and still in white-face,
It's just like the good old days,
On the air, Maxwell Coffee is still a big name
And Jello continues in radio fame
But in spite of Jack Benny it still tastes the same,
It's just like the good old days,
Just like the good old days.

REFRAIN 4

It's just like the good old days,
Our country's just the same,
It's just like the good old days
We're still playing the game,
The landmarks we always loved
Haven't changed their charming ways.
Tommy Manville still pays 'em by certified check,
Twenty One still provides you with Pommery Sec,
The Hope diamond still bruises poor Evalyn's neck,
It's just like the good old days
Doris Duke still tells Cromwell she won't pay the price,
Bertrand Russell still preaches the virtue of vice,
Pa Devine is still God and and so everything's nice,
It's just like the good old days,
Just like the good old days.

REFRAIN 5

It's just like the good old days,
Our country's just the same,
It's just like the good old days
We're still playing the game,
The landmarks we always loved
Haven't changed their charming ways,
Louie Bromfield is still raising Cain with his crops,
Miss Dietrich is still raising hell with her props,
The gangsters are still raising dough with the cops,
It's just like the good old days
Dick Tracy still runs his habitual risk,
Bing Crosby still costs you a nickel a disc,
Polly Adler still tells me that business is brisk,
It's just like the good old days,
Just like the good old days.

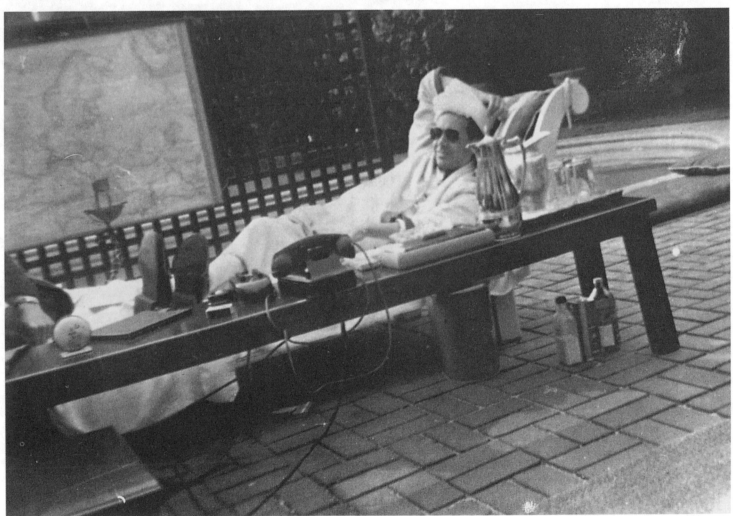

Brentwood, California, Summer 1944

SEVEN LIVELY ARTS (1944)

WHEN I WAS A LITTLE CUCKOO

VERSE

Last year down in dear Miami
I picked up such a sweet Hindu swami
And as by the sea we'd gayly stroll
He'd talk of the transmigration of the soul,
I found since the world's beginning,
I'd had many an outing and inning,
I'd been ev'ry sort of person and ev'ry kind of thing,
But my greatest success was as a bird on the wing.

REFRAIN 1

When I was a little cuckoo
Was I full of mischief? Oh boy!
Flitting hither and thither
Far from mither and fither,
I lived in a dither
Of joy.
Each night meant a new flirtation,
Each dawn another fond goodbye,
And if my wings became singed
And my tail, a bit fringed,
Just a little cuckoo was I.

Singing "Cuckoo,
Cuckoo,"
As I soared through the heavens of blue,
Singing "Cuckoo,
Cuckoo,
Cuckoo, cuckoo
And how are you?"

To return to the soul and its trick transmigrations,
Let us now make a list of my many incarnations:

PATTER

I first lived on earth as a crab-apple tree
And Adam and Eve used to romp under me,
I soon re-appeared as Methuselah's wife
And slowly but certainly shortened his life,
Next, in Troy, I pursued a more frivolous course
As a fly on the tail of a big wooden horse,
As a royal snake-charmer I made Egypt gasp
When I struck Cleopatra for kicking my asp,
And when Rome caught on fire I wasn't dismayed
For I was the G-string on which Nero played,
In days medieval I had lots of sport
As a cute little cockroach in King Arthur's Court,
As Catherine of Russia I never once guessed

That I'd, one day, appear on the stage as Mae West
And under Napoleon I was more glamorous
As a tiny jade button on the emperor's truss.

REFRAIN 2

But
When I was a little cuckoo
Was I full of mischief? Oh boy!
Flitting hither and thither
Far from mither and fither,
I lived in a dither
Of joy.
There was Bob White, Tom-Tit, Cock Robin
And Bertie, what a dirty old jay
And if you think I was wrong
To be had for a song,
Just a little cuckoo was Ay.

Singing "Cuckoo,
Cuckoo,"
As I sailed through the heavens of blue,
Singing "Cuckoo,
Cuckoo,
Cuckoo, cuckoo
And how are you?"

Bert Lahr

198

The opening-night audience at
"Seven Lively Arts," at the Ziegfeld Theatre,
December 7, 1944. Among those present
are Mr. and Mrs. James Farley,
Miss Beth Leary, William Robinson,
Mr. and Mrs. William Rhinelander Stewart,
Mr. and Mrs. Bennett Cerf, Mr. and Mrs.
George S. Kaufman, Mr. and Mrs.
Oscar Hammerstein II, Lucius Beebe, Ward
Morehouse, Mr. and Mrs. Gilbert Miller, Ben Hecht, Mrs.
Lytle Hull, Mr. and Mrs. Robert Considine, Mrs.
Martin Beck, Mr. and Mrs. Jules Stein,
Mrs. Bert Lahr, Mrs. Kate Porter, Miss Libby Holman,
John Chapman, Joseph Mankiewicz, William
Weintraub, and Mr. and Mrs. Jules Brulatour, who
are to be seen in their front row seats (nearest
the camera) and who for many years
were never *not* present at opening nights.

Beatrice Lillie and Bert Lahr in the sketch *Fragonard in Pink*

DANCIN' TO A JUNGLE DRUM (LET'S END THE BEGUINE)

INTRODUCTION

A broken-down oriental dancer am I,
So take out your 'kerchiefs, children, and
    prepare to cry:

VERSE

If you ask me, as a dancer,
Why my life can't last for long
I can quickly give the answer,
I've been wrecked by a Broadway song.
For wherever I'm seen
Some orchestra guy
Begins the Beguine
Accompanied by
Drums,
Those jungle drums.
When I left my home in Bali
For a show in NYC
Some cheroot in Tin Pan Alley
Wrote this song espeshly for me,
So wherever I'm seen
Some orchestra guy
Begins the Beguine
Accompanied by
Drums,
Those jungle drums.

REFRAIN

I've a twisted neck and a twisted back
And a crack in my sacro-iliac,
What from?
How come?
From dancin' to a jungle drum,
On this hand no more can I wear a glove,
Just regard the sad expression of
That thumb,
How come?
From dancin' to a jungle drum,
How I'd love to do a polka to violins
And without these bangles bruisin' my little shins,
Yes, the jungle's more than I can take,
I'm so muscle-bound I can hardly shake
My tum,
How come?
From dancin' to a jungle drum.

PATTER

Due to that Beguine
I detest those songs
Where the groaners go for calico sarongs,
Due to that Beguine, I resent each tune
That involves an actor with an acter-oon,
I hate grass skirts, I hate grass huts,
I hate palm trees and as for cocoa, nuts!
In a Bob Hope picture, I hate that scene

Where a finished baritone begins The Beguine.
I'm tired of *not* seein' that old rope trick
And the mammal called a camel makes me slightly sick,
When I hear those off-key temple bells
"Hell's Bells" is what Ah yells,
I resent pineapples as a form of dress,
I detest bananas even more—or less,
Why doesn't dear Dorothy Lamour relax
And exchange that diaper for a pair of slacks?
How I hate to sleep in the bright moonlight
With a lizard on my gizzard through the perfumed night,
But the thing that leaves me completely numb
Is the beat, beat, beat,
And the tick, tick, tock,
And the drip, drip, drip
Of a jungle drum,
Oh those drums!
    [Drums]
Those jungle drums!
    [Drums]
Those boring drums!
    [Drums]
Those dreadful drums!
    [Drums]
Those bloody drums!
    [Drums]
Oh those Bim-bam
    Flim-flam,
    Slim-slam,
    Jim-jam,
    [Drums]
Beg your pardon, mam,
God damn drums!

PRETTY LITTLE MISSUS BELL

INTRODUCTION

Have you heard the tale they tell
Of the pretty little Missus Bell?

VERSE 1

Now pretty little Missus Bell
Was a bride in Happy Harbor
And she felt she'd married very well
When she got Bill Bell, the barber,
(In the town of Happy Harbor
Mister Bell was quite a barber).

REFRAIN 1

On Sunday nights, he'd take his bride
For a stroll around the city
And how he'd gloat when people cried
"Gee whitakers, ain't she pretty!"
No wonder ev'rybody fell
When she came to Happy Harbor
For a nifty chick was Missus Bell,
Married to Mister Bell, the barber.

Yes, married very well
Was the pretty little Missus Bell.

VERSE 2

Missus Bell, one day on the beach was out
For her daily dozen rehearsal
When along came a Hollywood talent scout
From a firm called Universal.
Cried the scout from Universal
"What a juicy little mersel!"

REFRAIN 2

Then he said he'd put her on the screen
And he swore from next October on
She'd be famous as a cross between
Patsy Kelly and Lady Oberon
So as soon as she could leave the sand,
Quite forgetting her rehearsal,
She divorced Bill Bell, the barber, and
Married the scout from Universal.
Yes, headed straight for hell
Was the former little Missus Bell.

VERSE 3

To the coast with him she quickly ran
But his heart became another's
So she found herself a cam'ra man
From a firm called Warner Brothers,
(All the stars at Warner Brothers
Much preferred him to the others).

REFRAIN 3

He was such a master of his craft,
This magician of magicians,
That she soon was being photographed
And in several new positions,
When she left his big projection room
Full of oh such cozy corners,
She divorced the talent scout and voom!
Married the cam'ra man from Warners.
Getting closer still to hell
Was the former little Missus Bell.

VERSE 4

Up the ladder now she thought she'd go
But he started to neglect her,
So one night she told her tale of woe
To a Paramount director
(As a Paramount director
He immediately necked her).

REFRAIN 4

Then he ordered wine and he ordered more
And it proved such a soothing ointment
That she stood next day at his office door
With a Chippendale couch appointment,
And when he said his only wish
Was to help her and protect her
She divorced the cam'ra man and swish!
Married the Paramount director.
At the very gates of hell
Was the former little Missus Bell.

VERSE 5

When he found she had no temp-rament,
He proceeded to vamoose her,
Then she chanced to meet a perfect gent
Called an M-G-M producer,
(As an M-G-M producer
He was qualified to goose her).

REFRAIN 5

Then he promised he would make her life
Even greater than Greer Garson's
And he said if she would be his wife
He'd show her Louella Parsons,
So as soon as he had ceased to spank
Her derrière, entre nous, sir,
She divorced the Paramountebank
And married the M-G-M producer.
So they stoked the fires in hell
For the former little Missus Bell.

VERSE 6

To be starred she never ceased to beg
So in self defense he starred her,
But our glamour girl laid such an egg
Even Mike Romanoff barred her,
(And when Mike Romanoff scrams you
It definitely damns you).

REFRAIN 6

Then she got divorced and, if you please,
Hurried back to Happy Harbor,
And you'll all be glad to hear that she's
Just been remarried to the barber.
She's back in Happy Harbor,
Remarried to the barber,
Thus ends the tale they tell
Of the pretty, itty, bitty Missus Bell,
Of the pretty, itty, bitty Missus Bell.

Beatrice Lillie and Billy Rose

DAINTY, QUAINTY ME

VERSE

I was such a fragile precocious little elf
When we still had a family tree
That my nanny taught me to call my little self
"Dainty, Quainty Me."
And although today I am sixty-two
And I soon'll be sixty-three,
I continue always to think about myself
As "Dainty, Quainty Me."

REFRAIN 1

I'm "Dainty, Quainty Me"
And from care completely free.
You may ask me how I can still feel gay,
Why, by merely ignoring the world of today.
I never answer the telephone
For a 'phone, I refuse to own.
So like the lark, I'm as happy as can be,
I'm "Dainty, Quainty Me."

PATTER

In the morning, after taking a bath,
Not a shower, I put on dear grand-papá's dressing-gown
And have a breakfast consisting of one coddled egg
And a cup of very weak jasmine tea;
Then after dusting my jades and writing a letter
To the Times, I embark
On a long walk in Gramercy Park.

My favorite flowers are sweetheart roses,
White violets, petunias, forget-me-nots, jack-in-the-pulpits,
And baby's breath;
As for tiger lilies they frighten me to death.

I lunch every day at Schrafft's on chicken broth,
A green salad and a Triscuit
And pistachio ice cream when I dare risk it.

I never accept an invitation to dinner unless
I can dine in a room that has pastel shades, with Adam furniture,
Queen Anne silver, Dresden china,
Georgian candle-sticks and the finest of damask napery;
I shun everything Dorothy Drapery.

In contrast to the paintings of Botticelli,
I consider the works of Picasso,
Van Gogh, Cézanne, Renoir, Matisse, Manet, and Monet
So much balonay.

When people talk about those columnists,
Such as Walter Winchell, Ed Sullivan, Westbrook Pegler,
Hedda Hopper, Dorothy Thompson,
Dorothy Kilgallen, and that frightfully
Vulgar girl they all call "Elsa,"
I take a Bromo-Seltza.

When any one mentions Martha Raye, Carmen Miranda,
Lana Turner, Anita Louise, Joan Davis, Betty Hutton,
Gregory Ratoff, Red Skelton, Monty Woolley, Don Ameche,

Jack Oakie, Sir Cedric Hardwicke, and other stars of the cinema,
I have to take an inema.

REFRAIN 2

I'm "Dainty, Quainty Me"
And from care completely free.
You may ask me how I can still feel gay,
Why, by merely ignoring the world of today.
Whene'er I feel like mis-behaving
I go out and buy a French engraving
So like the lark, I'm as happy as can be,
Little old "Dainty, Quainty Me."

PATTER

As against those currently popular women novelists,
Such as Edna Ferber, Fannie Hurst, Kathleen Norris, and
Lillian Smith; (you know her book
Strange Fruit has recently been banned in Boston),
Give me Jane Austen.

Though such poets as Archibald MacLeish,
Edna St. Vincent Millay, Gertrude Stein, Ogden Nash,
And Dorothy Parker may be wiser and wittier,
Give me John Greenleaf Whittier.

On Sunday, when everybody else is following Dick Tracy,
Terry and the Pirates, Flash Gordon, Super-man,
The Gumps, Barney Google, Joe Palooka, Pop-eye, Lil Abner,
And all those other menaces,
I'm reading either Deuteronomy, Leviticus, Exodus, or Genesis.

I far prefer hearing a string quartet by Bach, Beethoven,
Mozart, Haydn, or Handel
Than listening to Lady Mendl.

When I dine alone, I prefer The Brevoort, The LaFayette,
The Murray Hill Hotel, or the Union (that's my one New York Club),
To dining at the Stork Club.

Last night I had a sick headache
While I was standing in the graveyard of Trinity Church
Looking at the steeple, but I wasn't afraid
Because I always carry with me, Lydia Pinkham's Pink
Pills for Pale People.

Those magazines like the Cosmopolitan,
The Red Book, the New Yorker, Collier's, McCall's, True Detective,
True Love Stories, and True Confessions,
I consider trash infernal,
Personally, I only read the Ladies Home Journal.

As for the women folk, rather than spend an evening
With those advanced girls such as Nancy Astor, Anne Morgan,
Helen Gahagan, and Clare Booth Luce,
That green-eyed leopardess, I'd much rather climb some
Arcadian hill and dally with a shepherdess.

The Times is my favorite newspaper.
I also like The Tribune and The Sun.
I tolerate the World-Telegram.
But somebody should certainly condemn
The News, The Mirror,
The Journal-American, The Post, and for Marshall's
If not for Heaven's sake, PM.

HENCE IT DON'T MAKE SENSE

VERSE

When we use words like scat, cat,
Skin, fin, reet, pleat,
The squares want to give up the heat-seat
For the jive we talk today,
But when I hear those hicks talk
That straight-from-the-sticks talk
It don't make sense, I say,
When they use the slang of yesterday,
In the following way:

REFRAIN 1

Now a girl is a babe
And a babe is a chick
And a chick is a bird
And a bird is a fowl
And a fowl is a ball
And a ball is a great big dance,
But a girl ain't a great big dance,
Hence it don't make sense.

EXTRA REFRAINS

Now a skirt is a gal
And a gal is a doll
And a doll is a dear
And a deer is a buck
And a buck is a man
And a man is a pair of pents
But a skirt ain't a pair of pents,
Hence it don't make sense.

Now a skunk is a fur
And a fur is a fleece
And a fleece is a theft
And a theft is a sin
And a sin is taboo,
And Tabu is perfume from France
But a skunk ain't perfume from France,
Hence it don't make sense.

Now a jerk is a pull
And a pull is a tug
And a tug is a craft
And a craft is a trick
And a trick is a gal
And a gal is a big romence
But a jerk ain't a big romence,
Hence it don't make sense.

Now a bra is a lift
And a lift is a boost
And a boost is a plug
And a plug is a stop
And a stop is a block
And a block is a good defense
But a bra ain't a good defense,
Hence it don't make sense.

Now a virgin's a miss
And a miss is a strike
And a strike is a blow
And a blow is a toot
And a toot is a jag
And a jag is a big expense
But a virgin ain't a big expense,
Hence it don't make sense.

First act finale—Benny Goodman and Ensemble

EV'RY TIME WE SAY GOODBYE

VERSE

We love each other so deeply
That I ask you this, sweetheart,
Why should we quarrel ever,
Why can't we be enough clever
Never to part?

REFRAIN

Ev'ry time we say goodbye
I die a little,
Ev'ry time we say goodbye

I wonder why a little,
Why the gods above me
Who must be in the know
Think so little of me
They allow you to go,
When you're near there's such an air
Of Spring about it
I can hear a lark somewhere
Begin to sing about it,
There's no love-song finer
But how strange
The change
From major to minor
Ev'ry time we say goodbye.
Ev'ry single time we say goodbye.

Cole's sketches for the opening and finish of *Ev'rytime We Say Goodbye*

I WROTE A PLAY

I wrote a play
And it took me many a day,
It took me many a month, hear, hear!
It took me many a hungry year,
Yet I still thrill when I say
That I wrote a play.

When I finished my play
I said to myself one day
"It must have a title with sweep and swirl."
Then I suddenly thought of it, "Boy Loves Girl,"
So "Boy Loves Girl" right away
Became the name of my play.

Then I packed my play
And carried it quick to Broadway
Where I dug up a millionaire friend of mine
Who took Gilbert Miller somewhere to dine
And filled the great gourmet so full of feed
That finally Gilbert agreed to read
Without a moment's delay,
"Boy Loves Girl," my pearl of a play.

A year passed and a day
Then Gilbert 'phoned me to say
"I think your play is excellent stuff
But hardly European enough
Yet with slight alterations it ought to go far,
So it's being re-written by Shaw and Molnar
And I'm changing the title from 'Boy Loves Girl'
To 'Hungarian Princess Loves British Earl.' "
So I went to his office that day
And stole my pretty play away.

I next took my play
To the Theatre Guild, heigh, heigh!
They read it and said "It's charming stuff
But, of course, for the Guild not long enough,
So Eugene O'Neill will re-write the whole thing
And when it's longer than Wagner's Ring
We'll start rehearsing your play at once
As we've simply got to revive the Lunts,
But as 'Boy Loves Girl' doesn't quite fit in
We have changed the title to 'Alfred Loves Lynn.' "
So I rushed to their office that day
And snatched my darling play away.

Then heavy-hearted I trod
With my play to Michael Todd,
He read it and said "It's terrific stuff
But for Broadway it ain't big and dirty enough,
Still I'm gonna produce it, just for a lark,
I'm taking the Mall in Central Park,
It's being re-written by Gypsy Rose,

I'm hiring a nudist to do the clo'es,
The cast will consist of Man Mountain Dean
And a boat-load of babes from the Argentine
And I've changed the title, so help me God,
To 'The Love Life of Michael Todd.' "
So I ran to his office that day
And plucked my precious play away.

Then I sent to the coast my play,
And Sam Goldwyn 'phoned me to say
"Hello, my boy, and au revoir,
Now listen slowly and have a cigar.

Your lousy play is a stinkeroo,
I just read part of it all the way through
But I like the title extremely much,
Somehow 'Boy Loves Girl' has the Goldwyn touch,
Now I've bought a play that was tough to get
Called 'Romeo and Juliet'
But if the title was 'Boy Loves Girl'
What a helluva picture for Milton Berle!
And if you'll sell me that title, by heck,
I'll wire you at once a blanket check."
So I sold him the title that day
And that's what became of my play,
Yes, that's what became of my play.

Orson Welles produced, directed, and performed in this musical comedy extravaganza version of Jules Verne's *Around the World in Eighty Days*. Cole thoroughly enjoyed working with Orson Welles; he said later that he never knew anyone in the theater who worked harder than Welles or was kinder to his cast. Michael Todd, who had been the show's original producer but had withdrawn before the opening, retained the screen rights and subsequently made a fortune from the movie version.

AROUND THE WORLD IN EIGHTY DAYS (1946)

LOOK WHAT I FOUND

VERSE

So wrong seemed the world
I faced it with rage,
While hopeless I whirled
Like a mouse in a cage,
Till you came in range
Not that! life was worth!
Then presto change,
I'm the happiest girl
On earth.

REFRAIN

Flow, sweet music,
Flow in rippling sound.
Flow, sweet music,
Look, look, look what I have found,
Sing, you song birds,
Make the hills resound,
Sing higher, oh song bird,
Look, look, look what I found.
From nights of care
And dismal despair
With days only lonely in view
I woke to see
How sweet life could be,
That great big moment when I found you,
So chime, gay joy-bells,
Chime the world around,
Chime, all the time, joy-bells,
Look, look, look,
Look, look, look,
Look, look, look, look what I found.

PIPE DREAMING

On this lonely night
When my pipe I light,
Through the rings of white

You're there as before,
As I see you, dear,
All my hopes re-appear
For again I am near
The one I adore.
Once our lips have met
I completely forget
All the sun-down till dawn.
Heartaches I've gone
Through,
Love is life sublime,
Ev'ry moment that I'm
Only wasting my time
Pipe-dreaming of you,
Pipe-dreaming of you,
Far away you,
Far away you,
Precious you,
Precious you,
Far away you,
Far away you.
You,
You.

THE PIRATE (1948)

BE A CLOWN

VERSE

I'll remember forever,
When I was but three,
Mama, who was clever
Remarking to me:
If, son, when you're grown up,
You want ev'rything nice,
I've got your future sewn up
If you take this advice:

REFRAIN 1

Be a clown, be a clown,
All the world loves a clown,
Act the fool, play the calf
And you'll always have the last laugh.
Wear the cap and the bells
And you'll rate with all the great swells,
If you become a doctor, folks'll face you
    with dread,
If you become a dentist, they'll be glad
    when you're dead,
You'll get a bigger hand if you can stand
    on your head,
Be a clown, be a clown, be a clown.

REFRAIN 2

Be a clown, be a clown,
All the world loves a clown,
Be a crazy buffoon
And the 'demoiselles'll all swoon.
Dress in huge, baggy pants
And you'll ride the road to romance.
A butcher or a baker, ladies never embrace,
A barber for a beau would be a social disgrace,
They all'll come to call if you can fall
    on your face,
Be a clown, be a clown, be a clown.

REFRAIN 3

Be a clown, be a clown,
All the world loves a clown,
Show 'em tricks, tell 'em jokes
And you'll only stop with top folks.
Be a crack jackanapes
And they'll imitate you like apes.
Why be a great composer with your rent
    in arrears?
Why be a major poet and you'll owe
    it for years?
When crowds'll pay to giggle if you wiggle
    your ears,
Be a clown, be a clown, be a clown.

REFRAIN 4

Be a clown, be a clown,
All the world loves a clown,
If you just make 'em roar
Watch your mountebank account soar.
Wear a painted mustache
And you're sure to make a big splash.
A college education I should never propose,
A bachelor's degree won't even keep
    you in clo'es,
But millions you will win if you can spin
    on your nose,
Be a clown, be a clown, be a clown.

REFRAIN 5

Be a clown, be a clown,
All the world loves a clown,
Be the poor silly ass
And you'll always travel first class,
Give 'em quips, give 'em fun,
And they'll pay to say you're A-1.
If you become a farmer you've the weather
    to buck,
If you become a gambler, you'll be stuck
    with your luck,
But jack you'll never lack if you can
    quack like a duck,
(Quack, quack, quack, quack)
Be a clown, be a clown, be a clown.

Gene Kelly and Judy Garland

Annabelle Hill leads the Ensemble in *Another Op'nin', Another Show*

The New Century Theater

Producer Lemuei Ayers designed the sets

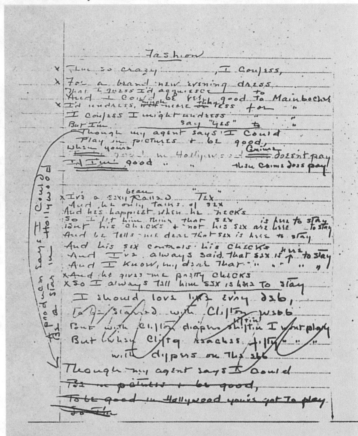

Sketches for *Always True to You in My Fashion*

Harold Lang and Lisa Kirk

Patricia Morison and Alfred Drake sing *Wunderbar*

KISS ME, KATE (1948)

ANOTHER OP'NIN', ANOTHER SHOW

Another op'nin', another show
In Philly, Boston or Baltimo'e,
A chance for stage-folks to say "hello,"
Another op'nin' of another show.
Another job that you hope, at last,
Will make your future forget your past,
Another pain where the ulcers grow,
Another op'nin' of another show.
Four weeks, you rehearse and rehearse,
Three weeks, and it couldn't be worse,
One week, will it ever be right?
Then out o' the hat, it's that big
        first night!
The overture is about to start,
You cross your fingers and hold your heart,
It's curtain time and away we go.
Another op'nin',
Just another op'nin' of another show.

WUNDERBAR

VERSE

Gazing down on the Jungfrau
From our secret chalet for two,
Let us drink, Liebchen mein,
In the moonlight benign,
To the joy of our dream come true.

REFRAIN

Wunderbar, wunderbar!
What a perfect night for love,
Here am I, here you are,
Why, it's truly wunderbar!
Wunderbar, wunderbar!
We're alone and hand in glove,
Not a cloud near or far,
Why, it's more than wunderbar!
Say you care, dear,
For you madly,
Say you long, dear,
For your kiss,
Do you swear, dear?
Darling, gladly,
Life's divine, dear!
And you're mine, dear!
Wunderbar, wunderbar!
There's our fav'rite star above,
What a bright shining star,
Like our love, it's wunderbar!

WHY CAN'T YOU BEHAVE?

Why can't you behave?
Oh, why can't you behave?
After all the things you told me
And the promises that you gave
Oh, why can't you behave?

Why can't you be good?
And do just as you should?
Won't you turn that new leaf over
So your baby can be your slave?
Oh, why can't you behave?

There's a farm I know near my old home town
Where we two can go and try settlin' down.
There I'll care for you forever,
Well at least 'til you dig my grave.
Oh, why can't you behave?

WE OPEN IN VENICE

VERSE

A troupe of strolling players are we,
Not stars like L.B. Mayer's are we
But just a simple band
Who roams about the land
Dispensing fol-de-rol frivolitee,
Mere folk who give distraction are we,
No Theatre Guild attraction are we
But just a crazy group
That never ceases to troop
Around the map of little Italee.

REFRAIN 1

We open in Venice,
We next play Verona,
Then on to Cremona.
Lotsa laughs in Cremona.
Our next jump is Parma,
That dopey, mopey menace,
Then Mantua, then Padua,
Then we open again, where?

REFRAIN 2

We open in Venice,
We next play Verona,
Then on to Cremona.
Lotsa bars in Cremona.
The next jump is Parma,
That beerless, cheerless menace,
Then Mantua, then Padua,
Then we open again, where?

REFRAIN 3

We open in Venice,
We next play Verona,
Then on to Cremona.
Lotsa dough in Cremona.
Our next jump is Parma,
That stingy, dingy menace,
Then Mantua, then Padua,
Then we open again, where?

REFRAIN 4

We open in Venice,
We next play Verona,
Then on to Cremona.
Lotsa quail in Cremona.
Our next jump is Parma,
That heartless, tartless menace
Then Mantua, then Padua
Then we open again, where?
In Venice.

SO IN LOVE

Strange, dear, but true, dear,
When I'm close to you, dear,
The stars fill the sky,
So in love with you am I.
Even without you
My arms fold about you.
You know darling why,
So in love with you am I.
In love with the night mysterious
The night when you first were there,
In love with my joy delirious
When I knew that you could care.
So taunt me and hurt me,
Deceive me, desert me,
I'm yours 'til I die,
So in love,
So in love,
So in love with you, my love, am I.

WERE THINE THAT SPECIAL FACE

VERSE

I wrote a poem
In classic style.
I wrote it with my tongue in my cheek
And my lips in a smile,
But today my poem
Has a meaning so new
For to my surprise
It suddenly applies
To my darling—to you.

REFRAIN

Were thine that special face
The face that fills my dreaming,
Were thine the rhythm'd grace,
Were thine the form so lithe and slender,
Were thine the arms so warm, so tender,
Were thine the kiss divine,
Were thine the love for me,
The love that fills my dreaming,
When all these charms are thine
Then you'll be mine, all mine.

① 11

W.v.s

If my wife has a bag of gold
Do I care if the bag be old

I'm A good woman, so 'tis said
Is none who's completely dead   but
(There are many good woman but they are all dead)
A viper's Tongue
Take away the light + all women are the same.   alike.

chorus
If she cold as
the rage like the winter breeze
On the rough Adriatic seas
Tho she rage like an angry boar
spit a Tiger cat
Do I mind if she's wild or Tame
In the dark, they are all the same

I should not feel
Should I feel disturbed one bit
If she be but a quarter wit

There are good women so 'tis said
" " " when they're dead
(II) She hiss like a cornered rat
" Kiss " tiger cat
But they're bad women when they're not in bed

②

W.v.s

decrease my joy
(Should she make for the baker's boy)
Twouldn't give me the slightest shock
now + then should
If her knees should at moments, knock

completely
If her eyes were a wee bit crossed
with this deal I shall feel content
If my bride can provide the rent
I've come to find a wealthy wife in Padua
If wealthy she then happily me in Padua   healthy

can
If she only could talk of clo'es
she powders
While a powdring her god-damned nose
she's a bloody bore
If she fight like a raging boar
I have oft stuck a boar before
There are wise women so 'tis said
They are fools when they're not in bed
but
If her looks make me cry "For shame!"   teeth
In the dark they are all the same
odjooks - zounds gadzooks, hoity-toity
plague take you,

I've come to wive it wealthily in Padua,
If wealthily then happily in Padua.
If my wife has a bag of gold
Do I care if the bag be old?
I've come to wive it wealthily in Padua.

I've come to wive it wealthily in Padua,
I heard you mutter "Zounds, a loathsome lad you are."
I shall not be disturbed one bit
If she be but a quarter-wit
If she only can talk of clo'es
While she powders her God-damned nose,
I've come to wive it wealthily in Padua.

I've come to wive it wealthily in Padua,
I heard you say "Gadzooks, completely mad you are!"
'Twouldn't give me the slightest shock
If her knees, now and then, should knock,
If her eyes were a wee bit crossed,
Were she wearing the hair she'd lost,
Still the damsel I'll make my dame,
In the dark they are all the same,
I've come to wive it wealthily in Padua.

I've come to wive it wealthily in Padua.
I heard you say "Good gad but what a cad you are!"
Do I mind if she fret and fuss
If she fume like Vesuvius
If she roar like a winter breeze
On the rough Adriatic seas,
If she scream like a teething brat,
If she scratch like a tiger cat,
If she fight like a raging boar,
I have oft stuck a pig before,
I've come to wive it wealthily in Padua.
With a hunny, nunny, nunny
And a hey, hey, hey,
Not to mention money, money
For a rainy day,
I've come to wive it wealthily in Padua.

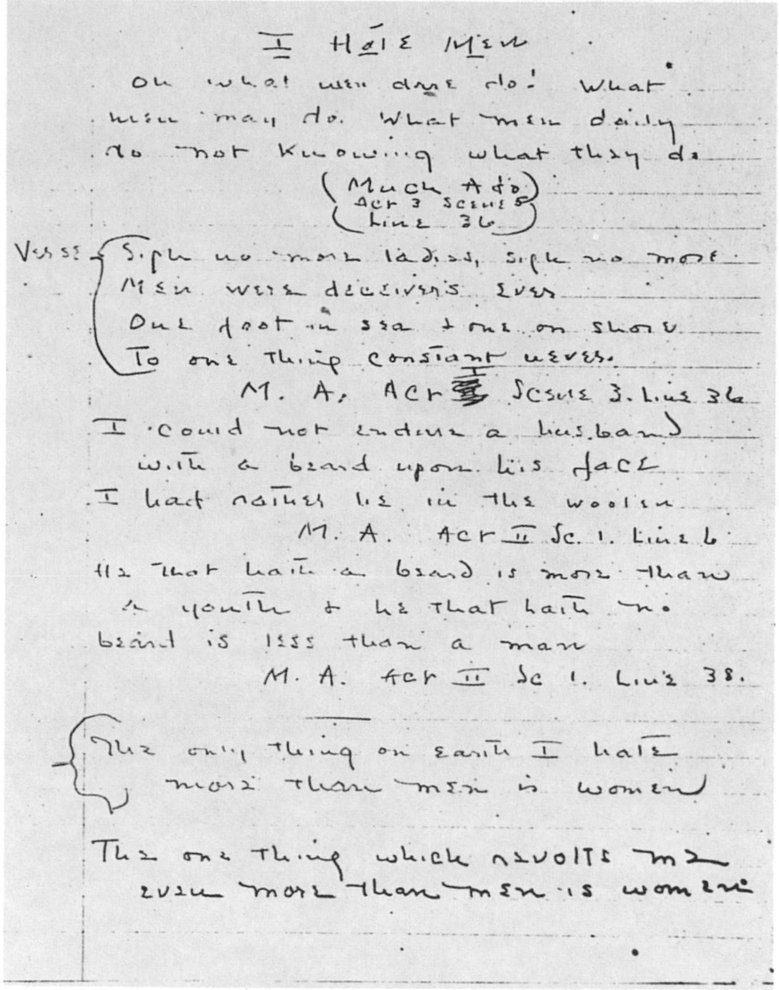

I HATE MEN

REFRAIN 1

I hate men.
I can't abide 'em even now and then,
Than ever marry one of them, I'd rest a virgin rather,
For husbands are a boring lot and only give you bother.
Of course, I'm awf'ily glad that Mother had to marry Father
But I hate men.
I hate 'em all, from modern man 'way back to Father Adam,
He sired Cain and Abel though the Lord above forbade 'em,
I'd hate both Cain and Abel though Betty Grable had 'em,
Oh, I hate men!

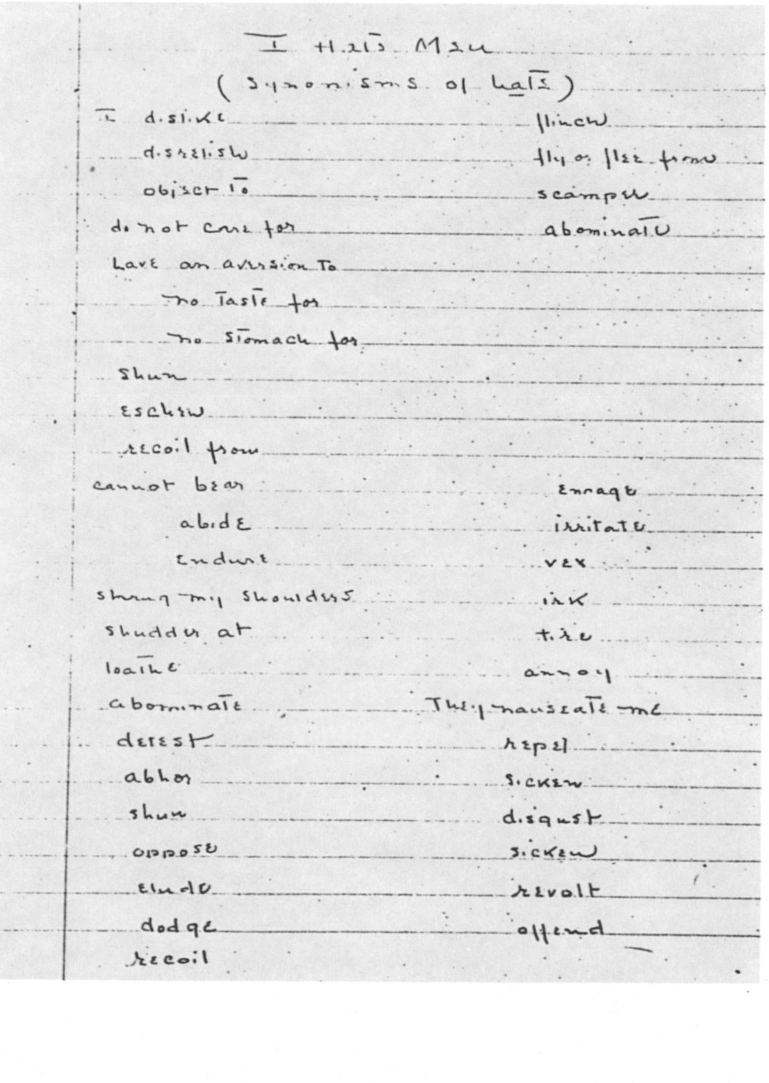

REFRAIN 2

I hate men.
They should be kept like piggies in a pen.
You may be wooed by Jack the Tar, so charming and so chipper,
But it you take him for a mate, be sure that you're the skipper
For Jack the Tar can go too far. Remember Jack the Ripper?
Oh, I hate men.
Of all the types I've ever met within our democracy,
I hate the most the athlete with his manner bold and brassy,
He may have hair upon his chest but, sister, so has Lassie.
Oh, I hate men!

REFRAIN 3

I hate men.
Their worth upon this earth I dinna ken.
Avoid the trav'ling salesman though a tempting Tom he may be,
From China he will bring you jade and perfume from Araby
But don't forget 'tis he who'll have the fun and thee the baby,
Oh, I hate men.
If thou shouldst wed a bus'ness man, be wary, oh be wary.
He'll tell you he's detained in town on bus'ness necessary,
His bus'ness is the bus'ness which he gives his secretary,
Oh, I hate men!

REFRAIN 4

I hate men.
Though roosters they, I will not play the hen.
If you espouse an older man through girlish optimism,
He'll always stay at home at night and make no criticism,
Though you may call it "love," the doctors call it "rheumatism."
Oh, I hate men.
From all I've read, alone in bed, from A to Zed, about 'em.
Since love is blind, then from the mind, all womankind
should rout 'em,
But, ladies, you must answer too, what would we do without 'em?
Still, I hate men!

TOO DARN HOT

VERSE 1

It's too darn hot,
It's too darn hot,
I'd like to sup with my baby tonight
And play the pup with my baby tonight
I'd like to sup with my baby tonight
And play the pup with my baby tonight
But I ain't up to my baby tonight
'Cause it's too darn hot.

It's too darn hot,
It's too darn hot,
I'd like to stop for my baby tonight
And blow my top with my baby tonight
I'd like to stop for my baby tonight
And blow my top with my baby tonight
But I'd be a flop with my baby tonight
'Cause it's too darn hot.

It's too darn hot,
It's too darn hot,
I'd like to fool with my baby tonight
Break ev'ry rule with my baby tonight
I'd like to fool with my baby tonight
Break ev'ry rule with my baby tonight
But pillow, you'll be my baby tonight
'Cause it's too darn hot.

REFRAIN 1

According to the Kinsey report
Ev'ry average man you know
Much prefers to play his favorite sport
When the temperature is low
But when the thermometer goes 'way up
And the weather is sizzling hot
Mister Adam
For his madam,
Is not
'Cause it's too, too,
Too darn hot,
It's too darn hot.

VERSE 2

It's too darn hot,
It's too darn hot,
I'd like to call on my baby tonight
And give my all to my baby tonight
I'd like to call on my baby tonight
And give my all to my baby tonight
But I can't play ball with my baby tonight
'Cause it's too darn hot.

It's too darn hot,
It's too darn hot,
I'd like to meet with my baby tonight
Get off my feet with my baby tonight
I'd like to meet with my baby tonight
Get off my feet with my baby tonight
But no repeat with my baby tonight
'Cause it's too darn hot.

It's too darn hot,
It's too darn hot,
I'd like to coo with my baby tonight
And pitch the woo with my baby tonight
I'd like to coo with my baby tonight
And pitch the woo with my baby tonight
But, brother, you bite my baby tonight
'Cause it's too darn hot.

REFRAIN 2

According to the Kinsey report
Ev'ry average man you know
Much prefers to play his favorite sport
When the temperature is low
But when the thermometer goes 'way up
And the weather is sizzling hot
Mister Gob
For his squab,
A marine
For his queen,
A G.I.

For his cutie-pie
Is not
'Cause it's too, too,
Too darn hot,
It's too darn hot.

WHERE IS THE LIFE THAT LATE I LED?

VERSE

Since I reached the charming age of puberty
And began to finger feminine curls,
Like a show that's typically Shuberty
I have always had a multitude of girls
But now that a married man, at last, am I,
How aware of my dear, departed past am I.

Cole and Bella Spewack at rehearsal of "Kiss Me, Kate"

Late

Delizia	Lucia (stiletta from)	Teresina
Della	Lucretia	Trista
Delphine	Luella	Una
Diana	Lydia	Valentina
Docilla, Docila	Margarita	Vera
Donata	Marina	Vittoria
Doncella	Marta	Zerlina
Doria	Maria	Zita
Edita	Miranda	
Elena	Monica	
Elisa, Elsia	Nella	
Eva	Nora	
Fedra	Norma	
Flora	Octavia	
Francesca	Olivia	
Gabriella	Patricia	
Isabella	Primavera	
Juanita	Regina	
Josephina	Rosa	
Julia (Apulia)	Rosalia	
Justina	Rosalina	
Lavinia	Rosanna	
Lelia	Sabina	
Lena	Serafina	
Letitia	Susanna	
Livia		

REFRAIN 1

Where is the life that late I led?
Where is it now? Totally dead.
Where is the fun I used to find?
Where has it gone? Gone with the wind.
A married life may all be well
But raising an heir
Could never compare
With raising a bit of hell
So I repeat what first I said,
Where is the life that late I?

PATTER 1

In dear Milano, where are you, Momo,
Still selling those pictures of the scriptures in the duomo?
And Carolina, where are you, Lina,
Still peddling your pizza in the streets o' Taormina?
And in Firenze, where are you, Alice,
Still there is your pretty, itty-bitty Pitti palace?
And sweet Lucretia, so young and gay-ee?
What scandalous doin's in the ruins of Pompeii!

REFRAIN 2

Where is the life that late I led?
Where is it now? Totally dead.
Where is the fun I used to find?
Where has it gone? Gone with the wind.
The marriage game is quite alright,
Yes, during the day
It's easy to play
But oh what a bore at night
So I repeat what first I said,
Where is the life that late I?

PATTER 2

Where is Rebecca, my Becki-weckio,
Again is she cruising that amusing Ponte Vecchio?
Where is Fedora, the wild virago?
It's lucky I missed her gangster sister from Chicago,
Where is Venetia who loved to chat so,
Could still she be drinkin, in her stinkin', pink palazzo?
And lovely Lisa, I thank you, Lisa,
You gave a new meaning to the leaning tow'r of Pisa.

REFRAIN 3

Where is the life that late I led?
Where is it now? Totally dead.
Where is the fun I used to find?
Where has it gone? Gone with the wind.
I've oft been told of nuptial bliss
But what do you do,
A quarter to two,
With only a shrew to kiss?
So I repeat what first I said,
Where is the life that late I led?

ALWAYS TRUE TO YOU IN MY FASHION

VERSE

Oh Bill,
Why can't you behave
Why can't you behave?
How in hell can you be jealous
When you know, baby, I'm your slave?
I'm just mad for you,
And I'll always be
But naturally.

REFRAIN 1

If a custom-tailored vet
Asks me out for something wet,
When the vet begins to pet, I cry "Hooray!"
But I'm always true to you, darlin', in my fashion,
Yes, I'm always true to you, darlin', in my way.
I enjoy a tender pass
By the boss of Boston, Mass.
Though his pass is middle-class and notta Backa Bay
But I'm always true to you, darlin', in my fashion,
Yes, I'm always true to you, darlin', in my way.
There's a madman known as "Mack"
Who is planning to attack,
If his mad attack means a Cadillac, Okay!
But I'm always true to you, darlin', in my fashion,
Yes, I'm always true to you, darlin', in my way.

REFRAIN 2

I've been asked to have a meal
By a big tycoon in steel,
If the meal includes a deal, accept I may.
But I'm always true to you, darlin', in my fashion,
Yes, I'm always true to you, darlin', in my way.
I could never curl my lip
To a dazzlin' diamond clip
Though the clip meant "let 'er rip," I'd not say "Nay!"

But I'm always true to you, darlin', in my fashion,
Yes, I'm always true to you, darlin', in my way.
There's an oil man known as "Tex"
Who is keen to give me checks
And his checks, I fear, mean that sex is here to stay!
But I'm always true to you, darlin', in my fashion,
Yes, I'm always true to you, darlin', in my way.

REFRAIN 3

There's a wealthy Hindu priest
Who's a wolf, to say the least,
When the priest goes too far east, I also stray.
But I'm always true to you, darlin', in my fashion,
Yes, I'm always true to you, darlin', in my way.
There's a lush from Portland, Ore.
Who is rich but sich a bore
When the bore falls on the floor, I let him lay.
But I'm always true to you, darlin', in my fashion,
Yes, I'm always true to you, darlin', in my way.
Mister Harris, plutocrat
Wants to give my cheek a pat,
If the Harris pat
Means a Paris hat,

Bébé, Oolala!
Mais je suis toujours fidéle, darlin', in my fashion,
Oui, je suis toujours fidéle, darlin', in my way.

REFRAIN 4

From Ohio Mister Thorne
Calls me up from night 'til morn,
Mister Thorne once cornered corn and that ain't hay.
But I'm always true to you, darlin', in my fashion,
Yes, I'm always true to you, darlin', in my way.
From Milwaukee, Mister Fritz
Often moves me to the Ritz,
Mister Fritz is full of Schlitz and full of play.
But I'm always true to you, darlin', in my fashion,
Yes, I'm always true to you, darlin', in my way.
Mister Gable, I mean Clark,
Wants me on his boat to park,
If the Gable boat
Means a sable coat,
Anchors aweigh!
But I'm always true to you, darlin', in my fashion,
Yes, I'm always true to you, darlin', in my way.

BIANCA

VERSE 1

While rehearsing with Bianca
(She's the darling I adore),
Off stage I found
She's been around
But I still love her more and more;
So I've written her a love-song
Though I'm just an amateur,
I'll sing it through
For all of you
To see if it's worthy of her,
Are yuh list'nin'?

REFRAIN

Bianca, Bianca,
Oh, baby, will you be mine?
Bianca, Bianca,
You'd better answer yes or Poppa spanka,
To win you, Bianca,
There's nothing I would not do,
I would gladly give up coffee for Sanka,
Even Sanka, Bianca, for you.

VERSE 2

In the street called "Tin-pan Alley"
I have suffered endless wrongs
For I'm the dog
Who writes incog.
All of Cole Porter's Broadway songs.
Here's a new one to Bianca,
Bless her heart and bless her soul,
I'll sing it through
For all of you
Then take it away, Cole.

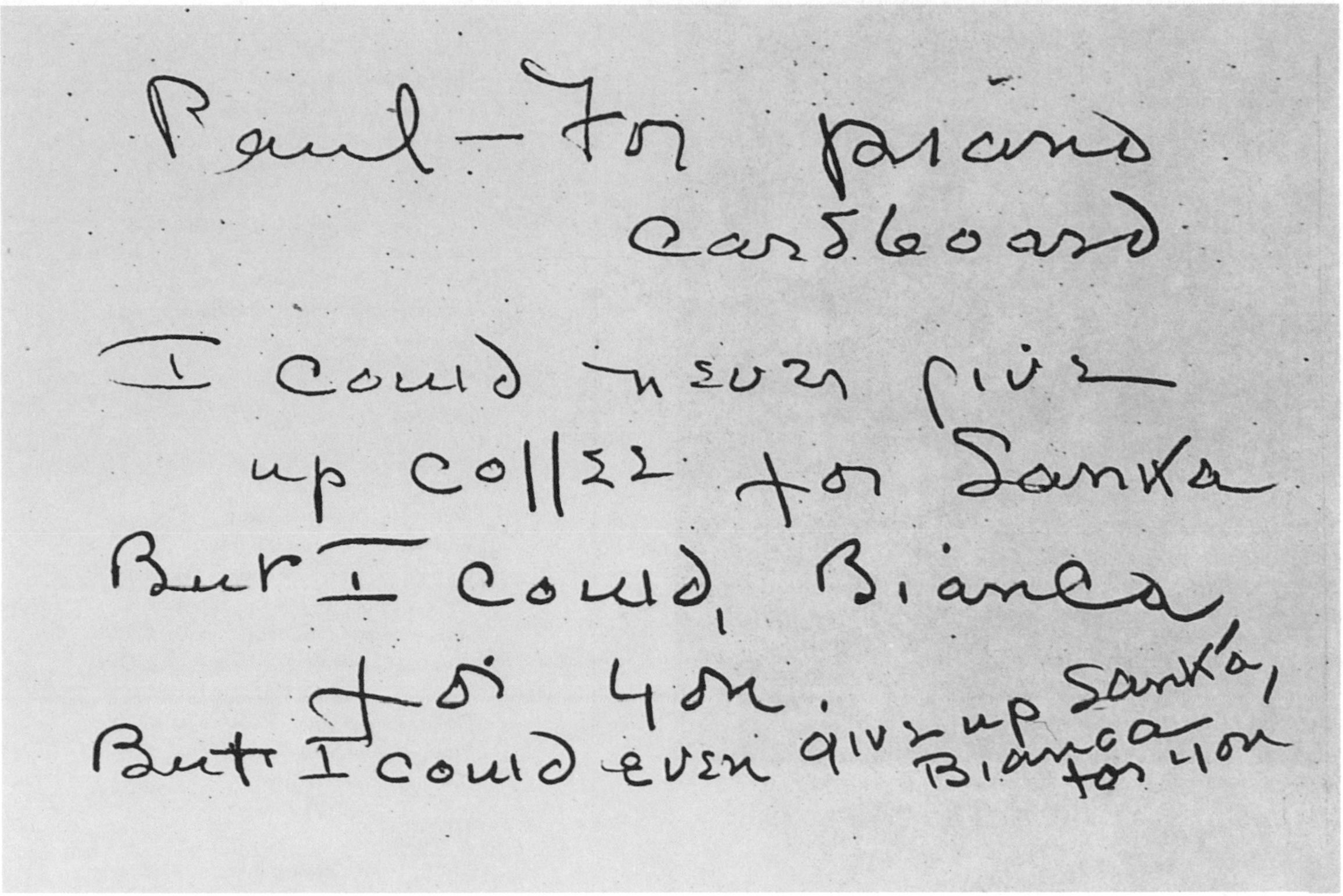

Paul — For piano
cardboard

I could never give
up coffee for Sanka
But I could, Bianca
for you.
But I could even give up Sanka,
Bianca for you

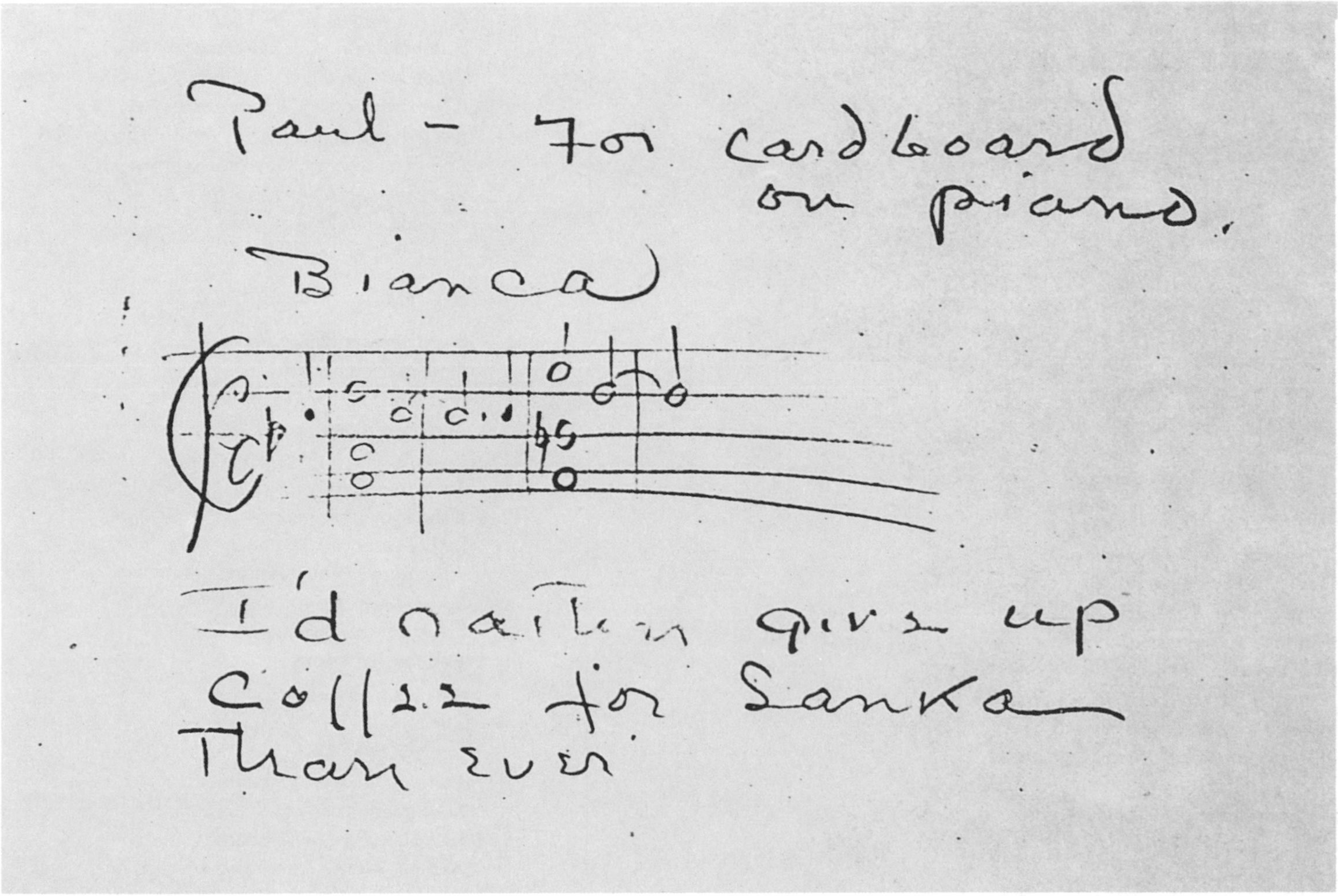

Paul — For cardboard
on piano.
Bianca

I'd rather give up
coffee for Sanka
Than ever

Jack Diamond and Harry Clark in *Brush Up Your Shakespeare*

BRUSH UP YOUR SHAKESPEARE

VERSE

The girls today in society
Go for classical poetry
So to win their hearts one must quote with ease
Aeschylus and Euripides.
One must know Homer and, b'lieve me, bo,
Sophocles, also Sappho-ho.
Unless you know Shelley and Keats and Pope,
Dainty debbies will call you a dope.
But the poet of them all
Who will start 'em simply ravin'
Is the poet people call
"The bard of Stratford-on-Avon."

REFRAIN 1

Brush up your Shakespeare,
Start quoting him now,
Brush up your Shakespeare
And the women you will wow.
Just declaim a few lines from "Othella"
And they'll think you're a helluva fella,
If your blonde won't respond when you flatter 'er
Tell her what Tony told Cleopaterer,
If she fights when her clothes you are mussing,
What are clothes? "Much Ado About Nussing."
Brush up your Shakespeare
And they'll all kowtow.

REFRAIN 2

Brush up your Shakespeare,
Start quoting him now,
Brush up your Shakespeare
And the women you will wow.
With the wife of the British embessida
Try a crack out of "Troilus and Cressida,"
If she says she won't buy it or tike it
Make her tike it, what's more, "As You Like It."
If she says your behavior is heinous
Kick her right in the "Coriolanus,"
Brush up your Shakespeare
And they'll all kowtow.

REFRAIN 3

Brush up your Shakespeare,
Start quoting him now,
Brush up your Shakespeare
And the women you will wow.
If you can't be a ham and do "Hamlet"
They will not give a damn or a damnlet,
Just recite an occasional sonnet
And your lap'll have "Honey" upon it,
When your baby is pleading for pleasure
Let her sample your "Measure for Measure"
Brush up your Shakespeare
And they'll all kowtow.

REFRAIN 4

Brush up your Shakespeare,
Start quoting him now,
Brush up your Shakespeare
And the women you will wow.
Better mention "The Merchant of Venice"
When her sweet pound o'flesh you would menace,
If her virtue, at first, she defends—well,
Just remind her that "All's Well That End's Well,"
And if still she won't give you a bonus
You know what Venus got from Adonis!
Brush up your Shakespeare
And they'll all kowtow.

REFRAIN 5

Brush up your Shakespeare
Start quoting him now,
Brush up your Shakespeare
And the women you will wow.
If your goil is a Washington Heights dream
Treat the kid to "A Midsummer Night's Dream,"
If she then wants an all-by-herself night
Let her rest ev'ry 'leventh or "Twelfth Night,"
If because of your heat she gets huffy
Simply play on and "Lay on, Macduffy!"
Brush up your Shakespeare
And they'll all kowtow.

Second Act Finale

ENCORE CURTAIN

Brush up your Shakespeare,
Start quoting him now,
Brush up your Shakespeare
And the women you will wow.

So tonight just recite to your matey
"Kiss me, Kate, Kiss me, Kate, Kiss me, Katey,"
Brush up your Shakespeare
And they'll all kowtow.

I AM ASHAMED THAT WOMEN ARE SO SIMPLE

I am ashamed that women are so simple
To offer war where they should kneel for peace
Or seek for rule, supremacy, and sway
When they are bound to serve, love, and obey.
Why are our bodies soft and weak, and smooth,
Unapt to toil and trouble in the world,
But that our soft conditions and our hearts
Should well agree with our external parts?
So wife, hold your temper and meekly put
Your hand 'neath the sole of your husband's foot,
In token of which duty, if he please,
My hand is ready,
Ready,
May it do him ease.

ADAM'S RIB (1949)

FAREWELL, AMANDA

VERSE

I loved you madly, you know it well,
Which makes my story too tough to tell,
So why not forget it all,
Just leave it unsaid,
And I'll merely sing to you instead:

REFRAIN

Farewell, Amanda,
Adios, Addio, Adieu.
Farewell, Amanda,
It all was great fun but it's done, it's through.
Still now and then, fair Amanda,
When you're stepping on the stars above,
Please recall that wonderful night on the veranda,
Sweet Amanda, and our love.

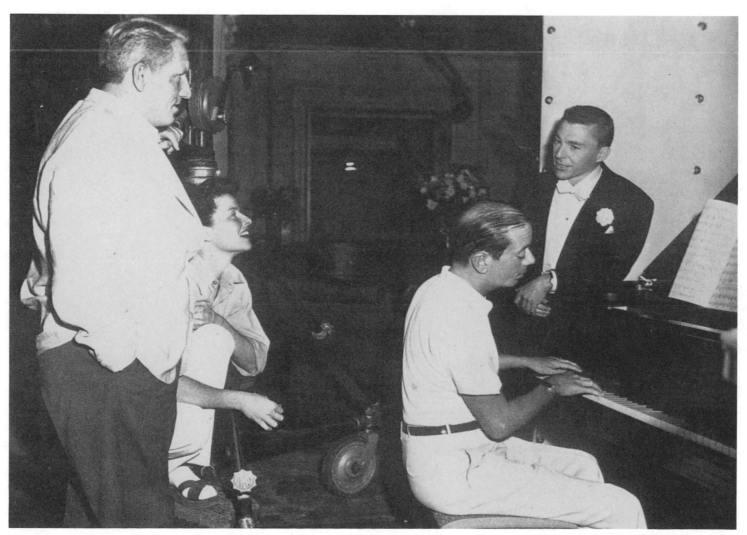

Playing Farewell, Amanda

OUT OF THIS WORLD (1950)

A version of the Amphitryon
legend starring Charlotte Greenwood as Juno.

Lemuel Ayers' setting for the Arcadia Inn and
Heaven provides the background for the finale, *Use Your
Imagination*. Priscilla Gillette (Helen) and William
Eythe (Art) as the happily reunited American
couple stand stage center. Charlotte Greenwood (Juno) and
George Jongeyans (Jupiter) are back on their Olympian
cloud, while William Redfield (Mercury) is
up a tree again. David Burns (Niki), a gangster, sits on a
step (left-center), while Barbara Ashley (Chloe) stands
directly across from him and underneath Mercury.

USE YOUR IMAGINATION

VERSE

What is, what is this song?
What can it be?
I wonder why
It seems to apply
To me,

REFRAIN

Use your imagination,
Just take this motto for your theme
And soon ev'ry night
Will be crowded with delight
And ev'ry day will be a dream.
Use your imagination,
You'll see such wonders if you do.
Around you there lies
Pure enchantment in disguise
And endless joys you never knew.
Behind ev'ry cloud
There's a so lovely star,
Behind ev'ry star
There's a lovelier one by far
So use your imagination,

Just take this motto for your theme
And soon you will dance
On the road to sweet romance
And ev'ry day will be a dream.

YOU DON'T REMIND ME

VERSE

I have tried my best sweet words to combine
To tell you all I feel,
And you must believe me, dearest mine,
That my love is entirely real,
So bear with me when I say
In my poor poetic,
Apologetic
Way:

REFRAIN

You don't remind me
Of the iris in spring,
Or of dawn on the mountain
When the bluebird starts to sing.
You don't remind me
Of the breeze on the bay,
Or of stars in the fountain
Where the silver fishes play,
To the moon-glow in September
You reveal no resemblance,
Of the first snow in November
You've not even a semblance.
No, you don't remind me
Of the world around me or behind me
For so much does my love for you blind me
That, my darling, you only remind me
Of you,
Of you,
Of you.

CHERRY PIES OUGHT TO BE YOU

VERSE

Mercury: Oh, by Jove and by Jehovah,
        You have set my heart aflame,
  Chloe: And to you, young Casanova,
        My reactions are the same,
Mercury: I would sing you tender verses
        But the flair, alas, I lack,
  Chloe: Oh, go on, try
        To versify
        And I'll versify back.

REFRAIN 1

Mercury: Cherry pies ought to be you,
  Chloe: Autumn skies ought to be you,
Mercury: Mister Pulitzer's prize ought to be you,
  Chloe: Romeo in disguise ought to be you,
Mercury: Columbine ought to be you,
  Chloe: Sparkling wine ought to be you,

Mercury: All of Beethoven's nine ought to be you,
Chloe: Ev'ry Will Shakespeare line ought to be you.
Mercury: Your are so enticing, I'm starting to shake,
Chloe: You are just the icing to put on my cake,
Mercury: To continue,
 Whistler's ma ought to be you,
Chloe: Elliot's pa ought to be you,
Mercury: Ev'rything hip-hoorah ought to be you.
Chloe: French perfumes ought to be you,
Mercury: Texas booms ought to be you,
Chloe: Early Egyptian tombs ought to be you,
Mercury: Super Chief drawing rooms ought to be you,
Chloe: Hot Don Juan ought to be you,
Mercury: Yasmin Khan ought to be you,
Chloe: Cupid with nothing on ought to be you,
Mercury: Leda without her swan ought to be you.
Chloe: You may come a cropper, you're losing your breath,
Mercury: Were I not so proper, I'd squeeze you to death,
Chloe: To continue,
 Cary's chin ought to be you,
Mercury: Hepburn's grin ought to be you,
Chloe: Ev'rything sure to win ought to be you.
Mercury: Ought to be you,
Chloe: Ought to be you,
Mercury: Ought to be you,
Chloe: Ought to be you,
Mercury: Ought to be you,
Chloe: Ought to be you,
Mercury: Ought to be you,
Both: Ought to be
 You!

REFRAIN 2

Chloe: 'rabian nights ought to be you,
Mercury: Brooklyn Heights ought to be you,
Chloe: Joe Di Maggio in lights ought to be you,
Mercury: Garbo in Grable's tights ought to be you,
Chloe: Bergen's doll ought to be you,
Mercury: Parsons Loll ought to be you,
Chloe: India's Taj Mahal ought to be you,
Mercury: Fibber Magee's pet moll ought to be you.
Chloe: You have so much talent, you should be in shows,
Mercury: Were I not so gallant, I'd rip off your clo'es,
Chloe: To continue,
 Heaven's blue ought to be you,
Mercury: Heaven too ought to be you,
Chloe: Ev'rything super-do ought to be you.
Mercury: Ought to be you,
Chloe: Ought to be you,
Mercury: Ought to be you,
Chloe: Ought to be you,
Mercury: Ought to be you,
Chloe: Ought to be you,
Mercury: Ought to be you,
Both: Ought to be
 You!

REFRAIN 3

Mercury: Asphodels ought to be you,
Chloe: Orson Welles ought to be you,
Mercury: Ankles like Kit Cornell's ought to be you,
Chloe: Towels from Ritz hotels ought to be you,
Mercury: Sweet Snow White ought to be you,

Chloe: Ambrose Light ought to be you,
Mercury: Eleanor, wrong or right, ought to be you,
Chloe: Erroll Flynn, loose or tight, ought to be you.
Mercury: You are so exciting, I can't even laugh,
Chloe: If you're fond of biting, I'll bite you in half,
Mercury: To continue,
 Truman's Bess ought to be you,
Chloe: His success ought to be you,
Mercury: All except Truman's press ought to be you.
Chloe: Ought to be you,
Mercury: Ought to be you,
Chloe: Ought to be you,
Mercury: Ought to be you,
Chloe: Ought to be you,
Mercury: Ought to be you,
Chloe: Ought to be you,
Both: Ought to be
 You!

REPRISE 1

Niki: Shooting pains ought to be you,
Juno: Addled brains ought to be you,
Niki: Florida, when it rains, ought to be you,
Juno: Pinchers in subway trains ought to be you,
Niki: Withered grass ought to be you,
Juno: Lethal gas ought to be you,
Niki: Sour old applesass ought to be you,
Juno: Gabby old Balaam's ass ought to be you,
Niki: You, you look so fearful,
 You give me de joiks,
Juno: Kid, if you're not keerful,
 I'll give you de woiks,
Niki: To continue,
 Horse-meat steak ought to be you,
Juno: Pickled snake ought to be you,
Niki: Ev'rything I can't take ought to be you,
Juno: Ought to be you,
Niki: Ought to be you,
Juno: Ought to be you,
Niki: Ought to be you,
Juno: Ought to be you,
Niki: Ought to be you,
Juno: Ought to be you,
Both: Ought to be
 You!

REPRISE 2

Niki: Corn that's tough ought to be you,
Juno: In the rough ought to be you,
Niki: Ev'ry old powder puff ought to be you,
Juno: Ev'rything not enough ought to be you,
Niki: No one's bride ought to be you,
Juno: No one's pride ought to be you,
Niki: Just an old chicken fried ought to be you,
Juno: Cyanide, on the side, ought to be you,
Niki: That's the darndest get-up
 That I've seen in years.
Juno: Kid, if you don't shet up,
 I'll pull off your ears.
Niki: To continue,
 No one's girl ought to be you,
Juno: Milton Berle ought to be you,
Niki: Salad with castor erl ought to be you,

WHERE, OH WHERE

VERSE

I often ask
Because I feel
I've ev'ry right to ask
"Will time take on the task
To reveal,
Yes or no,
My beau
Ideal?"
For even though,

When I'm abed,
I dream he holds me tight,
Awake, I never light
On the man
I plan
One day, to wed.

REFRAIN 1

Where, oh where
Is that combination so rare,
A cute knight in armor,
Completely a charmer
Who'd still be a millionaire?
Where, oh where
Is that combination so rare,

A youth who is able
To wrap me in sable
Who'd still be a love affair?
I could accept a cottage small
By a roaring waterfall,
Yet I'd much prefer a castle cool
By a marble swimming pool,
But where, oh where
Is that combination so rare,
A highly admissible, kissable boy
To fill me with, practic'lly kill me with joy
Who'd still be a millionaire?
Tell me where,
Oh, where,
Oh, where.

Charlotte Greenwood and George Jongeyans

REFRAIN 2

Where, oh where
Is that combination so rare,
A swain even sweller
Than John Rockefeller,
Who'd still be a love affair?
Where, oh where
Is that combination so rare,
A God's-gift-to-women,
With passion a-brimmin
Who'd still be a millionaire?
If I should own a castle cool
By a marble swimming pool,
I might often miss that cottage small
By a roaring waterfall,
So where, oh where
Is that combination so rare,
A tip-top tycoon, silver-spoon sort of egg,
Who's batty for dresses by Hattie Carneg.
Who'd still be a love affair,
Tell me, where
Oh, where,
Oh, where.

I AM LOVED

VERSE

Yesterday was a dull day,
Yesterday was a gray day,
But oh today,
Today is a gay day,
You ask me, darling, why?
And I answer

REFRAIN

I am loved,
I am loved
By the one I love in ev'ry way,
I am loved,
Absolutely loved,
What a wonderful thing to be able to say,
I'm adored,
I'm adored
By the one who first led my heart astray,
I'm adored,
Absolutely adored,
What a wonderful thing to be able to say.
So ring out the bells
And let the trumpets blow
And beat on the drums
For now I know I know
I am loved,
I am loved,
What a wonderful thing,
What a glorious thing,
What a beautiful thing to be able to say.

NO LOVER

VERSE

So many wives I meet today,
Complain because their husbands
won't play,
So many wives, to catch romance,
Rush off to Paris,
But not for dresses,
But for caresses,
Made in France.
Let them live their lives,
I'm the most contented of wives.

REFRAIN 1

No lover,
No lover for me,
My husband
Suits me to a T.
No lover,
No fiddle-dee-dee,
My husband
Is but heavenly.
Since the moment his kisses
Upon me were hurled,
It's been all hits, no misses,
For he's just out of this world.
Yes, my husband
Suits me to a T.
So no, no, no,
No, no, no, no, no,
No
Lover
For me.

REFRAIN 2

No lover,
No lover for me,
My husband
Suits me to a T.
No lover,
No fiddle-dee-dee,
My husband
Is but heavenly.
There is something about him,
With glamour so glossed,
That each moment without him,
Why, it's just Paradise lost.
Yes, my husband
Suits me to a T.
So no, no, no,
No, no, no, no, no,
No
Lover
For me.

From This Moment On
was ignored by every Philadelphia
reviewer and dropped from the show.
It was published and recorded,
and in a short time became the best
known song from the score.

FROM THIS MOMENT ON

VERSE

Now that we are close,
No more nights morose,
Now that we are one,
The beguine has just begun,
Now that we're side by side,
The future looks so gay,
Now we are alibi-ed
When we say:

REFRAIN

From this moment on,
You for me, dear,
Only two for tea, dear,
From this moment on,
From this happy day,
No more blue songs,
Only whoop-dee-doo songs,
From this moment on,
For you've got the love I need
so much,
Got the skin I love to touch,
Got the arms to hold me tight,
Got the sweet lips to kiss me
goodnight,
From this moment on,
You and I, babe,
We'll be ridin' high, babe,
Ev'ry care is gone
From this moment on.

INTERLUDE

My dear one,
My fair one,
My sunbeam,
My moonbeam,
My blue bird,
My love bird,
My dream-boat,
My cream-puff,
My ducky,
My wucky,
My poopsy,
My woopsy,
My tootsy,
My wootsy,
My cooky,
My wooky,
My piggy,
My wiggy,
My sugar,
My sweet,
No wonder we rewonder
we rewonder
we repeat.

THEY COULDN'T COMPARE TO YOU

VERSE

Mercury: Oh, what a bevy of beauties,
Oh, what a school of fish,
Oh, what a covey of cuties,
Oh, what a dish delish,
I've known but litters of minxes,
All of 'em fun for a while,
Yet now, for the nonce, what
methinks is
Girls: You've got 'em,
We've got 'em
All: Beat a mile:

REFRAIN 1

Mercury: They couldn't compare to you,
They couldn't compare to you,
Although I've played
Many, many a maid,
They couldn't compare to you.
I've thoroughly pitched the woo,
From the heights of Valhalla
to Kalamazoo,
And though they all
Had a lot on the ball,
They couldn't compare to you.
Of ladies fair,
I've loved more than my share,
And strange but true
I hereby declare,

From tiptoe to hair,
They couldn't compare
To you.

MERCURY'S PATTER

After playing the local sirens
Who resided in my environs,
I decided to learn the art of
Cupid's trickery,
So, at once, I started cruising,
Found the Muses so amusing
That I even got a kick outa
Terpsichore.
After her, I met Calypso
Who was definitely a dipso,
Then I fled to big Brünnhilde,
she was German,
After snitching Eve from Adam,
I attended "Call Me Madam,"
And shortly began to nestle
Essel Merman.
I admired the silken body
Of the chic Scheherazade,
Then of Lady Godiva I became
the lord,
After that I staged an orgy
For some friends o'
Lucretia Borgie,
And ended up at The Stork with
Fanny Ward.
After having had a party
With Phoenicia's goddess
Astarte,
Well, I raised a bit of hell with
Penelope,
After quieting all my urgin's

For several Vestal Virgins,
I put on a strip for
Gypsy Rose Lee
Though I liked the Queen of
Sheba,
She was mentally an amoeba,
As for Beatrice d'Este,
She was a pest and far too
chesty,
As for the passionate wife of
Nero,
My reaction was frankly zero,
As for that sorceress known
as Circe,
She was so hot I hollered
for mercy!
Girls: So hot he hollered for mercy!
Mercury: There was Galatea,
And mean Medea,
And Sappho, one of the best,
There was Nefertiti,
A perfect sweetie,
And gay Mae West.
I was a helluva fella
With Cinderella,
And Isabella of Spain.
And I used to caress
Both Lola Montez
And that damn Calamity Jane.
When betwixt Nell Gwyn,
And Anne Boleyn,
I was forced to make my choice,
I became so confused
I was even amused,
And abused by Peggy Joyce.
There was Melisande,
A platinum blonde,
(How I loved to ruffle her locks.)
There was bright Aurora,
Then Pandora
Who let me open her box!

REFRAIN 2

Girls: They couldn't compare to us,
Mercury: They couldn't compare to you,
Girls: Although he's played
Many, many a maid,
Mercury: They couldn't compare to you.
I've thoroughly pitched the woo,
From Galli-pippo-lippy
to Tippecanoe,
Girls: And though they all
Had a lot on the ball,
Mercury: They couldn't compare to you.
Of ladies fair,
I've loved more than my share,
Girls: And strange but true,
Mercury: I hereby declare,
From tiptoe to hair,
Girls: From hep-cat to square,
Mercury: From dressed-up to bare,
They couldn't compare,
To you.

Gisella Svetlik and dancers

CITY OF BOSTON
OFFICE OF THE MAYOR
CITY HALL

JOHN B. HYNES
Mayor

LICENSING DIVISION

WALTER R. MILLIKEN
Chief

November 29, 1950

Mr. Michael Kavanaugh
Shubert Theatre
Boston

Dear Mr. Kavanaugh:
     We would appreciate the following eliminations being made in "Out Of This World" at the Shubert Theatre.

     All irreverent use of "God"

     Act 1 Costume worn by "Night" and that consisting principally of white doves are to be more heavily lined so as to obliterate body creases in front and back of costume; particularly the white as it is worn on a brightly lighted stage.
Dance of "Night" to be modified.
Position and actions of girl in "Dove" costume to be less suggestive, particularly when she is at right of stage draped over three men. Unless much is done to improve costume, we would prefer her not making her exit by crossing extreme front of stage.

     # 7 "They Couldn't Compare To You" Suggest a substitution for line that sounded like "saving my urgings for Vestal Virgins" Mercury at completion of song to modify action with hands on girls leg.

     Ballet at end of Act 1 to be greatly modified.

     Act 2 Scene 1 Juno "old bag"

     Helen "sexual insecurity"

     Niki Scene 3 Blessing himself after shooting Juno.

     Scene 8 "Nobody's Chasing Me" cut "goosing me"

     Thanking you for your past cooperation, I am

                         Very truly yours

                         Beatrice J. Whelton

Charlotte Greenwood in "The Passing Show of 1912." Cole might have seen this show when it played
New Haven. At any rate, it was Cole who persuaded her to return to the stage.

Charlotte stops the show with *Nobody's Chasing Me*

I love this show—the freedom of it. When I'm waiting to go on I'm dancing in the wings. Of course my favorite is Nobody's Chasing Me. *Cole epitomized the whole theme of the show in one song. When you stop to think about it, everybody is chasing somebody in the entire cast. . . . Relearning takes a considerable amount of thinking. For instance, Cole would say, "Take that line and put it down next to closing in the fourth stanza." You aren't always sure you can, but somehow you do it. . . . I started out as a singer of sad songs but when they became songs with gestures that changed everything. I didn't mean people to laugh, but they did. You see, the audience found comedy for me. They actually made me what they wanted me to be.*

Charlotte Greenwood
New York Herald Tribune, *January 21, 1951*

NOBODY'S CHASING ME

REFRAIN 1

The breeze is chasing the zephyr,
The moon is chasing the sea,
The bull is chasing the heifer,
But nobody's chasing me.

The cock is chasing the chicken,
The pewee, some wee pewee,
The cat is taking a lickin',
But nobody's taking me.
Nobody wants to own me,
And I object.
Nobody wants to 'phone me,
Even collect.
The leopard's chasing the leopard,
The chimp, some champ chimpanzee,
The sheep is chasing the shepherd,
But nobody's chasing me.
Nobody,
Nobody's chasing me.

REFRAIN 2

The flood is chasing the levee,
The wolf is out on a spree,
The Ford is chasing the Chevvy,
But nobody's chasing me.
The bee is chasing Hymettus,
The queen is chasing the bee,
The worm is chasing the lettuce,
But nobody's chasing me.
Each night I get the mirror
From off the shelf.
Each night I'm getting queerer,
Chasing myself.
Ravel is chasing Debussy,
The aphis chases the pea,
The gander's chasing the goosey
But nobody's goosing me.
Nobody,
Nobody's chasing me.

REFRAIN 3

The rain's pursuing the roses,
The snow, the trim Christmas tree,

Big dough pursues Grandma Moses,
But no one's pursuing me.
While Isis chases Osiris,
And Pluto, Proserpine,
My doc is chasing my virus,
But nobody's chasing me.
I'd like to learn canasta
Yet how can I?
What wife without her masta
Can multiply?
The clams are almost a-mixin',
The hams are chasing T.V.,
The fox is chasing the vixen,
But nobody's vixin' me.
Nobody,
Nobody's chasing me.

REFRAIN 4

The llama's chasing the llama,
Papa is chasing Mama,
Monsieur is chasing Madame
But nobody's chasing moi.
The dove, each moment, is bolda,
The lark sings "Ich liebe dich,"
Tristan is chasing Isolda,
But nobody's chasing mich.
Although I may be Juno,
B'lieve it or not,
I've got a lot of you-know,
And you know what!
The snake with passion is shakin',
The pooch is chasing the flea,
The moose his love call is makin'
[Sung with head cold]
But dobody's baki'd be.
Dobody, (sneeze),
Nobody's chasing me.

Telegram to C.P.

COLE DEAR DID NOT BELIEVE IT WOULD HAPPEN
BUT WHEN MY TRANSPORTATION TO CALIFORNIA
WAS HANDED ME THEN I KNEW IT WAS TRUE WE
WOULD CLOSE.   THIS IS TO EXPRESS MY
GRATITUDE TO YOU FOR SELECTING ME FOR
JUNO AND TO SING YOUR LOVELY SONGS WHICH
I LOVE TO SING AND ALWAYS WILL MY SINCERE
GRATITUDE AND LOVE ALWAYS.

CHARLOTTE
May 3, 1951

"Out of This World" closed on May 19, 1951,
after a run of 157 performances.

CAN-CAN (1953)

"Can-Can," a nostalgic recreation of Paris in the early 1890's, was Cole's second longest running musical. It is also remembered as the show that brought overnight stardom to Gwen Verdon.

```
                    IRVING BERLIN



                                        July 30th, 1953



Dear Cole:

Elizabeth (my youngest) and I went to see "Can-Can"
last night and along with a packed house of satis-
fied customers, we loved it.

It's a swell show and I still say, to paraphrase
an old bar-room ballad, "anything I can do, you
can do better".

                              Love,


                              [signature]




Mr. Cole Porter
416 N. Rockingham Avenue
W. Los Angeles 24, Calif.
```

WHO SAID GAY PAREE?

REFRAIN

Who spread the rumor Paris was fun?
Who had such fantasy?
Who never knew
Paris minus you?
Who said Gay Paree?
Who said, of all towns under the sun,
All lovers here should be?
Who failed to add
Paris could be sad?

Who said Gay Paree?
I thought our love, so brightly begun,
Would burn through eternity.
Who told the lie,
Love can never die?
Who said Gay Paree,
Who said Gay Paree?

C'EST MAGNIFIQUE

VERSE 1

Pistache: Love is such a fantastic affair,
When it comes to call,
After taking you up in the air,
Down it lets you fall,
But be patient and soon you will find,
If you follow your heart, not your mind,
Love is waiting there again,
To take you up in the air again.

REFRAIN

When love comes in
And takes you for a spin,
Oo-la, lala, c'est magnifi-que.
When, ev'ry night,
Your loved one holds you tight,
Oo-la, lala, c'est magnifi-que.
But when, one day,
Your loved one drifts away,
Oo-la, lala, it is so tragi-que,
But when, once more,
He whispers "Je t'adore"
C'est magnifi-quel

VERSE 2

Aristide: When you began of love to speak,
I followed every word.
But when you called love magnifique,
I would have called it absurd
And when you said it was often tragique,
I would have said it was always comique.
So, mad'moiselle, be sweet to me
And kindly do not repeat to me.

Our hero is going to fall in love with the girl and he is going to be astounded by this fact. I should think it would be a good idea if the lyrics would contain, in addition to the hero's happiness, something about the fact that he is surprised by all this. This is a fellow who never thought he would fall in love with a woman, never thought he was capable of emotions like that. He was sure that his only interest was the law. Consequently, when love hits this man, his reactions will be slightly atomic. He'll be frightened, happy, chilled, warmed, ecstatic, puzzled, upset, shocked, and delighted.

*Abe Burrows in a letter to Cole,
July 8, 1952.*

I AM IN LOVE

VERSE

Sit down, mad'moiselle,
And from laughing refrain.
Sit down, mad'moiselle,
And, I beg you, try
To listen while I
Explain.

REFRAIN

I am dejected,
I am depressed,
Yet resurrected
And sailing the crest.
Why this elation,
Mixed with deflation?
What explanation?
I am in love!
Such conflicting questions ride
Around in my brain,
Should I order cyanide
Or order champagne?
Oh what is this sudden jolt?
I feel like a frightened colt,
Just hit by a thunderbolt,
I am in love!
I knew the odds
Were against me before.
I had no flair

For flaming desire,
But since the gods
Gave me you to adore,
I may lose
But I refuse to fight the—fire!
So come and enlighten my days
And never depart.
You only can brighten the blaze
That burns in my heart
For I am wildly in love with you,
And so in need of
A stampede of
Love!

ALLEZ-VOUS-EN
(GO AWAY)

VERSE

Since the moment when first
Like a rocket you burst
In my hitherto tranquil skies,
I am startled to find
I am not color blind
When I view the hue of your eyes,
Therefore please do not take me to task
If the following favor I ask:

REFRAIN

Allez-vous-en, allez-vous-en, {mam'selle, monsieur,
Allez-vous-en, go away,

Allez-vous-en, allez-vous-en, {mam'selle, monsieur,
I have no time for you today,
Do be a dear, just disappear, {mam'selle, monsieur,
Bid me goodbye, do, do, do,
Allez-vous-en, please go away, {mam'selle, monsieur,
Or I may go away with you.

I LOVE PARIS

VERSE

Ev'ry time I look down
On this timeless town
Whether blue or gray be her skies,
Whether loud be her cheers
Or whether soft be her tears,
More and more do I realize

REFRAIN

I love Paris in the springtime,
I love Paris in the fall,
I love Paris in the winter when it drizzles,
I love Paris in the summer when it sizzles,
I love Paris ev'ry moment,
Ev'ry moment of the year.
I love Paris,
Why, oh why do I love Paris?
Because my love is near.

C'est Magnifique. Lilo (Pistache) and Peter Cookson (Aristide)

Lilo sings *I Love Paris* in front of Jo Mielziner's backdrop, which inspired the writing of the song.

IT'S ALL RIGHT WITH ME

It's the wrong time and the wrong place,
Though your face is charming, it's the wrong face,
It's not her face but such a charming face
That it's all right with me.
It's the wrong song in the wrong style,
Though your smile is lovely, it's the wrong smile,
It's not her smile but such a lovely smile

That it's all right with me.
You can't know how happy I am that we met,
I'm strangely attracted to you,
There's someone I'm trying so hard to forget,
Don't you want to forget someone too?
It's the wrong game with the wrong chips,
Though your lips are tempting they're the wrong lips,
They're not her lips but they're such tempting lips
That if some night you're free,
Dear, it's all right,
It's all right
With me.

CAN-CAN

VERSE

Ev'rybody,
    Chic or shoddy,
Ev'rybody loves to dance
Since that big dance,
    Infra-dig dance
Called the "Can-Can" captivated France.
Why does it kill ev'ry care?
Why is it done ev'rywhere?

REFRAIN 1

There is no trick to a can-can,
It is so simple to do,
When you once kick to a can-can,
'Twill be so easy for you.
If a lady in Iran can,
If a shady African can,
If a Jap with a slap of her fan can,
Baby, you can can-can too.
If an English Dapper Dan can,
If an Irish Callahan can,
If an Afghan in Afghanistan can,
Baby, you can can-can too.

REFRAIN 2

Takes no art to do a can-can,
It is so simple to do,
When you start to do a can-can,
'Twill be so easy for you.
If a slow Mohammedan can,
If a kilted Scottish clan can,
If in Wagner a Valkyrian can,
Baby, you can can-can too.
If a lass in Michigan can,
If an ass in Astrakhan can,
If a bass in the Saskatchewan can,
Baby, you can can-can too.

REFRAIN 3

If in Deauville ev'ry swell can,
It is so simple to do,
If Debussy and Ravel can,
'Twill be so easy for you.
If the Louvre custodian can,
If the Guard Republican can,
If Van Gogh and Matisse and Cézanne can,
Baby, you can can-can too.
If a chief in the Sudan can,
If the hefty Aga Khan can,
If the camels in his caravan can,
Baby, you can can-can too.

REFRAIN 4

If the waltz king Johann Strauss can,
It is so simple to do,
If his gals in *Fledermaus* can,
'Twill be so easy for you.
Lovely Duse in Milan can,
Lucien Guitry and Réjane can,
Sarah Bernhardt upon a divan can,
Baby, you can can-can too.
If a holy Hindu man can,
If a gangly Anglican can,
If in Lesbos, a pure Lesbian can,
Baby, you can can-can too.

REFRAIN 5

If an ape gargantuan can,
It is so simple to do,
If a clumsy pelican can,
'Twill be so easy for you.
If a dachshund in Berlin can,
If a tom-cat in Pekin can,
If a crowded sardine in a tin can,
Baby, you can can-can too.
If a rhino with a crash can,
If a hippo with a splash can,
If an elm and an oak and an ash can,
Baby, you can can-can too.

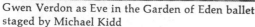

Gwen Verdon as Eve in the Garden of Eden ballet
staged by Michael Kidd

Can-Can

FILM: KISS ME, KATE (1953)

Back row, left to right: George Sidney (director), Howard Keel,
Jack Cummings (producer); front row: Cole, Kathryn Grayson, Ann Miller

Ann Miller, Cole, Jack Cummings, and Kathryn Grayson on the MGM lot

SILK STOCKINGS (1955)

PARIS LOVES LOVERS

VERSE

Gaze on those glist'ning lights
Below and above,
Oh what a night of nights
For people in love.
No city but this, my friend,
No city I know
Gives romance
Such a chance
To grow and grow.

REFRAIN 1

Paris loves lovers,
For lovers it's heaven above,
Paris tells lovers,
"Love is supreme,
Wake up your dream
And make love!"
Only in Paris one discovers,
The urge to merge with the splurge
    of the spring,
Paris loves lovers,
For lovers know that
Love is
Ev'ry
Thing.

REFRAIN 2

He: Paris
She: Capitalistic,
He: Loves lovers,
She: Characteristic,
He: For lovers
She: Sensualistic,
He: It's Heaven above.
She: They should be atheistic.
He: Paris
She: Imperialistic,
He: Tells lovers,
She: I'm pessimistic,
He: "Love is supreme,
    Wake up your dream
    And make love!"
She: That's anti-communistic.
He: Only in Paris
She: Militaristic,
He: One discovers
She: You're optimistic.
He: The urge to merge
    With the splurge
    Of the spring.

She: Bourgeois propaganda!
He: Paris
She: Unrealistic,
He: Loves lovers
For lovers know that
Love
She: Is individualistic.
He: Is ev-
She: And not at all collectivistic.
He: ry thing.
She: But a low totalitarianistic thing!

AS ON THROUGH THE SEASONS WE SAIL

VERSE

He: Love me, darling?
She: Love you, darling,
With all my soul I guarantee.
He: Will you, darling,
Marry me, darling?
She: I'll marry you so willingly!
He: Baby,

REFRAIN

I love you, oh I do
And this I'll prove to you
As on through the seasons we sail.
Remote from crazy crowds,
We'll float above the clouds,
As on through the seasons we sail.
When we are man and wife
I swear to make our life
A revolutionary fairy tale.
How happy we will be
Once we are one, two, or three
As on through the seasons we sail.

ALL OF YOU

VERSE

After watching her appeal from ev'ry angle,
There's a big romantic deal I've got to wangle
For I've fallen for a certain luscious lass
And it's not a passing fancy or a fancy pass.

REFRAIN

I love the looks of you, the lure of you,
I'd love to make a tour of you,
The eyes, the arms, the mouth of you,
The east, west, north, and the south of you,
I'd love to gain complete control of you,
And handle even the heart and soul of you,
So love, at least, a small per cent of me, do,
For I love all of you.

NINOTCHKA   August 15, 1953

ALL OF YOU
notes
Refrain

I love the looks of you, the touch of you,
I'd love to dream too much of you,
~~The dream I dream too much of you,~~

The arms, the eyes, the mouth of you,

The east, west, north and the south of you,
You couldn't know what I would give for you,
~~You can't imagine all I'd give for you,~~

I'd die for you but I'd rather live for you,

So love at least a little bit of me do

For I love all of you.

A. (substitute for first two lines)

I love the looks of you, the glow of you,
The "yes" of you, the "no" of you,

B. (substitute for 5th line)

You couldn't guess how much I'd give for you,

C. (substitute for 5th line)

You couldn't dream how much I'd give for you,

D. (substitute for 7th line)

So give a gent a small percent of you, do,

E. (substitute for 5th line)

I'd love to laze with you and doze with you,

F. (substitute for 6th line)

And solve the secret of sweet repose with you,

G - (substitute for 2nd line)

I'd love to dream too much of you.

H - (substitute for 6th line)

And fondle even the heart and soul of you.

I - (substitutes for 5th and 6th lines)

I worship each and ev'ry part of you

_____ till I reach the heart of you

J - (substitute for 3rd line)

The face, the grace, the charm of you

K - (substitute for 4 th line)

The two, three, four, five alarm of you.

L - (substitute for 3rd line)
The sweet of you, the pure of you,

M. (substitute for line)
And manage even the heart &
soul of you

GEORGE S. KAUFMAN
1035 PARK AVENUE
NEW YORK CITY

Monday

Dear Cole:

leading to the Song

Here is the revised scene for the three boys.
And here are at least some subjects for the Siberia song:

There is good skating all year ~~through~~ round. You
can cut figure eights and your/throat.

You meet all the best people there. Nicer than the
ones you meet in the rest of Russia.

Something about electric blankets and how wonderful
they are.

You get rid of your in-laws.

You never get that letter from your dentist, saying
"Come in and see me." You never get any mail at all,
not even the ones asking for money. And so you never
have to write answers.

You don't get phone calls saying "Guess who this is!"
Or wrong numbers either, in the middle of the
night. There are no phones at all.

There are wonderful hockey games.

Take along plenty of anti-freeze.

Wonderful cold drinks.

No traffic problem.

You never burn your tongue on the soup, because it is
always cold.

Beautiful mountains to climb -- bracing air.

———

Our love.

where
~~I understand~~ all day the sun shines bright
~~And~~ I'm also told that it shines all night —
Sincy Tartar

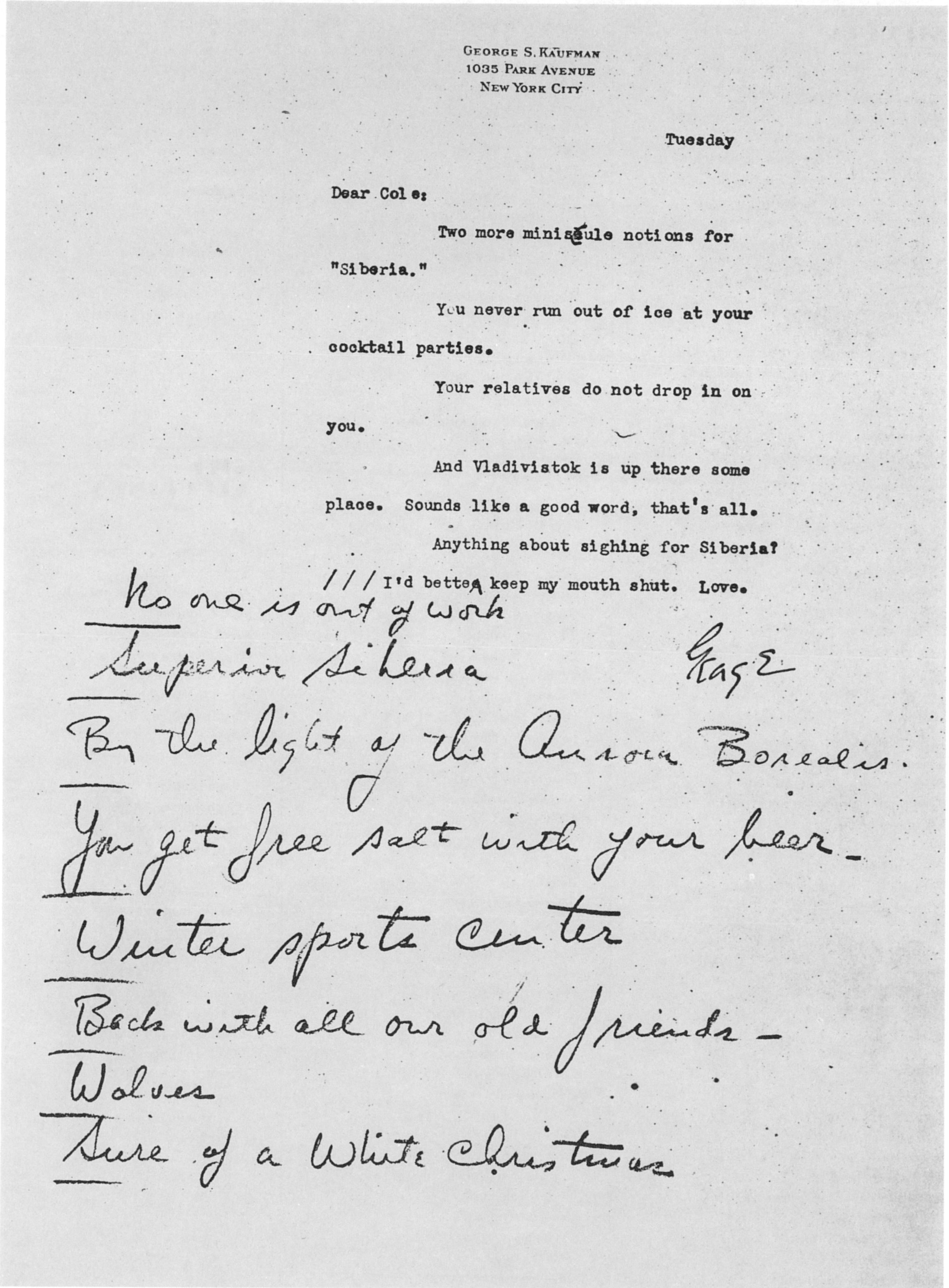

GEORGE S. KAUFMAN
1035 PARK AVENUE
NEW YORK CITY

Tuesday

Dear Cole:

Two more miniscule notions for "Siberia."

You never run out of ice at your cocktail parties.

Your relatives do not drop in on you.

And Vladivistok is up there some place. Sounds like a good word, that's all.

Anything about sighing for Siberia?

/// I'd better keep my mouth shut. Love.

No one is out of work

Superior Siberia   Geo E

By the light of the Aurora Borealis.

You get free salt with your beer.

Winter sports center

Back with all our old friends -

Wolves

Sure of a White Christmas

SIBERIA

REFRAIN 1

When we're sent to dear Siberia,
To Siberi—eri—a,
When it's cocktail time 'twill be so nice
Just to know you'll not have to phone for ice,
When we meet in sweet Siberia,
Far from communist hysteria,
We'll go on a tear
For our buddies all are there
In cheery Siberi ———a.

REFRAIN 2

When we're sent to dear Siberia,
To Siberi—eri—a,
Where they say all day the sun shines bright,
And they also say that it shines all night,
The aurora borealis is
Not as heated as a palace is.
If on heat you dote
You can shoot a sable coat
In cheery Siberi ———a.

REFRAIN 3

When we're sent to dear Siberia,
To Siberi—eri—a,
Where the labor laws are all so fair
That you never have unemployment there,
When we meet in sweet Siberia
To protect us from diphtheria,
We can toast our toes
On the lady Eskimos
In cheery Siberi ———a.

REFRAIN 4

When we're sent to dear Siberia,
To Siberi—eri—a,
Since the big salt mines will be so near
We can all have salt to put in our beer,
When we meet in sweet Siberia
Where the snow is so superia
You can bet, all right
That your Christmas will be white
In cheery Siberi ———a.

GIVE ME THE LAND

REFRAIN 1

Give me the land
Of malted milk and honey,
Give me the land
Where life is still a joke,
Give me the land
Where ev'ryone makes money,
Give me the land
Where ev'ryone is broke.
Give me her prairies,
Give me her valleys,
Give me her mountains
And her little ole soda fountains,
Give me the land
Where ev'rything's okay,
Give me
My pet country,
Give me the U. S. A.

REFRAIN 2

Give me the land
Of dough and B. O. Plenty,
Give me the land
Of Lux and Listerine,
Give me the land
Where no one's over twenty,
Give me the land
Of bop and Bishop Sheen.
Give me Jack Benny,
Give me Bob Hope,
Give me Fred Allen
And that little ole Kil-kilgatten,
Give me the land
Where ev'rything's okay,
Give me
Publicity.
Give me the U. S. A.

REFRAIN 3

Give me the land
Of chili-burgers juicy,
Give me the land
Of frozen orange juice,
Give me the land
Where people all love Lucy,
Give me the land
Where *Time* and *Life* love Luce.
Give me my clam-bake,
Give me my fish-ball,
Give me my chowder,
And my little old room called "powder,"
Give me the land
Where ev'rything's okay
Give me
Acidity,
Give me the U. S. A.

REFRAIN 4

Give me the land
Where rooms are over-heated,
Give me the land
Where influenza grows,
Give me the land
Where men are not conceited,
Give me the land
Of lovely Billy Rose.
Give me Chicago,
Give me El Paso,
Give me Savannah
And some little ole marijuana,
Give me the land
Where ev'rything's okay.
Give me
Delinquency,
Give me the U. S. A.

REFRAIN 5

Give me the land
Where singers get big sal'ries,
Give me the land
Of Ezio and Bing,
Give me the land
Where people count their cal'ries,
Give me the land
Of chicken a la king.
Give me her forests
Soothing and silent
Where robins nestle
Far from little ole Georgie Jessel.
Give me the land
Where ev'rything's okay,
Give me
Variety,
Give me the U. S. A.

SILK STOCKINGS

VERSE

So the dream was doomed to die,
So it's over, dear,
And you sent a sweet good-bye
With a souvenir,
What a heart-warming souvenir,
For again you are there
On the smiling night
When to my delight,
I first saw you dare
Wear

REFRAIN

Silk stockings,
I touch them and find
The joys that remind
Me of you.
Silk stockings
That give me again
Your shy laughter when
They were new.
Silk stockings,
What bliss they recall
When love promised all
Forevermore.
A pair of silk stockings,
So soft and so sheer,
The dear silk stockings
You wore.

Siberia
Will go on a tear,
All our — u friends are there
      buddies
where the parties are superia
   when it's cocktail time —
      it will be nice
To know you'll never run(s)
         one
      out of ice
            more ice
To know you'll not have to phone for ice

MEMORANDUM

The WALDORF-ASTORIA NEW YORK

One of the most famous rooms ever designed in America—the library of 33-A, Cole's nine-room apartment on the thirty-third floor of the Waldorf Towers, which "Billy" Baldwin designed for him in 1955. The walls were of tortoise-shell leather and the bookcases of brass tubing. Cole gave Baldwin *carte blanche* except in two respects: he wished for (and got) a red bed and he wanted Baldwin always to bear in mind in the course of his decorating that Cole was, so he said and uncannily believed, "Broadway."

Gretchen Wyler as Josephine and Stanley Simmonds as Napoleon

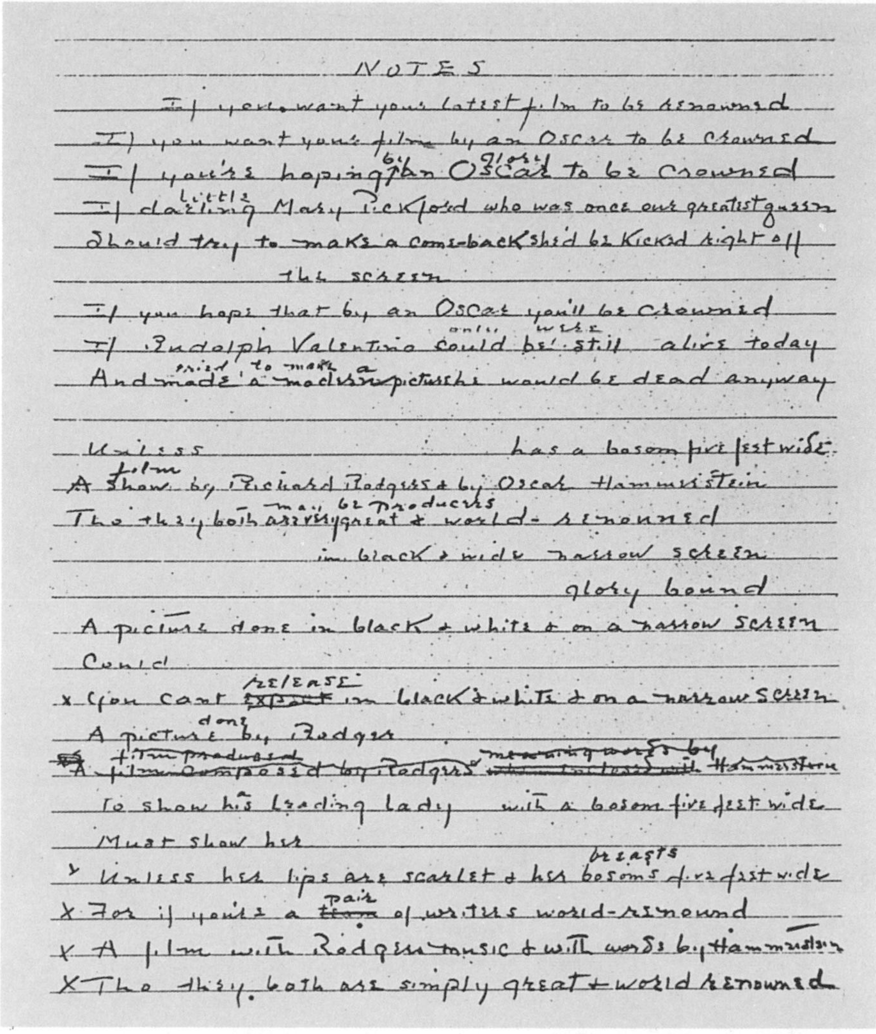

The left portion of this page reproduces handwritten manuscript draft notes:

NOTES

If you want your latest film to be renowned
If you want your film by an Oscar to be crowned
If you're hoping by an Oscar glory to be crowned
If darling Mary Pickford who was once our greatest guess
Should try to make a come-back she'd be kicked right off
the screen
If you hope that by an Oscar you'll be crowned
If Rudolph Valentino could be still alive today
And made a modern picture he would be dead anyway

Unless _____ has a bosom five feet wide
A film show by Richard Rodgers & by Oscar Hammerstein
The they both are may be producers great & world-renowned
in black & wide narrow screen
glory bound
A picture done in black & white & on a narrow screen
Could
x You can't expect release in black & white & on a narrow screen
A picture done by Rodgers
A film composed by Rodgers now words by Hammerstein
To show his leading lady with a bosom five feet wide
Must show her
x Unless her lips are scarlet & her bosoms breasts five feet wide
x For if you're a pair of writers world-renowned
x A film with Rodgers music & with words by Hammerstein
x The they both are simply great & world renowned

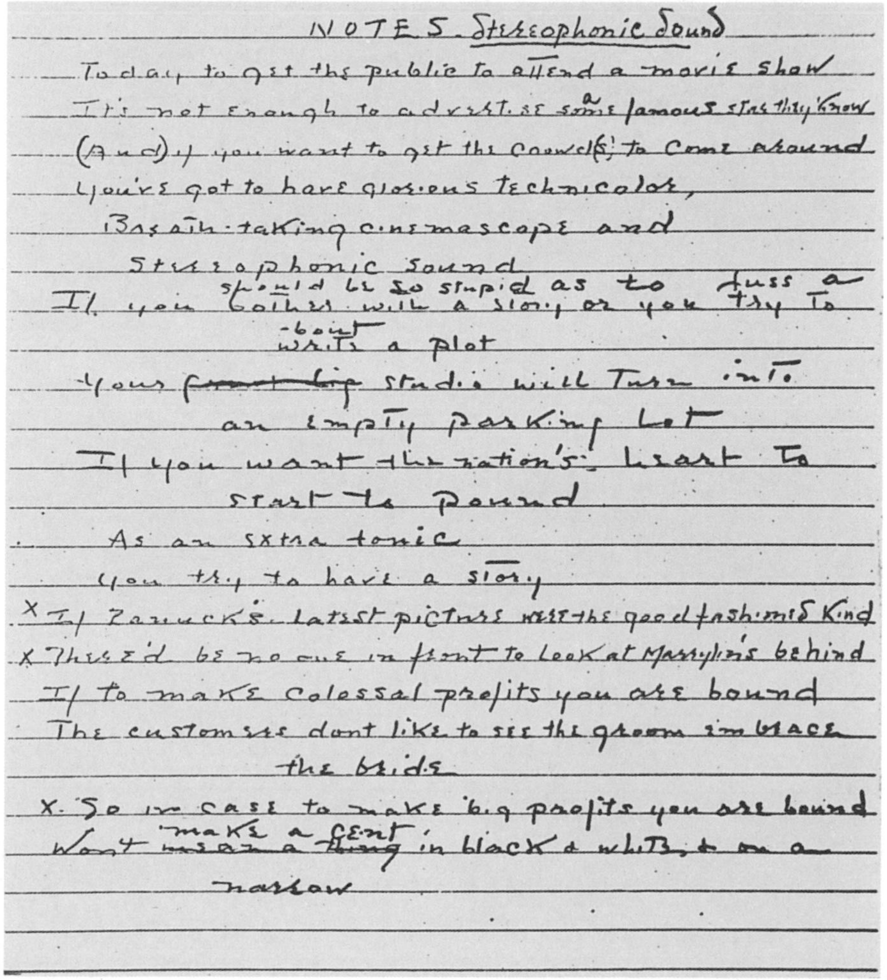

NOTES. Stereophonic Sound

Today, to get the public to attend a movie show
It's not enough to advertise some famous star they know
(And) if you want to get the crowd(s) to come around
You've got to have glorious technicolor,
Breath-taking cinemascope and
Stereophonic sound
If you should be so stupid as to fuss a bother with a story or you try to write a plot
Your studio will turn into
an empty parking lot
If you want the nation's heart to
start to pound
As an extra tonic
You try to have a story
x If Zanuck's latest picture were the good fashioned kind
x There'd be no one in front to look at Marilyn's behind
If to make colossal profits you are bound
The customers don't like to see the groom embrace the bride
x So in case to make big profits you are bound
Won't make a cent in black & white & on a narrow

STEREOPHONIC SOUND

REFRAIN 1

Today to get the public to attend a picture show
It's not enough to advertise a famous star they know.
If you want to get the crowd to come around
You've got to have glorious technicolor,
Breath-taking cinemascope and
Stereophonic sound.
If Zanuck's latest picture were the good
old-fashioned kind
There'd be no one in front to look at Marilyn's behind.
If you want to hear applauding hands resound
You've got to have glorious technicolor,
Breath-taking cinemascope and
Stereophonic sound.
The customers don't like to see the groom embrace
the bride
Unless her lips are scarlet and her bosom's five
feet wide.
You've got to have glorious technicolor,
Breath-taking cinemascope or
Cinerama, vistavision, superscope or Toddao and
Stereophonic sound,
And stereophonic sound.

REFRAIN 2

You all remember Lassie, that beloved canine star.
To see her wag her tail the crowds would come from
near and far,
But at present she'd be just another hound
Unless she had glorious technicolor,
Breath-taking cinemascope and
Stereophonic sound.
I lately did a picture at the bottom of the sea
I rassled with an octopus and licked an anchovee,
But the public wouldn't care if I had drowned
Unless I had glorious technicolor,
Breath-taking cinemascope and
Stereophonic sound.
If Ava Gardner played Godiva riding on a mare
The people wouldn't pay a cent to see her in the bare
Unless she had glorious technicolor or
Cinecolor or
Warnercolor or
Pathécolor or
Eastmancolor or
Kodacolor or
Any color and
Stereophonic sound
And stereophonic,
As an extra tonic,
Stereophonic sound.

IN MEMORY OF LINDA

Exhausted by the tryout difficulties of "Silk
Stockings," Cole flew to Switzerland five days before the
New York opening. Some friends presented him with a
cigarette case in memory of Linda, who had died
the previous year.

Telegramm - Télégramme - Telegramma

46

von - de - da	No.	Wörter Mots Parole	Aufgegeben den Consigné le Consegnato il	Stunde Heure Ora 26.11.55.

66046 NEWYORK TW501 60 25/2 1148A VIA CIA

	Erhalten - Reçu - Ricevuto			Befördert - Transmis - Trasmesso		
von - de - da	Stunde-Heure-Ora	Name - Nom - Nome	nach - d - a	Stunde-Heure-Ora	Name - Nom - Nome
K	66.521		Feb.25-1955		

No. 1783

= LT = COLE PORTER PALACE

HOTEL ST MORITZ ENGADIN

OPENING GIGANTIC SUCCESS BROOKS ATKINSON RAVING ESPECIALLY

ABOUT WORDS AND MUSIC ALL OTHER PAPERS SIMPLY WONDERFUL

ABE BURROUGHS AND CY HAVE ACHIEVED A THEATRICAL MIRACLE

AUDIENCE MOST ELEGANT IN YEARS GRETCHEN WYLER STOPPED

SHOW TWICE WITH JOSEPHINE AND STEREOPHONIC YOU HAVE EVERY

— XII. 51. Auf Wunsch werden die Telegramme zutelephoniert - Sur demande, les télégrammes sont téléphonés - A richiesta, i telegrammi sono telefonati   A 5 (210 × 148). — Qu. O 70.

No

REASON TO BE HAPPY AND PROUD LOVE AND KISSES = SIRMAY +

Dr. Albert Sirmay was Cole's music editor and close friend

Linda, 1954

HIGH SOCIETY (1956)

YOU'RE SENSATIONAL

VERSE

A thorough knowledge I've got
    about girls,
I've been around,
And after learning a lot about girls,
This is the important fact I found:

REFRAIN

I've no proof
When people say you're more or less aloof
But you're sensational.
I don't care
If you are called "The Fair
    Miss Frigid Air"
'Cause you're sensational.
Making love is quite an art,
What you require is the proper squire to
    fire your heart
And if you say
That one fine day you'll let me come to call
We'll have a ball
'Cause you're sensational,
Sensational,
That's all, that's all, that's all.

TRUE LOVE

VERSE

Sun-tanned, wind-blown
Honeymooners at last alone,
Feeling far above par,
Oh how lucky we are
While

REFRAIN

I give to you and you give to me
True love, true love.
So on and on it will always be
True love, true love.
For you and I
Have a guardian angel on high
With nothing to do
But to give to you and to give to me
Love forever true.

I LOVE YOU, SAMANTHA

VERSE

Samantha, you're all
I'll ever adore
So forgive me do
If I say to you
What I've said so often before.

REFRAIN

I love you, Samantha,
And my love will never die.
Remember, Samantha,
I'm a one-gal guy.

Together, Samantha,
We could ride a star and ride it high.

Frank Sinatra and Grace Kelly

Remember, Samantha,
I'm a one-gal guy.

And if some distant day
You decided to say:
"Get along, go away, good-bye!"
Remember, Samantha,
I'm a one-gal guy.

LES GIRLS (1957)

HIGH FLYIN' WINGS ON MY SHOES

VERSE

With your looks so attractive

And your charm so radio-active
You're my dream supreme in ev'ry way.
So I long to possess you,
To be close to you and caress you,
Twenty-four hours per day.

REFRAIN

Whenever, darling, by chance,
Together we dance,
Although I've been battling the blues,
You give me stars in my eyes,
Love in my heart
And high flyin' wings on my shoes.
I so adore you, my dear,
That when you appear,
No matter what moment you choose,
You give me stars in my eyes,
Love in my heart
And high flyin' wings on my shoes,
So if you care for me,
I guarantee
Our life could be
Forever good news
Including stars in our eyes,

Love in our hearts
And high flyin' wings on our shoes.

ÇA, C'EST L'AMOUR

REFRAIN

When suddenly you sight
Someone for whom you yearn,
Ça, c'est l'amour.
And when to your delight
She loves you in return,
Ça, c'est l'amour.
Then dawns a dreary day,
Your darling goes away
And all is over you are sure,
But oh when she returns
And loves you as before,
You take her in your lonely arms
And want her even more,
Ça, c'est l'amour,
Ça, c'est l'amour.

Mitzi Gaynor, Kay Kendall, and Taina Elg

Sunday, April 28

Bad luck in Lucca. Being Sunday, we thought all the churches would be open all day, but no. We were able, however, to see the Duomo because of an obliging priest. Once inside, we saw the painting of Ghirlandaio, *The Virgin and Saints.* Also the beautiful tomb of a naughty girl named Ilaria del Caretto by Iacopo della Quercia. There she lies, resting her feet on her little dog. The priest told us that she was not faithful to her husband but she was always faithful to her dog.

Over to Montecatini for lunch at the hotel, *La Pace,* where Sturges always stayed when he took the cure.

At 5:00 PM to Settignano to see my old friend, B. B. Berenson. I talked to him for nearly an hour in his bedroom. Or rather, he talked to me mostly about Linda. He summed her up: "A great beauty with great brains." He asked my age. I told him "65 years old." He said, "A mere child; I'm 92." Later I went downstairs to tea where his secretary, the charming Nikki Mariano, was presiding at tea. There were several people there, all of them obviously scholars. Then B.B. appeared. He was delighted to meet Bob Bray and asked him penetrating questions about moving pictures. Nikki—I don't know how to spell her nickname—has been his secretary since 1919. She is so attractive, and while I was upstairs with B. B. she showed Bob Bray through the villa, including its paintings—mostly Italian primitives and its eleven libraries.

Thursday, May 2nd

Off to Padua (and after Padua to dear Venice). On arriving in Venice, Beppino, our gondolier, met us. He was so young when Linda and I were Venetians—but no more. Arrived by motor-boat at the Gritti, a bang-up hotel.

Friday, May 3rd

In San Marco and all through the Doge's Palace during the morning. Lunch at Quadri on the Piazza San Marco with Daisy Fellowes (a joy to see her again and she so attractive and fascinating). Then to San Giorgio degli Schiavoni to see the Carpaccios (episodes from the lives of St. George and the dragon, St. Tryphon and St. Jerome). On the way back, by the small canals, we saw again the great equestrian statue of Colleoni by Verrocchio. How Monty Woolley used to love this statue!

Monday, May 6th

After lunch we stopped at the Rezzonico, which is now a museum containing many Tiepolos, Longhis, and other 18th-century artists. The interiors have been so altered that I hardly recognized it as the dear palazzo where we had such happy years.

ALADDIN (1958)

WOULDN'T IT BE FUN

REFRAIN 1

Wouldn't it be fun not to be famous,
Wouldn't it be fun not to be rich!
Wouldn't it be pleasant
To be a simple peasant
And spend a happy day digging a ditch!
Wouldn't it be fun not to be known as
    an important VIP,
Wouldn't it be fun to be nearly anyone
Except me, mighty me!

PATTER

Yesterday I had to endure a kite-flying match
And rushed to an execution downtown
Then I gave a luncheon for some horrible hectic Huns
Who proceeded to drink too much and fall down.
After lunch I went to inspect a slave labor camp
And opened a new wing in my dungeon keep,
Then I gave a feast for a lofty lama from Tibet
And he stayed so late I never got to sleep,
So help me Buddha!

REFRAIN 2

Wouldn't it be fun not to be wealthy,
Wouldn't it be fun not to be great!
How I'd love it dearly
To be a beggar merely
And not be bored to death living in state!
Wouldn't it be fun not to have always deadly
    diplomats for tea,
Wouldn't it be fun to be nearly anyone
Except me, mixed-up me!

Thursday, May 9th
Goodbye to Venice on a most beautiful day.

APPENDICES

CHRONOLOGY OF COLE PORTER SONGS AND PRODUCTIONS

(*indicates published songs)

1910-1919

CORA

Produced by the Phi Opera Company as the fall initiation play at the Delta Kappa Epsilon fraternity house, November 28, 1911. One performance. Book by T. Gaillard Thomas, II. Directed by Peter C. Bryce and Thomas. Cast, starring Cole Porter and Thomas, included Arnold Whitridge, L. C. Hanna, Jr., H. H. Parsons, J. Lytton, W. Doolittle, Reginald LeG. Auchincloss, and Fletcher Van W. Blood.

MUSICAL NUMBERS

POKER
CONCENTRATION
SATURDAY NIGHT
HELLO, MISS CHAPEL STREET
CORA, THE FAIR CHORINE
MY HOME TOWN GIRL
QUEEN OF THE YALE DRAMAT
WE'RE OFF
GOODBYE BOYS
CABLEGRAM
THE OLD RAT MORT
MA PETITE NINETTE
LE REVE D'ABSINTHE
FAR, FAR AWAY
FAIR ONE
ROSEBUD
ROLLING, ROLLING
MOTHER PHI

AND THE VILLAIN STILL PURSUED HER

Produced by the Yale University Dramatic Association at the New Haven Lawn Club, April 24, 1912 and at Yale Club of New York City, May 10, 1912. Two performances. Book by T. Gaillard Thomas, II. Staged by Messrs. Thomas and Porter. Cast, starring Monty Woolley, included Rufus F. King, Irving G. Beebe, Arnold Whitridge, Johnfritz Achelis, Hay Langenheim, Joseph Kelleher, and Lawrence M. Cornwall.

MUSICAL NUMBERS

WE ARE THE CHORUS OF THE SHOW
STROLLING
THE LOVELY HEROINE
I'M THE VILLAIN
TWILIGHT

LLEWELLYN
THAT ZIP CORNWALL COOCH
CHARITY
QUEENS OF TERPSICHORE
LEADERS OF SOCIETY
SUBMARINE
BARCELONA
SILVER MOON
DEAR DOCTOR
ANYTIME
COME TO BOHEMIA
DANCING
FARE THEE WELL

THE POT OF GOLD

Produced as the fall initiation play at the Delta Kappa Epsilon fraternity house, November 26, 1912, and at the Hotel Taft, New Haven, Connecticut, Dec. 4, 1912. Two performances. Book by Almet F. Jenks, Jr. Staged by Messrs. Jenks and Porter. Cast, starring Cole Porter, included T. Gaillard Thomas, II, Fletcher Van W. Blood, H. H. Parsons, Arnold Whitridge, and A. Clark.

MUSICAL NUMBERS

AT THE RAINBOW
BELLBOYS
LONGING FOR DEAR OLD BROADWAY
WHEN I USED TO LEAD THE BALLET
MY HOUSEBOAT ON THE THAMES
SHE WAS A FAIR YOUNG MERMAID
WHAT AN AWFUL HULLABALOO
WHAT A CHARMING AFTERNOON
SINCE WE'VE MET
EXERCISE
WE ARE SO AESTHETIC
SCANDAL
I WONDER WHERE MY GIRL IS NOW
MY SALVATION ARMY QUEEN
IT'S AWFULLY HARD WHEN MOTHER'S NOT ALONG
I WANT TO BE MARRIED (TO A DELTA KAPPA EPSILON MAN)
HA, HA, THEY MUST SAIL FOR SIBERIA
I LOVE YOU SO
LOIE AND CHLODO
SO LET US HAIL

Unused
THAT RAINBOW RAG
IF I WERE A FOOTBALL MAN

THE KALEIDOSCOPE

Produced by the Yale University Dramatic Association at the Hotel Taft, New Haven, April 30, 1913, and at the Yale Club of New York City, May 7, 1913. Two performances. Billed as "A Home Play in Two Acts." Cast, starring Newbold Noyes and Rufus F. King, included Archibald MacLeish, Howard T. Cumming, Arnold Whitridge, Johnfritz Achelis, Joseph Kelleher, and Hay Langenheim.

MUSICAL NUMBERS

AT THE DAWN TEA
WE ARE PROM GIRLS
CHAPERONS
IN THE LAND WHERE MY HEART WAS BORN
MEET ME BESIDE THE RIVER
BEWARE OF THE SOPHOMORE

RICK-CHICK-A-CHICK
GOOD-BYE MY TRUE LOVE
ON MY YACHT
WE'RE A GROUP OF NONENTITIES
FLOWER MAIDENS
ABSINTHE
THE ABSINTHE DRIP
MAID OF SANTIAGO
AS I LOVE YOU
DUODESSIMALOGUE
OH, WHAT A PRETTY PAIR OF LOVERS
A MEMBER OF THE YALE ELIZABETHAN CLUB
MOON MAN
MY GEORGIA GAL

PARANOIA

Produced by the Yale University Dramatic Association at the Hotel Taft, New Haven, April 24, 1914. One performance. Book, music and lyrics by Thomas Lawrason Riggs and Cole Porter. Directed by Monty Woolley. Cast, starring Newbold Noyes and Rufus F. King, included William S. Innis, Percival Dodge, Archibald MacLeish, Stoddard King, and Hay Langenheim.

MUSICAL NUMBERS

PARANOIA
FUNNY LITTLE TRACKS IN THE SNOW
INNOCENT, INNOCENT MAIDS
OH, WHAT A LOVELY PRINCESS
WON'T YOU COME CRUSADING WITH ME
I WANT TO ROW ON THE CREW
WHAT LOVE IS
DOWN IN A DUNGEON DEEP
SLOW SINKS THE SUN
THE PREP SCHOOL WIDOW
IDYLL
I'VE A SHOOTING-BOX IN SCOTLAND
DOWN LOVERS LANE
FLOWER SONG
DRESDEN CHINA SOLDIERS
NAUGHTY, NAUGHTY
HAIL TO CYRIL

WE'RE ALL DRESSED UP AND WE DON'T KNOW HUERTO GO

Produced by members of the Yale University Dramatic Association at the Hotel Gibson, Cincinnati, Ohio, May 22, 1914, at the annual dinner of the Associated Western Yale Clubs. The cast included Cole Porter, Phelps Newberry, Monty Woolley, Hay Langenheim, Newbold Noyes, Johnfritz Achelis, and Lawrence Cornwall. The songs, with the exception of "Cincinnati," are unknown and lost.

SEE AMERICA FIRST

Tryout: Van Curler Opera House, Schenectady, New York, February 22, 1916, Harmanus Bleecker Hall, Albany, New York, February 24, 1916, Lyceum Theatre, Rochester, New York, February 28, 1916, Shubert Theatre, New Haven, Connecticut, March 22, 1916, Grand Opera House, Providence, Rhode Island, March 23, 1916.

Produced by Miss Elisabeth Marbury at the Maxine Elliott Theatre, New York, March 28, 1916. Fifteen performances. A comic opera with book, music and lyrics by T. Lawrason Riggs and Cole Porter. Staged by Benrimo. Cast, starring Dorothie Bigelow and John Goldsworthy, included Clifton Webb, Jeanne Cartier, Clara Palmer, Sam Edwards, and Felix Adler.

MUSICAL NUMBERS LISTED IN NEW YORK PROGRAM

DAWN MUSIC
INDIAN GIRLS CHANT
BAD MEN
TO FOLLOW EVERY FANCY
INDIAN MAIDEN'S CHORUS
*SOMETHING'S GOT TO BE DONE
*I'VE GOT AN AWFUL LOT TO LEARN
BEAUTIFUL, PRIMITIVE INDIAN GIRLS
HOLD-UP ENSEMBLE
*SEE AMERICA FIRST
*THE LANGUAGE OF FLOWERS
*DAMSEL, DAMSEL (PRITHEE COME CRUSADING WITH ME)
THE LADY I'VE VOWED TO WED
FINALE (HAIL THE FEMALE RELATIVE)
MIRROR, MIRROR
*EVER AND EVER YOURS
*LIMA
WILL YOU LOVE ME WHEN MY FLIVVER IS A WRECK?
WOODLAND DANCE
*BUY HER A BOX AT THE OPERA
*I'VE A SHOOTING-BOX IN SCOTLAND
*WHEN I USED TO LEAD THE BALLET
FINALE ACT 2

Unused
*OH, BRIGHT FAIR DREAM
*PITY ME PLEASE
*SLOW SINKS THE SUN
DINNER
STROLLING QUITE FANCY FREE
IF IN SPITE OF OUR ATTEMPTS
THE SOCIAL COACH OF ALL THE FASHIONABLE FUTURE
    DEBUTANTES
SERENADE
LADY FAIR, LADY FAIR
LOVE CAME AND CROWNED ME
WHEN A BODY'S IN LOVE
REVELATION ENSEMBLE
BICHLORIDE OF MERCURY
STEP WE GRANDLY
SWEET SIMPLICITY
WAKE, LOVE, WAKE

It is difficult to know whether the various soliloquys, recitatives, and ensembles which were written for the show actually appeared in the New York production.

HITCHY-KOO OF 1919

Tryout: Nixon's Apollo Theatre, Atlantic City, N. J., August 18, 1919, Colonial Theatre, Boston, Massachusetts, September 1, 1919.

Produced by Raymond Hitchcock at the Liberty Theatre, New York, October 6, 1919. Fifty-six performances. Book by George V. Hobart. Staged by Julian Alfred. Cast, starring Raymond Hitchcock, included Lillian Kemble Cooper, Ruth Mitchell, Joe Cook, and Florence O'Denishawn.

MUSICAL NUMBERS

PAGLIACCI
WHEN BLACK SALLIE SINGS PAGLIACCI
*I INTRODUCED
*HITCHY'S GARDEN OF ROSES
*WHEN I HAD A UNIFORM ON
*I'VE GOT SOMEBODY WAITING
*PETER PIPER
*THE SEA IS CALLING
I'M AN ANAESTHETIC DANCER
*MY COZY LITTLE CORNER IN THE RITZ
*OLD-FASHIONED GARDEN
*BRING ME BACK MY BUTTERFLY

Unused

*ANOTHER SENTIMENTAL SONG
*THAT BLACK AND WHITE BABY OF MINE
AH FONG LOW
SINCE MA GOT THE CRAZE ESPAGNOLE

MISCELLANEOUS SONGS
1910-1919

*BRIDGET MCGUIRE
WHEN THE SUMMER MOON COMES 'LONG
*BINGO ELI YALE
*FLA DE DAH
*HAIL TO YALE (Music by Arthur Troostwyck)
*BEWARE OF YALE
*ELI
*BULL DOG
*A FOOTBALL KING
*THE MOTOR CAR
PERFECTLY TERRIBLE
MERCY PERCY
NO SHOW THIS EVENING
MUSIC WITH MEALS
I WANT TO BE A YALE BOY
IT PAYS TO ADVERTISE
WHEN I'M EATING AROUND WITH YOU
YELLOW MELODRAMA
*ANTOINETTE BIRBY
CLASS OF 1913 SONG
*ESMERELDA (Hands-Up, 1915)
*TWO BIG EYES (Miss Information, 1915)
WAR SONG
KATIE OF THE Y.M.C.A.
IT PUZZLES ME SO
CLEVELAND
*ALONE WITH YOU (Very Good Eddie, England, 1918)
*ALTOGETHER TOO FOND OF YOU, co-authors: Melville Gideon
    and James Heard (Telling the Tale, England, 1918)
*CHELSEA (The Eclipse, England 1919)
*I NEVER REALIZED (The Eclipse, 1919, and Buddies, 1919)
TIRED OF LIVING ALONE
*WASHINGTON SQUARE (As You Were, 1920)
WIDOW'S CRUISE
VENUS OF MILO
YOU MAKE UP
A TABLE FOR TWO
OH, HONEY

1920-1929

A NIGHT OUT

Cole wrote the music, Clifford Grey the lyrics, for the following songs from this English production, which opened at the Winter Garden Theatre, London, September 18, 1920, and ran for 309 performances.

MUSICAL NUMBERS

*LOOK AROUND
*OUR HOTEL
*WHY DIDN'T WE MEET BEFORE

MAYFAIR AND MONTMARTRE

Produced by Charles B. Cochran at London's New Oxford Theatre, March 9, 1922. Seventy-seven performances. A revue by John Hastings Turner, which starred Alice Delysia and which contained a number of songs by other composers. Cole's songs included:

MUSICAL NUMBERS

*OLGA (COME BACK TO THE VOLGA)
*COCKTAIL TIME
*THE BLUE BOY BLUES

Unused

THE SPONGE
THE BANDIT BAND
WOND'RING NIGHT AND DAY

HITCHY-KOO OF 1922

(Opened and closed out of town)

Produced by the Messrs. Lee and J. J. Shubert at the Sam S. Shubert Theatre, Philadelphia, October 10, 1922, for a run of less than two weeks. Book by Harold Atteridge. Directed by J. C. Huffman. The entire production staged under the personal direction of Mr. J. J. Shubert. Cast, starring Raymond Hitchcock, included Benny Leonard, Edythe Baker, Jack Pearl, May Boley, Jack Squires, Helen Dahlia, El Brendel, and Florence Bert.

MUSICAL NUMBERS

MARYLAND SCENE
OH, MARY
AH FONG LOW
*WHEN MY CARAVAN COMES HOME
*THE AMERICAN PUNCH
PLAY ME A TUNE
*LOVE LETTTER WORDS
*THE BANDIT BAND
THE SPONGE
*THE HARBOR DEEP DOWN IN MY HEART

Since the program is incomplete, the following may or may not have been used in the show:

THE OLD-FASHIONED WALTZ
PITTER-PATTER
SCOTCH TWINS
SOUTH SEA ISLES
TWIN SISTERS

WITHIN THE QUOTA

World premiere, October 25, 1923, of ballet-sketch.

GREENWICH VILLAGE FOLLIES

Tryout: Nixon's Apollo Theatre, Atlantic City, September 8, 1924.

Produced by A. L. Jones and Morris Green at the Sam S. Shubert Theatre, New York, September 16, 1924. 127 performances. Book by Lew Fields, Irving Caesar, William K. Wells, Arthur Caesar, and others. The entire production devised and staged by John Murray Anderson. The cast, starring The Dolly Sisters, included Moran and Mack, Georgie Hale, Bobbe Arnst, Vincent Lopez and his orchestra.

MUSICAL NUMBERS

*BRITTANY
 I WANT TWINS
 THE DOLLYS AND THEIR COLLIES
 TOY OF DESTINY
*TWO LITTLE BABES IN THE WOOD
 BRING ME A RADIO
 BROADCAST A JAZZ
*WAIT FOR THE MOON
 SYNCOPATED PIPES OF PAN
*MY LONG AGO GIRL
*MAKE EVERY DAY A HOLIDAY
*I'M IN LOVE AGAIN (added after N.Y. opening)

Unused
THE LIFE OF A SAILOR
UNDERSTUDIES

OUT O' LUCK

Produced in 1925 and 1926 by the Yale University Dramatic Association. Book by Tom Cushing. Directed by Monty Woolley. Cast included Henry C. Potter, John McA. Hoysradt, Edward R. Wardwell, Theodore S. Ryan, and Roger V. Stearns.

MUSICAL NUMBERS

BUTTERFLIES
MADEMAZELLE
OPERA STAR

LA REVUE DES AMBASSADEURS

Produced by Edmond Sayag at des Ambassadeurs Cafe, May 10, 1928. Number of performances unknown. Directed by Bobby Connolly. Cast, starring Buster and John West and Fred Waring's orchestra, included Evelyn Hoey, Mary Leigh, Carter Wardell, Morton Downey, Katheryn Ray, Frances Gershwin, the Pearson Brothers, Eleanor Shaler, Basil Howes, Muriel Harrisson, and the Three Eddies.

MUSICAL NUMBERS

 KEEP MOVING
*THE LOST LIBERTY BLUES
 OMNIBUS
*PILOT ME
*IN A MOORISH GARDEN
*ALMIRO
*YOU AND ME
*FISH
*MILITARY MAIDS
*BLUE HOURS
*ALPINE ROSE
 GERSHWIN SPECIALTY
 BOULEVARD BREAK
*HANS
*BABY, LET'S DANCE
*AN OLD-FASHIONED GIRL
*FOUNTAIN OF YOUTH

PARIS

Tryout: Nixon's Apollo Theatre, Atlantic City, February 6, 1928, Adelphi Theatre, Philadelphia, February 13, 1928, Wilbur Theatre, Boston, May 7, 1928, Poli Theatre, Washington, D.C. September 30, 1928.

Produced by Gilbert Miller in association with E. Ray Goetz at the Music Box Theatre, New York, October 8, 1928. 195 performances. Book by Martin Brown. Staged by W. H. Gilmore. Cast, starring Irene Bordoni, included Arthur Margetson, Louise Closser Hale, and Irving Aaronson's Commanders.

MUSICAL NUMBERS

*TWO LITTLE BABES IN THE WOOD
*DON'T LOOK AT ME THAT WAY
*LET'S DO IT, LET'S FALL IN LOVE
*VIVIENNE
*THE HEAVEN HOP

Unused
*QUELQUE-CHOSE
*LET'S MISBEHAVE
*WHICH
 DIZZY BABY

WAKE UP AND DREAM

Tryout: Palace Theatre, Manchester, England, March 5, 1929.

Produced by Charles B. Cochran at the London Pavilion, March 27, 1929. 263 performances. American production, Selwyn Theatre, New York, December 30, 1929. 136 performances. Book by John Hastings Turner. Staged by Frank Collins under the personal direction of Charles B. Cochran. Cast, starring Jessie Matthews, Sonnie Hale, Tilly Losch and George Metaxa, included Toni Birkmayer, Douglas Byng, William Stephens, Moya Nugent, Tina Meller, Elsie Carlisle, and Chester Fredericks (original English cast).

MUSICAL NUMBERS

*WAKE UP AND DREAM
 I'VE GOT A CRUSH ON YOU
*I LOVED HIM BUT HE DIDN'T LOVE ME
*LOOKING AT YOU
*THE BANJO THAT MAN JOE PLAYS
 DANCE OF THE CRINOLINE LADIES

DANCE OF THE RAGAMUFFINS
ENTRANCE OF EMIGRANTS
*AQUA SINCOPADA TANGO
*WHAT IS THIS THING CALLED LOVE?
WAIT UNTIL IT'S BEDTIME
OPERATIC PILLS
AFTER ALL, I'M ONLY A SCHOOLGIRL
*LET'S DO IT, LET'S FALL IN LOVE
*I DREAM OF A GIRL IN A SHAWL
NIGHT CLUB OPENING
*I'M A GIGOLO
*I WANT TO BE RAIDED BY YOU
*WHICH

Unused
THE EXTRA MAN
THE LADY I LOVE
MY LOUISA

THE BATTLE OF PARIS

Produced by Paramount Pictures. Released November 30, 1929. Screen play by Gene Markey. Directed by Robert Florey. Cast, starring Gertrude Lawrence, included Charles Ruggles, Walter Petrie, Gladys Du Bois, Arthur Treacher, and Joe King.

MUSICAL NUMBERS

*HERE COMES THE BANDWAGON
*THEY ALL FALL IN LOVE

FIFTY MILLION FRENCHMEN

Tryout: Colonial Theatre, Boston, November 14, 1929.

Produced by E. Ray Goetz at the Lyric Theatre, New York, November 27, 1929. 254 performances. Book by Herbert Fields. Directed by Monty Woolley. Cast, starring William Gaxton and Genevieve Tobin, included Helen Broderick, Evelyn Hoey, Betty Compton, and Jack Thompson.

MUSICAL NUMBERS

A TOAST TO VOLSTEAD
*YOU DO SOMETHING TO ME
THE AMERICAN EXPRESS
*YOU'VE GOT THAT THING
*FIND ME A PRIMITIVE MAN
WHERE WOULD YOU GET YOUR COAT?
DO YOU WANT TO SEE PARIS?
AT LONGCHAMPS TODAY
YANKEE DOODLE
*THE HAPPY HEAVEN OF HARLEM
WHY SHOULDN'T I HAVE YOU?
SOMEBODY'S GOING TO THROW A BIG PARTY
IT ISN'T DONE
*I'M IN LOVE
THE TALE OF AN OYSTER
*PAREE, WHAT DID YOU DO TO ME?
*YOU DON'T KNOW PAREE
*I'M UNLUCKY AT GAMBLING

Unused
*I WORSHIP YOU
*PLEASE DON'T MAKE ME BE GOOD
*THE QUEEN OF TERRE HAUTE

WATCHING THE WORLD GO BY
DOWN WITH EVERYBODY BUT US
THE SNAKE IN THE GRASS (Ballet)
WHY DON'T WE TRY STAYING HOME
THAT'S WHY I LOVE YOU
THE HEAVEN OF HARLEM
MY HARLEM WENCH

Added after New York opening
*LET'S STEP OUT
THE BOY FRIEND BACK HOME

MISCELLANEOUS SONGS
1920-1929

*RAGTIME PIPES OF PAN (Phi-Phi, 1922)
*HOT-HOUSE ROSE (1927)
*WEREN'T WE FOOLS (1927)
*THE LAZIEST GAL IN TOWN (1927)
SEX APPEAL
*LET'S MISBEHAVE
ITALIAN STREET SINGERS
POOR YOUNG MILLIONAIRE
DON'T TELL ME WHO YOU ARE
THE SCAMPI
I'M DINING WITH ELSA
THAT LITTLE OLD BAR AT THE RITZ
LOVE 'EM AND LEAVE 'EM

1930-1939

THE NEW YORKERS

Tryout: Chestnut Street Opera House, Philadelphia, November 12, 1930, Shubert Theatre, Newark, November 24, 1930.

Produced by E. Ray Goetz at B. S. Moss' Broadway Theatre, December 8, 1930. 168 performances. Book by Herbert Fields, based on a story by E. Ray Goetz and Peter Arno. Directed by Monty Woolley. Cast, starring Hope Williams, Charles King and Jimmy Durante, included Ann Pennington, Frances Williams, Marie Cahill, Lou Clayton, Eddie Jackson, Richard Carle, and Fred Waring and his orchestra.

MUSICAL NUMBERS

GO INTO YOUR DANCE
*WHERE HAVE YOU BEEN?
SAY IT WITH GIN
VENICE
*I'M GETTING MYSELF READY FOR YOU
*LOVE FOR SALE
*THE GREAT INDOORS
SING SING FOR SING SING
*TAKE ME BACK TO MANHATTAN
*LET'S FLY AWAY
*I HAPPEN TO LIKE NEW YORK

Unused
*JUST ONE OF THOSE THINGS (not the familiar song
    with the same title)
MONA AND HER KIDDIES
THE POOR RICH
YOU'RE TOO FAR AWAY

YOU'VE GOT TO BE HARD-BOILED
MY LOUISA
WE'VE BEEN SPENDING THE SUMMER WITH OUR FAMILIES
WHY TALK ABOUT SEX?

STAR DUST

Unproduced musical which E. Ray Goetz planned to present in 1931. The book was by Herbert Fields. The following songs were intended for the show:

MUSICAL NUMBERS

AUF WIEDERSEHN
BUT HE NEVER SAYS HE LOVES ME
I STILL LOVE THE RED, WHITE AND BLUE
I WORSHIP YOU
MYSTERIOUSLY
PICK ME UP AND LAY ME DOWN
I'VE GOT YOU ON MY MIND
I GET A KICK OUT OF YOU
MISTER AND MISSUS FITCH
IT'S PROBABLY JUST AS WELL

GAY DIVORCE

Tryout: Wilbur Theatre, Boston, November 7, 1932, Shubert Theatre, New Haven, November 21, 1932.

Produced by Dwight Deere Wiman and Tom Weatherly at the Ethel Barrymore Theatre, November 29, 1932. 248 performances. Book by Dwight Taylor. Directed by Howard Lindsay. Cast, starring Fred Astaire, included Claire Luce, Luella Gear, Betty Starbuck, Erik Rhodes, Eric Blore, and G. P. Huntley, Jr.

MUSICAL NUMBERS

*AFTER YOU, WHO?
WHY MARRY THEM
SALT AIR
I STILL LOVE THE RED, WHITE AND BLUE
*NIGHT AND DAY
*HOW'S YOUR ROMANCE?
WHAT WILL BECOME OF OUR ENGLAND?
*I'VE GOT YOU ON MY MIND
*MISTER AND MISSUS FITCH
*YOU'RE IN LOVE

Unused
FATE
A WEEKEND AFFAIR

Numbers added to London production, Palace Theatre, November 2, 1933

I LOVE ONLY YOU
NEVER SAY NO
WAITERS v. WAITRESSES

NYMPH ERRANT

Tryout: The Opera House, Manchester, England, September 11, 1933.

Produced by Charles B. Cochran at the Adelphi Theatre, London, October 6, 1933. 154 performances. Book by Romney Brent, based on the novel by James Laver. Directed by Romney Brent under the personal supervision of Charles B. Cochran. Cast, starring Gertrude Lawrence, included Iris Ashley, Doris Carson, Walter Crisham, Austin Trevor, David Burns, and Elizabeth Welch.

MUSICAL NUMBERS

*EXPERIMENT
*IT'S BAD FOR ME
 NEAUVILLE SUR MER
 THE COCOTTE
*HOW COULD WE BE WRONG
 THEY'RE ALWAYS ENTERTAINING
 GEORGIA SAND
 CASANOVA
*NYMPH ERRANT
 RUINS
*THE PHYSICIAN
*SOLOMON
 BACK TO NATURE
 PLUMBING
 SI VOUS AIMEZ LES POITRINES
*YOU'RE TOO FAR AWAY

Unused
*WHEN LOVE COMES YOUR WAY
 SWEET NUDITY
 MY LOUISA

ONCE UPON A TIME
(EVER YOURS)

An unproduced musical intended for presentation by Gilbert Miller. Book by Guy Bolton, late 1933 and early 1934, based on a novel by Lily Hatvany. Cole Porter wrote the following songs:

MUSICAL NUMBERS

GYPSY SONG
ILSA'S SONG
YOURS
THE NIGHT OF THE BALL
ONCE UPON A TIME
IT ALL SEEMS SO LONG AGO
THANK YOU
COFFEE
SUCCESS
TECHNIQUE
WHEN LOVE COMES YOUR WAY
WALTZ DOWN THE AISLE
LEAD ME ON

ANYTHING GOES

Tryout: Colonial Theatre, Boston, November 5, 1934.

Produced by Vinton Freedley at the Alvin Theatre, New York, November 21, 1934. 420 performances. Book by Guy Bolton and P. G. Wodehouse, revised by Howard Lindsay and Russel Crouse. Directed by Howard Lindsay. Cast, starring William Gaxton, Ethel Merman and Victor Moore, included Bettina Hall, Vivian Vance, and Leslie Barrie.

MUSICAL NUMBERS (Complete piano-vocal score published)

*I GET A KICK OUT OF YOU
 BON VOYAGE
*ALL THROUGH THE NIGHT
*THERE'LL ALWAYS BE A LADY FAIR
 WHERE ARE THE MEN?
*YOU'RE THE TOP
*ANYTHING GOES
 PUBLIC ENEMY NUMBER ONE
*BLOW, GABRIEL, BLOW
 BE LIKE THE BLUEBIRD
*BUDDIE BEWARE
*THE GYPSY IN ME

Unused

*WALTZ DOWN THE AISLE
 WHAT A JOY TO BE YOUNG
 KATE THE GREAT
 THERE'S NO CURE LIKE TRAVEL

ADIOS ARGENTINA

Unproduced Fox Film for which Cole wrote the following songs in late 1934 and early 1935.

MUSICAL NUMBERS

 ADIOS ARGENTINA
 THE CHIRIPAH
*DON'T FENCE ME IN (Based on poem by Bob Fletcher)
 IF YOU COULD LOVE ME
 THE SIDE CAR
 SINGING IN THE SADDLE

JUBILEE

Tryout: Shubert Theatre, Boston, September 21, 1935.

Produced by Sam H. Harris and Max Gordon at the Imperial Theatre, New York, October 12, 1935. 169 performances. Book by Moss Hart. Directed by Monty Woolley. Entire production supervised, staged, and lighted by Hassard Short. Cast, starring Mary Boland, included Melville Cooper, June Knight, Derek Williams, May Boley, Charles Walters, Margaret Adams, Mark Plant, and Montgomery Clift.

MUSICAL NUMBERS

 OUR CROWN
 WE'RE OFF TO FEATHERMORE
*WHY SHOULDN'T I?
 ENTRANCE OF ERIC
*THE KLING-KLING BIRD ON THE DIVI-DIVI TREE
*WHEN LOVE COMES YOUR WAY
 WHAT A NICE MUNICIPAL PARK
 WHEN ME, MOWGLI, LOVE
 GATHER YE AUTOGRAPHS WHILE YE MAY
 MY LOULOU
*BEGIN THE BEGUINE
 CABINET MUSIC
 GOOD MONING, MISS STANDING
 MY MOST INTIMATE FRIEND
*A PICTURE OF ME WITHOUT YOU
 EV'RYBOD-EE WHO'S ANYBOD-EE
 THE JUDGMENT OF PARIS

SWING THAT SWING
SUNDAY MORNING, BREAKFAST TIME
MR. AND MRS. SMITH
GAY LITTLE WIVES (SIX LITTLE WIVES)
TO GET AWAY
BEACH SCENE
*ME AND MARIE
*JUST ONE OF THOSE THINGS
JUBILEE PRESENTATION

Unused

WALTZ DOWN THE AISLE
THERE'S NOTHING LIKE SWIMMING
GREEK SCENE
YOURS
SING JUBILEE

BORN TO DANCE

Produced by Jack Cummings for MGM in 1936. Released in November, 1936. Screenplay by Jack McGowan and Sid Silvers, based on an original story by McGowan, Silvers and B. G. De Sylva. Directed by Roy del Ruth. Cast, starring Eleanor Powell, included James Stewart, Virginia Bruce, Una Merkel, Sid Silvers, Frances Langford, Raymond Walburn, Buddy Ebsen, Georges and Jalna, and Reginald Gardiner.

MUSICAL NUMBERS

*ROLLING HOME
*RAP TAP ON WOOD
*HEY BABE HEY
 ENTRANCE OF LUCY JAMES
*LOVE ME, LOVE MY PEKINESE
*EASY TO LOVE
*I'VE GOT YOU UNDER MY SKIN
*SWINGIN' THE JINX AWAY

RED, HOT AND BLUE

Tryout: Colonial Theatre, Boston, October 7, 1936. Shubert Theatre, New Haven, October 19, 1936.

Produced by Vinton Freedley at the Alvin Theatre, New York, October 29, 1936. 183 performances. Book by Howard Lindsay and Russel Crouse. Directed by Howard Lindsay. Cast, starring Ethel Merman and Jimmy Durante, included Bob Hope, Polly Walters, Grace and Paul Hartman, Dorothy Vernon, and Thurston Crane.

MUSICAL NUMBERS

 AT YE OLDE COFFEE SHOPPE IN CHEYENNE
 IT'S A GREAT LIFE
*PERENNIAL DEBUTANTES
*OURS
*DOWN IN THE DEPTHS
 CARRY ON
*YOU'VE GOT SOMETHING
*IT'S DE-LOVELY
*A LITTLE SKIPPER FROM HEAVEN ABOVE
 FIVE HUNDRED MILLION
*RIDIN' HIGH
 WE'RE ABOUT TO START BIG REHEARSIN'
 HYMN TO HYMEN
*WHAT A GREAT PAIR WE'LL BE
*YOU'RE A BAD INFLUENCE ON ME
*THE OZARKS ARE CALLIN' ME HOME
*RED, HOT AND BLUE

Unused
*GOOD-BYE, LITTLE DREAM, GOOD-BYE
WHEN YOUR TROUBLES HAVE STARTED
BERTIE AND GERTIE
WHO, BUT YOU
THAT'S THE NEWS I'M WAITING TO HEAR
WHERE?
LONELY STAR

ROSALIE

Produced by William Anthony McGuire for MGM in 1937. Released, December 24, 1937. Screenplay by William Anthony McGuire, based on the musical comedy libretto by McGuire and Guy Bolton. Directed by W. S. Van Dyke. Cast, starring Nelson Eddy and Eleanor Powell, included Frank Morgan, Edna May Oliver, Ray Bolger, and Ilona Massey.

MUSICAL NUMBERS

*CLOSE (may not have been sung in film)
*IN THE STILL OF THE NIGHT
IT'S ALL OVER BUT THE SHOUTING
*I'VE A STRANGE NEW RHYTHM IN MY HEART
*ROSALIE
SPRING LOVE IS IN THE AIR
*WHO KNOWS?
*WHY SHOULD I CARE?

Unused (or probably unused)
A FOOL THERE WAS
ENTRANCE OF PRINCE PAUL
TO LOVE OR NOT TO LOVE
I KNOW IT'S NOT MEANT FOR ME

BREAK THE NEWS

Produced by René Clair for Monogram Pictures, England, 1937. Released in 1938 and in the United States in 1941. Screenplay by Geoffrey Kerr. Directed by René Clair. Cast headed by Maurice Chevalier, Jack Buchanan, and June Knight.

MUSICAL NUMBER

*IT ALL BELONGS TO YOU

GREEK TO YOU

Unproduced musical intended for presentation by Vinton Freedley, 1937-38. Unfinished book by Howard Lindsay and Russel Crouse. Cole wrote a few numbers, which included:

GREEK TO YOU
MELOS, THAT LOVELY SMILING ISLE
WILD WEDDING BELLS
IT NEVER ENTERED MY HEAD

YOU NEVER KNOW

Tryout: Shubert Theatre, New Haven, March 3, 1938; Shubert Theatre, Boston, March 7, 1938; National Theatre, Washington, March 21, 1938; Forrest Theatre, Philadelphia, March 28, 1938; Nixon Theatre, Pittsburgh, April 18, 1938; Cass Theatre, Detroit, April 24, 1938; Grand Opera House, Chicago, May 1, 1938; Shrine Auditorium, Des Moines, May 22, 1938; English's Theatre, Indianapolis, May 23, 1938; Hartman Theatre, Columbus, May 27, 1938; Erlanger Theatre, Buffalo, May 29, 1938; Bushnell Auditorium, Hartford, Sept. 16, 1938.

Produced by Lee and J. J. Shubert, in association with John Shubert, at the Winter Garden Theatre, September 21, 1938. Seventy-eight performances. Book adapted by Rowland Leigh from *By Candlelight*. Directed by Rowland Leigh. Cast, starring Clifton Webb, Lupe Velez and Libby Holman, included Toby Wing, Rex O'Malley, Charles Kemper, and June Preisser.

MUSICAL NUMBERS

I AM GASTON
AU REVOIR, CHER BARON
*MARIA
*YOU NEVER KNOW
*WHAT IS THAT TUNE?
*FOR NO RHYME OR REASON
*FROM ALPHA TO OMEGA
DON'T LET IT GET YOU DOWN
*WHAT SHALL I DO?
*AT LONG LAST LOVE
YES, YES, YES
GOOD EVENING, PRINCESS

Unused
I'LL BLACK HIS EYES
I'M YOURS
WHAT A PRICELESS PLEASURE
ONE STEP AHEAD OF LOVE
HA, HA, HA
BY CANDLELIGHT
I'M BACK IN CIRCULATION
I'M GOING IN FOR LOVE
IT'S NO LAUGHING MATTER

LEAVE IT TO ME

Tryout: Shubert Theatre, New Haven, October 13, 1938; Shubert Theatre, Boston, October 17, 1938.

Produced by Vinton Freedley at the Imperial Theatre, New York, November 9, 1938. 307 performances. Book by Bella and Samuel Spewack. Directed by Samuel Spewack. Cast, starring William Gaxton and Victor Moore, included Sophie Tucker, Tamara, Mary Martin, and Gene Kelly.

MUSICAL NUMBERS

HOW DO YOU SPELL AMBASSADOR
WE DRINK TO YOU, J. H. BRODY
VITE, VITE, VITE
*I'M TAKING THE STEPS TO RUSSIA
*GET OUT OF TOWN
WHEN IT'S ALL SAID AND DONE
*MOST GENTLEMEN DON'T LIKE LOVE
COMRADE ALONZO
RECALL GOODHUE
*FROM NOW ON
*I WANT TO GO HOME

*MY HEART BELONGS TO DADDY
*TOMORROW
*FAR AWAY
 FROM THE U.S.A. TO THE U.S.S.R.

Unused
WHEN THE HEN STOPS LAYING
JUST ANOTHER PAGE IN YOUR DIARY
INFORMATION PLEASE
THERE'S A FAN
WILD WEDDING BELLS
AS LONG AS IT'S NOT ABOUT LOVE

BROADWAY MELODY OF 1940

Produced by Jack Cummings for MGM in 1939. Released February 9, 1940. Screenplay by Leon Gordon and George Oppenheimer, based on a book by Jack McGowan and Dore Schary. Directed by Norman Taurog. Cast, starring Fred Astaire and Eleanor Powell, included George Murphy, Frank Morgan, Douglas McPhail, and Carmen D'Antonio and her vocal group.

MUSICAL NUMBERS

*BETWEEN YOU AND ME
*I CONCENTRATE ON YOU
*I'VE GOT MY EYES ON YOU
*PLEASE DON'T MONKEY WITH BROADWAY
*BEGIN THE BEGUINE (motion picture premiere)

Unused
*I HAPPEN TO BE IN LOVE
 I'M SO IN LOVE WITH YOU

DU BARRY WAS A LADY

Tryout: Shubert Theatre, New Haven, November 9, 1939; Shubert Theatre, Boston, November 13, 1939; Forrest Theatre, Philadelphia, November 27, 1939.

Produced by B. G. De Sylva at the 46th Street Theatre on December 6, 1939. 408 performances. Book by Herbert Fields and B. G. De Sylva. Directed by Edgar MacGregor. Cast, starring Bert Lahr and Ethel Merman, included Betty Grable, Benny Baker, Charles Walters, and Ronald Graham.

MUSICAL NUMBERS

 WHERE'S LOUIE?
*EV'RY DAY A HOLIDAY
 IT AIN'T ETIQUETTE
*WHEN LOVE BECKONED
*COME ON IN
 DREAM SONG
 MESDAMES AND MESSIEURS
 GAVOTTE
*BUT IN THE MORNING, NO
*DO I LOVE YOU?
 DANSE VICTOIRE
 DANSE EROTIQUE
 DU BARRY WAS A LADY
 DANSE TZIGANE
*GIVE HIM THE OO-LA-LA
*WELL, DID YOU EVAH!

*IT WAS WRITTEN IN THE STARS
 L'APRES MIDI D'UN BOEUF
*KATIE WENT TO HAITI
*FRIENDSHIP

Unused
WHAT HAVE I?
IN THE BIG MONEY

MISCELLANEOUS SONGS 1930-1939

 WHAT'S MY MAN GONNA BE LIKE (The Vanderbilt Revue, 1930)
*MISS OTIS REGRETS
*THANK YOU SO MUCH MRS. LOWSBOROUGH-GOODBY
 JAVA
*GOOD-BYE, LITTLE DREAM, GOOD-BYE
    (O Mistress Mine, England 1936)
*RIVER GOD (The Sun Never Sets, England 1938)
 WHAT AM I TO DO (The Man Who Came to Dinner, 1939)
 AT LAST IN YOUR ARMS
 HOW DO THEY DO IT?
 MAYBE YES, MAYBE NO
 THE UPPER PARK AVENUE

1940-1949

PANAMA HATTIE

Tryout: Shubert Theatre, New Haven, October 3, 1940; Shubert Theatre, Boston, October 8, 1940.

Produced by B. G. De Sylva at the 46th Street Theatre, New York, October 30, 1940. 501 performances. Book by Herbert Fields and B. G. De Sylva. Staged by Edgar MacGregor. Cast, starring Ethel Merman, included Arthur Treacher, Betty Hutton, James Dunn, Phyllis Brooks, Joan Carroll, Rags Ragland, Pat Harrington, and Frank Hyers.

MUSICAL NUMBERS

 A STROLL ON THE PLAZA SANT 'ANA
 JOIN IT RIGHT AWAY
*VISIT PANAMA
*MY MOTHER WOULD LOVE YOU
*I'VE STILL GOT MY HEALTH
*FRESH AS A DAISY
 WELCOME TO JERRY
*LET'S BE BUDDIES
 THEY AIN'T DONE RIGHT BY OUR NELL
 I'M THROWING A BALL TONIGHT
 WE DETEST A FIESTA
*WHO WOULD HAVE DREAMED
*MAKE IT ANOTHER OLD-FASHIONED, PLEASE
*ALL I'VE GOT TO GET NOW IS MY MAN
 YOU SAID IT
 GOD BLESS THE WOMEN

Unused
HERE'S TO PANAMA HATTIE
AMERICANS ALL DRINK COFFEE

264

YOU'LL NEVER GET RICH

Produced by Samuel Bischoff for Columbia Pictures in 1941. Released October 23, 1941. Screenplay by Michael Fessier and Ernest Pagano. Directed by Sidney Lanfield. Cast, starring Fred Astaire and Rita Hayworth, included Robert Benchley and Martha Tilton.

MUSICAL NUMBERS

*BOOGIE BARCAROLLE
*DREAM DANCING
*SHOOTIN' THE WORKS FOR UNCLE SAM
*SINCE I KISSED MY BABY GOODBYE
*SO NEAR AND YET SO FAR
*THE WEDDING CAKE-WALK
 A-STAIRABLE RAG (may not have been used)

LET'S FACE IT

Tryout: Colonial Theatre, Boston, October 9, 1941.

Produced by Vinton Freedley at the Imperial Theatre, New York, October 29, 1941. 547 performances. Book by Herbert and Dorothy Fields. Staged by Edgar MacGregor. Cast, starring Danny Kaye, included Eve Arden, Benny Baker, Mary Jane Walsh, Edith Meiser, Vivian Vance, Sunnie O'Dea, Nanette Fabray, and Jack Williams.

MUSICAL NUMBERS

 LET'S FACE IT
 MILK, MILK, MILK
 A LADY NEEDS A REST
*JERRY, MY SOLDIER BOY
*FARMING
*EV'RYTHING I LOVE
*ACE IN THE HOLE
*YOU IRRITATE ME SO
 BABY GAMES
*RUB YOUR LAMP
 I'VE GOT SOME UNFINISHED BUSINESS WITH YOU
*LET'S NOT TALK ABOUT LOVE
*A LITTLE RUMBA NUMBA
*I HATE YOU, DARLING
 GET YOURSELF A GIRL

Unused
REVENGE
WHAT ARE LITTLE HUSBANDS MADE OF
PETS
MAKE A DATE WITH A GREAT PSYCHOANALYST
UP TO HIS OLD TRICKS AGAIN
YOU CAN'T BEAT MY BILL

SOMETHING TO SHOUT ABOUT

Produced by Gregory Ratoff for Columbia Pictures in 1942. Released in February, 1943. Screenplay by Lou Breslow and Edward Eliscu. Directed by Gregory Ratoff. Cast, starring Don Ameche and Janet Blair, included William Gaxton, Jack Oakie, Hazel Scott, Cobina Wright, Jr., and Veda Ann Borg.

MUSICAL NUMBERS

*HASTA LUEGO
*I ALWAYS KNEW
*LOTUS BLOOM
*SOMETHING TO SHOUT ABOUT

 THROUGH THICK AND THIN
*YOU'D BE SO NICE TO COME HOME TO

Unused
*IT MIGHT HAVE BEEN
 I CAN DO WITHOUT TEA IN MY TEAPOT
 COULDN'T BE
 TAKE IT EASY
 LET DOCTOR SCHMET VET YOUR PET

SOMETHING FOR THE BOYS

Tryout: Shubert Theatre, Boston, December 18, 1942.

Produced by Michael Todd at the Alvin Theatre, New York, January 7, 1943. 422 performances. Book by Herbert and Dorothy Fields. Staged and lighted by Hassard Short. Cast, starring Ethel Merman, included, Paula Laurence, Bill Johnson, Betty Garrett, Betty Bruce, and Allen Jenkins.

MUSICAL NUMBERS

 ANNOUNCEMENT OF INHERITANCE
*SEE THAT YOU'RE BORN IN TEXAS
*WHEN MY BABY GOES TO TOWN
*SOMETHING FOR THE BOYS
 WHEN WE'RE HOME ON THE RANGE
*COULD IT BE YOU?
*HEY, GOOD LOOKIN'
*HE'S A RIGHT GUY
*THE LEADER OF A BIG-TIME BAND
*I'M IN LOVE WITH A SOLDIER BOY
 THERE'S A HAPPY LAND IN THE SKY
*BY THE MISSISSINEWAH

Unused
RIDDLE DIDDLE ME THIS
SO LONG, SAN ANTONIO
WASHINGTON, D.C.
OH, HOW I COULD GO FOR YOU
TEXAS WILL MAKE YOU A MAN
WELL, I JUST WOULDN'T KNOW
WOULDN'T IT BE CRAZY

MISSISSIPPI BELLE

Unproduced musical film written for Warner Brothers in 1943 and abandoned in 1944. Cole wrote the following musical numbers, all unused.

AMO AMAS
CLOSE TO ME
HIP, HIP HOORAY FOR ANDY JACKSON
I LIKE PRETTY THINGS
I'M NOT MYSELF AT ALL
IN THE GREEN HILLS OF COUNTY MAYO
KATHLEEN
LOADING SONG
MAMIE MAGDALIN
MISSISSIPPI BELLE
MY BROTH OF A BOY
SCHOOL, SCHOOL, HEAVEN-BLESSED SCHOOL
SO LONG
WHEN A WOMAN'S IN LOVE
WHEN McKINLEY MARCHES ON
WHEN YOU AND I WERE STRANGERS
WHO'LL BID

MEXICAN HAYRIDE

Tryout: Shubert Theatre, Boston, December 29, 1943.

Produced by Michael Todd at the Winter Garden Theatre, New York, January 28, 1944. 481 performances. Book by Herbert and Dorothy Fields. Entire production staged and lighted by Hassard Short. Cast, starring Bobby Clark, included June Havoc, George Givot, Wilbur Evans, Luba Malina, Corinna Mura, and Paul Haakon.

MUSICAL NUMBERS

 ENTRANCE OF MONTANA
*SING TO ME GUITAR
*THE GOOD-WILL MOVEMENT
*I LOVE YOU
*THERE MUST BE SOMEONE FOR ME
*CARLOTTA
*GIRLS
 WHAT A CRAZY WAY TO SPEND SUNDAY
*ABRACADABRA
*COUNT YOUR BLESSINGS

Unused
HEREAFTER
*IT MUST BE FUN TO BE YOU
 HERE'S A CHEER FOR DEAR OLD CIRO'S
 TEQUILA
 WE'RE OFF FOR A HAYRIDE IN MEXICO
 HE CERTAINLY KILLS THE WOMEN
 A HUMBLE HOLLYWOOD EXECUTIVE
 IT'S A BIG NIGHT
 IT'S JUST LIKE THE GOOD OLD DAYS
 IT'S JUST YOURS
 OCTET
 PUT A SACK OVER THEIR HEADS
 A SIGHT SEEING TOUR
 THAT'S WHAT YOU MEAN TO ME
 I'M AFRAID I LOVE YOU
 I'M SO GLAHD TO MEET YOU

SEVEN LIVELY ARTS

Tryout: Forrest Theatre, Philadelphia, November 24, 1944.

Produced by Billy Rose at the Ziegfeld Theatre, New York, December 7, 1944. 183 performances. Book by Moss Hart, George S. Kaufman, Robert Pirosh, Joseph Schrank, Charles Sherman, and Ben Hecht. Staged and lighted by Hassard Short. Cast, starring Beatrice Lillie, Bert Lahr, Benny Goodman, Alicia Markova, and Anton Dolin, included Teddy Wilson, Red Norvo, Bill Tabbert, Nan Wynn, Jere McMahon, Dolores Grey, Billie Worth, Paula Bane, Mary Roche, and, in her Broadway debut, Helen Gallagher.

MUSICAL NUMBERS

 BIG TOWN
*IS IT THE GIRL? (OR IS IT THE GOWN?)
*ONLY ANOTHER BOY AND GIRL
*WOW-OOH-WOLF
 DRINK
*WHEN I WAS A LITTLE CUCKOO
*FRAHNGEE-PAHNEE
 DANCIN' TO A JUNGLE DRUM (LET'S END THE BEGUINE)
*EV'RYTIME WE SAY GOODBYE
*HENCE IT DON'T MAKE SENSE
*THE BAND STARTED SWINGING A SONG
 THE BIG PARADE

Unused
PRETTY LITTLE MISSUS BELL
DAINTY, QUAINTY ME
YOURS FOR A SONG
I WROTE A PLAY
IF I HADN'T A HUSBAND
WHERE DO WE GO FROM HERE?
CAFE SOCIETY STILL CARRIES ON

AROUND THE WORLD IN EIGHTY DAYS

Tryout: Boston Opera House, Boston, April 28, 1946; Shubert Theatre, New Haven, May 7, 1946; Shubert Theatre, Philadelphia, May 14, 1946.

Produced by Orson Welles as a Mercury Theatre Production at the Adelphi Theatre, New York, May 31, 1946. Seventy-five performances. Book adapted by Orson Welles from the Jules Verne novel. Directed by Orson Welles. Cast, starring Orson Welles, included Arthur Margetson, Mary Healy, Julie Warren, Larry Laurence (Enzo Stuarti), and Victoria Cordova.

MUSICAL NUMBERS

*LOOK WHAT I FOUND
*THERE HE GOES, MR. PHILEAS FOGG
 MEERAHLAH
 SUTTEE PROCESSION
 SUEZ DANCE
 SEA CHANTEY
*SHOULD I TELL YOU I LOVE YOU
*PIPE DREAMING
 OKA SAKA CIRCUS
 CALIFORNIA SCENE DANCE
*IF YOU SMILE AT ME
*WHEREVER THEY FLY THE FLAG OF OLD ENGLAND

Unused
 MISSUS AOUDA
 SLAVE AUCTION
 SNAGTOOTH GERTIE

Note: Much of the incidental music is not listed in the program but may have been used in the show.

THE PIRATE

Produced by Arthur Freed for MGM in 1948. Released March 24. Screenplay by Albert Hackett and Frances Goodrich, based on S. N. Behrman's play. Directed by Vincente Minelli. Cast, starring Judy Garland and Gene Kelly, included Walter Slezak, Gladys Cooper, and Reginald Owen.

MUSICAL NUMBERS

*BE A CLOWN
*LOVE OF MY LIFE
*MACK THE BLACK
*NINA
*YOU CAN DO NO WRONG

Unused
VOODOO
MANUELA
MARTINIQUE

KISS ME, KATE

Tryout: Shubert Theatre, Philadelphia, December 2, 1948.

Produced by Saint Subber and Lemuel Ayers at the New Century Theatre, December 30, 1948. 1077 performances. Book by Sam and Bella Spewack, inspired and based loosely on Shakespeare's *Taming of the Shrew*. Production staged by John C. Wilson. Cast, starring Alfred Drake, Patricia Morison, Harold Lang and Lisa Kirk, included Annabelle Hill, Lorenzo Fuller, Harry Clark, and Jack Diamond.

MUSICAL NUMBERS (Complete vocal score published)

*ANOTHER OP'NIN', ANOTHER SHOW
*WHY CAN'T YOU BEHAVE
*WUNDERBAR
*SO IN LOVE
*WE OPEN IN VENICE
*TOM, DICK OR HARRY
*I'VE COME TO WIVE IT WEALTHILY IN PADUA
*I HATE MEN
*WERE THINE THAT SPECIAL FACE
 I SING OF LOVE
 KISS ME KATE
*TOO DARN HOT
*WHERE IS THE LIFE THAT LATE I LED?
*ALWAYS TRUE TO YOU IN MY FASHION
*BIANCA
*BRUSH UP YOUR SHAKESPEARE
*I AM ASHAMED THAT WOMEN ARE SO SIMPLE

Unused
 IT WAS GREAT FUN THE FIRST TIME
 WE SHALL NEVER BE YOUNGER
 A WOMAN'S CAREER
 WHAT DOES YOUR SERVANT DREAM ABOUT
 I'M AFRAID, SWEETHEART, I LOVE YOU
 IF EVER MARRIED I'M

ADAM'S RIB

Produced by Lawrence Weingarten for MGM in 1949. Released in 1949. Screenplay by Ruth Gordon and Garson Kanin. Directed by George Cukor. Cast, starring Spencer Tracy and Katharine Hepburn, included Judy Holliday, Tom Ewell, David Wayne, and Jean Hagen.

MUSICAL NUMBER

*FAREWELL, AMANDA

MISCELLANEOUS SONGS
1940-1949

SO LONG, SAMOA
*GLIDE, GLIDER, GLIDE (Written for Armed Forces)
*SAILORS OF THE SKY (Written for Armed Forces)
GOLD DUSTERS SONG

1950-1958

OUT OF THIS WORLD

Tryout: Shubert Theatre, Philadelphia, November 4, 1950; Shubert Theatre, Boston, November 28, 1950.

Produced by Saint Subber and Lemuel Ayers at the New Century Theatre, New York, December 21, 1950. 157 performances. Book by Dwight Taylor and Reginald Lawrence. Entire production staged by Agnes de Mille. Cast, starring Charlotte Greenwood, included William Eythe, Priscilla Gillette, William Redfield, Barbara Ashley, Janet Collins, George Jongeyans (George Gaynes), Ray Harrison, and David Burns.

MUSICAL NUMBERS

PROLOGUE
 I JUPITER, I REX
*USE YOUR IMAGINATION
 HAIL, HAIL, HAIL
 I GOT BEAUTY
 MAIDEN FAIR
*WHERE, OH WHERE?
*I AM LOVED
 THEY COULDN'T COMPARE TO YOU
 WHAT DO YOU THINK ABOUT MEN?
 I SLEEP EASIER NOW
*CLIMB UP THE MOUNTAIN
*NO LOVER
*CHERRY PIES OUGHT TO BE YOU
*HARK TO THE SONG OF THE NIGHT
*NOBODY'S CHASING ME

Unused
 WE'RE ON THE ROAD TO ATHENS
*FROM THIS MOMENT ON
*YOU DON'T REMIND ME
 HUSH, HUSH, HUSH
 AWAY FROM IT ALL
 MIDSUMMER NIGHT
 OH, IT MUST BE FUN
 TO HELL WITH EVERYONE BUT US
 TONIGHT I LOVE YOU MORE
 WHY DO YOU WANT TO HURT ME SO?

CAN-CAN

Tryout: Shubert Theatre, Philadelphia, March 23, 1953.

Produced by Cy Feuer and Ernest Martin at the Sam S. Shubert Theatre, New York, May 7, 1953. 892 performances. Book and direction by Abe Burrows. Dances and musical numbers staged by Michael Kidd. Cast, starring Lilo and Peter Cookson, included Hans Conreid, Gwen Verdon, and Erik Rhodes.

MUSICAL NUMBERS (Complete vocal score published)

 MAIDENS TYPICAL OF FRANCE
*NEVER GIVE ANYTHING AWAY
*C'EST MAGNIFIQUE
 QUADRILLE
*COME ALONG WITH ME
*LIVE AND LET LIVE
*I AM IN LOVE
*IF YOU LOVED ME TRULY
*MONTMART'
 THE GARDEN OF EDEN
*ALLEZ-VOUS-EN (Go Away)
 NEVER, NEVER BE AN ARTIST
*IT'S ALL RIGHT WITH ME
 EVERY MAN IS A STUPID MAN
 THE APACHES
*I LOVE PARIS
*CAN-CAN

Unused
THE LAW
I SHALL POSITIVELY PAY YOU NEXT MONDAY
A MAN MUST HIS HONOR DEFEND
NOTHING TO DO BUT WORK
LAUNDRY SCENE
HER HEART WAS IN HER WORK
WHO SAID GAY PAREE?
WHAT A FAIR THING IS A WOMAN
AM I IN LOVE?
TO THINK THAT THIS COULD HAPPEN TO ME
I DO
IF ONLY YOU COULD LOVE ME
WHEN LOVE COMES TO CALL

SILK STOCKINGS

Tryout: Shubert Theatre, Philadelphia, November 26, 1954; Shubert Theatre, Boston, January 4, 1955; Shubert Theatre, Detroit, February 1, 1955.

Produced by Cy Feuer and Ernest Martin at the Imperial Theatre, New York, February 24, 1955. 477 performances. Book by George S. Kaufman, Leueen MacGrath, and Abe Burrows. Directed by Cy Feuer. Dances and musical numbers staged by Eugene Loring. Cast, starring Don Ameche and Hildegarde Neff, included Gretchen Wyler and Julie Newmar.

MUSICAL NUMBERS

TOO BAD
*PARIS LOVES LOVERS
*STEREOPHONIC SOUND
*IT'S A CHEMICAL REACTION, THAT'S ALL
*ALL OF YOU
*SATIN AND SILK
*WITHOUT LOVE
HAIL BIBINSKI
*AS ON THROUGH THE SEASONS WE SAIL
*JOSEPHINE
*SIBERIA
*SILK STOCKINGS
THE RED BLUES

Unused
ART
THERE'S A HOLLYWOOD THAT'S GOOD
GIVE ME THE LAND
IF EVER WE GET OUT OF JAIL
LET'S MAKE IT A NIGHT
THE PERFUME OF LOVE
UNDER THE DRESS
WHAT A BALL
WHY SHOULD I TRUST YOU?
BEBE OF GAY PAREE
KEEP YOUR CHIN UP
I'M THE QUEEN THAMAR

Written for film version 1957
*FATED TO BE MATED
*RITZ ROLL AND ROCK

HIGH SOCIETY

Produced for Sol C. Siegel for MGM in 1956. Released August 3, 1956. Based on Philip Barry's stage play, *The Philadelphia Story*. Screenplay by John Patrick. Director, Charles Walters. Cast, starring Bing Crosby, Grace Kelly and Frank Sinatra, included Celeste Holm, John Lund, Louis Calhern, Sidney Blackmer, and Louis Armstrong.

MUSICAL NUMBERS

*HIGH SOCIETY CALYPSO
*I LOVE YOU, SAMANTHA
*LITTLE ONE
*WHO WANTS TO BE A MILLIONAIRE?
*TRUE LOVE
*YOU'RE SENSATIONAL
*NOW YOU HAS JAZZ
*WELL, DID YOU EVAH! (revised)
*MIND IF I MAKE LOVE TO YOU

Unused
A STEP MONTAGE
CAROLINE
LET'S VOCALIZE
SO WHAT?
HEY SEXY

LES GIRLS

Produced by Sol C. Siegel for MGM in 1957. Released in November, 1957. Associate Producer Saul Chaplin. Screenplay, John Patrick. Director, George Cukor. Cast starred Gene Kelly, Mitzi Gaynor, Kay Kendall, and Taina Elg.

MUSICAL NUMBERS

*ÇA C'EST L'AMOUR
*LES GIRLS
LADIES IN WAITING
*WHY AM I SO GONE ABOUT THAT GAL
*YOU'RE JUST TOO, TOO

Unused
DRINKING SONG
HIGH FLYIN' WINGS ON MY SHOES
I COULD KICK MYSELF
IS IT JOY?
MY DARLING NEVER IS LATE
MY LITTLE PIECE O' PIE
PER FAVORE
WHAT FUN
YOU'RE THE PRIZE GUY OF GUYS

ALADDIN

Produced by Richard Lewine for CBS Television's DuPont Show of the Month on February 21, 1958. Book by S. J. Perelman. Directed by Ralph Nelson. Cast, starring Cyril Ritchard and Dennis King, included Sal Mineo, Anna Maria Alberghetti, Basil Rathbone, Una Merkel, and George Hall.

MUSICAL NUMBERS

*TRUST YOUR DESTINY TO YOUR STAR
*ALADDIN
*COME TO THE SUPERMARKET IN OLD PEKING
*I ADORE YOU
*MAKE WAY FOR THE EMPEROR
*NO WONDER TAXES ARE HIGH
*OPPORTUNITY KNOCKS BUT ONCE
*WOULDN'T IT BE FUN
GENIE'S THEME

ALPHABETICAL LIST OF COLE PORTER SONGS

(Page numbers refer to lyrics in this volume)

ABRACADABRA
June Havoc and ensemble,
Mexican Hayride 1944

ABSINTHE
Ensemble, *The Kaleidoscope* 1913

THE ABSINTHE DRIP
Ensemble, *The Kaleidoscope* 1913

ACE IN THE HOLE
Mary Jane Walsh, Sunnie O'Dea, Nanette
Fabray and ensemble, *Let's Face It* 1941

ADIOS ARGENTINA
Unused. Unproduced film *Adios Argentina*
1934-35

AFTER ALL,
I'M ONLY A SCHOOLGIRL
Jessie Matthews and ensemble,
Wake Up and Dream 1929

AFTER YOU, WHO?
Fred Astaire, *Gay Divorce* 1932 (p. 111)

AH FONG LOW
Ensemble, *Hitchy-Koo of 1922*

ALADDIN
Anna Maria Alberghetti and ensemble,
Aladdin 1958

ALL I'VE GOT
TO GET NOW IS MY MAN
Betty Hutton and ensemble,
Panama Hattie 1940

ALL OF YOU
Don Ameche, *Silk Stockings* 1955 (p. 239)

ALL THROUGH THE NIGHT
Bettina Hall and William Gaxton,
Anything Goes 1934 (p. 122)

ALLEZ-VOUS-EN
  (Go Away)
Lilo, *Can-Can* 1953 (p. 235)

ALMIRO
Basil Howes, *La Revue des Ambassadeurs* 1928

ALONE WITH YOU.
Nelson Keys, English production,
Very Good Eddie 1918

ALPINE ROSE
Eleanor Shaler and ensemble,
La Revue des Ambassadeurs 1928

ALTOGETHER TOO FOND OF YOU
(Co-authors: Melville
Gideon and James Heard)
English production, *Telling the Tale* 1918

ALWAYS TRUE TO YOU
IN MY FASHION
Lisa Kirk, *Kiss Me Kate* 1948 (p. 217)

AM I IN LOVE?
Unused. *Can-Can* 1953

THE AMERICAN EXPRESS
Ensemble, *Fifty Million Frenchmen* 1929

THE AMERICAN PUNCH
Raymond Hitchcock, Benny Leonard and
ensemble, *Hitchy-Koo of 1922.* Used later in
The Dancing Girl 1923

AMERICANS
ALL DRINK COFFEE
Unused. *Panama Hattie* 1940 (p. 177)

AMO AMAS
Unused. Unproduced film *Mississippi Belle*
1943-44

ANNOUNCEMENT
OF INHERITANCE
Jed Prouty, Paula Laurence, Allen Jenkins and
Ethel Merman, *Something for the Boys* 1943

ANOTHER OP'NIN', ANOTHER SHOW
Annabelle Hill and ensemble,
Kiss Me Kate 1948 (p. 211)

ANOTHER SENTIMENTAL SONG
Unused. *Hitchy-Koo of 1919*

ANTOINETTE BIRBY
Cole Porter, Yale Glee Club, c. 1912 (p. 12)

ANYTHING GOES
Ethel Merman and ensemble,
Anything Goes 1934 (p. 127)

ANYTIME
Ensemble, *And the Villain Still
Pursued Her* 1912

THE APACHES
Danced by Gwen Verdon, Ralph Beaumont
and ensemble, *Can-Can* 1953

AQUA SINCOPADA TANGO
Danced by June Roper and Jack Kinney,
Wake Up and Dream 1929

ART
Unused. *Silk Stockings* 1955

AS I LOVE YOU
Newbold Noyes, *The Kaleidoscope* 1913

AS LONG AS IT'S NOT
ABOUT LOVE
Unused. *Leave It To Me* 1938

AS ON THROUGH
THE SEASONS WE SAIL
Don Ameche and Hildegarde Neff,
Silk Stockings 1955 (p. 239)

A-STAIRABLE RAG
Unused. *You'll Never Get Rich* 1941

AT LAST IN YOUR ARMS
Unused. *Balalaika* 1939

AT LONG LAST LOVE
Clifton Webb, *You Never Know* 1938 (p. 150)

AT LONGCHAMPS TODAY
Ensemble, *Fifty Million Frenchmen* 1929

AT THE DAWN TEA
Ensemble, *The Kaleidoscope* 1913

AT THE RAINBOW
Ensemble, *The Pot of Gold* 1912

AT YE OLDE COFFEE
SHOPPE IN CHEYENNE
Ensemble, *Red, Hot and Blue* 1936

AU REVOIR, CHER BARON
Ensemble, *You Never Know* 1938

AUF WIEDERSEHN
Unused. Unproduced musical *Star Dust* 1931

AWAY FROM IT ALL
Unused. *Out of This World* 1950

BABY GAMES
Danny Kaye, Eve Arden, Benny Baker,
Edith Meiser, Vivian Vance and Jack Williams,
Let's Face It 1941

BABY, LET'S DANCE
Buster West and ensemble,
La Revue des Ambassadeurs 1928

BACK TO NATURE
Gertrude Lawrence and Walter Crisham,
Nymph Errant 1933

BAD MEN
Ensemble, *See America First* 1916

THE BAND STARTED
SWINGING A SONG
Nan Wynn, *Seven Lively Arts* 1944

THE BANDIT BAND
Llora Hoffman and ensemble,
Hitchy-Koo of 1922

THE BANJO
THAT MAN JOE PLAYS
William Stephens, *Wake Up and Dream* 1929

BARCELONA
Irving G. Beebe, *And the Villain
Still Pursued Her* 1912

BE A CLOWN
Gene Kelly, Judy Garland and ensemble,
The Pirate 1948 (p. 208)

BE LIKE THE BLUEBIRD
Victor Moore, *Anything Goes* 1934

BEACH SCENE
Dorothy Fox and ensemble, *Jubilee* 1935

BEAUTIFUL,
PRIMITIVE INDIAN GIRLS
Clifton Webb, Roma June, Betty Brewster,
Gypsy O'Brien and ensemble,
See America First 1916

BEBE OF GAY PAREE
Unused. *Silk Stockings* 1955

BEGIN THE BEGUINE
June Knight, danced by June Knight and
Charles Walters, *Jubilee* 1935 (p. 134)

BELLBOYS
Ensemble, *The Pot of Gold* 1912

BERTIE AND GERTIE
Unused. *Red, Hot and Blue* 1936

BETWEEN YOU AND ME
George Murphy, danced by George Murphy
and Eleanor Powell, *Broadway Melody
of 1940* (p. 157)

FROM THE U.S.A. TO THE U.S.S.R.
Victor Moore, Sophie Tucker and ensemble,
Leave It To Me 1938

FROM THIS MOMENT ON
Unused. *Out of This World* 1950
Later introduced in the film version of
Kiss Me Kate 1953 (p. 227)

FUNNY LITTLE TRACKS
IN THE SNOW
William S. Innis and ensemble, *Paranoia* 1914

THE GARDEN OF EDEN
Danced by Gwen Verdon and ensemble,
Can-Can 1953

GATHER YE AUTOGRAPHS
WHILE YE MAY
Ensemble, *Jubilee* 1935

GAVOTTE
Betty Grable and ensemble,
Du Barry Was a Lady 1939

GAY LITTLE WIVES (SIX LITTLE WIVES)
Ensemble, *Jubilee* 1935

GENIE'S THEME
Instrumental, *Aladdin* 1958

GEORGIA SAND
Doris Carson, *Nymph Errant* 1933

GERSHWIN SPECIALTY
Frances Gershwin, *La Revue des
Ambassadeurs* 1928

GET OUT OF TOWN
Tamara, *Leave It To Me* 1938 (p. 154)

GET YOURSELF A GIRL
Tommy Gleason and The Royal Guards,
Let's Face It 1941

GIRLS
Bobby Clark and ensemble,
Mexican Hayride 1944

GIVE HIM THE OO-LA-LA
Ethel Merman, *Du Barry Was a Lady* 1939
(p. 160)

GIVE ME THE LAND
Unused. *Silk Stockings* 1955 (p. 242)

GLIDE, GLIDER, GLIDE
Song for the Armed Forces, 1942

GO INTO YOUR DANCE
Frances Williams and ensemble,
The New Yorkers 1930

GOD BLESS THE WOMEN
Rags Ragland, Frank Hyers and Pat
Harrington, *Panama Hattie* 1940

GOLD DUSTERS SONG
Written for Vassar College Singing Group,
1946

GOOD EVENING, PRINCESS
Clifton Webb and Lupe Velez,
You Never Know 1938

GOOD MORNING, MISS STANDING
May Boley and ensemble, *Jubilee* 1935

GOOD-BYE BOYS
T. Gaillard Thomas, II, and Cole Porter,
Cora 1911

GOOD-BYE,
LITTLE DREAM, GOOD-BYE
Yvonne Printemps, English production,
O Mistress Mine 1936 (p. 140)

GOOD-BYE MY TRUE LOVE
Newbold Noyes, *The Kaleidoscope* 1913

THE GOOD-WILL MOVEMENT
Wilbur Evans and ensemble,
Mexican Hayride 1944

THE GREAT INDOORS
Frances Williams and ensemble,
The New Yorkers 1930 (p. 103)

GREEK SCENE
Unused. *Jubilee* 1935

GREEK TO YOU
Unused. Unproduced musical,
Greek To You 1937-38

THE GYPSY IN ME
Bettina Hall and ensemble,
Anything Goes 1934

GYPSY SONG
Unused. Unproduced musical, *Once Upon
a Time (Ever Yours)* 1933-34

HA, HA, HA
Unused, *You Never Know* 1938

HA, HA, THEY MUST
SAIL FOR SIBERIA
Ensemble, *The Pot of Gold* 1912

HAIL BIBINSKI
Henry Lascoe, Leon Belasco, David Opatoshu
and ensemble, *Silk Stockings* 1955

HAIL, HAIL, HAIL
Peggy Rea, William Redfield and ensemble,
Out of This World 1950

HAIL THE FEMALE RELATIVE
Ensemble, *See America First* 1916

HAIL TO CYRIL
Ensemble, *Paranoia* 1914

HAIL TO YALE
(Music by Arthur Troostwyck)
Yale football song, 1911

HANS
Katheryn Ray, Jack Pearson, ensemble,
La Revue des Ambassadeurs 1928

THE HAPPY HEAVEN OF HARLEM
Billy Reed, *Fifty Million Frenchmen* 1929

THE HARBOR DEEP
DOWN IN MY HEART
Hitchy-Koo of 1922

HARK TO THE SONG
OF THE NIGHT
George Jongeyans (Gaynes),
Out of This World 1950

HASTA LUEGO
Janet Blair, David Lichine and ensemble,
Something to Shout About 1943

HE CERTAINLY KILLS THE WOMEN
Unused. *Mexican Hayride* 1944

THE HEAVEN HOP
Irving Aaronson and his Commanders,
Paris 1928

THE HEAVEN OF HARLEM
Unused. *Fifty Million Frenchmen* 1929

HELLO, MISS CHAPEL STREET
Ensemble, *Cora* 1911 (p. 13)

HENCE IT DON'T MAKE SENSE
Nan Wynn, Mary Roche, Dolores Gray,
Billie Worth and Jere McMahon,
Seven Lively Arts 1944 (p. 205)

HER HEART WAS IN HER WORK
Unused. *Can-Can* 1953

HERE COMES THE BANDWAGON
Gertrude Lawrence, *The Battle of Paris* 1929

HEREAFTER
Unused. *Mexican Hayride* 1944

HERE'S A CHEER FOR DEAR OLD CIRO'S
Unused. *Mexican Hayride* 1944

HERE'S TO PANAMA HATTIE
Unused. *Panama Hattie* 1940

HE'S A RIGHT GUY
Ethel Merman, *Something for the Boys* 1943
(p. 192)

HEY BABE HEY
Ensemble, *Born To Dance* 1936

HEY, GOOD LOOKIN'
Ethel Merman and Bill Johnson,
Something for the Boys 1943

HEY SEXY
Unused. *High Society* 1956

HIGH FLYIN' WINGS ON MY SHOES
Unused. *Les Girls* 1957 (p. 249)

HIGH SOCIETY CALYPSO
Louis Armstrong and band, *High Society* 1956

HIP, HIP HOORAY FOR ANDY JACKSON
Unused. Unproduced film
Mississippi Belle 1943-44

HITCHY'S GARDEN OF ROSES
Lillian Kemble Cooper and ensemble,
Hitchy-Koo of 1919

HOLD-UP ENSEMBLE
Clara Palmer, Sam Edwards and ensemble,
See America First 1916

HOT-HOUSE ROSE
Unused. Written for Fanny Brice, 1927 (p. 80)

HOW COULD WE BE WRONG?
Gertrude Lawrence, *Nymph Errant* 1933

HOW DO THEY DO IT?
Unused. Written during 1930's

HOW DO YOU SPELL AMBASSADOR
Ensemble, *Leave It To Me* 1938

HOW'S YOUR ROMANCE?
Erik Rhodes and ensemble, *Gay Divorce* 1932
(p. 113)

A HUMBLE HOLLYWOOD EXECUTIVE
Unused. *Mexican Hayride* 1944

HUSH, HUSH, HUSH
Unused. *Out of This World* 1950

HYMN TO HYMEN
Ensemble, *Red, Hot and Blue* 1936

I ADORE YOU
Sal Mineo and Anna Maria Alberghetti,
Aladdin 1958

I ALWAYS KNEW
Janet Blair and Jaye Martin,
Something to Shout About 1943

I AM ASHAMED THAT
WOMEN ARE SO SIMPLE
Patricia Morison, *Kiss Me Kate* 1948 (p. 221)

I AM GASTON
Clifton Webb, *You Never Know* 1938

I AM IN LOVE
Peter Cookson, *Can-Can* 1953 (p. 235)

I AM LOVED
Priscilla Gillette, *Out of This World* 1950
(p. 227)

I CAN DO WITHOUT TEA
IN MY TEAPOT
Unused. *Something to Shout About* 1943

I CONCENTRATE ON YOU
Douglas McPhail, *Broadway Melody of 1940*
(p. 159)

I COULD KICK MYSELF
Unused. *Les Girls* 1957

I DO
Unused. *Can-Can* 1953

I DREAM OF A GIRL IN A SHAWL
William Stephens, Sonnie Hale, George
Metaxa, Tilly Losch, Polly Ward, Tina Meller
and Antonio Rodriguez, *Wake Up and Dream*
1929

I GET A KICK OUT OF YOU
Ethel Merman to William Gaxton,
Anything Goes 1934 (p. 122)

I GOT BEAUTY
Charlotte Greenwood and ensemble,
Out of This World 1950

I HAPPEN TO BE IN LOVE
Unused. *Broadway Melody of 1940*

I HAPPEN TO LIKE NEW YORK
Oscar Ragland, *The New Yorkers* 1930 (p. 106)

I HATE MEN
Patricia Morison, *Kiss Me Kate* 1948 (p. 213)

I HATE YOU, DARLING
Vivian Vance, James Todd, Mary Jane Walsh
and Danny Kaye, *Let's Face It* 1941

I INTRODUCED
Raymond Hitchcock and ensemble,
Hitchy-Koo of 1919

I JUPITER, I REX
George Jongeyans (Gaynes) and ensemble,
Out of This World 1950

I KNOW IT'S NOT MEANT FOR ME
Unused. *Rosalie* 1937

I LIKE PRETTY THINGS
Unused. Unproduced film *Mississippi Belle*
1943-44

I LOVE ONLY YOU
Erik Rhodes, English production,
Gay Divorce 1933

I LOVE PARIS
Lilo, *Can-Can* 1953 (p. 235)

I LOVE YOU
Wilbur Evans, *Mexican Hayride* 1944 (p. 194)

I LOVE YOU, SAMANTHA
Bing Crosby, *High Society* 1956 (p. 248)

I LOVE YOU SO
Ensemble, *The Pot of Gold* 1912

I LOVED HIM BUT HE DIDN'T LOVE ME
Jessie Matthews, *Wake Up and Dream* 1929
(p. 92)

I NEVER REALIZED
Nancy Gibbs and F. Pope Stamper,
The Eclipse 1919

I SHALL POSITIVELY PAY YOU
NEXT MONDAY
Unused. *Can-Can* 1953

I SING OF LOVE
Lisa Kirk, Harold Lang and ensemble,
Kiss Me Kate 1948

I SLEEP EASIER NOW
Charlotte Greenwood, *Out of This World* 1950

I STILL LOVE THE RED, WHITE AND BLUE
Luella Gear, *Gay Divorce* 1932

I WANT TO BE A YALE BOY
Cole Porter, Yale Glee Club, 1912

I WANT TO BE MARRIED (TO A DELTA
KAPPA EPSILON MAN)
Cole Porter and ensemble,
The Pot of Gold 1912

I WANT TO BE RAIDED BY YOU
Sonnie Hale, *Wake Up and Dream* 1929

I WANT TO GO HOME
Victor Moore, *Leave It To Me* 1938

I WANT TO ROW ON THE CREW
Newbold Noyes, *Paranoia* 1914 (p. 24)

I WANT TWINS
James Clemons, James Naulty and ensemble,
Greenwich Village Follies of 1924

I WONDER WHERE MY GIRL IS NOW
T. Gaillard Thomas, II, *The Pot of Gold* 1912

I WORSHIP YOU
Unused. *Fifty Million Frenchmen* 1929 (p. 96)

I WROTE A PLAY
Unused. *Seven Lively Arts* 1944 (p. 206)

IDYLL
Hay Langenheim, *Paranoia* 1914

IF EVER MARRIED I'M
Unused. *Kiss Me Kate* 1948

IF EVER WE GET OUT OF JAIL
Unused. *Silk Stockings* 1955. Same music as
AS ON THROUGH THE SEASONS WE SAIL

IF I HADN'T A HUSBAND
Unused. *Seven Lively Arts* 1944

IF I WERE A FOOTBALL MAN
Unused. *The Pot of Gold* 1912. Rewritten as
A FOOTBALL KING

IF IN SPITE OF OUR ATTEMPTS
Ensemble, *See America First* 1916

IF ONLY YOU COULD LOVE ME
Unused. *Can-Can* 1953

IF YOU COULD LOVE ME
Unused. Unproduced film *Adios Argentina*
1934-35

IF YOU LOVED ME TRULY
Hans Conreid, Gwen Verdon, Phil Leeds,
Robert Penn, Richard Purdy, Mary Anne
Cohan, Jean Kramer and Beverly Purvin,
Can-Can 1953

IF YOU SMILE AT ME
Victoria Cordova, reprised by Julie Warren,
Around the World in Eighty Days 1946

I'LL BLACK HIS EYES
Unused. *You Never Know* 1938

ILSA'S SONG
Unused. Unproduced musical *Once Upon
a Time (Ever Yours)* 1933-34

I'M A GIGOLO
William Stephens, *Wake Up and Dream* 1929
(p. 94)

I'M AFRAID I LOVE YOU
Unused. *Mexican Hayride* 1944

I'M AFRAID, SWEETHEART, I LOVE YOU
Unused. *Kiss Me Kate* 1948

I'M AN ANESTHETIC DANCER
Sylvia Clark, *Hitchy-Koo of 1919*

I'M BACK IN CIRCULATION
Unused. *You Never Know* 1938

I'M DINING WITH ELSA
Unused, 1920's

I'M GETTING MYSELF READY FOR YOU
Frances Williams, Barrie Oliver, Ann
Pennington and Maurice Lapue,
The New Yorkers 1930

I'M GOING IN FOR LOVE
Unused. *You Never Know* 1938

I'M IN LOVE
Genevieve Tobin and ensemble,
Fifty Million Frenchmen 1929

I'M IN LOVE AGAIN
Sung by Rosie and Jennie Dolly; danced by
James Naulty and Robert Alton,
Greenwich Village Follies of 1924 (p. 70)

I'M IN LOVE WITH A SOLDIER BOY
Betty Garrett and ensemble,
Something for the Boys 1943

I'M NOT MYSELF AT ALL
Unused. Unproduced film *Mississippi Belle*
1943-44

I'M SO GLAHD TO MEET YOU
Unused. *Mexican Hayride* 1944

I'M SO IN LOVE WITH YOU
Unused. *Broadway Melody of 1940*

I'M TAKING THE STEPS TO RUSSIA
Sophie Tucker and ensemble,
Leave It To Me 1938

I'M THE QUEEN THAMAR
Unused. *Silk Stockings* 1955

I'M THE VILLAIN
Monty Woolley, *And the Villain Still Pursued Her* 1912 (p. 14)

I'M THROWING A BALL TONIGHT
Ethel Merman and ensemble, *Panama Hattie* 1940 (p. 175)

I'M UNLUCKY AT GAMBLING
Evelyn Hoey and Larry Ceballos' Hollywood Dancers, *Fifty Million Frenchmen* 1929 (p. 98)

I'M YOURS
Unused. *You Never Know* 1938

IN A MOORISH GARDEN
Morton Downey, *La Revue des Ambassadeurs* 1928

IN THE BIG MONEY
Unused. *Du Barry Was a Lady* 1939

IN THE GREEN HILLS OF COUNTY MAYO
Unused. Unproduced film *Mississippi Belle* 1943-44

IN THE LAND WHERE MY HEART WAS BORN
Hay Langenheim, *The Kaleidoscope* 1913

IN THE STILL OF THE NIGHT
Nelson Eddy, *Rosalie* 1937 (p. 147)

INDIAN GIRLS CHANT
Ensemble, *See America First* 1916

INDIAN MAIDENS CHORUS
Ensemble, *See America First* 1916

INFORMATION PLEASE
Unused. *Leave It To Me* 1938

INNOCENT, INNOCENT MAIDS
Ensemble. *Paranoia* 1914

IS IT JOY?
Unused. *Les Girls* 1957

IS IT THE GIRL?
(OR IS IT THE GOWN?)
Dolores Gray and ensemble, *Seven Lively Arts* 1944

IT AIN'T ETIQUETTE
Bert Lahr and Jean Moorhead, *Du Barry Was a Lady* 1939 (p. 159)

IT ALL BELONGS TO YOU
Maurice Chevalier, Jack Buchanan and ensemble, *Break the News* 1938

IT ALL SEEMS SO LONG AGO
Unused. Unproduced musical *Once Upon a Time (Ever Yours)* 1933-34

IT ISN'T DONE
Ensemble, *Fifty Million Frenchmen* 1929

IT MIGHT HAVE BEEN
Unused. *Something to Shout About* 1943

IT MUST BE FUN TO BE YOU
Unused. *Mexican Hayride* 1944

IT NEVER ENTERED MY HEAD
Unused. Unproduced musical *Greek To You* 1937-38

IT PAYS TO ADVERTISE
Cole Porter, Yale Glee Club, 1912

IT PUZZLES ME SO
Unused. Written around 1918 (p. 40)

IT WAS GREAT FUN THE FIRST TIME
Unused. *Kiss Me Kate* 1948

IT WAS WRITTEN IN THE STARS
Ronald Graham and ensemble, *Du Barry Was a Lady* 1939

ITALIAN STREET SINGERS
Unused. Written in the late 1920's

IT'S A BIG NIGHT
Unused. *Mexican Hayride* 1944

IT'S A CHEMICAL REACTION, THAT'S ALL
Hildegarde Neff, *Silk Stockings* 1955

IT'S A GREAT LIFE
Ensemble. *Red, Hot and Blue* 1936

IT'S ALL OVER BUT THE SHOUTING
Ensemble. *Rosalie* 1937

IT'S ALL RIGHT WITH ME
Peter Cookson, *Can-Can* 1953 (p. 236)

IT'S AWFULLY HARD WHEN MOTHER'S NOT ALONG
Fletcher Van W. Blood, *The Pot of Gold* 1912

IT'S BAD FOR ME
Gertrude Lawrence, *Nymph Errant* 1933 (p. 118)

IT'S DE-LOVELY
Ethel Merman and Bob Hope, *Red, Hot and Blue* 1936 (p. 143)

IT'S JUST LIKE THE GOOD OLD DAYS
Unused. *Mexican Hayride* 1944 (p. 195)

IT'S JUST YOURS
Unused. *Mexican Hayride* 1944 (p. 194)

IT'S NO LAUGHING MATTER
Unused. *You Never Know* 1938

IT'S PROBABLY JUST AS WELL
Unused. Written in early 1930's, possibly for *Star Dust*

I'VE A SHOOTING-BOX IN SCOTLAND
Newbold Noyes and Rufus F. King, *Paranoia* 1914; Dorothie Bigelow and John Goldsworthy, *See America First* 1916 (p. 35)

I'VE A STRANGE NEW RHYTHM IN MY HEART
Eleanor Powell, *Rosalie* 1937

I'VE COME TO WIVE IT WEALTHILY IN PADUA
Alfred Drake and ensemble, *Kiss Me Kate* 1948 (p. 212)

I'VE GOT A CRUSH ON YOU
Margie Finley, Chester Fredericks and ensemble, *Wake Up and Dream* 1929

I'VE GOT AN AWFUL LOT TO LEARN
Dorothie Bigelow and ensemble, *See America First* 1916

I'VE GOT MY EYES ON YOU
Fred Astaire and Eleanor Powell, *Broadway Melody of 1940*

I'VE GOT SOME UNFINISHED BUSINESS WITH YOU
Mary Jane Walsh, Nanette Fabray, Sunnie O'Dea, Helen Devlin, Betty Moran, Joseph Macaulay and Fred Irving Lewis, *Let's Face It* 1941

I'VE GOT SOMEBODY WAITING
Ruth Mitchell and ensemble, *Hitchy-Koo of 1919*

I'VE GOT YOU ON MY MIND
Fred Astaire and Claire Luce, *Gay Divorce* 1932 (p. 113)

I'VE GOT YOU UNDER MY SKIN
Virginia Bruce to James Stewart; danced by Georges and Jalna, *Born To Dance* 1936 (p. 141)

I'VE STILL GOT MY HEALTH
Ethel Merman and ensemble, *Panama Hattie* 1940 (p. 174)

JAVA
Unused. Written in 1930's

JERRY, MY SOLDIER BOY
Mary Jane Walsh, *Let's Face It* 1941

JOIN IT RIGHT AWAY
Rags Ragland, Pat Harrington, Frank Hyers and ensemble, *Panama Hattie* 1940

JOSEPHINE
Gretchen Wyler and ensemble, *Silk Stockings* 1955

JUBILEE PRESENTATION
Entire company, *Jubilee* 1935

JUDGMENT OF PARIS
Danced by David Preston, Kay Cameron, Rose Gale, June Knight and ensemble, *Jubilee* 1935

JUST ANOTHER PAGE IN YOUR DIARY
Unused. *Leave It To Me* 1938

JUST ONE OF THOSE THINGS
Unused. *The New Yorkers* 1930

JUST ONE OF THOSE THINGS
[Entirely Different Song]
June Knight, Charles Walters, *Jubilee* 1935 (p. 139)

KATE THE GREAT
Unused. *Anything Goes* 1934 (p. 123)

KATHLEEN
Unused. Unproduced film *Mississippi Belle* 1943-44

KATIE OF THE Y.M.C.A.
Unused. Written around 1918 (p. 40)

KATIE WENT TO HAITI
Ethel Merman and ensemble, *Du Barry Was a Lady* 1939 (p. 162)

KEEP MOVING
Muriel Harrisson, *La Revue des Ambassadeurs* 1928

KEEP YOUR CHIN UP
Unused. *Silk Stockings* 1955

KISS ME KATE
Alfred Drake, Patricia Morison and ensemble, *Kiss Me Kate* 1948

THE KLING-KLING BIRD ON THE
DIVI-DIVI TREE
Derek Williams, *Jubilee* 1935

LADIES IN WAITING
Mitzi Gaynor, Kay Kendall and Taina Elg,
Les Girls 1957

LADY FAIR, LADY FAIR
Unused. *See America First* 1916 (p. 36)

THE LADY I LOVE
Unused. *Wake Up and Dream* 1929

THE LADY I'VE VOWED TO WED
Ensemble, *See America First* 1916

A LADY NEEDS A REST
Eve Arden, Vivian Vance and Edith Meiser,
Let's Face It 1941 (p. 185)

THE LANGUAGE OF FLOWERS
Clifton Webb and Jeanne Cartier,
See America First 1916

L'APRES-MIDI D'UN BOEUF
Danced by Benny Baker and Harold Cromer,
Du Barry Was a Lady 1939

LAUNDRY SCENE
Unused. *Can-Can* 1953

THE LAW
Unused. *Can-Can* 1953

THE LAZIEST GAL IN TOWN
Marlene Dietrich, *Stage Fright* 1950
Written in 1927 (p. 87)

LE REVE D'ABSINTHE
H. H. Parsons, *Cora* 1911

LEAD ME ON
Unused. Written in 1930's

THE LEADER OF A BIG-TIME BAND
Ethel Merman, danced by Bill Callahan and
ensemble, *Something for the Boys* 1943 (p. 189)

LEADERS OF SOCIETY
Ensemble, *And the Villain Still Pursued Her*
1912

LES GIRLS
Gene Kelly, *Les Girls* 1957

LET DOCTOR SCHMETT VET YOUR PET
Unused. *Something to Shout About* 1943

LET'S BE BUDDIES
Ethel Merman and Joan Carroll, *Panama
Hattie* 1940 (p. 176)

LET'S DO IT, LET'S FALL IN LOVE
Irene Bordoni and Arthur Margetson, *Paris*
1928 (p. 88)

LET'S FACE IT
Tommy Gleason and The Royal Guards,
Let's Face It 1941

LET'S FLY AWAY
Charles King and Hope Williams, *The New
Yorkers* 1930 (p. 104)

LET'S MAKE IT A NIGHT
Unused. *Silk Stockings* 1955

LET'S MISBEHAVE
Irving Aaronson and his Commanders at
Les Ambassadeurs in Paris, 1927; Irene

Bordoni in pre-Broadway tryout of *Paris* 1928,
then dropped from show (p. 87)

LET'S NOT TALK ABOUT LOVE
Danny Kaye and Eve Arden, *Let's Face It* 1941
(p. 183)

LET'S STEP OUT
Evelyn Hoey and Gertrude McDonald, *Fifty
Million Frenchmen* 1929

LET'S VOCALIZE
Unused. *High Society* 1956

THE LIFE OF A SAILOR
Unused. *Greenwich Village Follies of 1924*

LIMA
Clara Palmer, *See America First* 1916

LITTLE ONE
Bing Crosby, *High Society* 1956

A LITTLE RUMBA NUMBA
Tommy Gleason and the Royal Guards,
Marguerite Benton, Mary Parker and
Billy Daniel, *Let's Face It* 1941

A LITTLE SKIPPER FROM HEAVEN ABOVE
Jimmy Durante and ensemble, *Red, Hot
and Blue* 1936

LIVE AND LET LIVE
Lilo, *Can-Can* 1953

LLEWELLYN
Johnfritz Achelis, *And the Villain Still
Pursued Her* 1912

LOADING SONG
Unused. Unproduced film *Mississippi Belle*
1943-44

LOIE AND CHLODO
Ensemble, *The Pot of Gold* 1912

LONELY STAR
Unused. *Red, Hot and Blue* 1936

LONGING FOR DEAR OLD BROADWAY
Cole Porter, *The Pot of Gold* (p. 18)

LOOK AROUND
(Lyric by Clifford Grey)
Lily St. John, *A Night Out* 1920

LOOK WHAT I FOUND
Julie Warren, Larry Laurence (Enzo Stuarti)
and ensemble, *Around the World in Eighty
Days* 1946 (p. 208)

LOOKING AT YOU
Jessie Matthews, Sonnie Hale and ensemble,
Wake Up and Dream 1929; first presented by
Clifton Webb and Dorothy Dickson with
Noble Sissle's Orchestra at Les Ambassadeurs,
Paris, 1928 (p. 92)

THE LOST LIBERTY BLUES
Evelyn Hoey, *La Revue des Ambassadeurs*
1928

LOVE CAME AND CROWNED ME
Unused. *See America First* 1916

LOVE OF MY LIFE
Judy Garland, *The Pirate* 1948

LOTUS BLOOM
Sung by Janet Blair, danced by David Lichine
and Lily Norwood, *Something to Shout
About* 1943

LOVE 'EM AND LEAVE 'EM
Unused. Written during early 1920's

LOVE FOR SALE
Kathryn Crawford and Three Girl Friends
(June Shafer, Ida Pearson and Stella Friend),
The New Yorkers 1930 (p. 103)

LOVE LETTER WORDS
Ensemble, *Hitchy-Koo of 1922*

LOVE ME, LOVE MY PEKINESE
Virginia Bruce and ensemble, *Born To
Dance* 1936

THE LOVELY HEROINE
Rufus F. King, *And the Villain Still Pursued
Her* 1912

MA PETITE NINETTE
Ensemble, *Cora* 1911

MACK THE BLACK
Judy Garland and ensemble, *The Pirate* 1948

MADEMAZELLE
Henry C. Potter, *Out O' Luck* 1925

MAID OF SANTIAGO
Hay Langenheim, *The Kaleidoscope* 1913

MAIDEN FAIR
Ensemble, *Out of This World* 1950

MAIDENS TYPICAL OF FRANCE
Ensemble, *Can-Can* 1953

MAKE A DATE WITH A GREAT
PSYCHOANALYST
Unused. *Let's Face It* 1941 (p. 187)

MAKE EVERY DAY A HOLIDAY
Julia Silvers and ensemble, *Greenwich
Village Follies of 1924*

MAKE IT ANOTHER OLD-FASHIONED,
PLEASE
Ethel Merman, *Panama Hattie* 1940 (p. 176)

MAKE WAY FOR THE EMPEROR
George Hall, *Aladdin* 1958

MAMIE MAGDALIN
Unused. Unproduced film *Mississippi Belle*
1943-44

A MAN MUST HIS HONOR DEFEND
Unused. *Can-Can* 1953

MANUELA
Unused. *The Pirate* 1948

MARIA
Clifton Webb and ensemble,
You Never Know 1938

MARTINIQUE
Unused. *The Pirate* 1948

MARYLAND SCENE
Ensemble, *Hitchy-Koo of 1922*

MAYBE YES, MAYBE NO
Unused. Written during 1930's

ME AND MARIE
Mary Boland and Melville Cooper, *Jubilee*
1935 (p. 138)

MEERAHLAH
Ensemble, *Around the World in Eighty Days*
1946

MEET ME BESIDE THE RIVER
Joseph Kelleher, *The Kaleidoscope* 1913

MELOS, THAT LOVELY SMILING ISLE
Unused. Unproduced musical, *Greek to You*
1937-38

A MEMBER OF THE
YALE ELIZABETHAN CLUB
Arnold Whitridge, *The Kaleidoscope* 1913
(p. 23)

MERCY PERCY
Cole Porter, Yale Glee Club, c. 1912

MESDAMES ET MESSIEURS
Ensemble, *Du Barry Was a Lady* 1939

MIDSUMMER NIGHT
Unused. *Out of This World* 1950

MILITARY MAIDS
Evelyn Hoey and ensemble, *La Revue
des Ambassadeurs* 1928

MILK, MILK, MILK
Ensemble, *Let's Face It* 1941

MIND IF I MAKE LOVE TO YOU
Frank Sinatra, *High Society* 1956

MIRROR, MIRROR
Ensemble, *See America First* 1916

MISS OTIS REGRETS
Published 1934, dedicated to Miss Elsa
Maxwell. Sung in *Hi Diddle Diddle* in England
by Douglas Byng, 1934 (p. 116)

MISSISSIPPI BELLE
Unused. Unproduced film
Mississippi Belle 1943-44

MISSUS AOUDA
Unused. *Around the World in Eighty Days*
1946

MISTER AND MISSUS FITCH
Luella Gear, *Gay Divorce* 1932 (p. 110)

MONA AND HER KIDDIES
Unused. *The New Yorkers* 1930

MONTMART'
Ensemble, *Can-Can* 1953

MOON MAN
Joseph Kelleher, *The Kaleidoscope* 1913

MOST GENTLEMEN DON'T LIKE LOVE
Sophie Tucker and ensemble, *Leave It To Me*
1938 (p. 153)

MOTHER PHI
Ensemble, *Cora* 1911

THE MOTOR CAR
Cole Porter, Yale Glee Club, 1911 (p. 10)

MR. AND MRS. SMITH
Mary Boland, Melville Cooper, Margaret
Adams, Charles Walters, June Knight, May
Boley, Derek Williams and Mark Plant, *Jubilee*
1935

MUSIC WITH MEALS
Cole Porter, Yale Glee Club, 1912

MY BROTH OF A BOY
Unused. Unproduced film *Mississippi Belle*
1943-44

MY COZY LITTLE CORNER IN THE RITZ
Raymond Hitchcock and ensemble,
Hitchy-Koo of 1919

MY DARLING NEVER IS LATE
Unused. *Les Girls* 1957

MY GEORGIA GAL
Johnfritz Achelis, *The Kaleidoscope* 1913

MY HARLEM WENCH
Unused. *Fifty Million Frenchmen* 1929

MY HEART BELONGS TO DADDY
Mary Martin, *Leave It To Me* 1938 (p. 152)

MY HOME TOWN GIRL
Cole Porter, *Cora* 1911

MY HOUSEBOAT ON THE THAMES
H. H. Parsons, *The Pot of Gold* 1912

MY LITTLE PIECE O' PIE
Unused. *Les Girls* 1957

MY LONG AGO GIRL
George Rasely, *Greenwich Village Follies
of 1924*

MY LOUISA
Unused. *Wake Up and Dream* 1929

MY LOULOU
Ensemble, *Jubilee* 1935

MY MOST INTIMATE FRIEND
May Boley, *Jubilee* 1935

MY MOTHER WOULD LOVE YOU
Ethel Merman and James Dunn, *Panama
Hattie* 1940

MY SALVATION ARMY QUEEN
Cole Porter and ensemble, *The Pot of Gold*
1912

MYSTERIOUSLY
Unused. Unproduced show *Star Dust* c. 1931

NAUGHTY, NAUGHTY
Ensemble, *Paranoia* 1914

NEAUVILLE SUR MER
Gerald Nodin, Annabel Gibson, Kenneth
Ware and Betty Hare, *Nymph Errant* 1933

NEVER GIVE ANYTHING AWAY
Lilo, *Can-Can* 1953

NEVER, NEVER BE AN ARTIST
Hans Conreid, Phil Leeds, Richard Purdy
and Pat Turner, *Can-Can* 1953

NEVER SAY NO
Joan Gardner and ensemble, English
production, *Gay Divorce* 1933

NIGHT AND DAY
Sung by Fred Astaire, danced by Fred Astaire
and Claire Luce, *Gay Divorce* 1932 (p. 110)

NIGHT CLUB OPENING
Sonnie Hale, George Metaxa, William
Stephens and Chester Fredericks, *Wake Up
and Dream* 1929

THE NIGHT OF THE BALL
Unused. Unproduced show *Once Upon a Time
(Ever Yours)* 1933-34

NINA
Gene Kelly, *The Pirate* 1948

NO LOVER
Priscilla Gillette, *Out of This World* 1950
(p. 227)

NO SHOW THIS EVENING
Cole Porter, Yale Glee Club, 1911

NO WONDER TAXES ARE HIGH
Cyril Ritchard and ensemble, *Aladdin* 1958

NOBODY'S CHASING ME
Charlotte Greenwood and ensemble, *Out of
This World* 1950 (p. 231)

NOTHING TO DO BUT WORK
Unused. *Can-Can* 1953

NOW YOU HAS JAZZ
Bing Crosby and Louis Armstrong,
High Society 1956

NYMPH ERRANT
Gertrude Lawrence, *Nymph Errant* 1933
(p. 121)

OCTET
Unused. *Mexican Hayride* 1944

OH, BRIGHT FAIR DREAM
Unused. *See America First* 1916

OH, HONEY
Unused. Written about 1919

OH, HOW I COULD GO FOR YOU
Unused. *Something for the Boys* 1943

OH, IT MUST BE FUN
Unused. *Out of This World* 1950

OH, MARY
Ensemble. *Hitchy-Koo of 1922*

OH, WHAT A LOVELY PRINCESS
Rufus F. King and ensemble, *Paranoia* 1914

OH, WHAT A PRETTY PAIR OF LOVERS
Rufus F. King and Newbold Noyes, *The
Kaleidoscope* 1913 (p. 22)

OKA SAKA CIRCUS
Incidental music for ensemble, *Around the
World in Eighty Days* 1946

OLD-FASHIONED GARDEN
Lillian Kemble Cooper and ensemble,
Hitchy-Koo of 1919 (p. 47)

AN OLD-FASHIONED GIRL
Mary Leigh, Basil Howes and ensemble,
La Revue des Ambassadeurs 1928

THE OLD-FASHIONED WALTZ
Unused. *Hitchy-Koo of 1922*

THE OLD RAT MORT
Ensemble, *Cora* 1911

OLGA (COME BACK TO THE VOLGA)
Nikitina, *Mayfair and Montmartre* 1922

OMNIBUS
Eleanor Shaler, Jack Pearson and ensemble
La Revue des Ambassadeurs 1928 (p. 87)

ON MY YACHT
Howard Cumming, *The Kaleidoscope* 1913

ONCE UPON A TIME
Unused. Unproduced musical *Once Upon a Time (Ever Yours)* 1933-34

ONE STEP AHEAD OF LOVE
Unused. *You Never Know* 1938

ONLY ANOTHER BOY AND GIRL
Mary Roche and Bill Tabbert, *Seven Lively Arts* 1944

OPERA STAR
John Hoysradt, *Out O' Luck* 1925 (p. 72)

OPERATIC PILLS
Sonnie Hale and ensemble,
Wake Up and Dream 1929

OPPORTUNITY KNOCKS BUT ONCE
Cyril Ritchard and ensemble, *Aladdin* 1958

OUR CROWN
Entire company, *Jubilee* 1935

OUR HOTEL (Lyric by Clifford Grey)
Ensemble, *A Night Out* 1920

OURS
Dorothy Vernon and Thurston Crane; danced by Grace and Paul Hartman and ensemble, *Red, Hot and Blue* 1936 (p. 144)

THE OZARKS ARE CALLIN' ME HOME
Ethel Merman, *Red, Hot and Blue* 1936

PAGLIACCI
Lillian Kemble Cooper, Elaine Palmer, Ursula O'Hare and ensemble, *Hitchy-Koo of 1919*

PARANOIA
Ensemble, *Paranoia* 1914

PAREE, WHAT DID YOU DO TO ME?
Betty Compton and Jack Thompson, *Fifty Million Frenchmen* 1929

PARIS LOVES LOVERS
Don Ameche and Hildegarde Neff, *Silk Stockings* 1955 (p. 238)

PER FAVORE
Unused. *Les Girls* 1957

PERENNIAL DEBUTANTES
Ensemble, *Red, Hot and Blue* 1936

PERFECTLY TERRIBLE
Cole Porter, Yale Glee Club, 1910

THE PERFUME OF LOVE
Unused. *Silk Stockings* 1955

PETER PIPER
Raymond Hitchcock and ensemble,
Hitchy-Koo of 1919

PETS
Unused. *Let's Face It* 1941 (p. 188)

THE PHYSICIAN
Gertrude Lawrence, *Nymph Errant* 1933 (p. 118)

PICK ME UP AND LAY ME DOWN
Unused. Unproduced show *Star Dust* c. 1931 (p. 107)

A PICTURE OF ME WITHOUT YOU
June Knight and Charles Walters, *Jubilee* 1935 (p. 134)

PILOT ME
Muriel Harrisson, Carter Wardell and ensemble, *La Revue des Ambassadeurs* 1928 (p. 55)

PIPE DREAMING
Larry Laurence (Enzo Stuarti) and ensemble, *Around the World in Eighty Days* 1946 (p. 208)

PITTER PATTER
Unused. *Hitchy-Koo of 1922*

PITY ME PLEASE
Dorothie Bigelow, *See America First* 1916

PLAY ME A TUNE
Edythe Baker, *Hitchy-Koo of 1922*, *The Dancing Girl* 1923, and *One Dam Thing After Another* 1927

PLEASE DON'T MAKE ME BE GOOD
Unused. *Fifty Million Frenchmen* 1929

PLEASE DON'T MONKEY WITH BROADWAY
Fred Astaire and George Murphy, *Broadway Melody of 1940*

PLUMBING
Walter Crisham, *Nymph Errant* 1933

POKER
Ensemble, *Cora* 1911 (p. 13)

THE POOR RICH
Unused. *The New Yorkers* 1930

POOR YOUNG MILLIONAIRE
Unused. Written during 1920's (p. 62)

THE PREP SCHOOL WIDOW
Rufus F. King, *Paranoia* 1914

PRETTY LITTLE MISSUS BELL
Unused. *Seven Lively Arts* 1944 (p. 201)

PRITHEE COME CRUSADING WITH ME (DAMSEL, DAMSEL)
Dorothie Bigelow and John Goldsworthy, *See America First* 1916

PROLOGUE
William Redfield, *Out of This World* 1950

PUBLIC ENEMY NUMBER ONE
Ensemble, *Anything Goes* 1934

PUT A SACK OVER THEIR HEADS
Unused. *Mexican Hayride* 1944

QUADRILLE
Danced by Gwen Verdon, Bert May and ensemble, *Can-Can* 1953

THE QUEEN OF TERRE HAUTE
Unused. *Fifty Million Frenchmen* 1929

QUEEN OF THE YALE DRAMAT
Cole Porter, *Cora* 1911

QUEENS OF TERPSICHORE
Ensemble, *And the Villain Still Pursued Her* 1912

QUELQUE-CHOSE
Unused. *Paris* 1928

THE RAGTIME PIPES OF PAN
Clifton Webb, *Phi-Phi* 1922

RAP TAP ON WOOD
Eleanor Powell, *Born to Dance* 1936

RECALL GOODHUE
Ensemble, *Leave It To Me* 1938

THE RED BLUES
Ensemble, *Silk Stockings* 1955

RED, HOT AND BLUE
Ethel Merman and ensemble, *Red, Hot and Blue* 1936

REVELATION ENSEMBLE
Unused. *See America First* 1916

REVENGE
Unused. *Let's Face It* 1941

RICK-CHICK-A-CHICK
Johnfritz Achelis, *The Kaleidoscope* 1913

RIDDLE DIDDLE ME THIS
Unused, *Something for the Boys* 1943

RIDIN' HIGH
Ethel Merman and ensemble, *Red, Hot and Blue* 1936 (p. 145)

RITZ ROLL AND ROCK
Fred Astaire, film version of *Silk Stockings* 1957

RIVER GOD
Todd Duncan, *The Sun Never Sets* 1938

ROLLING HOME
Ensemble, *Born To Dance* 1936

ROLLING, ROLLING
Cole Porter, Arnold Whitridge, T. Gaillard Thomas, II, Fletcher Van W. Blood and ensemble, *Cora* 1911

ROSALIE (several versions)
Final version sung by Nelson Eddy, *Rosalie* 1937 (p. 147)

ROSEBUD
Fletcher Van W. Blood, *Cora* 1911

RUB YOUR LAMP
Mary Jane Walsh and ensemble; danced by Mary Parker and Billy Daniel *Let's Face It* 1941

RUINS
Gerald Nodin, Annabel Gibson, Kenneth Ware and Betty Hare, *Nymph Errant* 1933 (p. 50)

SAILORS OF THE SKY
Song for Armed Forces 1942

SALT AIR
G. P. Huntley, Jr., Betty Starbuck and ensemble, *Gay Divorce* 1932

SATIN AND SILK
Gretchen Wyler, *Silk Stockings* 1955

SATURDAY NIGHT
Ensemble, *Cora* 1911 (p. 13)

SAY IT WITH GIN
Ensemble, *The New Yorkers* 1930

THE SCAMPI
Written in Venice in 1926 (p. 74)

SCANDAL
Fletcher Van W. Blood and ensemble,
The Pot of Gold 1912

SCHOOL, SCHOOL, HEAVEN-BLESSED
SCHOOL
Unused. Unproduced film *Mississippi Belle*
1943-44

SCOTCH TWINS
Unused. *Hitchy-Koo of 1922*

SEA CHANTEY
Ensemble. *Around the World in Eighty Days*
1946

THE SEA IS CALLING
Ruth Mitchell and ensemble, *Hitchy-Koo of
1919*

SEE AMERICA FIRST
Sam Edwards, *See America First* 1916 (p. 34)

SEE THAT YOU'RE BORN IN TEXAS
Ensemble, *Something for the Boys* 1943

SERENADE
Unused. *See America First* 1916

SEX APPEAL
Written around 1927, it may have been
performed at *Des Ambassadeurs*

SHE WAS A FAIR YOUNG MERMAID
Cole Porter, *The Pot of Gold* 1912

SHOOTIN' THE WORKS FOR UNCLE SAM
Fred Astaire and ensemble, *You'll Never Get
Rich* 1941

SHOULD I TELL YOU I LOVE YOU
Mary Healy, *Around the World in Eighty
Days* 1946

SI VOUS AIMEZ LES POITRINES
Iris Ashley, *Nymph Errant* 1933 (p. 121)

SIBERIA
Henry Lascoe, Leon Belasco and David
Opatoshu, *Silk Stockings* 1955 (p. 242)

THE SIDECAR
Unused. Unproduced film *Adios Argentina*
1934-35

A SIGHT-SEEING TOUR
Unused. *Mexican Hayride* 1944

SILK STOCKINGS
Don Ameche, *Silk Stockings* 1955 (p. 242)

SILVER MOON
Gurney Smith, *And the Villain Still Pursued
Her* 1912

SINCE I KISSED MY BABY GOODBYE
The Delta Rhythm Boys; danced by Fred
Astaire, *You'll Never Get Rich* 1941 (p. 178)

SINCE MA GOT THE CRAZE ESPAGNOLE
Unused. *Hitchy-Koo of 1919* (p. 46)

SINCE WE'VE MET
Ensemble, *The Pot of Gold* 1912

SING JUBILEE
Unused. *Jubilee* 1935

SING SING FOR SING SING
Charles King and ensemble, *The New Yorkers*
1930

SING TO ME GUITAR
Corinna Mura and ensemble, *Mexican
Hayride* 1944

SINGING IN THE SADDLE
Unused. Unproduced film *Adios Argentina*
1934-35

SLAVE AUCTION
Unused. Ensemble, *Around the World in
Eighty Days* 1946

SLOW SINKS THE SUN
Ensemble, *Paranoia* 1914; unused, *See
America First* 1916

SNAGTOOTH GERTIE
Unused. *Around the World in Eighty Days*
1946

THE SNAKE IN THE GRASS
Unused ballet music danced by ensemble
Fifty Million Frenchmen 1929, during the
pre-Broadway tryout, but dropped before the
New York opening. The choreography was
by Leonide Massine.

SO IN LOVE
Patricia Morison; reprised by Alfred Drake,
Kiss Me Kate 1948 (p. 211)

SO LET US HAIL
Ensemble, *The Pot of Gold* 1912

SO LONG
Unused. Unproduced film *Mississippi Belle*
1943-44

SO LONG, SAMOA
Unused. Written on cruise 1940 (p. 170)

SO LONG, SAN ANTONIO
Unused. *Something for the Boys* 1943

SO NEAR AND YET SO FAR
Sung by Fred Astaire; danced by Fred Astaire
and Rita Hayworth, *You'll Never Get Rich*
1941 (p. 178)

SO WHAT?
Unused. *High Society* 1956

THE SOCIAL COACH OF ALL THE
FASHIONABLE FUTURE DEBUTANTES
Unused. *See America First* 1916

SOLOMON
Elizabeth Welch, *Nymph Errant* 1933

SOMEBODY'S GOING TO THROW A
BIG PARTY
Ensemble, *Fifty Million Frenchmen* 1929

SOMETHING FOR THE BOYS
Ethel Merman and ensemble, *Something for
the Boys* 1943

SOMETHING TO SHOUT ABOUT
Jack Oakie, Don Ameche, William Gaxton,
Janet Blair, Veda Ann Borg and ensemble,
Something to Shout About 1943

SOMETHING'S GOT TO BE DONE
Felix Adler and ensemble, *See America First*
1916

SOUTH SEA ISLES
Unused. *Hitchy-Koo of 1922*

THE SPONGE
Helene Dahlia, *Hitchy-Koo of 1922*

SPRING LOVE IS IN THE AIR
Ilona Massey and ensemble, *Rosalie* 1937

A STEP MONTAGE
Unused. *High Society* 1956

STEP WE GRANDLY
Unused. *See America First* 1916

STEREOPHONIC SOUND
Gretchen Wyler, *Silk Stockings* 1955 (p. 245)

A STROLL ON THE PLAZA SANT'ANA
Ensemble, *Panama Hattie* 1940

STROLLING
Ensemble, *And the Villain Still Pursued Her*
1912

STROLLING QUITE FANCY FREE
Unused. *See America First* 1916

SUBMARINE
Johnfritz Achelis, *And the Villain Still
Pursued Her* 1912

SUCCESS
Unused. Unproduced musical *Once Upon a
Time (Ever Yours)* 1933-34

SUEZ DANCE
Danced by Dorothy Bird and ensemble,
Around the World in Eighty Days 1946

SUNDAY MORNING, BREAKFAST TIME
Ensemble, *Jubilee* 1935

SUTTEE PROCESSION
Mary Healy and ensemble, *Around the
World in Eighty Days* 1946

SWEET NUDITY
Unused. *Nymph Errant* 1933

SWEET SIMPLICITY
Unused. *See America First* 1916

SWING THAT SWING
Entire company, *Jubilee* 1935

SWINGIN' THE JINX AWAY
Sung by Frances Langford and the Foursome
Quartet; danced by Eleanor Powell and
ensemble, *Born To Dance* 1936

SYNCOPATED PIPES OF PAN
Rosie and Jennie Dolly, Georgie Hale and
ensemble, *Greenwich Village Follies of 1924*

A TABLE FOR TWO
Unused. Probably written c. 1920

TAKE IT EASY
Unused. *Something to Shout About* 1943

TAKE ME BACK TO MANHATTAN
Frances Williams, *The New Yorkers* 1930

THE TALE OF AN OYSTER
Helen Broderick, *Fifty Million Frenchmen*
1929 (p. 98)

TECHNIQUE
Unused. Unproduced musical *Once Upon a
Time (Ever Yours)* 1933-34

TEQUILA
Unused. *Mexican Hayride* 1944

TEXAS WILL MAKE YOU A MAN
Unused. *Something for the Boys* 1943

THANK YOU
Unused. Unproduced musical *Once Upon a Time (Ever Yours)* 1933-34

THANK YOU SO MUCH, MRS. LOWSBOROUGH-GOODBY
Published 1934 as an independent song (p. 113)

THAT BLACK AND WHITE BABY OF MINE
Unused. *Hitchy-Koo of 1919* (p. 47)

THAT LITTLE OLD BAR AT THE RITZ
Unused. Written during the 1920's

THAT RAINBOW RAG
Unused. *The Pot of Gold* 1912

THAT ZIP CORNWALL COOCH
Jack Stevens, *And the Villain Still Pursued Her* 1912

THAT'S THE NEWS I'M WAITING TO HEAR
Unused. *Red, Hot and Blue* 1936

THAT'S WHAT YOU MEAN TO ME
Unused. *Mexican Hayride* 1944

THAT'S WHY I LOVE YOU
Unused. *Fifty Million Frenchmen* 1929

THERE HE GOES, MR. PHILEAS FOGG
Arthur Margetson and Larry Laurence (Enzo Stuarti), *Around the World in Eighty Days* 1946

THERE MUST BE SOMEONE FOR ME
June Havoc, *Mexican Hayride* 1944 (p. 194)

THERE'LL ALWAYS BE A LADY FAIR
The Foursome Quartet (Marshall Smith, Ray Johnson, Dwight Snyder, Del Porter), *Anything Goes* 1934

THERE'S A FAN
Unused. *Leave It To Me* 1938

THERE'S A HAPPY LAND IN THE SKY
Ethel Merman, Paula Laurence, Allen Jenkins, William Lynn and Bill Johnson, *Something for the Boys* 1943

THERE'S A HOLLYWOOD THAT'S GOOD
Unused. *Silk Stockings* 1955

THERE'S NO CURE LIKE TRAVEL
Unused. *Anything Goes* 1934

THERE'S NOTHING LIKE SWIMMING
Unused. *Jubilee* 1935

THEY AIN'T DONE RIGHT BY OUR NELL
Betty Hutton and Arthur Treacher, *Panama Hattie* 1940

THEY ALL FALL IN LOVE
Gertrude Lawrence, *The Battle of Paris* 1929

THEY COULDN'T COMPARE TO YOU
William Redfield and ensemble, *Out of This World* 1950 (p. 228)

THEY'RE ALWAYS ENTERTAINING
Gerald Nodin, Annabel Gibson, Kenneth Ware, Sheila Marlyn, David Shenstone and Betty Hare, *Nymph Errant* 1933 (p. 73)

THROUGH THICK AND THIN
Hazel Scott and Janet Blair, *Something to Shout About* 1943

TIRED OF LIVING ALONE
Unused. Probably written c. 1919

TO FOLLOW EVERY FANCY
John Goldsworthy and ensemble, *See America First* 1916

TO GET AWAY
Ensemble, *Jubilee* 1935

TO HELL WITH EVERYONE BUT US
Unused. *Out of This World* 1950

TO LOVE OR NOT TO LOVE
Nelson Eddy and ensemble, *Rosalie* 1937

TO THINK THAT THIS COULD HAPPEN TO ME
Unused, *Can-Can* 1953

A TOAST TO VOLSTEAD
Ensemble, *Fifty Million Frenchmen* 1929

TOM, DICK OR HARRY
Lisa Kirk, Harold Lang, Edwin Clay, Charles Wood, *Kiss Me Kate* 1948

TOMORROW
Sophie Tucker and ensemble, *Leave It To Me* 1938 (p. 154)

TONIGHT I LOVE YOU MORE
Unused. *Out of This World* 1950

TOO BAD
Harry Lascoe, Leon Belasco, David Opatoshu and ensemble. *Silk Stockings* 1955

TOO DARN HOT
Lorenzo Fuller, Eddie Sledge and Fred Davis, *Kiss Me Kate* 1948 (p. 215)

TOY OF DESTINY
Julia Silvers, *Greenwich Village Follies of 1924*

TRUE LOVE
Bing Crosby and Grace Kelly, *High Society* 1956 (p. 248)

TRUST YOUR DESTINY TO YOUR STAR
Dennis King, *Aladdin* 1958

TWILIGHT
Irving G. Beebe and Hay Langenheim, *And the Villain Still Pursued Her* 1912

TWIN SISTERS
Unused. *Hitchy-Koo of 1922*

TWO BIG EYES
(Words by John Golden)
Elsie Janis, *Miss Information* 1915

TWO LITTLE BABES IN THE WOOD
Sung by Julia Silvers and Georgie Hale with Rosie and Jennie Dolly as the Hans Christian Andersen Babes; James Clemons as the Roué and James Naulty as his chauffeur; and Rosie and Jennie Dolly as the John Murray Andersen Babes, *Greenwich Village Follies of 1924*. Also Irene Bordoni, *Paris* 1928 (p. 68)

UNDER THE DRESS
Unused. *Silk Stockings* 1955

UNDERSTUDIES
Unused. *Greenwich Village Follies of 1924*

UP TO HIS OLD TRICKS AGAIN
Unused. *Let's Face It* 1941

THE UPPER PARK AVENUE
Unused. Written during 1930's

USE YOUR IMAGINATION
William Redfield and Priscilla Gillette, *Out of This World* 1950 (p. 224)

VENICE
Hope Williams, Jimmy Durante, Lou Clayton, Eddie Jackson, *The New Yorkers* 1930

VENUS OF MILO
Unused. Written around 1920

VISIT PANAMA
Ethel Merman and ensemble, *Panama Hattie* 1940

VITE, VITE, VITE
Ensemble, *Leave It To Me* 1938

VIVIENNE
Irving Aaronson and The Commanders, *Paris* 1928

VOODOO
Unused. *The Pirate* 1948

WAIT FOR THE MOON
Jennie Dolly and George Rasely, *Greenwich Village Follies of 1924*

WAIT UNTIL IT'S BEDTIME
Jessie Matthews and ensemble, *Wake Up and Dream* 1929

WAITERS v. WAITRESSES
Eric Blore and ensemble, English production, *Gay Divorce* 1933

WAKE, LOVE, WAKE
Unused. *See America First* 1916

WAKE UP AND DREAM
George Metaxa, *Wake Up and Dream* 1929

WALTZ DOWN THE AISLE
Unused. Unproduced musical *Once Upon a Time (Ever Yours)* 1933-34; *Anything Goes* 1934; *Jubilee* 1935.

WAR SONG
Cole's lyric parody of *They Didn't Believe Me* used in the score of *Oh What A Lovely War*. Written c. 1918 (p. 40)

WASHINGTON, D.C.
Unused. *Something for the Boys* 1943

WASHINGTON SQUARE
Used. *Buddies* 1919. Same song as CHELSEA.

WATCHING THE WORLD GO BY
Unused. *Fifty Million Frenchmen* 1929

WE ARE PROM GIRLS
Ensemble, *The Kaleidoscope* 1913

WE ARE SO AESTHETIC
Ensemble, *The Pot of Gold* 1912

WE ARE THE CHORUS OF THE SHOW
Ensemble, *And the Villain Still Pursued Her* 1912

WE DETEST A FIESTA
Ensemble, *Panama Hattie* 1940

WE DRINK TO YOU J. H. BRODY
William Gaxton and ensemble, *Leave It To Me* 1938

WE OPEN IN VENICE
Alfred Drake, Patricia Morison, Lisa Kirk,
and Harold Lang, *Kiss Me Kate* 1948 (p. 211)

WE SHALL NEVER BE YOUNGER
Unused. *Kiss Me Kate* 1948

THE WEDDING CAKE-WALK
Sung by Martha Tilton; danced by Fred
Astaire and Rita Hayworth; ensemble, *You'll
Never Get Rich* 1941

A WEEKEND AFFAIR
Unused. *Gay Divorce* 1932

WELCOME TO JERRY
Ensemble. *Panama Hattie* 1940

WELL, DID YOU EVAH!
Betty Grable and Charles Walters, *Du Barry
Was a Lady* 1939. Sung with revised lyric by
Bing Crosby and Frank Sinatra, *High Society*
1956 (p. 164)

WELL, I JUST WOULDN'T KNOW
Unused. *Something for the Boys* 1943

WERE THINE THAT SPECIAL FACE
Alfred Drake and ensemble, *Kiss Me Kate*
1948 (p. 211)

WE'RE A GROUP OF NONENTITIES
Ensemble, *The Kaleidoscope* 1913 (p. 22)

WE'RE ABOUT TO START BIG REHEARSIN'
Ensemble, *Red, Hot and Blue* 1936

WE'RE OFF
T. Gaillard Thomas, II, and Cole Porter, *Cora*
1911

WE'RE OFF FOR A HAYRIDE IN MEXICO
Unused. *Mexican Hayride* 1944

WE'RE OFF TO FEATHERMORE
Melville Cooper, Mary Boland, Charles
Walters and Margaret Adams, *Jubilee* 1935

WE'RE ON THE ROAD TO ATHENS
Unused. *Out of This World* 1950

WEREN'T WE FOOLS
Fanny Brice, Palace Theatre, New York, 1927

WE'VE BEEN SPENDING THE SUMMMER
WITH OUR FAMILIES
Unused. *The New Yorkers* 1930

WHAT A BALL
Unused. *Silk Stockings* 1955

WHAT A CHARMING AFTERNOON
Ensemble, *The Pot of Gold* 1912

WHAT A CRAZY WAY TO SPEND SUNDAY
Ensemble, *Mexican Hayride* 1944

WHAT A FAIR THING IS A WOMAN
Unused. *Can-Can* 1953

WHAT A GREAT PAIR WE'LL BE
Dorothy Vernon, Thurston Crane; danced by
Grace and Paul Hartman and ensemble,
Red, Hot and Blue 1936

WHAT A JOY TO BE YOUNG
Unused. *Anything Goes* 1934

WHAT A NICE MUNICIPAL PARK
Jack Whitney and ensemble, *Jubilee* 1935

WHAT A PRICELESS PLEASURE
Unused. *You Never Know* 1938

WHAT AM I TO DO
John Hoysradt in *The Man Who Came to
Dinner* 1939 (p. 156)

WHAT AN AWFUL HULLABALOO
Ensemble, *The Pot of Gold* 1912

WHAT ARE LITTLE HUSBANDS MADE OF
Unused. *Let's Face It* 1941

WHAT DO YOU THINK ABOUT MEN?
Charlotte Greenwood, Priscilla Gillette,
Barbara Ashley, *Out of This World* 1950

WHAT DOES YOUR SERVANT
DREAM ABOUT?
Unused. *Kiss Me Kate* 1948

WHAT FUN
Unused. *Les Girls* 1957

WHAT HAVE I?
Unused. *Du Barry Was a Lady* 1939

WHAT IS THAT TUNE?
Libby Holman, *You Never Know* 1938

WHAT IS THIS THING CALLED LOVE?
Sung by Elsie Carlisle in a sketch performed
by Tilly Losch, Toni Birkmayer, Alanova and
William Cavanagh, *Wake Up and Dream* 1929
(p. 93)

WHAT LOVE IS
Hay Langenheim, *Paranoia* 1914

WHAT SHALL I DO?
Lupe Velez, *You Never Know* 1938

WHAT WILL BECOME OF OUR ENGLAND?
Eric Blore and ensemble, *Gay Divorce* 1932

WHAT'S MY MAN GONNA BE LIKE?
Evelyn Hoey; Jacques Fray and Mario
Braggiotti at the pianos; *The Vanderbilt
Revue* 1930

WHEN A BODY'S IN LOVE
Unused. *See America First* 1916

WHEN A WOMAN'S IN LOVE
Unused. Unproduced film *Mississippi Belle*
1943-44

WHEN BLACK SALLIE SINGS PAGLIACCI
Ruth Mitchell and ensemble, *Hitchy-Koo of
1919*

WHEN I HAD A UNIFORM ON
Joseph Cook, Eleanor Sinclair and ensemble,
Hitchy-Koo of 1919 (p. 46)

WHEN I USED TO LEAD THE BALLET
T. Gaillard Thomas, II, *The Pot of Gold* 1912;
Felix Adler and ensemble, *See America First*
1916 (p. 18)

WHEN I WAS A LITTLE CUCKOO
Beatrice Lillie, *Seven Lively Arts* 1944 (p. 197)

WHEN I'M EATING AROUND WITH YOU
Cole Porter, Yale Glee Club, 1912

WHEN IT'S ALL SAID AND DONE
William Gaxton, Mary Martin and ensemble,
Leave It To Me 1938

WHEN LOVE BECKONED
Ethel Merman, *Du Barry Was a Lady* 1939

WHEN LOVE COMES TO CALL
Unused. *Can-Can* 1953

WHEN LOVE COMES YOUR WAY
Derek Williams and Margaret Adams, *Jubilee*
1935. Originally written for *Nymph Errant*
1933

WHEN MCKINLEY MARCHES ON
Unused. Unproduced film *Mississippi Belle*
1943-44

WHEN ME, MOWGLI, LOVE
Mark Plant, *Jubilee* 1935

WHEN MY BABY GOES TO TOWN
Bill Johnson and ensemble, *Something for
the Boys* 1943

WHEN MY CARAVAN COMES HOME
Jack Squires, *Hitchy-Koo of 1922*

WHEN THE HEN STOPS LAYING
Unused. *Leave It To Me* 1938

WHEN THE SUMMER MOON
COMES 'LONG
Written at Yale, 1910 (p. 7)

WHEN WE'RE HOME ON THE RANGE
Ethel Merman, Paula Laurence and Allen
Jenkins, *Something for the Boys* 1943

WHEN YOU AND I WERE STRANGERS
Unused. Unproduced film *Mississippi Belle*
1943-44

WHEN YOUR TROUBLES HAVE STARTED
Unused. *Red, Hot and Blue* 1936

WHERE?
Unused. *Red, Hot and Blue* 1936

WHERE ARE THE MEN?
Vera Dunn, Houston Richards, and ensemble,
Anything Goes 1934

WHERE DO WE GO FROM HERE?
Unused. *Seven Lively Arts* 1944

WHERE HAVE YOU BEEN?
Charles King and Hope Williams, *The New
Yorkers* 1930 (p. 103)

WHERE IS THE LIFE THAT LATE I LED?
Alfred Drake, *Kiss Me Kate* 1948 (p. 216)

WHERE, OH WHERE
Barbara Ashley and ensemble, *Out of This
World* 1950 (p. 226)

WHERE WOULD YOU GET YOUR COAT?
Helen Broderick, *Fifty Million Frenchmen*
1929 (p. 97)

WHERE'S LOUIE?
Ensemble, *Du Barry Was a Lady* 1939

WHEREVER THEY FLY THE FLAG OF
OLD ENGLAND
Arthur Margetson and ensemble, *Around the
World in Eighty Days* 1946

WHICH
Originally intended for *Paris* 1928,
it was introduced in *Wake Up and Dream*
1929 by Jessie Matthews (p. 89)

WHO, BUT YOU
Unused. *Red, Hot and Blue* 1936

WHO KNOWS?
Unknown female vocalist, *Rosalie* 1937

WHO SAID GAY PAREE?
Unused. *Can-Can* 1953 (p. 234)

WHO WANTS TO BE A MILLIONAIRE?
Frank Sinatra and Celeste Holm, *High
Society* 1956

WHO WOULD HAVE DREAMED?
Janis Carter and Lipman Duckat (Larry
Douglas), *Panama Hattie* 1940

WHO'LL BID
Unused. Unproduced film *Mississippi Belle*
1943-44

WHY AM I SO GONE ABOUT THAT GAL
Gene Kelly, *Les Girls* 1957

WHY CAN'T YOU BEHAVE
Sung by Lisa Kirk; danced by Harold Lang,
Kiss Me Kate 1948 (p. 211)

WHY DIDN'T WE MEET BEFORE
(Lyric by Clifford Grey)
Lily St. John and Leslie Henson *A Night
Out* 1920

WHY DO YOU WANT TO HURT ME SO?
Unused. *Out of This World* 1950

WHY DON'T WE TRY STAYING HOME?
Unused. *Fifty Million Frenchmen* 1929

WHY MARRY THEM
Betty Starbuck and ensemble, *Gay Divorce*
1932

WHY SHOULD I CARE?
Frank Morgan, *Rosalie* 1937

WHY SHOULD I TRUST YOU?
Unused. *Silk Stockings* 1955

WHY SHOULDN'T I?
Margaret Adams, *Jubilee* 1935 (p. 137)

WHY SHOULDN'T I HAVE YOU?
Betty Compton and Jack Thompson, *Fifty
Million Frenchmen* 1929

WHY TALK ABOUT SEX?
Unused. *The New Yorkers* 1930

WIDOW'S CRUISE
Unused. Written before 1920

WILD WEDDING BELLS
Unused. Unproduced musical *Greek To You*
1937-38

WILL YOU LOVE ME WHEN MY FLIVVER
IS A WRECK?
Felix Adler, *See America First* 1916. This may
not be a Cole Porter song.

WITHOUT LOVE
Hildegarde Neff, *Silk Stockings* 1955

A WOMAN'S CAREER
Unused. *Kiss Me Kate* 1948

WOND'RING NIGHT AND DAY
Unused. *Mayfair and Montmartre* 1922

WON'T YOU COME CRUSADING
WITH ME
Newbold Noyes and Rufus King, *Paranoia*
1914. Revised and retitled PRITHEE COME
CRUSADING WITH ME. Used in *See
America First* 1916

WOODLAND DANCE
Danced by Clifton Webb and Jeanne Cartier,
See America First 1916

WOULDN'T IT BE CRAZY
Unused. *Something for the Boys* 1943

WOULDN'T IT BE FUN
Basil Rathbone, *Aladdin* 1958 (p. 250)

WOW-OOH-WOLF
Nan Wynn, Dolores Gray and Mary Roche,
Seven Lively Arts 1944

WUNDERBAR
Patricia Morison and Alfred Drake, *Kiss Me
Kate* 1948 (p. 211)

YANKEE DOODLE
Ensemble, *Fifty Million Frenchmen* 1929

YELLOW MELODRAMA
Cole Porter, Yale Glee Club 1911 (p. 10)

YES, YES, YES
Toby Wing and ensemble, *You Never Know*
1938

YOU AND ME
Mary Leigh and Basil Howes, *La Revue des
Ambassadeurs* 1928

YOU CAN DO NO WRONG
Judy Garland, *The Pirate* 1948

YOU CAN'T BEAT MY BILL
Unused. *Let's Face It* 1941

YOU DO SOMETHING TO ME
William Gaxton and Genevieve Tobin,
Fifty Million Frenchmen 1929 (p. 94)

YOU DON'T KNOW PAREE
William Gaxton, *Fifty Million Frenchmen*
1929 (p. 98)

YOU DON'T REMIND ME
Unused. *Out of This World* 1950 (p. 224)

YOU IRRITATE ME SO
Nanette Fabray and Jack Williams, *Let's Face
It* 1941

YOU MAKE UP
Unused. Written c. 1920

YOU NEVER KNOW
Libby Holman, *You Never Know* 1938

YOU SAID IT
Ethel Merman, Arthur Treacher, Rags
Ragland, Pat Harrington and Frank Hyers,
Panama Hattie 1940

YOU'D BE SO NICE TO COME HOME TO
Janet Blair and Don Ameche, *Something to
Shout About* 1943 (p. 188)

YOU'RE A BAD INFLUENCE ON ME
Ethel Merman, *Red, Hot and Blue* 1936

YOU'RE IN LOVE
Fred Astaire, Claire Luce and Erik Rhodes,
Gay Divorce 1932

YOU'RE JUST TOO, TOO
Gene Kelly and Kay Kendall, *Les Girls* 1957

YOU'RE SENSATIONAL
Frank Sinatra, *High Society* 1956 (p. 248)

YOU'RE THE PRIZE GUY OF GUYS
Unused. *Les Girls* 1957

YOU'RE THE TOP
Ethel Merman and William Gaxton, *Anything
Goes* 1934 (p. 123)

YOU'RE TOO FAR AWAY
Unused. *Nymph Errant* 1933

YOURS
Unused. Unproduced musical *Once Upon a
Time (Ever Yours)* 1933-34; unused, *Jubilee*
1935

YOURS FOR A SONG
Unused. *Seven Lively Arts* 1944

YOU'VE GOT SOMETHING
Bob Hope and Ethel Merman, *Red, Hot and
Blue* 1936

YOU'VE GOT THAT THING
Jack Thompson and Betty Compton, *Fifty
Million Frenchmen* 1929 (p. 94)

YOU'VE GOT TO BE HARD-BOILED
Unused, *The New Yorkers* 1930

DISCOGRAPHY OF ORIGINAL CAST AND SELECTED HISTORICAL RECORDINGS OF COLE PORTER SONGS

(Prepared with the assistance of Miles Kreuger)

78 RPM RECORDINGS

SEE AMERICA FIRST
(1916)

I'VE A SHOOTING-BOX IN SCOTLAND
Joseph C. Smith & his orchestra
Victor 18165

Note: This is the earliest known commercial recording of a Cole Porter song.

THE ECLIPSE
(1919)
England
Original Cast Recordings

CHELSEA
Nancy Gibbs and F. Pope Stamper
English Columbia F-1033

I NEVER REALIZED
Nancy Gibbs and F. Pope Stamper
English Columbia F-1033

THE ECLIPSE
Selection, Garrick Theatre Orchestra
English Columbia 783 (12-inch)
Selection includes: Chelsea, I Never Realized

A NIGHT OUT
(1920)
England
Original Cast Recordings. Music by Cole Porter;
Lyrics by Clifford Grey.

WHY DIDN'T WE MEET BEFORE
Lily St. John, Leslie Henson
English Columbia F-1061

LOOKING AROUND (LOOK AROUND)
Lily St. John
English Columbia F-1062

PARIS
(1928)
Original Cast Recordings

LET'S MISBEHAVE
Irving Aaronson and his Commanders
Victor 21260

DON'T LOOK AT ME THAT WAY
Irene Bordoni with Irving Aaronson and
his Commanders
Victor 21742

LET'S DO IT, Let's Fall in Love
Irving Aaronson and his Commanders
Victor 21745

WAKE UP AND DREAM
(1929)
England
Original Cast Recordings

WAKE UP AND DREAM
George Metaxa with orchestra
HMV B-3016

WHAT IS THIS THING CALLED LOVE?
George Metaxa with orchestra
HMV B-3016

LET'S DO IT, Let's Fall in Love
Leslie Hutchinson, piano-vocal
Parlophone R-342, F-242

LOOKING AT YOU
Leslie Hutchinson, piano-vocal
Parlophone R-342, F-242

I'M A GIGOLO
Leslie Hutchinson, piano-vocal
Parlophone R-343, F-243

WHAT IS THIS THING CALLED LOVE?
Leslie Hutchinson, piano-vocal
Parlophone R-343, F-243

SELECTIONS (WAKE UP AND DREAM)
Orchestra conducted by Leslie Hutchinson
12 inch Parlophone E-10869

THE NEW YORKERS
(1930)
Original Cast Recordings

LOVE FOR SALE
Fred Waring's Pennsylvanians with the
Three Waring Girls
Victor 22598, 25080

WHERE HAVE YOU BEEN?
Fred Waring's Pennsylvanians with the
Three Waring Girls
Victor 22598

GAY DIVORCE
(1932)
Original Cast Recordings

NIGHT AND DAY
Fred Astaire with Leo Reisman's Orchestra
Victor 24193, 24716

I'VE GOT YOU ON MY MIND
Fred Astaire with Leo Reisman's Orchestra
Victor 24193

English Production (1933) Original Cast Recordings

NIGHT AND DAY
Fred Astaire
English Columbia DB 1215, FB 1255

AFTER YOU, WHO?
Fred Astaire
English Columbia DB 1215, FB 1255

NYMPH ERRANT
(1933)
England
Original Cast Recordings

EXPERIMENT
Gertrude Lawrence
HMV B 8029, Victor 25224

THE PHYSICIAN
Gertrude Lawrence
HMV B 8029, Victor 25224

HOW COULD WE BE WRONG?
Gertrude Lawrence
HMV B 8030, Victor 25225

IT'S BAD FOR ME
Gertrude Lawrence
HMV B 8030, Victor 25225

NYMPH ERRANT
Gertrude Lawrence
HMV B 8031, Victor 25226

SOLOMON
Elisabeth Welch
HMV B 8031, Victor 25226

HI DIDDLE DIDDLE
(1934)
England
Original Cast Recording

MISS OTIS REGRETS
Douglas Byng
English Decca F-5249

ANYTHING GOES
(1934)
Original Cast Recordings

I GET A KICK OUT OF YOU
YOU'RE THE TOP
Ethel Merman with Johnny Green's Orchestra
Liberty L-261, Brunswick 7342

THERE'LL ALWAYS BE A LADY FAIR
THE GYPSY IN ME
Anything Goes Foursome
Victor 24817

COLE PORTER PIANO VOCALS

Cole Porter made his only commercial recordings in late 1934 and early 1935.

THANK YOU SO MUCH,
MRS. LOWSBOROUGH-GOODBY
Victor 24766

YOU'RE THE TOP
Victor 24766

ANYTHING GOES
Victor 24825

TWO LITTLE BABES IN THE WOOD
Victor 24825

BE LIKE THE BLUEBIRD
Victor 24843

I'M A GIGOLO
Victor 24843

THE PHYSICIAN
Victor 24859

THE COCOTTE
Victor 24859

JUBILEE
(1935)

BEGIN THE BEGUINE
Xavier Cugat and his Waldorf-Astoria
Orchestra
Victor 25133
Note: The first recording

BEGIN THE BEGUINE
Artie Shaw and his Orchestra
Bluebird 7746
Note: The recording brought fame to both
Shaw and the song in 1938.

BORN TO DANCE
(1936)
Original Cast Recordings

I'VE GOT YOU UNDER MY SKIN
Virginia Bruce
Brunswick 7765

EASY TO LOVE
Virginia Bruce
Brunswick 7765

I'VE GOT YOU UNDER MY SKIN
Frances Langford
Decca 939

RAP TAP ON WOOD
Frances Langford
Decca 939

EASY TO LOVE
Frances Langford
Decca 940

SWINGIN' THE JINX AWAY
Frances Langford
Decca 940

RED, HOT AND BLUE
(1936)
Original Cast Recordings

DOWN IN THE DEPTHS
Ethel Merman
Liberty L-206

IT'S DE-LOVELY
Ethel Merman
Liberty L-206

RIDIN' HIGH
Ethel Merman
Liberty L-207

RED, HOT AND BLUE
Ethel Merman
Liberty L-207

O MISTRESS MINE
(1936)
England
Original Cast Recording

GOOD-BYE, LITTLE DREAM, GOOD-BYE
Yvonne Printemps, Pierre Fresnay
HMV DA 1539

THE SUN NEVER SETS
(1938)
England
Original Cast Recording

RIVER GOD
Todd Duncan
English Columbia DB-1778

LEAVE IT TO ME
(1938)
Original Cast Recordings

MY HEART BELONGS TO DADDY
Mary Martin, Eddie Duchin's Orchestra
Brunswick 8282

MOST GENTLEMEN DON'T LIKE LOVE
Mary Martin, Eddie Duchin's Orchestra
Brunswick 8282

PANAMA HATTIE
(1940)
Original Cast Recordings

LET'S BE BUDDIES
Ethel Merman, Joan Carroll
Decca 23199

MAKE IT ANOTHER OLD-FASHIONED,
  PLEASE
Ethel Merman
Decca 23199

MY MOTHER WOULD LOVE YOU
Ethel Merman
Decca 23200

I'VE STILL GOT MY HEALTH
Ethel Merman
Decca 23200

YOU'LL NEVER
GET RICH
(1941)
Original Cast Recordings

SO NEAR AND YET SO FAR
Fred Astaire
Decca 18187

SINCE I KISSED MY BABY GOODBYE
Fred Astaire, Delta Rhythm Boys
Decca 18187

DREAM DANCING
Fred Astaire
Decca 18188

THE WEDDING CAKE WALK
Fred Astaire, Delta Rhythm Boys
Decca 181888
Martha Tilton
Decca 4029

LET'S FACE IT
(1941)
Original Cast Recordings

LET'S NOT TALK ABOUT LOVE
Danny Kaye
Columbia 36582

FARMING
Danny Kaye
Columbia 36583

FARMING
Mary Jane Walsh, Max Meth conducting
Liberty L-343

I HATE YOU, DARLING
Mary Jane Walsh, Max Meth conducting
Liberty L-343

EV'RYTHING I LOVE
Mary Jane Walsh, Max Meth conducting
Liberty L-344

ACE IN THE HOLE
Mary Jane Walsh, Max Meth conducting
Liberty L-344

SOMETHING
FOR THE BOYS
(1943)
Original Cast Recordings

SOMETHING FOR THE BOYS
Paula Laurence
Decca 23363

BY THE MISSISSINEWAH
Betty Garrett, Paula Laurence
Decca 23363

MEXICAN HAYRIDE
(1944)
Original Cast Recordings

SING TO ME, GUITAR
Corinna Mura
Decca 23336

CARLOTTA
Corinna Mura
Decca 23336

I LOVE YOU
Wilbur Evans
Decca 23337

GIRLS
Wilbur Evans
Decca 23337

THERE MUST BE SOMEONE FOR ME
June Havoc
Decca 23338

ABRACADABRA
June Havoc
Decca 23338

COUNT YOUR BLESSINGS
June Havoc
Decca 23339

WHAT A CRAZY WAY TO SPEND SUNDAY
Chorus
Decca 23339

SEVEN LIVELY ARTS
(1944)
Original Cast Recordings

EV'RYTIME WE SAY GOODBYE
Benny Goodman Quintet, vocal Peggy Mann
Columbia 36767

ONLY ANOTHER BOY AND GIRL
Benny Goodman Quintet, vocal Jane Harvey
Columbia 36767

EV'RYTIME WE SAY GOODBYE
Teddy Wilson Quintet
Musicraft 317

AROUND THE WORLD IN EIGHTY DAYS
(1946)
Original Cast Recordings

SHOULD I TELL YOU I LOVE YOU
Larry Laurence, Ray Carter and Orchestra
Real 1195A

LOOK WHAT I FOUND
Larry Laurence, Ray Carter and Orchestra
Real 1195B

IF YOU SMILE AT ME
Larry Laurence, Ray Carter and Orchestra
Real 1195C

PIPE DREAMING
Larry Laurence, Ray Carter and Orchestra
Real 1195D

THE PIRATE
(1948)
Original Cast Recordings

BE A CLOWN
Gene Kelly, Judy Garland
MGM 30097

LOVE OF MY LIFE
Judy Garland
MGM 30098

YOU CAN DO NO WRONG
Judy Garland
MGM 30098

NINA
Gene Kelly
MGM 30099

MACK THE BLACK
Judy Garland
MGM 30099

33⅓ LONG-PLAYING RECORDS

KISS ME, KATE
(1948)
Original Cast Recordings

Columbia OL 4140, OS 2300 (1949);
Capitol TAO-1267, STAO-1267,
original cast reassembled (1959).
MGM E-3077, Metro 525, S-395,
film soundtrack (1953).

OUT OF THIS WORLD
(1950)
Original Cast Recording

Columbia OL-4390 (Issued, January, 1951;
deleted, December, 1969)

CAN-CAN
(1953)
Original Cast Recordings

Capitol S-452, DW-452 (Issued, June, 1953)
Capitol W-1301, SW-1301 (Issued, April, 1960;
deleted, April, 1964) film soundtrack

SILK STOCKINGS
(1955)
Original Cast Recordings

RCA Victor LOC-1016 (Issued, March, 1955;
deleted, April, 1960)
RCA Victor LOC-1102, LSO-1102
(Reissued, May, 1965)
MGM E-3542 (Issued, June, 1957;
deleted, November, 1959) film soundtrack

HIGH SOCIETY
(1956)
Original Cast Recording

Capitol W-750, SW-750 (Issued, May, 1956)

LES GIRLS
(1957)
Original Cast Recording

MGM E-3590 (Issued, November, 1957;
deleted, January, 1965)

ALADDIN
(1958)
Original Cast Recording

Columbia CL-1117 (Issued, February, 1958;
deleted, December, 1959)